High Performance Spark
Best Practices for Scaling and
Optimizing Apache Spark

Holden Karau and Rachel Warren

Beijing · Boston · Farnham · Sebastopol · Tokyo

High Performance Spark

by Holden Karau and Rachel Warren

Published by O'Reilly Media, Inc., 1005 Gravenstein Highway North, Sebastopol, CA 95472.

O'Reilly books may be purchased for educational, business, or sales promotional use. Online editions are also available for most titles (*http://oreilly.com/safari*). For more information, contact our corporate/institutional sales department: 800-998-9938 or *corporate@oreilly.com*.

Editor: Shannon Cutt
Production Editor: Kristen Brown
Copyeditor: Kim Cofer
Proofreader: James Fraleigh

Indexer: Ellen Troutman-Zaig
Interior Designer: David Futato
Cover Designer: Karen Montgomery
Illustrator: Rebecca Demarest

June 2017:   First Edition

Revision History for the First Edition
2017-05-22:   First Release
2017-10-20:   Second Release

978-1-491-94320-5

[LSI]

Table of Contents

Preface. ix

1. Introduction to High Performance Spark. 1
   What Is Spark and Why Performance Matters   1
   What You Can Expect to Get from This Book   2
   Spark Versions   3
   Why Scala?   3
      To Be a Spark Expert You Have to Learn a Little Scala Anyway   3
      The Spark Scala API Is Easier to Use Than the Java API   4
      Scala Is More Performant Than Python   4
      Why Not Scala?   4
      Learning Scala   5
   Conclusion   6

2. How Spark Works. 7
   How Spark Fits into the Big Data Ecosystem   8
      Spark Components   8
   Spark Model of Parallel Computing: RDDs   10
      Lazy Evaluation   11
      In-Memory Persistence and Memory Management   13
      Immutability and the RDD Interface   14
      Types of RDDs   16
      Functions on RDDs: Transformations Versus Actions   17
      Wide Versus Narrow Dependencies   17
   Spark Job Scheduling   19
      Resource Allocation Across Applications   20
      The Spark Application   20
   The Anatomy of a Spark Job   22

The DAG   22
Jobs   23
Stages   23
Tasks   24
Conclusion   26

3. DataFrames, Datasets, and Spark SQL.   27
Getting Started with the SparkSession (or HiveContext or SQLContext)   28
Spark SQL Dependencies   30
    Managing Spark Dependencies   31
    Avoiding Hive JARs   32
Basics of Schemas   33
DataFrame API   36
    Transformations   36
    Multi-DataFrame Transformations   48
    Plain Old SQL Queries and Interacting with Hive Data   49
Data Representation in DataFrames and Datasets   49
    Tungsten   50
Data Loading and Saving Functions   51
    DataFrameWriter and DataFrameReader   51
    Formats   52
    Save Modes   61
    Partitions (Discovery and Writing)   62
Datasets   62
    Interoperability with RDDs, DataFrames, and Local Collections   63
    Compile-Time Strong Typing   64
    Easier Functional (RDD "like") Transformations   65
    Relational Transformations   65
    Multi-Dataset Relational Transformations   65
    Grouped Operations on Datasets   66
Extending with User-Defined Functions and Aggregate Functions (UDFs,
    UDAFs)   67
Query Optimizer   69
    Logical and Physical Plans   69
    Code Generation   70
    Large Query Plans and Iterative Algorithms   70
Debugging Spark SQL Queries   71
JDBC/ODBC Server   71
Conclusion   72

4. Joins (SQL and Core).   75
Core Spark Joins   75

Choosing a Join Type   77
Choosing an Execution Plan   78
Spark SQL Joins   81
DataFrame Joins   82
Dataset Joins   85
Conclusion   86

5. **Effective Transformations**. **87**
Narrow Versus Wide Transformations   88
Implications for Performance   90
Implications for Fault Tolerance   91
The Special Case of coalesce   92
What Type of RDD Does Your Transformation Return?   92
Minimizing Object Creation   94
Reusing Existing Objects   94
Using Smaller Data Structures   97
Iterator-to-Iterator Transformations with mapPartitions   100
What Is an Iterator-to-Iterator Transformation?   101
Space and Time Advantages   102
An Example   103
Set Operations   106
Reducing Setup Overhead   107
Shared Variables   108
Broadcast Variables   108
Accumulators   109
Reusing RDDs   114
Cases for Reuse   114
Deciding if Recompute Is Inexpensive Enough   117
Types of Reuse: Cache, Persist, Checkpoint, Shuffle Files   118
Alluxio (nee Tachyon)   122
LRU Caching   123
Noisy Cluster Considerations   124
Interaction with Accumulators   125
Conclusion   126

6. **Working with Key/Value Data**. **127**
The Goldilocks Example   129
Goldilocks Version 0: Iterative Solution   130
How to Use PairRDDFunctions and OrderedRDDFunctions   132
Actions on Key/Value Pairs   133
What's So Dangerous About the groupByKey Function   134
Goldilocks Version 1: groupByKey Solution   134

Choosing an Aggregation Operation   138
    Dictionary of Aggregation Operations with Performance Considerations   138
Multiple RDD Operations   141
    Co-Grouping   141
Partitioners and Key/Value Data   142
    Using the Spark Partitioner Object   144
    Hash Partitioning   144
    Range Partitioning   144
    Custom Partitioning   145
    Preserving Partitioning Information Across Transformations   146
    Leveraging Co-Located and Co-Partitioned RDDs   146
    Dictionary of Mapping and Partitioning Functions PairRDDFunctions   148
Dictionary of OrderedRDDOperations   149
    Sorting by Two Keys with SortByKey   151
Secondary Sort and repartitionAndSortWithinPartitions   151
    Leveraging repartitionAndSortWithinPartitions for a Group by Key and
        Sort Values Function   152
    How Not to Sort by Two Orderings   155
    Goldilocks Version 2: Secondary Sort   156
    A Different Approach to Goldilocks   159
    Goldilocks Version 3: Sort on Cell Values   164
Straggler Detection and Unbalanced Data   165
    Back to Goldilocks (Again)   167
    Goldilocks Version 4: Reduce to Distinct on Each Partition   167
Conclusion   173

7. Going Beyond Scala. 175
Beyond Scala within the JVM   176
Beyond Scala, and Beyond the JVM   180
    How PySpark Works   181
    How SparkR Works   189
    Spark.jl (Julia Spark)   191
    How Eclair JS Works   192
    Spark on the Common Language Runtime (CLR)—C# and Friends   193
Calling Other Languages from Spark   193
    Using Pipe and Friends   193
    JNI   195
    Java Native Access (JNA)   198
    Underneath Everything Is FORTRAN   199
    Getting to the GPU   200
The Future   201
Conclusion   201

8. **Testing and Validation**... **203**
    Unit Testing 203
      General Spark Unit Testing 204
      Mocking RDDs 208
    Getting Test Data 210
      Generating Large Datasets 210
      Sampling 211
    Property Checking with ScalaCheck 213
      Computing RDD Difference 213
    Integration Testing 216
      Choosing Your Integration Testing Environment 216
    Verifying Performance 217
      Spark Counters for Verifying Performance 217
      Projects for Verifying Performance 218
    Job Validation 219
    Conclusion 220

9. **Spark MLlib and ML**... **221**
    Choosing Between Spark MLlib and Spark ML 221
    Working with MLlib 222
      Getting Started with MLlib (Organization and Imports) 222
      MLlib Feature Encoding and Data Preparation 223
      Feature Scaling and Selection 228
      MLlib Model Training 228
      Predicting 229
      Serving and Persistence 230
      Model Evaluation 232
    Working with Spark ML 233
      Spark ML Organization and Imports 233
      Pipeline Stages 234
      Explain Params 235
      Data Encoding 236
      Data Cleaning 239
      Spark ML Models 239
      Putting It All Together in a Pipeline 240
      Training a Pipeline 241
      Accessing Individual Stages 241
      Data Persistence and Spark ML 242
      Extending Spark ML Pipelines with Your Own Algorithms 244
      Model and Pipeline Persistence and Serving with Spark ML 252
    General Serving Considerations 252
    Conclusion 253

10. Spark Components and Packages. **255**
    Stream Processing with Spark   257
        Sources and Sinks   257
        Batch Intervals   259
        Data Checkpoint Intervals   260
        Considerations for DStreams   261
        Considerations for Structured Streaming   262
        High Availability Mode (or Handling Driver Failure or Checkpointing)   270
    GraphX   271
    Using Community Packages and Libraries   271
        Creating a Spark Package   273
    Conclusion   274

A. Tuning, Debugging, and Other Things Developers Like to Pretend Don't Exist. **275**

Index. **325**

Preface

We wrote this book for data engineers and data scientists who are looking to get the most out of Spark. If you've been working with Spark and invested in Spark but your experience so far has been mired by memory errors and mysterious, intermittent failures, this book is for you. If you have been using Spark for some exploratory work or experimenting with it on the side but have not felt confident enough to put it into production, this book may help. If you are enthusiastic about Spark but have not seen the performance improvements from it that you expected, we hope this book can help. This book is intended for those who have some working knowledge of Spark, and may be difficult to understand for those with little or no experience with Spark or distributed computing. For recommendations of more introductory literature see "Supporting Books and Materials" on page x.

We expect this text will be most useful to those who care about optimizing repeated queries in production, rather than to those who are doing primarily exploratory work. While writing highly performant queries is perhaps more important to the data engineer, writing those queries with Spark, in contrast to other frameworks, requires a good knowledge of the data, usually more intuitive to the data scientist. Thus it may be more useful to a data engineer who may be less experienced with thinking critically about the statistical nature, distribution, and layout of data when considering performance. We hope that this book will help data engineers think more critically about their data as they put pipelines into production. We want to help our readers ask questions such as "How is my data distributed?", "Is it skewed?", "What is the range of values in a column?", and "How do we expect a given value to group?" and then apply the answers to those questions to the logic of their Spark queries.

However, even for data scientists using Spark mostly for exploratory purposes, this book should cultivate some important intuition about writing performant Spark queries, so that as the scale of the exploratory analysis inevitably grows, you may have a better shot of getting something to run the first time. We hope to guide data scientists, even those who are already comfortable thinking about data in a distributed way, to think critically about how their programs are evaluated, empowering them to explore their data more fully, more quickly, and to communicate effectively with any-one helping them put their algorithms into production.

Regardless of your job title, it is likely that the amount of data with which you are working is growing quickly. Your original solutions may need to be scaled, and your old techniques for solving new problems may need to be updated. We hope this book will help you leverage Apache Spark to tackle new problems more easily and old problems more efficiently.

First Edition Notes

You are reading the first edition of *High Performance Spark*, and for that, we thank you! If you find errors, mistakes, or have ideas for ways to improve this book, please reach out to us at *high-performance-spark@googlegroups.com*. If you wish to be included in a "thanks" section in future editions of the book, please include your preferred display name.

Supporting Books and Materials

For data scientists and developers new to Spark, *Learning Spark* by Karau, Konwin-ski, Wendell, and Zaharia is an excellent introduction,[1] and *Advanced Analytics with Spark* by Sandy Ryza, Uri Laserson, Sean Owen, and Josh Wills is a great book for interested data scientists. For individuals more interested in streaming, the upcoming *Learning Spark Streaming* by François Garillot may also be of use once it is available.

Beyond books, there is also a collection of intro-level Spark training material avail-able. For individuals who prefer video, Paco Nathan has an excellent introduction video series on O'Reilly (*http://shop.oreilly.com/product/0636920036807.do*). Com-mercially, Databricks (*https://databricks.com/spark/training*) as well as Cloudera (*https://www.cloudera.com/more/training/courses/developer-training-for-spark-and-hadoop.html*) and other Hadoop/Spark vendors offer Spark training. Previous recordings of Spark camps, as well as many other great resources, have been posted on the Apache Spark documentation page (*http://spark.apache.org/documenta tion.html*).

If you don't have experience with Scala, we do our best to convince you to pick up Scala in Chapter 1, and if you are interested in learning, *Programming Scala*, 2nd Edi-tion, by Dean Wampler and Alex Payne is a good introduction.[2]

---

1 Though we may be biased.

2 Although it's important to note that some of the practices suggested in this book are not common practice in Spark code.

Conventions Used in This Book

The following typographical conventions are used in this book:

Italic
> Indicates new terms, URLs, email addresses, filenames, and file extensions.

`Constant width`
> Used for program listings, as well as within paragraphs to refer to program elements such as variable or function names, databases, data types, environment variables, statements, and keywords.

`Constant width bold`
> Shows commands or other text that should be typed literally by the user.

`Constant width italic`
> Shows text that should be replaced with user-supplied values or by values determined by context.

This element signifies a tip or suggestion.

This element signifies a general note.

This element indicates a warning or caution.

Examples prefixed with "Evil" depend heavily on Apache Spark internals, and will likely break in future minor releases of Apache Spark. You've been warned—but we totally understand you aren't going to pay much attention to that because neither would we.

Using Code Examples

Supplemental material (code examples, exercises, etc.) is available for download from the High Performance Spark GitHub repository (*https://github.com/high-performance-spark/high-performance-spark-examples*) and some of the testing code is available at the "Spark Testing Base" GitHub repository (*https://github.com/holdenk/spark-testing-base*) and the Spark Validator repo (*https://github.com/holdenk/spark-validator*). Structured Streaming machine learning examples, which are generally in the "evil" category discussed under "Conventions Used in This Book" on page xi, are available at *https://github.com/holdenk/spark-structured-streaming-ml*.

This book is here to help you get your job done. In general, if example code is offered with this book, you may use it in your programs and documentation. You do not need to contact us for permission unless you're reproducing a significant portion of the code. For example, writing a program that uses several chunks of code from this book does not require permission. Selling or distributing a CD-ROM of examples from O'Reilly books does require permission. Answering a question by citing this book and quoting example code does not require permission. The code is also available under an Apache 2 License. Incorporating a significant amount of example code from this book into your product's documentation may require permission.

We appreciate, but do not require, attribution. An attribution usually includes the title, author, publisher, and ISBN. For example: "*High Performance Spark* by Holden Karau and Rachel Warren (O'Reilly). Copyright 2017 Holden Karau, Rachel Warren, 978-1-491-94320-5."

If you feel your use of code examples falls outside fair use or the permission given above, feel free to contact us at *permissions@oreilly.com*.

O'Reilly Safari

 *Safari* (formerly Safari Books Online) is a membership-based training and reference platform for enterprise, government, educators, and individuals.

Members have access to thousands of books, training videos, Learning Paths, interactive tutorials, and curated playlists from over 250 publishers, including O'Reilly Media, Harvard Business Review, Prentice Hall Professional, Addison-Wesley Professional, Microsoft Press, Sams, Que, Peachpit Press, Adobe, Focal Press, Cisco Press, John Wiley & Sons, Syngress, Morgan Kaufmann, IBM Redbooks, Packt, Adobe Press, FT Press, Apress, Manning, New Riders, McGraw-Hill, Jones & Bartlett, and Course Technology, among others.

For more information, please visit *http://oreilly.com/safari*.

How to Contact the Authors

For feedback, email us at *high-performance-spark@googlegroups.com*. For random ramblings, occasionally about Spark, follow us on twitter:

Holden: *http://twitter.com/holdenkarau*

Rachel: *https://twitter.com/warre_n_peace*

How to Contact Us

Please address comments and questions concerning this book to the publisher:

> O'Reilly Media, Inc.
> 1005 Gravenstein Highway North
> Sebastopol, CA 95472
> 800-998-9938 (in the United States or Canada)
> 707-829-0515 (international or local)
> 707-829-0104 (fax)

To comment or ask technical questions about this book, send email to *bookquestions@oreilly.com*.

For more information about our books, courses, conferences, and news, see our website at *http://www.oreilly.com*.

Find us on Facebook: *http://facebook.com/oreilly*

Follow us on Twitter: *http://twitter.com/oreillymedia*

Watch us on YouTube: *http://www.youtube.com/oreillymedia*

Acknowledgments

The authors would like to acknowledge everyone who has helped with comments and suggestions on early drafts of our work. Special thanks to Anya Bida, Jakob Odersky, and Katharine Kearnan for reviewing early drafts and diagrams. We'd like to thank Mahmoud Hanafy for reviewing and improving the sample code as well as early drafts. We'd also like to thank Michael Armbrust for reviewing and providing feedback on early drafts of the SQL chapter. Justin Pihony has been one of the most active early readers, suggesting fixes in every respect (language, formatting, etc.).

Thanks to all of the readers of our O'Reilly early release who have provided feedback on various errata, including Kanak Kshetri and Rubén Berenguel.

We'd also like to thank our dedicated (official) technical reviewers, Neelesh Srinivas Salian and Denny Lee, who read through every page providing detailed feedback and helped us decide what content belonged where.

Finally, thank you to our respective employers for being understanding as we've worked on this book. Especially Lawrence Spracklen who insisted we mention him here :p.

## CHAPTER 1

Introduction to High Performance Spark

This chapter provides an overview of what we hope you will be able to learn from this book and does its best to convince you to learn Scala. Feel free to skip ahead to Chapter 2 if you already know what you're looking for and use Scala (or have your heart set on another language).

What Is Spark and Why Performance Matters

Apache Spark is a high-performance, general-purpose distributed computing system that has become the most active Apache open source project, with more than 1,000 active contributors.[1] Spark enables us to process large quantities of data, beyond what can fit on a single machine, with a high-level, relatively easy-to-use API. Spark's design and interface are unique, and it is one of the fastest systems of its kind. Uniquely, Spark allows us to write the logic of data transformations and machine learning algorithms in a way that is parallelizable, but relatively system agnostic. So it is often possible to write computations that are fast for distributed storage systems of varying kind and size.

However, despite its many advantages and the excitement around Spark, the simplest implementation of many common data science routines in Spark can be much slower and much less robust than the best version. Since the computations we are concerned with may involve data at a very large scale, the time and resources that gains from tuning code for performance are enormous. Performance does not just mean run faster; often at this scale it means getting something to run at all. It is possible to construct a Spark query that fails on gigabytes of data but, when refactored and adjusted with an eye toward the structure of the data and the requirements of the cluster,

---

[1] From *http://spark.apache.org/*.

succeeds on the same system with terabytes of data. In the authors' experience writing production Spark code, we have seen the same tasks, run on the same clusters, run 100× faster using some of the optimizations discussed in this book. In terms of data processing, time is money, and we hope this book pays for itself through a reduction in data infrastructure costs and developer hours.

Not all of these techniques are applicable to every use case. Especially because Spark is highly configurable and is exposed at a higher level than other computational frameworks of comparable power, we can reap tremendous benefits just by becoming more attuned to the shape and structure of our data. Some techniques can work well on certain data sizes or even certain key distributions, but not all. The simplest example of this can be how for many problems, using groupByKey in Spark can very easily cause the dreaded out-of-memory exceptions, but for data with few duplicates this operation can be just as quick as the alternatives that we will present. Learning to understand your particular use case and system and how Spark will interact with it is a must to solve the most complex data science problems with Spark.

What You Can Expect to Get from This Book

Our hope is that this book will help you take your Spark queries and make them faster, able to handle larger data sizes, and use fewer resources. This book covers a broad range of tools and scenarios. You will likely pick up some techniques that might not apply to the problems you are working with, but that might apply to a problem in the future and may help shape your understanding of Spark more generally. The chapters in this book are written with enough context to allow the book to be used as a reference; however, the structure of this book is intentional and reading the sections in order should give you not only a few scattered tips, but a comprehensive understanding of Apache Spark and how to make it sing.

It's equally important to point out what you will likely not get from this book. This book is not intended to be an introduction to Spark or Scala; several other books and video series are available to get you started. The authors may be a little biased in this regard, but we think *Learning Spark* by Karau, Konwinski, Wendell, and Zaharia as well as Paco Nathan's introduction video series (*http://shop.oreilly.com/product/0636920036807.do*) are excellent options for Spark beginners. While this book is focused on performance, it is not an operations book, so topics like setting up a cluster and multitenancy are not covered. We are assuming that you already have a way to use Spark in your system, so we won't provide much assistance in making higher-level architecture decisions. There are future books in the works, by other authors, on the topic of Spark operations that may be done by the time you are reading this one. If operations are your show, or if there isn't anyone responsible for operations in your organization, we hope those books can help you.

Spark Versions

Spark follows semantic versioning with the standard [MAJOR].[MINOR].[MAINTE-NANCE] with API stability for public nonexperimental nondeveloper APIs within minor and maintenance releases. Many of these experimental components are some of the more exciting from a performance standpoint, including `Datasets`—Spark SQL's new structured, strongly-typed, data abstraction. Spark also tries for binary API compatibility between releases, using MiMa[2]; so if you are using the stable API you generally should not need to recompile to run a job against a new version of Spark unless the major version has changed.

 This book was created using the Spark 2.0.1 APIs, but much of the code will work in earlier versions of Spark as well. In places where this is not the case we have attempted to call that out.

Why Scala?

In this book, we will focus on Spark's Scala API and assume a working knowledge of Scala. Part of this decision is simply in the interest of time and space; we trust readers wanting to use Spark in another language will be able to translate the concepts used in this book without presenting the examples in Java and Python. More importantly, it is the belief of the authors that "serious" performant Spark development is most easily achieved in Scala.

To be clear, these reasons are very specific to using Spark with Scala; there are many more general arguments for (and against) Scala's applications in other contexts.

To Be a Spark Expert You Have to Learn a Little Scala Anyway

Although Python and Java are more commonly used languages, learning Scala is a worthwhile investment for anyone interested in delving deep into Spark development. Spark's documentation can be uneven. However, the readability of the codebase is world-class. Perhaps more than with other frameworks, the advantages of cultivating a sophisticated understanding of the Spark codebase is integral to the advanced Spark user. Because Spark is written in Scala, it will be difficult to interact with the Spark source code without the ability, at least, to read Scala code. Furthermore, the methods in the *Resilient Distributed Datasets* (RDD) class closely mimic those in the Scala collections API. RDD functions, such as `map`, `filter`, `flatMap`,

---

2 MiMa is the Migration Manager for Scala and tries to catch binary incompatibilities between releases.

reduce, and fold, have nearly identical specifications to their Scala equivalents.[3] Fundamentally Spark is a functional framework, relying heavily on concepts like immutability and lambda definition, so using the Spark API may be more intuitive with some knowledge of functional programming.

The Spark Scala API Is Easier to Use Than the Java API

Once you have learned Scala, you will quickly find that writing Spark in Scala is less painful than writing Spark in Java. First, writing Spark in Scala is significantly more concise than writing Spark in Java since Spark relies heavily on inline function definitions and lambda expressions, which are much more naturally supported in Scala (especially before Java 8). Second, the Spark shell can be a powerful tool for debugging and development, and is only available in languages with existing REPLs (Scala, Python, and R).

Scala Is More Performant Than Python

It can be attractive to write Spark in Python, since it is easy to learn, quick to write, interpreted, and includes a very rich set of data science toolkits. However, Spark code written in Python is often slower than equivalent code written in the JVM, since Scala is statically typed, and the cost of JVM communication (from Python to Scala) can be very high. Last, Spark features are generally written in Scala first and then translated into Python, so to use cutting-edge Spark functionality, you will need to be in the JVM; Python support for MLlib and Spark Streaming are particularly behind.

Why Not Scala?

There are several good reasons to develop with Spark in other languages. One of the more important constant reasons is developer/team preference. Existing code, both internal and in libraries, can also be a strong reason to use a different language. Python is one of the most supported languages today. While writing Java code can be clunky and sometimes lag slightly in terms of API, there is very little performance cost to writing in another JVM language (at most some object conversions).[4]

---

3 Although, as we explore in this book, the performance implications and evaluation semantics are quite different.

4 Of course, in performance, every rule has its exception. mapPartitions in Spark 1.6 and earlier in Java suffers some severe performance restrictions that we discuss in "Iterator-to-Iterator Transformations with mapPartitions" on page 100.

While all of the examples in this book are presented in Scala for the final release, we will port many of the examples from Scala to Java and Python where the differences in implementation could be important. These will be available (over time) at our GitHub (*https://github.com/high-performance-spark/high-performance-spark-examples*). If you find yourself wanting a specific example ported, please either email us or create an issue on the GitHub repo.

Spark SQL does much to minimize the performance difference when using a non-JVM language. Chapter 7 looks at options to work effectively in Spark with languages outside of the JVM, including Spark's supported languages of Python and R. This section also offers guidance on how to use Fortran, C, and GPU-specific code to reap additional performance improvements. Even if we are developing most of our Spark application in Scala, we shouldn't feel tied to doing everything in Scala, because specialized libraries in other languages can be well worth the overhead of going outside the JVM.

Learning Scala

If after all of this we've convinced you to use Scala, there are several excellent options for learning Scala. Spark 1.6 is built against Scala 2.10 and cross-compiled against Scala 2.11, and Spark 2.0 is built against Scala 2.11 and cross-compiled against Scala 2.10 until Spark 2.3 and may add 2.12 in the future. Depending on how much we've convinced you to learn Scala, and what your resources are, there are a number of different options ranging from books to massive open online courses (MOOCs) to professional training.

For books, *Programming Scala*, 2nd Edition, by Dean Wampler and Alex Payne can be great, although much of the actor system references are not relevant while working in Spark. The Scala language website also maintains a list of Scala books (*http://www.scala-lang.org/documentation/books.html*).

In addition to books focused on Spark, there are online courses for learning Scala. *Functional Programming Principles in Scala* (*https://www.coursera.org/course/progfun*), taught by Martin Ordersky, its creator, is on Coursera as well as Introduction to Functional Programming (*https://www.edx.org/course/introduction-functional-programming-delftx-fp101x-0*) on edX. A number of different companies also offer video-based Scala courses, none of which the authors have personally experienced or recommend.

For those who prefer a more interactive approach, professional training is offered by a number of different companies, including Lightbend (formerly Typesafe) (*https://www.typesafe.com/services/training*). While we have not directly experienced Typesafe training, it receives positive reviews and is known especially to help bring a team or group of individuals up to speed with Scala for the purposes of working with Spark.

Conclusion

Although you will likely be able to get the most out of Spark performance if you have an understanding of Scala, working in Spark does not require a knowledge of Scala. For those whose problems are better suited to other languages or tools, techniques for working with other languages will be covered in Chapter 7. This book is aimed at individuals who already have a grasp of the basics of Spark, and we thank you for choosing *High Performance Spark* to deepen your knowledge of Spark. The next chapter will introduce some of Spark's general design and evaluation paradigms that are important to understanding how to efficiently utilize Spark.

## CHAPTER 2

How Spark Works

This chapter introduces the overall design of Spark as well as its place in the big data ecosystem. Spark is often considered an alternative to Apache MapReduce, since Spark can also be used for distributed data processing with Hadoop.[1] As we will discuss in this chapter, Spark's design principles are quite different from those of MapReduce. Unlike Hadoop MapReduce, Spark does not need to be run in tandem with Apache Hadoop—although it often is. Spark has inherited parts of its API, design, and supported formats from other existing computational frameworks, particularly DryadLINQ.[2] However, Spark's internals, especially how it handles failures, differ from many traditional systems. Spark's ability to leverage lazy evaluation within memory computations makes it particularly unique. Spark's creators believe it to be the first high-level programming language for fast, distributed data processing.[3]

To get the most out of Spark, it is important to understand some of the principles used to design Spark and, at a cursory level, how Spark programs are executed. In this

---

1 MapReduce is a programmatic paradigm that defines programs in terms of *map* procedures that filter and sort data onto the nodes of a distributed system, and *reduce* procedures that aggregate the data on the mapper nodes. Implementations of MapReduce have been written in many languages, but the term usually refers to a popular implementation called *Hadoop MapReduce* (*http://hadoop.apache.org/*), packaged with the distributed filesystem, Apache Hadoop Distributed File System.

2 DryadLINQ is a Microsoft research project that puts the .NET Language Integrated Query (LINQ) on top of the Dryad distributed execution engine. Like Spark, the DryadLINQ API defines an object representing a distributed dataset, and then exposes functions to transform data as methods defined on that dataset object. DryadLINQ is lazily evaluated and its scheduler is similar to Spark's. However, DryadLINQ doesn't use in-memory storage. For more information see the DryadLINQ documentation (*http://research.microsoft.com/en-us/projects/DryadLINQ*).

3 See the original Spark Paper (*http://people.csail.mit.edu/matei/papers/2012/nsdi_spark.pdf*) and other Spark papers (*http://spark.apache.org/research.html*).

chapter, we will provide a broad overview of Spark's model of parallel computing and a thorough explanation of the Spark scheduler and execution engine. We will refer to the concepts in this chapter throughout the text. Further, we hope this explanation will provide you with a more precise understanding of some of the terms you've heard tossed around by other Spark users and encounter in the Spark documentation.

How Spark Fits into the Big Data Ecosystem

Apache Spark is an open source framework that provides methods to process data in parallel that are generalizable; the same high-level Spark functions can be used to perform disparate data processing tasks on data of different sizes and structures. On its own, Spark is not a data storage solution; it performs computations on Spark JVMs (Java Virtual Machines) that last only for the duration of a Spark application. Spark can be run locally on a single machine with a single JVM (called local mode). More often, Spark is used in tandem with a distributed storage system (e.g., HDFS, Cassandra, or S3) and a cluster manager—the storage system to house the data processed with Spark, and the cluster manager to orchestrate the distribution of Spark applications across the cluster. Spark currently supports three kinds of cluster managers: Standalone Cluster Manager, Apache Mesos, and Hadoop YARN (see Figure 2-1). The Standalone Cluster Manager is included in Spark, but using the Standalone manager requires installing Spark on each node of the cluster.

Figure 2-1. A diagram of the data processing ecosystem including Spark

Spark Components

Spark provides a high-level query language to process data. Spark Core, the main data processing framework in the Spark ecosystem, has APIs in Scala, Java, Python, and R. Spark is built around a data abstraction called *Resilient Distributed Datasets* (RDDs). RDDs are a representation of lazily evaluated, statically typed, distributed collections. RDDs have a number of predefined "coarse-grained" transformations (functions that are applied to the entire dataset), such as map, join, and reduce to manipulate the distributed datasets, as well as I/O functionality to read and write data between the distributed storage system and the Spark JVMs.

> While Spark also supports R, at present the RDD interface is not available in that language. We will cover tips for using Java, Python, R, and other languages in detail in Chapter 7.

In addition to Spark Core, the Spark ecosystem includes a number of other first-party components, including Spark SQL, Spark MLlib, Spark ML, Spark Streaming, and GraphX,[4] which provide more specific data processing functionality. Some of these components have the same generic performance considerations as the Core; MLlib, for example, is written almost entirely on the Spark API. However, some of them have unique considerations. Spark SQL, for example, has a different query optimizer than Spark Core.

Spark SQL is a component that can be used in tandem with Spark Core and has APIs in Scala, Java, Python, and R, and basic SQL queries. Spark SQL defines an interface for a semi-structured data type, called DataFrames, and as of Spark 1.6, a semi-structured, typed version of RDDs called called Datasets.[5] Spark SQL is a very important component for Spark performance, and much of what can be accomplished with Spark Core can be done by leveraging Spark SQL. We will cover Spark SQL in detail in Chapter 3 and compare the performance of joins in Spark SQL and Spark Core in Chapter 4.

Spark has two machine learning packages: ML and MLlib. MLlib is a package of machine learning and statistics algorithms written with Spark. Spark ML is still in the early stages, and has only existed since Spark 1.2. Spark ML provides a higher-level API than MLlib with the goal of allowing users to more easily create practical machine learning pipelines. Spark MLlib is primarily built on top of RDDs and uses functions from Spark Core, while ML is built on top of Spark SQL DataFrames.[6] Eventually the Spark community plans to move over to ML and deprecate MLlib. Spark ML and MLlib both have additional performance considerations from Spark Core and Spark SQL—we cover some of these in Chapter 9.

---

4 GraphX is not actively developed at this point, and will likely be replaced with GraphFrames or similar.

5 Datasets and DataFrames are unified in Spark 2.0. Datasets are DataFrames of "Row" objects that can be accessed by field number.

6 See the MLlib documentation (*http://spark.apache.org/docs/latest/mllib-guide.html*).

Spark Streaming uses the scheduling of the Spark Core for streaming analytics on minibatches of data. Spark Streaming has a number of unique considerations, such as the window sizes used for batches. We offer some tips for using Spark Streaming in "Stream Processing with Spark" on page 257.

GraphX is a graph processing framework built on top of Spark with an API for graph computations. GraphX is one of the least mature components of Spark, so we don't cover it in much detail. In future versions of Spark, typed graph functionality will be introduced on top of the Dataset API. We will provide a cursory glance at GraphX in "GraphX" on page 271.

This book will focus on optimizing programs written with the Spark Core and Spark SQL. However, since MLlib and the other frameworks are written using the Spark API, this book will provide the tools you need to leverage those frameworks more efficiently. Maybe by the time you're done, you will be ready to start contributing your own functions to MLlib and ML!

In addition to these first-party components, the community has written a number of libraries that provide additional functionality, such as for testing or parsing CSVs, and offer tools to connect it to different data sources. Many libraries are listed at *http://spark-packages.org/*, and can be dynamically included at runtime with spark-submit or the spark-shell and added as build dependencies to your maven or sbt project. We first use Spark packages to add support for CSV data in "Additional formats" on page 60 and then in more detail in "Using Community Packages and Libraries" on page 271.

Spark Model of Parallel Computing: RDDs

Spark allows users to write a program for the *driver* (or master node) on a cluster computing system that can perform operations on data in parallel. Spark represents large datasets as RDDs—immutable, distributed collections of objects—which are stored in the *executors* (or slave nodes). The objects that comprise RDDs are called partitions and may be (but do not need to be) computed on different nodes of a distributed system. The Spark cluster manager handles starting and distributing the Spark executors across a distributed system according to the configuration parameters set by the Spark application. The Spark execution engine itself distributes data across the executors for a computation. (See Figure 2-4.)

Rather than evaluating each transformation as soon as specified by the driver program, Spark evaluates RDDs lazily, computing RDD transformations only when the final RDD data needs to be computed (often by writing out to storage or collecting an aggregate to the driver). Spark can keep an RDD loaded in-memory on the executor nodes throughout the life of a Spark application for faster access in repeated computations. As they are implemented in Spark, RDDs are immutable, so transforming an

RDD returns a new RDD rather than the existing one. As we will explore in this chapter, this paradigm of lazy evaluation, in-memory storage, and immutability allows Spark to be easy-to-use, fault-tolerant, scalable, and efficient.

Lazy Evaluation

Many other systems for in-memory storage are based on "fine-grained" updates to mutable objects, i.e., calls to a particular cell in a table by storing intermediate results. In contrast, evaluation of RDDs is completely lazy. Spark does not begin computing the partitions until an action is called. An action is a Spark operation that returns something other than an RDD, triggering evaluation of partitions and possibly returning some output to a non-Spark system (outside of the Spark executors); for example, bringing data back to the driver (with operations like count or collect) or writing data to an external storage storage system (such as copyToHadoop). Actions trigger the scheduler, which builds a *directed acyclic graph* (called the DAG), based on the dependencies between RDD transformations. In other words, Spark evaluates an action by working backward to define the series of steps it has to take to produce each object in the final distributed dataset (each partition). Then, using this series of steps, called the execution plan, the scheduler computes the missing partitions for each stage until it computes the result.

 Not all transformations are 100% lazy. sortByKey needs to evaluate the RDD to determine the range of data, so it involves both a transformation and an action.

Performance and usability advantages of lazy evaluation

Lazy evaluation allows Spark to combine operations that don't require communication with the driver (called transformations with one-to-one dependencies) to avoid doing multiple passes through the data. For example, suppose a Spark program calls a map and a filter function on the same RDD. Spark can send the instructions for both the map and the filter to each executor. Then Spark can perform both the map and filter on each partition, which requires accessing the records only once, rather than sending two sets of instructions and accessing each partition twice. This theoretically reduces the computational complexity by half.

Spark's lazy evaluation paradigm is not only more efficient, it is also easier to implement the same logic in Spark than in a different framework—like MapReduce—that requires the developer to do the work to consolidate her mapping operations. Spark's clever lazy evaluation strategy lets us be lazy and express the same logic in far fewer lines of code: we can chain together operations with narrow dependencies and let the Spark evaluation engine do the work of consolidating them.

Consider the classic word count example that, given a dataset of documents, parses the text into words and then computes the count for each word. The Apache docs provide a word count example, which even in its simplest form comprises roughly fifty lines of code (*https://hadoop.apache.org/docs/r1.2.1/mapred_tutorial.html#Exam ple%3A+WordCount+v1.0*) (excluding import statements) in Java. A comparable Spark implementation is roughly fifteen lines of code in Java and five in Scala, available on the Apache website (*http://spark.apache.org/examples.html*). The example excludes the steps to read in the data mapping documents to words and counting the words. We have reproduced it in Example 2-1.

Example 2-1. Simple Scala word count example

```scala
def simpleWordCount(rdd: RDD[String]): RDD[(String, Int)] = {
  val words = rdd.flatMap(_.split(" "))
  val wordPairs = words.map((_, 1))
  val wordCounts = wordPairs.reduceByKey(_ + _)
  wordCounts
}
```

A further benefit of the Spark implementation of word count is that it is easier to modify and improve. Suppose that we now want to modify this function to filter out some "stop words" and punctuation from each document before computing the word count. In MapReduce, this would require adding the filter logic to the mapper to avoid doing a second pass through the data. An implementation of this routine for MapReduce can be found here: *https://github.com/kite-sdk/kite/wiki/WordCount-Version-Three*. In contrast, we can modify the preceding Spark routine by simply putting a `filter` step before the `map` step that creates the key/value pairs. Example 2-2 shows how Spark's lazy evaluation will consolidate the `map` and `filter` steps for us.

Example 2-2. Word count example with stop words filtered

```scala
def withStopWordsFiltered(rdd : RDD[String], illegalTokens : Array[Char],
    stopWords : Set[String]): RDD[(String, Int)] = {
  val separators = illegalTokens ++ Array[Char](' ')
  val tokens: RDD[String] = rdd.flatMap(_.split(separators).
    map(_.trim.toLowerCase))
  val words = tokens.filter(token =>
    !stopWords.contains(token) && (token.length > 0) )
  val wordPairs = words.map((_, 1))
  val wordCounts = wordPairs.reduceByKey(_ + _)
  wordCounts
}
```

Lazy evaluation and fault tolerance

Spark is fault-tolerant, meaning Spark will not fail, lose data, or return inaccurate results in the event of a host machine or network failure. Spark's unique method of fault tolerance is achieved because each partition of the data contains the dependency information needed to recalculate the partition. Most distributed computing paradigms that allow users to work with mutable objects provide fault tolerance by logging updates or duplicating data across machines.

In contrast, Spark does not need to maintain a log of updates to each RDD or log the actual intermediary steps, since the RDD itself contains all the dependency information needed to replicate each of its partitions. Thus, if a partition is lost, the RDD has enough information about its lineage to recompute it, and that computation can be parallelized to make recovery faster.

Lazy evaluation and debugging

Lazy evaluation has important consequences for debugging since it means that a Spark program will fail only at the point of action. For example, suppose that you were using the word count example, and afterwards were collecting the results to the driver. If the value you passed in for the stop words was null (maybe because it was the result of a Java program), the code would of course fail with a null pointer exception in the contains check. However, this failure would not appear until the program evaluated the collect step. Even the stack trace will show the failure as first occurring at the collect step, suggesting that the failure came from the collect statement. For this reason it is probably most efficient to develop in an environment that gives you access to complete debugging information.

 Because of lazy evaluation, stack traces from failed Spark jobs (especially when embedded in larger systems) will often appear to fail consistently at the point of the action, even if the problem in the logic occurs in a transformation much earlier in the program.

In-Memory Persistence and Memory Management

Spark's performance advantage over MapReduce is greatest in use cases involving repeated computations. Much of this performance increase is due to Spark's use of in-memory persistence. Rather than writing to disk between each pass through the data, Spark has the option of keeping the data on the executors loaded into memory. That way, the data on each partition is available in-memory each time it needs to be accessed.

Spark offers three options for memory management: in-memory as deserialized data, in-memory as serialized data, and on disk. Each has different space and time advantages:

In memory as deserialized Java objects

The most intuitive way to store objects in RDDs is as the original deserialized Java objects that are defined by the driver program. This form of in-memory storage is the fastest, since it reduces serialization time; however, it may not be the most memory efficient, since it requires the data to be stored as objects.

As serialized data

Using the standard Java serialization library, Spark objects are converted into streams of bytes as they are moved around the network. This approach may be slower, since serialized data is more CPU-intensive to read than deserialized data; however, it is often more memory efficient, since it allows the user to choose a more efficient representation. While Java serialization is more efficient than full objects, Kryo serialization (discussed in "Kryo" on page 290) can be even more space efficient.

On disk

RDDs, whose partitions are too large to be stored in RAM on each of the executors, can be written to disk. This strategy is obviously slower for repeated computations, but can be more fault-tolerant for long sequences of transformations, and may be the only feasible option for enormous computations.

The `persist()` function in the RDD class lets the user control how the RDD is stored. By default, `persist()` stores an RDD as deserialized objects in memory, but the user can pass one of numerous storage options to the `persist()` function to control how the RDD is stored. We will cover the different options for RDD reuse in "Types of Reuse: Cache, Persist, Checkpoint, Shuffle Files" on page 118. When persisting RDDs, the default implementation of RDDs evicts the least recently used partition (called LRU caching) if the space it takes is required to compute or to cache a new partition. However, you can change this behavior and control Spark's memory prioritization with the `persistencePriority()` function in the RDD class. See "LRU Caching" on page 123.

Immutability and the RDD Interface

Spark defines an RDD interface with the properties that each type of RDD must implement. These properties include the RDD's dependencies and information about data locality that are needed for the execution engine to compute that RDD. Since RDDs are statically typed and immutable, calling a transformation on one RDD will not modify the original RDD but rather return a new RDD object with a new definition of the RDD's properties.

RDDs can be created in three ways: (1) by transforming an existing RDD; (2) from a SparkContext, which is the API's gateway to Spark for your application; and (3) converting a `DataFrame` or `Dataset` (created from the `SparkSession`[7]). The `SparkCon text` represents the connection between a Spark cluster and one running Spark application. The `SparkContext` can be used to create an RDD from a local Scala object (using the `makeRDD` or `parallelize` methods) or by reading from stable storage (text files, binary files, a Hadoop Context, or a Hadoop file). `DataFrames` and `Data sets` can be read using the Spark SQL equivalent to a `SparkContext`, the `SparkSes sion`.

Internally, Spark uses five main properties to represent an RDD. The three required properties are the list of partition objects that make up the RDD, a function for computing an iterator of each partition, and a list of dependencies on other RDDs. Optionally, RDDs also include a partitioner (for RDDs of rows of key/value pairs represented as Scala tuples) and a list of preferred locations (for the HDFS file). As an end user, you will rarely need these five properties and are more likely to use predefined RDD transformations. However, it is helpful to understand the properties and know how to access them for debugging and for a better conceptual understanding. These five properties correspond to the following five methods available to the end user (you):

`partitions()`
> Returns an array of the partition objects that make up the parts of the distributed dataset. In the case of an RDD with a partitioner, the value of the index of each partition will correspond to the value of the `getPartition` function for each key in the data associated with that partition.

`iterator(p, parentIters)`
> Computes the elements of partition p given iterators for each of its parent partitions. This function is called in order to compute each of the partitions in this RDD. This is not intended to be called directly by the user. Rather, this is used by Spark when computing actions. Still, referencing the implementation of this function can be useful in determining how each partition of an RDD transformation is evaluated.

`dependencies()`
> Returns a sequence of dependency objects. The dependencies let the scheduler know how this RDD depends on other RDDs. There are two kinds of dependencies: *narrow dependencies* (`NarrowDependency` objects), which represent partitions that depend on one or a small subset of partitions in the parent, and *wide dependencies* (`ShuffleDependency` objects), which are used when a partition can

---

7 Prior to Spark 2.0, the `SparkSession` was called the `SQLContext`.

only be computed by rearranging all the data in the parent. We will discuss the types of dependencies in "Wide Versus Narrow Dependencies" on page 17.

partitioner()

> Returns a Scala option type of a partitioner object if the RDD has a function between element and partition associated with it, such as a hashPartitioner. This function returns None for all RDDs that are not of type tuple (do not represent key/value data). An RDD that represents an HDFS file (implemented in *NewHadoopRDD.scala*) has a partition for each block of the file. We will discuss partitioning in detail in "Using the Spark Partitioner Object" on page 144.

preferredLocations(p)

> Returns information about the data locality of a partition, p. Specifically, this function returns a sequence of strings representing some information about each of the nodes where the split p is stored. In an RDD representing an HDFS file, each string in the result of preferredLocations is the Hadoop name of the node where that partition is stored.

Types of RDDs

The implementation of the Spark Scala API contains an abstract class, RDD, which contains not only the five core functions of RDDs, but also those transformations and actions that are available to all RDDs, such as map and collect. Functions defined only on RDDs of a particular type are defined in several RDD function classes, including PairRDDFunctions, OrderedRDDFunctions, and GroupedRDDFunctions. The additional methods in these classes are made available by implicit conversion from the abstract RDD class, based on type information or when a transformation is applied to an RDD.

The Spark API also contains implementations of the RDD class that define more specific behavior by overriding the core properties of the RDD. These include the NewHadoopRDD class discussed previously—which represents an RDD created from an HDFS filesystem—and ShuffledRDD, which represents an RDD that was already partitioned. Each of these RDD implementations contains functionality that is specific to RDDs of that type. Creating an RDD, either through a transformation or from a SparkContext, will return one of these implementations of the RDD class. Some RDD operations have a different signature in Java than in Scala. These are defined in the JavaRDD.java class.

> Find out what type an RDD is by using the toDebugString function, which is defined on all RDDs. This will tell you what kind of RDD you have and provide a list of its parent RDDs.

We will discuss the different types of RDDs and RDD transformations in detail in Chapters 5 and 6.

Functions on RDDs: Transformations Versus Actions

There are two types of functions defined on RDDs: *actions* and *transformations*. Actions are functions that return something that is not an RDD, including a side effect, and transformations are functions that return another RDD.

Each Spark program must contain an action, since actions either bring information back to the driver or write the data to stable storage. Actions are what force evaluation of a Spark program. Persist calls also force evaluation, but usually do not mark the end of Spark job. Actions that bring data back to the driver include `collect`, `count`, `collectAsMap`, `sample`, `reduce`, and `take`.

 Some of these actions do not scale well, since they can cause memory errors in the driver. In general, it is best to use actions like `take`, `count`, and `reduce`, which bring back a fixed amount of data to the driver, rather than `collect` or `sample`.

Actions that write to storage include `saveAsTextFile`, `saveAsSequenceFile`, and `saveAsObjectFile`. Most actions that save to Hadoop are made available only on RDDs of key/value pairs; they are defined both in the `PairRDDFunctions` class (which provides methods for RDDs of tuple type by implicit conversion) and the `NewHa doopRDD` class, which is an implementation for RDDs that were created by reading from Hadoop. Some saving functions, like `saveAsTextFile` and `saveAsObjectFile`, are available on all RDDs, and they work by adding an implicit null key to each record (which is then ignored by the saving level). Functions that return nothing (*void* in Java, or `Unit` in Scala), such as `foreach`, are also actions: they force execution of a Spark job. `foreach` can be used to force evaluation of an RDD, but is also often used to write out to nonsupported formats (like web endpoints).

Most of the power of the Spark API is in its transformations. Spark transformations are coarse-grained transformations used to sort, reduce, group, sample, filter, and map distributed data. We will discuss transformations in detail in both Chapter 6, which deals exclusively with transformations on RDDs of key/value data, and Chapter 5.

Wide Versus Narrow Dependencies

For the purpose of understanding how RDDs are evaluated,the most important thing to know about transformations is that they fall into two categories: transformations with *narrow dependencies* and transformations with *wide dependencies*. The narrow versus wide distinction has significant implications for the way Spark evaluates a transformation and, consequently, for its performance. We will define narrow and wide transformations for the purpose of understanding Spark's execution paradigm in "Spark Job Scheduling" on page 19 of this chapter, but we will save the longer explanation of the performance considerations associated with them for Chapter 5.

Conceptually, narrow transformations are those in which each partition in the child RDD has simple, finite dependencies on partitions in the parent RDD. Dependencies are only narrow if they can be determined at design time, irrespective of the values of the records in the parent partitions, and if each parent has at most one child partition. Specifically, partitions in narrow transformations can either depend on one parent (such as in the `map` operator), or a unique subset of the parent partitions that is known at design time (`coalesce`). Thus narrow transformations can be executed on an arbitrary subset of the data without any information about the other partitions. In contrast, transformations with wide dependencies cannot be executed on arbitrary rows and instead require the data to be partitioned in a particular way, e.g., according the value of their key. In `sort`, for example, records have to be partitioned so that keys in the same range are on the same partition. Transformations with wide dependencies include `sort`, `reduceByKey`, `groupByKey`, `join`, and anything that calls the `rePartition` function.

In certain instances, for example, when Spark already knows the data is partitioned in a certain way, operations with wide dependencies do not cause a shuffle. If an operation will require a shuffle to be executed, Spark adds a `ShuffledDependency` object to the dependency list associated with the RDD. In general, shuffles are expensive. They become more expensive with more data and when a greater proportion of that data has to be moved to a new partition during the shuffle. As we will discuss at length in Chapter 6, we can get a lot of performance gains out of Spark programs by doing fewer and less expensive shuffles.

The next two diagrams illustrate the difference in the dependency graph for transformations with narrow dependencies versus transformations with wide dependencies. Figure 2-2 shows narrow dependencies in which each child partition (each of the blue squares on the bottom rows) depends on a known subset of parent partitions. Narrow dependencies are shown with blue arrows. The left represents a dependency graph of narrow transformations (such as `map`, `filter`, `mapPartitions`, and `flatMap`). On the upper right are dependencies between partitions for `coalesce`, a narrow transformation. In this instance we try to illustrate that a transformation can still qualify as narrow if the child partitions may depend on multiple parent partitions, so long as the set of parent partitions can be determined regardless of the values of the data in the partitions.

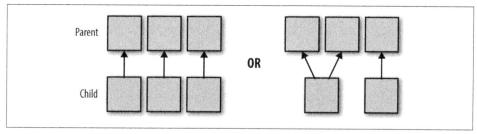

Figure 2-2. A simple diagram of dependencies between partitions for narrow transformations

Figure 2-3 shows wide dependencies between partitions. In this case the child partitions (shown at the bottom of Figure 2-3) depend on an arbitrary set of parent partitions. The wide dependencies (displayed as red arrows) cannot be known fully before the data is evaluated. In contrast to the `coalesce` operation, data is partitioned according to its value. The dependency graph for any operations that cause a shuffle (such as `groupByKey`, `reduceByKey`, `sort`, and `sortByKey`) follows this pattern.

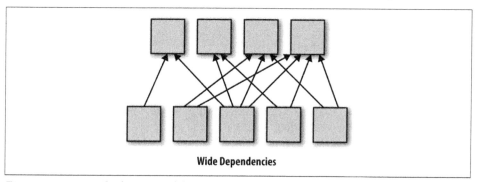

Wide Dependencies

Figure 2-3. A simple diagram of dependencies between partitions for wide transformations

The join functions are a bit more complicated, since they can have wide or narrow dependencies depending on how the two parent RDDs are partitioned. We illustrate the dependencies in different scenarios for the join operation in "Core Spark Joins" on page 75.

Spark Job Scheduling

A Spark application consists of a driver process, which is where the high-level Spark logic is written, and a series of executor processes that can be scattered across the nodes of a cluster. The Spark program itself runs in the driver node and sends some instructions to the executors. One Spark cluster can run several Spark applications concurrently. The applications are scheduled by the cluster manager and correspond to one SparkContext. Spark applications can, in turn, run multiple concurrent jobs. Jobs correspond to each action called on an RDD in a given application. In this section, we will describe the Spark application and how it launches Spark jobs: the processes that compute RDD transformations.

Resource Allocation Across Applications

Spark offers two ways of allocating resources across applications: *static allocation* and *dynamic allocation*. With static allocation, each application is allotted a finite maximum of resources on the cluster and reserves them for the duration of the application (as long as the SparkContext is still running). Within the static allocation category, there are many kinds of resource allocation available, depending on the cluster. For more information, see the Spark documentation for job scheduling (*http:// spark.apache.org/docs/latest/job-scheduling.html*).

Since 1.2, Spark offers the option of dynamic resource allocation, which expands the functionality of static allocation. In dynamic allocation, executors are added and removed from a Spark application as needed, based on a set of heuristics for estimated resource requirement. We will discuss resource allocation in "Allocating Cluster Resources and Dynamic Allocation" on page 281.

The Spark Application

A Spark application corresponds to a set of Spark jobs defined by one SparkContext in the driver program. A Spark application begins when a SparkContext is started. When the SparkContext is started, a driver and a series of executors are started on the worker nodes of the cluster. Each executor is its own Java Virtual Machine (JVM), and an executor cannot span multiple nodes although one node may contain several executors.

The SparkContext determines how many resources are allotted to each executor. When a Spark job is launched, each executor has slots for running the tasks needed to compute an RDD. In this way, we can think of one SparkContext as one set of configuration parameters for running Spark jobs. These parameters are exposed in the SparkConf object, which is used to create a SparkContext. We will discuss how to use the parameters in Appendix A. Applications often, but not always, correspond to users. That is, each Spark program running on your cluster likely uses one SparkContext.

> RDDs cannot be shared between applications. Thus transformations, such as join, that use more than one RDD must have the same SparkContext.

Figure 2-4 illustrates what happens when we start a `SparkContext`. First, the driver program pings the cluster manager. The cluster manager launches a number of Spark executors (JVMs shown as black boxes in the diagram) on the worker nodes of the cluster (shown as blue circles). One node can have multiple Spark executors, but an executor cannot span multiple nodes. An RDD will be evaluated across the executors in partitions (shown as red rectangles). Each executor can have multiple partitions, but a partition cannot be spread across multiple executors.

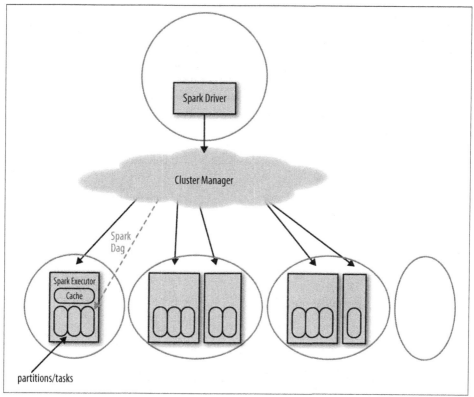

Figure 2-4. Starting a Spark application on a distributed system

Default Spark Scheduler

By default, Spark schedules jobs on a first in, first out basis. However, Spark does offer a fair scheduler, which assigns tasks to concurrent jobs in round-robin fashion, i.e., parceling out a few tasks for each job until the jobs are all complete. The fair scheduler ensures that jobs get a more even share of cluster resources. The Spark application then launches jobs in the order that their corresponding actions were called on the `SparkContext`.

The Anatomy of a Spark Job

In the Spark lazy evaluation paradigm, a Spark application doesn't "do anything" until the driver program calls an action. With each action, the Spark scheduler builds an execution graph and launches a *Spark job*. Each job consists of *stages*, which are steps in the transformation of the data needed to materialize the final RDD. Each stage consists of a collection of *tasks* that represent each parallel computation and are performed on the executors.

Figure 2-5 shows a tree of the different components of a Spark application and how these correspond to the API calls. An application corresponds to starting a `SparkCon text/SparkSession`. Each *application* may contain many jobs that correspond to one RDD action. Each *job* may contain several stages that correspond to each wide transformation. Each *stage* is composed of one or many tasks that correspond to a parallelizable unit of computation done in each stage. There is one *task* for each partition in the resulting RDD of that stage.

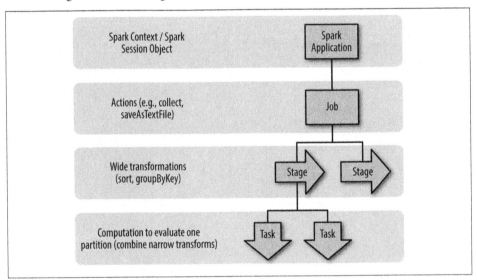

Figure 2-5. The Spark application tree

The DAG

Spark's high-level scheduling layer uses RDD dependencies to build a *Directed Acyclic Graph* (a DAG) of stages for each Spark job. In the Spark API, this is called the DAG Scheduler. As you have probably noticed, errors that have to do with connecting to your cluster, your configuration parameters, or launching a Spark job show up as DAG Scheduler errors. This is because the execution of a Spark job is handled by the DAG. The DAG builds a graph of stages for each job, determines the locations to run each task, and passes that information on to the `TaskScheduler`, which is responsible for running tasks on the cluster. The `TaskScheduler` creates a graph with dependencies between partitions.[8]

Jobs

A Spark job is the highest element of Spark's execution hierarchy. Each Spark job corresponds to one action, and each action is called by the driver program of a Spark application. As we discussed in "Functions on RDDs: Transformations Versus Actions" on page 17, one way to conceptualize an action is as something that brings data out of the RDD world of Spark into some other storage system (usually by bringing data to the driver or writing to some stable storage system).

The edges of the Spark execution graph are based on dependencies between the partitions in RDD transformations (as illustrated by Figures 2-2 and 2-3). Thus, an operation that returns something other than an RDD cannot have any children. In graph theory, we would say the action forms a "leaf" in the DAG. Thus, an arbitrarily large set of transformations may be associated with one execution graph. However, as soon as an action is called, Spark can no longer add to that graph. The application launches a job including those transformations that were needed to evaluate the final RDD that called the action.

Stages

Recall that Spark lazily evaluates transformations; transformations are not executed until an action is called. As mentioned previously, a job is defined by calling an action. The action may include one or several transformations, and wide transformations define the breakdown of jobs into *stages*.

Each stage corresponds to a shuffle dependency created by a wide transformation in the Spark program. At a high level, one stage can be thought of as the set of computations (tasks) that can each be computed on one executor without communication with other executors or with the driver. In other words, a new stage begins whenever network communication between workers is required; for instance, in a shuffle.

These dependencies that create stage boundaries are called `ShuffleDependencies`. As we discussed in "Wide Versus Narrow Dependencies" on page 17, shuffles are caused by those wide transformations, such as `sort` or `groupByKey`, which require the data to be redistributed across the partitions. Several transformations with narrow dependencies can be grouped into one stage.

---

8 See *https://jaceklaskowski.gitbooks.io/mastering-apache-spark/content/spark-TaskScheduler.html* for a more thorough description of the `TaskScheduler`.

As we saw in the word count example where we filtered stop words (Example 2-2), Spark can combine the flatMap, map, and filter steps into one stage since none of those transformations requires a shuffle. Thus, each executor can apply the flatMap, map, and filter steps consecutively in one pass of the data.

 Spark keeps track of how an RDD is partitioned, so that it does not need to partition the same RDD by the same partitioner more than once. This has some interesting consequences for the DAG: the same operations on RDDs with known partitioners and RDDs without a known partitioner can result in different stage boundaries, because there is no need to shuffle an RDD with a known partition (and thus the subsequent transformations happen in the same stage). We will discuss the evaluation consequence of known partitioners in Chapter 6.

Because the stage boundaries require communication with the driver, the stages associated with one job generally have to be executed in sequence rather than in parallel. It is possible to execute stages in parallel if they are used to compute different RDDs that are combined in a downstream transformation such as a join. However, the wide transformations needed to compute one RDD have to be computed in sequence. Thus it is usually desirable to design your program to require fewer shuffles.

Tasks

A stage consists of tasks. The *task* is the smallest unit in the execution hierarchy, and each can represent one local computation. All of the tasks in one stage execute the same code on a different piece of the data. One task cannot be executed on more than one executor. However, each executor has a dynamically allocated number of slots for running tasks and may run many tasks concurrently throughout its lifetime. The number of tasks per stage corresponds to the number of partitions in the output RDD of that stage.

Figure 2-6 shows the evaluation of a Spark job that is the result of a driver program that calls the simple Spark program shown in Example 2-3.

Example 2-3. Different types of transformations showing stage boundaries

```
def simpleSparkProgram(rdd : RDD[Double]): Long ={
//stage1
  rdd.filter(_< 1000.0)
    .map(x => (x, x) )
//stage2
    .groupByKey()
    .map{ case(value, groups) => (groups.sum, value)}
//stage 3
```

```
    .sortByKey()
    .count()
}
```

The stages (blue boxes) are bounded by the shuffle operations `groupByKey` and `sort ByKey`. Each stage consists of several tasks: one for each partition in the result of the RDD transformations (shown as red rectangles), which are executed in parallel.

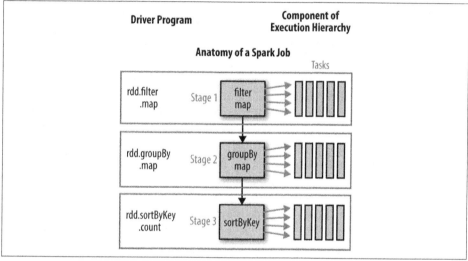

Figure 2-6. A stage diagram for the simple Spark program shown in Example 2-3

A cluster cannot necessarily run every task in parallel for each stage. Each executor has a number of cores. The number of cores per executor is configured at the application level, but likely corresponding to the physical cores on a cluster.[9] Spark can run no more tasks at once than the total number of executor cores allocated for the application. We can calculate the number of tasks from the settings from the Spark Conf as (total number of executor cores = # of cores per executor × number of executors). If there are more partitions (and thus more tasks) than the number of slots for running tasks, then the extra tasks will be allocated to the executors as the first round of tasks finish and resources are available. In most cases, all the tasks for one stage must be completed before the next stage can start. The process of distributing these tasks is done by the `TaskScheduler` and varies depending on whether the fair scheduler or FIFO scheduler is used (recall the discussion in "Default Spark Scheduler" on page 21).

---

9 See "Basic Spark Core Settings: How Many Resources to Allocate to the Spark Application?" on page 278 for information about configuring the number of cores and the relationship between Spark cores and the CPU on the cluster.

In some ways, the simplest way to think of the Spark execution model is that a Spark job is the set of RDD transformations needed to compute one final result. Each stage corresponds to a segment of work, which can be accomplished without involving the driver. In other words, one stage can be computed without moving data across the partitions. Within one stage, the tasks are the units of work done for each partition of the data.

Conclusion

Spark offers an innovative, efficient model of parallel computing that centers on lazily evaluated, immutable, distributed datasets, known as RDDs. Spark exposes RDDs as an interface, and RDD methods can be used without any knowledge of their implementation—but having an understanding of the details will help you write more performant code. Because of Spark's ability to run jobs concurrently, to compute jobs across multiple nodes, and to materialize RDDs lazily, the performance implications of similar logical patterns may differ widely, and errors may surface from misleading places. Thus, it is important to understand how the execution model for your code is assembled in order to write and debug Spark code. Furthermore, it is often possible to accomplish the same tasks in many different ways using the Spark API, and a strong understanding of how your code is evaluated will help you optimize its performance. In this book, we will focus on ways to design Spark applications to minimize network traffic, memory errors, and the cost of failures.

CHAPTER 3

DataFrames, Datasets, and Spark SQL

Spark SQL and its DataFrames and Datasets interfaces are the future of Spark performance, with more efficient storage options, advanced optimizer, and direct operations on serialized data. These components are super important for getting the best of Spark performance (see Figure 3-1).

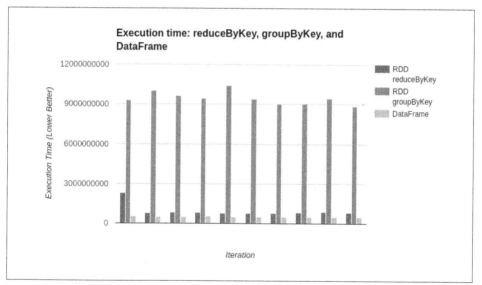

Figure 3-1. Relative performance for RDD versus DataFrames based on SimplePerfTest computing aggregate average fuzziness of pandas

These are relatively new components; Datasets were introduced in Spark 1.6, Data Frames in Spark 1.3, and the SQL engine in Spark 1.0. This chapter is focused on helping you learn how to best use Spark SQL's tools and how to intermix Spark SQL with traditional Spark operations.

 Spark's DataFrames have very different functionality compared to traditional DataFrames like Panda's and R's. While these all deal with structured data, it is important not to depend on your existing intuition surrounding DataFrames.

Like RDDs, DataFrames and Datasets represent distributed collections, with additional schema information not found in RDDs. This additional schema information is used to provide a more efficient storage layer (Tungsten), and in the optimizer (Catalyst) to perform additional optimizations. Beyond schema information, the operations performed on Datasets and DataFrames are such that the optimizer can inspect the logical meaning rather than arbitrary functions. DataFrames are Datasets of a special Row object, which doesn't provide any compile-time type checking. The strongly typed Dataset API shines especially for use with more RDD-like functional operations. Compared to working with RDDs, DataFrames allow Spark's optimizer to better understand our code and our data, which allows for a new class of optimizations we explore in "Query Optimizer" on page 69.

 While Spark SQL, DataFrames, and Datasets provide many excellent enhancements, they still have some rough edges compared to traditional processing with "regular" RDDs. The Dataset API, being brand new at the time of this writing, is likely to experience some changes in future versions.

Getting Started with the SparkSession (or HiveContext or SQLContext)

Much as the SparkContext is the entry point for all Spark applications, and the StreamingContext is for all streaming applications, the SparkSession serves as the entry point for Spark SQL. Like with all of the Spark components, you need to import a few extra components as shown in Example 3-1.

 If you are using the Spark Shell you will automatically get a Spark Session called spark to accompany the SparkContext called sc.

Example 3-1. Spark SQL imports

```
import org.apache.spark.sql.{Dataset, DataFrame, SparkSession, Row}
import org.apache.spark.sql.catalyst.expressions.aggregate._
import org.apache.spark.sql.expressions._
import org.apache.spark.sql.functions._
```

 Scala's type alias of DataFrame = Dataset[Row] is broken in Java
—you must use Dataset<Row> instead.

SparkSession is generally created using the builder pattern, along with getOr
Create(), which will return an existing session if one is already running. The builder
can take string-based configuration keys config(key, value), and shortcuts exist
for a number of common params. One of the more important shortcuts is enableHi
veSupport(), which will give you access to Hive UDFs and *does not require* a Hive
installation—but does require certain extra JARs (discussed in "Spark SQL Dependencies" on page 30). Example 3-2 shows how to create a SparkSession with Hive
support. The enableHiveSupport() shortcut not only configures Spark SQL to use
these Hive JARs, but it also eagerly checks that they can be loaded—leading to a
clearer error message than setting configuration values by hand. In general, using
shortcuts listed in the API docs (*http://spark.apache.org/docs/latest/api/scala/
index.html#org.apache.spark.package*), is advised when they are present, since no
checking is done in the generic config interface.

Example 3-2. Create a SparkSession

```
val session = SparkSession.builder()
  .enableHiveSupport()
  .getOrCreate()
// Import the implicits, unlike in core Spark the implicits are defined
// on the context.
import session.implicits._
```

 When using getOrCreate, if an existing session exists your configuration values may be ignored and you will simply get the existing
SparkSession. Some options, like master, will also only apply if
there is no existing SparkContext running; otherwise, the existing
SparkContext will be used.

Before Spark 2.0, instead of the SparkSession, two separate entry points (HiveCon
text or SQLContext) were used for Spark SQL. The names of these entry points can

be a bit confusing, and it is important to note the HiveContext *does not require* a Hive installation. The primary reason to use the SQLContext is if you have conflicts with the Hive dependencies that cannot be resolved. The HiveContext has a more complete SQL parser compared to the SQLContext as well as additional user-defined functions (UDFs).[1] Example 3-4 shows how to create a legacy HiveContext. The SparkSession should be preferred when possible, followed by the HiveContext, then SQLContext. Not all libraries, or even all Spark code, has been updated to take the SparkSession and in some cases you will find functions that still expect a SQLContext or HiveContext.

If you need to construct one of the legacy interfaces (SQLContext or HiveContext) the additional imports in Example 3-3 will be useful.

Example 3-3. Spark SQL legacy imports

```
import org.apache.spark.sql.SQLContext
import org.apache.spark.sql.hive.HiveContext
import org.apache.spark.sql.hive.thriftserver._
```

 Getting a HiveContext or SQLContext from a SparkSession is not well supported outside of the org.apache.spark scope—however, getOrCreate can be used.

Example 3-4. Creating the HiveContext

```
val hiveContext = new HiveContext(sc)
// Import the implicits, unlike in core Spark the implicits are defined
// on the context.
import hiveContext.implicits._
```

Spark SQL Dependencies

Like the other components in Spark, using Spark SQL requires adding additional dependencies. If you have conflicts with the Hive JARs you can't fix through shading, you can just limit yourself to the *spark-sql* JAR—although you want to have access to the Hive dependencies without also including the *spark-hive* JAR.

To enable Hive support in SparkSession or use the HiveContext you will need to add both Spark's SQL and Hive components to your dependencies.

---

[1] UDFs allow us to extend SQL to have additional powers, such as computing the geospatial distance between points.

For Maven-compatible build systems, the coordinates for Spark's `SQL` and `Hive` components in 2.2.0 are `org.apache.spark:spark-sql_2.11:2.2.0` and `org.apache.spark:spark-hive_2.11:2.2.0`. Example 3-5 shows how to add them to a "regular" sbt build, and Example 3-6 shows the process for Maven users.

Example 3-5. Add Spark SQL and Hive component to "regular" sbt build

```
libraryDependencies ++= Seq(
  "org.apache.spark" %% "spark-sql" % "2.2.0",
  "org.apache.spark" %% "spark-hive" % "2.2.0")
```

Example 3-6. Add Spark SQL and Hive component to Maven pom file

```
<dependency> <!-- Spark dependency -->
  <groupId>org.apache.spark</groupId>
  <artifactId>spark-sql_2.11</artifactId>
  <version>2.2.0</version>
</dependency>
<dependency> <!-- Spark dependency -->
  <groupId>org.apache.spark</groupId>
  <artifactId>spark-hive_2.11</artifactId>
  <version>2.2.0</version>
</dependency>
```

Managing Spark Dependencies

While managing these dependencies by hand isn't particularly challenging, sometimes mistakes can be made when updating versions. The sbt-spark-package (*https://github.com/databricks/sbt-spark-package*) plug-in can simplify managing Spark dependencies. This plug-in is normally used for creating community packages (discussed in "Creating a Spark Package" on page 273), but also assist in building software that depends on Spark. To add the plug-in to your sbt build you need to create a *project/plugins.sbt* file and make sure it contains the code in Example 3-7.

Example 3-7. Including sbt-spark-package in project/plugins.sbt

```
resolvers += ["Spark Package Main Repo" at
  "https://dl.bintray.com/spark-packages/maven"]

addSbtPlugin("org.spark-packages" % "sbt-spark-package" % "0.2.5")
```

> If you are starting a new Spark project, there is a g8 template, holdenk/sparkProjectTemplate (*https://github.com/holdenk/sparkProjectTemplate.g8*) you can use to bootstrap your new project by running sbt new holdenk/sparkProjectTemplate.

For `spark-packages` to work you will need to specify a Spark version and at least one Spark component (core), which can be done in sbt settings as shown in Example 3-8.

Example 3-8. Configuring Spark version and "core" component

```
sparkVersion := "2.2.0"
sparkComponents ++= Seq("core")
```

Once you have `sbt-spark-package` installed and set up, you can add the Spark components by just adding `SQL` and `Hive` to your list of `sparkComponents` as shown in Example 3-9.

Example 3-9. Add Spark SQL and Hive component to sbt-spark-package build

```
sparkComponents ++= Seq("sql", "hive", "hive-thriftserver", "hive-thriftserver")
```

While it's not required, if you do have an existing Hive Metastore to which you wish to connect with Spark, you can copy your *hive-site.xml* to Spark's *conf/* directory.

> The default Hive Metastore version is 1.2.1. For other versions of the Hive Metastore you will need to set the `spark.sql.hive.meta store.version` property to the desired versions as well as set `spark.sql.hive.metastore.jars` to either "maven" (to have Spark retrieve the JARs) or the system path where the Hive JARs are present.

Avoiding Hive JARs

If you can't include the Hive dependencies with your application, you can leave out Spark's Hive component and instead create a `SQLContext`, as shown in Example 3-10. This provides much of the same functionality, but uses a less capable SQL parser and lacks certain Hive-based user-defined functions (UDFs) and user-defined aggregate functions (UDAFs).

Example 3-10. Creating the SQLContext

```
val sqlContext = new SQLContext(sc)
// Import the implicits, unlike in core Spark the implicits are defined
// on the context.
import sqlContext.implicits._
```

As with the core `SparkContext` and `StreamingContext`, the `Hive/SQLContext` is used to load your data. JSON is a very popular format, in part because it can be easily loaded in many languages, and is at least semi–human-readable. Some of the sample data we've included in the book is in JSON format for exactly these reasons. JSON is especially interesting since it lacks schema information, and Spark needs to do some work to infer the schema from our data. JSON can also be expensive to parse; in some simple cases parsing the input JSON data can be greater than the actual operation. We will cover the full loading and saving API for JSON in "JSON" on page 52, but to get started, let's load a sample we can use to explore the schema (see Example 3-11).

Example 3-11. Load JSON sample

```
val df1 = session.read.json(path)
```

Feel free to load your own JSON data, but if you don't have any handy to test with, check out the examples GitHub (*https://github.com/high-performance-spark/high-performance-spark-examples*) resources directory (*https://github.com/high-performance-spark/high-performance-spark-examples/tree/master/resources*). Now that you've got the JSON data loaded you can start by exploring what schema Spark has managed to infer for your data.

Basics of Schemas

The schema information, and the optimizations it enables, is one of the core differences between Spark SQL and core Spark. Inspecting the schema is especially useful for DataFrames since you don't have the templated type you do with RDDs or Data sets. Schemas are normally handled automatically by Spark SQL, either inferred when loading the data or computed based on the parent DataFrames and the transformation being applied.

DataFrames expose the schema in both human-readable or programmatic formats. printSchema() will show us the schema of a DataFrame and is most commonly used when working in the shell to figure out what you are working with. This is especially useful for data formats, like JSON, where the schema may not be immediately visible by looking at only a few records or reading a header. For programmatic usage, you can get the schema by simply calling schema, which is often used in ML pipeline transformers. Since you are likely familiar with case classes and JSON, let's examine how the equivalent Spark SQL schema would be represented in Examples 3-12 and 3-13.

Example 3-12. JSON data that would result in an equivalent schema

```
{"name":"mission","pandas":[{"id":1,"zip":"94110","pt":"giant", "happy":true,
    "attributes":[0.4,0.5]}]}
```

Example 3-13. Equivalent case class

```
case class RawPanda(id: Long, zip: String, pt: String,
                        happy: Boolean, attributes: Array[Double])
case class PandaPlace(name: String, pandas: Array[RawPanda])
```

Now with the case classes defined you can create a local instance, turn it into a Data set, and print the schema as shown in Example 3-14, resulting in Example 3-15. The same can be done with the JSON data, but requires some configuration as discussed in "JSON" on page 52.

Example 3-14. Create a Dataset with the case class

```
def createAndPrintSchema() = {
  val damao = RawPanda(1, "M1B 5K7", "giant", true, Array(0.1, 0.1))
  val pandaPlace = PandaPlace("toronto", Array(damao))
  val df = session.createDataFrame(Seq(pandaPlace))
  df.printSchema()
}
```

Example 3-15. Sample schema information for nested structure (.printSchema())

```
root
 |-- name: string (nullable = true)
 |-- pandas: array (nullable = true)
 |    |-- element: struct (containsNull = true)
 |    |    |-- id: long (nullable = false)
 |    |    |-- zip: string (nullable = true)
 |    |    |-- pt: string (nullable = true)
 |    |    |-- happy: boolean (nullable = false)
 |    |    |-- attributes: array (nullable = true)
 |    |    |    |-- element: double (containsNull = false)
```

In addition to the human-readable schema, the schema information is also available for you to use programmatically. The programatic schema is returned as a Struct Field, as shown in Example 3-16.

Example 3-16. StructField case class

```
case class StructField(
    name: String,
    dataType: DataType,
    nullable: Boolean = true,
    metadata: Metadata = Metadata.empty)
 ....
```

Example 3-17 shows the same schema as Example 3-15, in machine-readable format.

Example 3-17. Sample schema information for nested structure (.schema())—manually formatted

```
org.apache.spark.sql.types.StructType = StructType(
  StructField(name,StringType,true),
  StructField(pandas,
    ArrayType(
      StructType(StructField(id,LongType,false),
                 StructField(zip,StringType,true),
                 StructField(pt,StringType,true),
                 StructField(happy,BooleanType,false),
                 StructField(attributes,ArrayType(DoubleType,false),true)),
              true),true))
```

From here you can dive into what this schema information means and look at how to construct more complex schemas. The first part is a `StructType`, which contains a list of fields. It's important to note you can nest `StructTypes`, like how a case class can contain additional case classes. The fields in the `StructType` are defined with `Struct Field`, which specifies the name, type (see Tables 3-1 and 3-2 for a listing of types), and a Boolean indicating if the field may be null/missing.

Table 3-1. Basic Spark SQL types

Scala type	SQL type	Details
Byte	ByteType	1-byte signed integers (−128,127)
Short	ShortType	2-byte signed integers (−32768,32767)
Int	IntegerType	4-byte signed integers (−2147483648,2147483647)
Long	LongType	8-byte signed integers (−9223372036854775808, 9223372036854775807)
java.math.BigDecimal	DecimalType	Arbitrary precision signed decimals
Float	FloatType	4-byte floating-point number
Double	DoubleType	8-byte floating-point number
Array[Byte]	BinaryType	Array of bytes
Boolean	BooleanType	true/false
java.sql.Date	DateType	Date without time information
java.sql.Timestamp	TimestampType	Date with time information (second precision)
String	StringType	Character string values (stored as UTF8)

Table 3-2. Complex Spark SQL types

Scala type	SQL type	Details	Example
`Array[T]`	`ArrayType(element Type, containsNull)`	Array of single type of element, containsNull true if any null elements.	`Array[Int] => Array Type(IntegerType, true)`
`Map[K, V]`	`MapType(elementType, valueType, valueCon tainsNull)`	Key/value map, valueCon tainsNull if any values are null.	`Map[String, Int] => Map Type(StringType, Integer Type, true)`
case class	`Struct Type(List[Struct Fields])`	Named fields of possible heterogeneous types, similar to a case class or JavaBean.	`case class Panda(name: String, age: Int) => StructType(List(Struct Field("name", StringType, true), StructField("age", IntegerType, true)))`

As you saw in Example 3-17, you can nest `StructFields` and all of the complex Spark SQL types.

Now that you've got an idea of how to understand and, if needed, specify schemas for your data, you are ready to start exploring the `DataFrame` interfaces.

Spark SQL schemas are eagerly evaluated, unlike the data underneath. If you find yourself in the shell and uncertain of what a transformation will do, try it and print the schema. See Example 3-15.

DataFrame API

Spark SQL's DataFrame API allows us to work with `DataFrames` without having to register temporary tables or generate SQL expressions. The DataFrame API has both transformations and actions. The transformations on `DataFrames` are more relational in nature, with the Dataset API (covered next) offering a more functional-style API.

Transformations

Transformations on `DataFrames` are similar in concept to RDD transformations, but with a more relational flavor. Instead of specifying arbitrary functions, which the optimizer is unable to introspect, you use a restricted expression syntax so the opti‐mizer can have more information. As with RDDs, we can broadly break down transformations into simple single `DataFrame`, multiple `DataFrame`, key/value, and grouped/windowed transformations.

 Spark SQL transformations are only partially lazy; the schema is eagerly evaluated.

Simple DataFrame transformations and SQL expressions

Simple `DataFrame` transformations allow us to do most of the standard things one can do when working a row at a time.[2] You can still do many of the same operations defined on RDDs, except using Spark SQL expressions instead of arbitrary functions. To illustrate this we will start by examining the different kinds of filter operations available on `DataFrame`s.

`DataFrame` functions, like `filter`, accept Spark SQL expressions instead of lambdas. These expressions allow the optimizer to understand what the condition represents, and with `filter`, it can often be used to skip reading unnecessary records.

To get started, let's look at a SQL expression to filter our data for unhappy pandas using our existing schema. The first step is looking up the column that contains this information. In our case it is `happy`, and for our `DataFrame` (called `df`) we access the column through the `apply` function (e.g., `df("happy")`). The `filter` expression requires the expression to return a boolean value, and if you wanted to select happy pandas, the entire expression could be retrieving the column value. However, since we want to find the unhappy pandas, we can check to see that `happy` isn't true using the `!==` operator as shown in Example 3-18.

Example 3-18. Simple filter for unhappy pandas

```
pandaInfo.filter(pandaInfo("happy") !== true)
```

 To look up the column, we can either provide the column name on the specific `DataFrame` or use the implicit `$` operator for column lookup. This is especially useful when the `DataFrame` is anonymous. The `!` binary negation function can be used together with `$` to simplify our expression from Example 3-18 down to `df.fil ter(!$("happy"))`.

---

2 A row at a time allows for narrow transformations with no shuffle.

This illustrates how to access a specific column from a DataFrame. For accessing other structures inside of DataFrames, like nested structs, keyed maps, and array elements, use the same apply syntax. So, if the first element in the attributes array represent squishiness, and you only want very squishy pandas, you can access that element by writing df("attributes")(0) >= 0.5.

Our expressions need not be limited to a single column. You can compare multiple columns in our "filter" expression. Complex filters like that shown in Example 3-19 are more difficult to push down to the storage layer, so you may not see the same speedup over RDDs that you see with simpler filters.

Example 3-19. More complex filter

```
pandaInfo.filter(
    pandaInfo("happy").and(pandaInfo("attributes")(0) > pandaInfo("attributes")(1))
)
```

 Spark SQL's column operators are defined on the column class, so a filter containing the expression 0 >= df.col("friends") will not compile since Scala will use the >= defined on 0. Instead you would write df.col("friend") <= 0 or convert 0 to a column literal with lit.[3]

Spark SQL's DataFrame API has a very large set of operators available. You can use all of the standard mathematical operators on floating points, along with the standard logical and bitwise operations (prefix with bitwise to distinguish from logical). Columns use === and !== for equality to avoid conflict with Scala internals. For columns of strings, startsWith/endsWith, substr, like, and isNull are all available. The full set of operations is listed in org.apache.spark.sql.Column (*http://spark.apache.org/docs/latest/api/scala/index.html#org.apache.spark.sql.Column*) and covered in Table 3-3 and Table 3-4.

---

3 A column literal is a column with a fixed value that doesn't change between rows (i.e., constant).

Table 3-3. Spark SQL Scala operators

Scala operator	Java equivalent	Input column types	Output type	Purpose	Sample	Result
!==	notEqual	Any	Boolean	Check if expressions not equal	`"hi" !== "bye"`	`true`
%	mod	Numeric	Numeric	Modulo	`10 % 5`	`0`
&&	and	Boolean	Boolean	Boolean and	`true && false`	`false`
*	multiply	Numeric	Numeric	Multiply expressions	`2 * 21`	`42`
+	plus	Numeric	Numeric	Sum expression	`2 + 2`	`4`
-	minus	Numeric	Numeric	Subtraction	`2 - 2`	`0`
-	unary_-	Numeric	Numeric	Unary subtraction	`-42`	`-42`
/	division	Numeric	Double	Division	`43/2`	`21.5`
<	lt	Comparable	Boolean	Less than	`"a" < "b"`	`true`
<=	leq	Comparable	Boolean	Less than or equal to	`"a" <= "a"`	`true`
===	equals	Any	Any	Equality test (unsafe on null values)	`"a" === "a"`	`true`
<=>	eqNullSafe	Any	Any	Equality test (safe on null values)	`"a" <=> "a"`	`true`
>	gt	Comparable	Boolean	Greater than	`"a" > "b"`	`false`
>=	ge	Comparable	Boolean	Greater than or equal to	`"a" >= "b"`	`false`

Table 3-4. Spark SQL expression operators

Operator	Input column types	Output type	Purpose	Sample	Result
apply	Complex types	Type of field accessed	Get value from complex type (e.g., structfield/map lookup or array index)	`[1,2,3].apply(0)`	`1`
bitwiseAND	Integral Type [a]	Same as input	Computes and bitwise	`21.bitwiseAND(11)`	`1`
bitwiseOR	Integral Type [a]	Same as input	Computes or bitwise	`21.bitwiseOR(11)`	`31`
bitwiseXOR	Integral Type [a]	Same as input	Computes bitwise exclusive or	`21.bitwiseXOR(11)`	`30`

[a] Integral types include `ByteType`, `IntegerType`, `LongType`, and `ShortType`.

Not all Spark SQL expressions can be used in every API call. For example, Spark SQL joins do not support complex operations, and `filter` requires that the expression result in a boolean, and similar.

In addition to the operators directly specified on the column, an even larger set of functions on columns exists in org.apache.spark.sql.functions (*https://spark.apache.org/docs/latest/api/scala/index.html#org.apache.spark.sql.functions$*), some of which we cover in Tables 3-5, 3-6, and 3-7. For illustration, this example shows the values for each column at a specific row, but keep in mind that these functions are called on columns, not values.

Table 3-5. Spark SQL standard functions

Function name	Purpose	Input types	Example usage	Result
lit(value)	Convert a Scala symbol to a column literal	Column & Symbol	lit(1)	Column(1)
array	Create a new array column	Must all have the same Spark SQL type	array(lit(1),lit(2))	array(1,2)
isNaN	Check if not a number	Numeric	isNan(lit(100.0))	false
not	Opposite value	Boolean	not(lit(true))	false

Table 3-6. Spark SQL common mathematical expressions

Function name	Purpose	Input types	Example usage	Result
abs	Absolute value	Numeric	abs(lit(-1))	1
sqrt	Square root	Numeric	sqrt(lit(4))	2
acos	Inverse cosine	Numeric	acos(lit(0.5))	1.04....[a]
asin	Inverse sine	Numeric	asin(lit(0.5))	0.523...[a]
atan	Inverse tangent	Numeric	atan(lit(0.5))	0.46...[a]
cbrt	Cube root	Numeric	sqrt(lit(8))	2
ceil	Ceiling	Numeric	ceil(lit(8.5))	9
cos	Cosine	Numeric	cos(lit(0.5))	0.877....[a]
sin	Sine	Numeric	sin(lit(0.5))	0.479...[a]
tan	Tangent	Numeric	tan(lit(0.5))	0.546...[a]
exp	Exponent	Numeric	exp(lit(1.0))	2.718...[a]
floor	Ceiling	Numeric	floor(lit(8.5))	8
least	Minimum value	Numerics	least(lit(1), lit(-10))	-10

[a] Truncated for display purposes.

Table 3-7. Functions for use on Spark SQL arrays

Function name	Purpose	Example usage	Result
array_contains	If an array contains a value.	array_contains(lit(Array(2,3,-1)), 3))	true
sort_array	Sort an array (ascending default).	sort_array(lit(Array(2,3,-1)))	Array(-1,2,3)
explode	Create a row for each element in the array—often useful when working with nested JSON records. Either takes a column name or additional function mapping from row to iterator of case classes.	explode(lit(Array(2,3,-1)), "murh")	Row(2), Row(3), Row(-1)

Beyond simply filtering out data, you can also produce a DataFrame with new columns or updated values in old columns. Spark uses the same expression syntax we discussed for filter, except instead of having to include a condition (like testing for equality), the results are used as values in the new DataFrame. To see how you can use select on complex and regular data types, Example 3-20 uses the Spark SQL explode function to turn an input DataFrame of PandaPlaces into a DataFrame of just PandaInfo as well as computing the "squishness" to "hardness" ratio of each panda.

Example 3-20. Spark SQL select and explode operators

```
val pandaInfo = pandaPlace.explode(pandaPlace("pandas")){
  case Row(pandas: Seq[Row]) =>
    pandas.map{
      case (Row(
        id: Long,
        zip: String,
        pt: String,
        happy: Boolean,
        attrs: Seq[Double])) =>
        RawPanda(id, zip, pt, happy, attrs.toArray)
    }}
pandaInfo.select(
  (pandaInfo("attributes")(0) / pandaInfo("attributes")(1))
    .as("squishyness"))
```

 When you construct a sequence of operations, the generated column names can quickly become unwieldy, so the as or alias operators are useful to specify the resulting column name.

While all of these operations are quite powerful, sometimes the logic you wish to express is more easily encoded with if/else semantics. Example 3-21 is a simple example of this, and it encodes the different types of panda as a numeric value.[4] The when and otherwise functions can be chained together to create the same effect.

Example 3-21. If/else in Spark SQL

```
/**
  * Encodes pandaType to Integer values instead of String values.
  *
  * @param pandaInfo the input DataFrame
  * @return Returns a DataFrame of pandaId and integer value for pandaType.
  */
def encodePandaType(pandaInfo: DataFrame): DataFrame = {
  pandaInfo.select(pandaInfo("id"),
    (when(pandaInfo("pt") === "giant", 0).
    when(pandaInfo("pt") === "red", 1).
    otherwise(2)).as("encodedType")
  )
}
```

Specialized DataFrame transformations for missing and noisy data

Spark SQL also provides special tools for handling missing, null, and invalid data. By using isNan or isNull along with filters, you can create conditions for the rows you want to keep. For example, if you have a number of different columns, perhaps with different levels of precision (some of which may be null), you can use coalesce(c1, c2, ..) to return the first nonnull column. Similarly, for numeric data, nanvl returns the first non-NaN value (e.g., nanvl(0/0, sqrt(-2), 3) results in 3). To simplify working with missing data, the na function on DataFrame gives us access to some common routines for handling missing data in DataFrameNaFunctions (*http:// spark.apache.org/docs/latest/api/scala/index.html#org.apache.spark.sql.DataFrameNa Functions*).

Beyond row-by-row transformations

Sometimes applying a row-by-row decision, as you can with filter, isn't enough. Spark SQL also allows us to select the unique rows by calling dropDuplicates, but as with the similar operation on RDDs (distinct), this can require a shuffle, so is often much slower than filter. Unlike with RDDs, dropDuplicates can optionally drop rows based on only a subset of the columns, such as an ID field, as shown in Example 3-22.

---

4 StringIndexer (*http://spark.apache.org/docs/latest/api/scala/index.html#org.apache.spark.ml.feature.StringIn dexer*) in the ML pipeline is designed for string index encoding.

Example 3-22. Drop duplicate panda IDs

```
pandas.dropDuplicates(List("id"))
```

This leads nicely into our next section on aggregates and groupBy since often the most expensive component of each is the shuffle.

Aggregates and groupBy

Spark SQL has many powerful aggregates, and thanks to its optimizer it can be easy to combine many aggregates into one single action/query. Like with Pandas' Data Frames, groupBy returns special objects on which we can ask for certain aggregations to be performed. In pre-2.0 versions of Spark, this was a generic GroupedData (*http:// spark.apache.org/docs/1.6.2/api/scala/index.html#org.apache.spark.sql.GroupedData*), but in versions 2.0 and beyond, DataFrames groupBy is the same as one Datasets.

Aggregations on Datasets have extra functionality, returning a GroupedDataset (*http://bit.ly/2pyMplR*) (in pre-2.0 versions of Spark) or a KeyValueGroupedDataset (*http://bit.ly/2oZ67oX*) when grouped with an arbitrary function, and a Relational GroupedDataset (*http://bit.ly/2pySePV*) when grouped with a relational/Dataset DSl expression. The additional typed functionality is discussed in "Grouped Operations on Datasets" on page 66, and the common "untyped" DataFrame and Dataset groupBy functionality is explored here.

min, max, avg, and sum are all implemented as convenience functions directly on GroupedData, and more can be specified by providing the expressions to agg. Example 3-23 shows how to compute the maximum panda size by zip code. Once you specify the aggregates you want to compute, you can get the results back as a DataFrame.

 If you're used to RDDs you might be concerned by groupBy, but it is now a safe operation on DataFrames thanks to the Spark SQL optimizer, which automatically pipelines our reductions, avoiding giant shuffles and mega records.

Example 3-23. Compute the max panda size by zip code

```
def maxPandaSizePerZip(pandas: DataFrame): DataFrame = {
  pandas.groupBy(pandas("zip")).max("pandaSize")
}
```

While Example 3-23 computes the max on a per-key basis, these aggregates can also be applied over the entire DataFrame or all numeric columns in a DataFrame. This is often useful when trying to collect some summary statistics for the data with which you are working. In fact, there is a built-in describe transformation which does just that, although it can also be limited to certain columns, which is used in Example 3-24 and returns Example 3-25.

Example 3-24. Compute some common summary stats, including count, mean, stddev, and more, on the entire DataFrame

```
// Compute the count, mean, stddev, min, max summary stats for all
// of the numeric fields of the provided panda infos. non-numeric
// fields (such as string (name) or array types) are skipped.
val df = pandas.describe()
// Collect the summary back locally
println(df.collect())
```

Example 3-25. Result of describe and collect on some small sample data (note: summarizes all of the numeric fields)

```
Array([count,3,3], [mean,1.3333333333333333,5.0],
   [stddev,0.5773502691896258,4.358898943540674], [min,1,2], [max,2,10])
```

> The behavior of groupBy has changed between Spark versions. Prior to Spark 1.3 the values of the grouping columns are discarded by default, while post 1.3 they are retained. The configuration parameter, spark.sql.retainGroupColumns, can be set to false to force the earlier functionality.

For computing multiple different aggregations, or more complex aggregations, you should use the agg API on the GroupedData instead of directly calling count, mean, or similar convenience functions. For the agg API, you either supply a list of aggregate expressions, a string representing the aggregates, or a map of column names to aggregate function names. Once we've called agg with the requested aggregates, we get back a regular DataFrame with the aggregated results. As with regular functions, they are listed in the org.apache.spark.sql.functions Scaladoc (*http://spark.apache.org/docs/latest/api/scala/index.html#org.apache.spark.sql.functions$*). Table 3-8 lists some common and useful aggregates. For our example results in these tables we will consider a DataFrame with the schema of name field (as a string) and age (as an integer), both nullable with values ({"ikea", null}, {"tube", 6}, {"real", 30}). Example 3-26 shows how to compute both the min and mean for the pandaSize column on our running panda example.

> Computing multiple aggregates with Spark SQL can be much simpler than doing the same tasks with the RDD API.

Example 3-26. Example aggregates using the agg API

```
def minMeanSizePerZip(pandas: DataFrame): DataFrame = {
  // Compute the min and mean
  pandas.groupBy(pandas("zip")).agg(
    min(pandas("pandaSize")), mean(pandas("pandaSize")))
}
```

Table 3-8. Spark SQL aggregate functions for use with agg API

Function name	Purpose	Storage requirement	Input types	Example usage	Example result
approxCount Distinct	Count approximate distinct values in column [a]	Configurable through rsd (which controls error rate)	All	`df.agg(approxCountDistinct (df("age"), 0.001))`	2
avg	Average	Constant	Numeric	`df.agg(avg(df("age")))`	18
count	Count number of items (excluding nulls). Special case of "*" counts number of rows	Constant	All	`df.agg(count(df("age")))`	2
countDistinct	Count distinct values in column	O(distinct elems)	All	`df.agg(countDistinct (df("age")))`	2
first	Return the first element [b]	Constant	All	`df.agg(first(df("age")))`	6
last	Return the last element	Constant	All	`df.agg(last(df("age")))`	30
stddev	Sample standard deviation [c]	Constant	Numeric	`df.agg(stddev(df("age")))`	16.97...
stddev_pop	Population standard deviation [c]	Constant	Numeric	`df.agg(stddev_pop(df("age")))`	12.0
sum	Sum of the values	Constant	Numeric	`df.agg(sum(df("age")))`	36
sumDistinct	Sum of the distinct values	O(distinct elems)	Numeric	`df.agg(sumDistinct (df("age")))`	36

Function name	Purpose	Storage requirement	Input types	Example usage	Example result
min	Select the minimum value	Constant	Sortable data	df.agg(min(df("age")))	5
max	Select the maximum value	Constant	Sortable data	df.agg(max(df("age")))	30
mean	Select the mean value	Constant	Numeric	df.agg(mean(df("age")))	18

[a] Implemented with HyperLogLog: *https://en.wikipedia.org/wiki/HyperLogLog*.
[b] This was commonly used in early versions of Spark SQL where the grouping column was not preserved.
[c] Added in Spark 1.6.

> In addition to using aggregates on groupBy, you can run the same aggregations on multidimensional cubes with cube and rollups with rollup.

If the built-in aggregation functions don't meet your needs, you can extend Spark SQL using UDFs as discussed in "Extending with User-Defined Functions and Aggregate Functions (UDFs, UDAFs)" on page 67, although things can be more complicated for aggregate functions.

Windowing

Spark SQL 1.4.0 introduced windowing functions to allow us to more easily work with ranges or windows of rows. When creating a window you specify what columns the window is over, the order of the rows within each partition/group, and the size of the window (e.g., K rows before and J rows after OR range between values). If it helps to think of this visually, Figure 3-2 shows a sample window and its results. Using this specification each input row is related to some set of rows, called a frame, that is used to compute the resulting aggregate. Window functions can be very useful for things like computing average speed with noisy data, relative sales, and more. A window for pandas by age is shown in Example 3-27.

Example 3-27. Define a window on the +/-10 closest (by age) pandas in the same zip code

```
val windowSpec = Window
  .orderBy(pandas("age"))
  .partitionBy(pandas("zip"))
  .rowsBetween(start = -10, end = 10) // can use rangeBetween for range instead
```

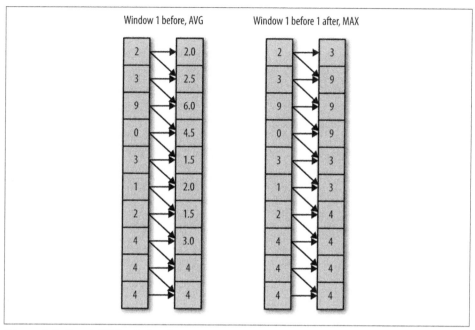

Figure 3-2. Spark SQL windowing

Once you've defined a window specification you can compute a function over it, as shown in Example 3-28. Spark's existing aggregate functions, covered in "Aggregates and groupBy" on page 43, can be computed on an aggregation over the window. Window operations are very useful for things like Kalman filtering or many types of relative analysis.

Example 3-28. Compute difference from the average using the window of +/-10 closest (by age) pandas in the same zip code

```
val pandaRelativeSizeCol = pandas("pandaSize") -
  avg(pandas("pandaSize")).over(windowSpec)

pandas.select(pandas("name"), pandas("zip"), pandas("pandaSize"), pandas("age"),
  pandaRelativeSizeCol.as("panda_relative_size"))
```

> As of this writing, windowing functions require Hive support to be enabled or using HiveContext.

Sorting

Sorting supports multiple columns in ascending or descending order, with ascending as the default. These sort orders can be intermixed, as shown in Example 3-29. Spark SQL has some extra benefits for sorting as some serialized data can be compared without deserialization.

Example 3-29. Sort by panda age and size in opposite orders

```
pandas.orderBy(pandas("pandaSize").asc, pandas("age").desc)
```

When limiting results, sorting is often used to only bring back the top or bottom K results. When limiting you specify the number of rows with limit(numRows) to restrict the number of rows in the DataFrame. Limits are also sometimes used for debugging without sorting to bring back a small result. If, instead of limiting the number of rows based on a sort order, you want to sample your data, "Sampling" on page 211 covers techniques for Spark SQL sampling as well.

Multi-DataFrame Transformations

Beyond single DataFrame transformations you can perform operations that depend on multiple DataFrames. The ones that first pop into our heads are most likely the different types of joins, which are covered in Chapter 4, but beyond that you can also perform a number of set-like operations between DataFrames.

Set-like operations

The DataFrame set-like operations allow us to perform many operations that are most commonly thought of as set operations. These operations behave a bit differently than traditional set operations since we don't have the restriction of unique elements. While you are likely already familiar with the results of set-like operations from regular Spark and *Learning Spark*, it's important to review the cost of these operations in Table 3-9.

Table 3-9. Set operations

Operation name	Cost
unionAll	Low
intersect	Expensive
except	Expensive
distinct	Expensive

Plain Old SQL Queries and Interacting with Hive Data

Sometimes, it's better to use regular SQL queries instead of building up our operations on `DataFrames`. If you are connected to a Hive Metastore we can directly write SQL queries against the Hive tables and get the results as a `DataFrame`. If you have a `DataFrame` you want to write SQL queries against, you can register it as a temporary table, as shown in Example 3-30 (or save it as a managed table if you intend to reuse it between jobs). `Datasets` can also be converted back to `DataFrames` and registered for querying against.

Example 3-30. Registering/saving tables

```
def registerTable(df: DataFrame): Unit = {
  df.registerTempTable("pandas")
  df.write.saveAsTable("perm_pandas")
}
```

Querying tables is the same, regardless of whether it is a temporary table, existing Hive table, or newly saved Spark table, and is illustrated in Example 3-31.

Example 3-31. Querying a table (permanent or temporary)

```
def querySQL(): DataFrame = {
  sqlContext.sql("SELECT * FROM pandas WHERE size > 0")
}
```

In addition to registering tables you can also write queries directly against a specific file path, as shown in Example 3-32.

Example 3-32. Querying a raw file

```
def queryRawFile(): DataFrame = {
  sqlContext.sql("SELECT * FROM parquet.`path_to_parquet_file`")
}
```

Data Representation in DataFrames and Datasets

`DataFrames` are more than RDDs of `Row` objects; `DataFrames` and `Datasets` have a specialized representation and columnar cache format. The specialized representation is not only more space efficient, but also can be much faster to encode than even Kryo serialization. To be clear, like RDDs, `DataFrames` and `Datasets` are generally lazily evaluated and build up a lineage of their dependencies (except in `DataFrames` this is called a logical plan and contains more information).

Tungsten

Tungsten is a new Spark SQL component that provides more efficient Spark operations by working directly at the byte level. Looking back on Figure 3-1, we can take a closer look at the space differences between the RDDs and DataFrames when cached in Figure 3-3. Tungsten includes specialized in-memory data structures tuned for the types of operations required by Spark, improved code generation, and a specialized wire protocol.

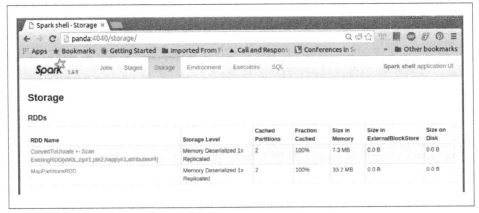

Figure 3-3. RDD versus DataFrame storage space for same data

For those coming from Hadoop, you can think of Tungsten data types as being `WritableComparable` types on steroids.

Tungsten's representation is substantially smaller than objects serialized using Java or even Kryo serializers. As Tungsten does not depend on Java objects, both on-heap and off-heap allocations are supported. Not only is the format more compact, but serialization times can be substantially faster than with native serialization.

Since Tungsten no longer depends on working with Java objects, you can use either on-heap (in the JVM) or off-heap storage. If you use off-heap storage, it is important to leave enough room in your containers for the off-heap allocations, which you can get an approximate idea for from the web UI.

Tungsten's data structures are also created closely in mind with the kind of processing for which they are used. The classic example of this is with sorting, a common and expensive operation. The on-wire representation is implemented so that sorting can be done without having to deserialize the data again.

 In the future Tungsten may make it more feasible to use certain non-JVM libraries. For many simple operations the cost of using BLAS, or similar linear algebra packages, from the JVM is dominated by the cost of copying the data off-heap.

By avoiding the memory and GC overhead of regular Java objects, Tungsten is able to process larger datasets than the same handwritten aggregations. Tungsten became the default in Spark 1.5 and can be enabled in earlier versions by setting `spark.sql.tung sten.enabled` to true (or disabled in later versions by setting this to false). Even without Tungsten, Spark SQL uses a columnar storage format with Kryo serialization to minimize storage cost.

Data Loading and Saving Functions

Spark SQL has a different way of loading and saving data than core Spark. To be able to push down certaintypes of operations to the storage layer, Spark SQL has its own Data Source API (*https://databricks.com/blog/2015/01/09/spark-sql-data-sources-api-unified-data-access-for-the-spark-platform.html*). Data sources are able to specify and control which type of operations should be pushed down to the data source. As developers, you don't need to worry too much about the internal activity going on here, unless the data sources you are looking for are not supported.

 Data loading in Spark SQL is not quite as lazy as in regular Spark, but is still generally lazy. You can verify this by quickly trying to load from a data source that doesn't exist.

DataFrameWriter and DataFrameReader

The DataFrameWriter (*http://spark.apache.org/docs/latest/api/scala/index.html#org.apache.spark.sql.DataFrameWriter*) and the DataFrameReader (*http://spark.apache.org/docs/latest/api/scala/index.html#org.apache.spark.sql.Data FrameReader*) cover writing and reading from external data sources. The `DataFrame Writer` is accessed by calling `write` on a `DataFrame` or `Dataset`. The `DataFrameReader` can be accessed through `read` on a `SQLContext`.

Spark SQL updated the load/save API in Spark 1.4, so you may see code still using the old-style API without the `DataFrame` reader or writer classes, but under the hood it is implemented as a wrapper around the new API.

Formats

When reading or writing you specify the format by calling `format(formatName)` on the `DataFrameWriter`/`DataFrameReader`. Format-specific parameters, such as number of records to be sampled for JSON, are specified by either providing a map of options with `options` or setting option-by-option with `option` on the reader/writer.

The first-party formats `JSON`, `JDBC`, `ORC`, and `Parquet` methods are directly defined on the reader/writers taking the path or connection info. These methods are for convenience only and are wrappers around the more general methods we illustrate in this chapter.

JSON

Loading and writing JSON is supported directly in Spark SQL, and despite the lack of schema information in JSON, Spark SQL is able to infer a schema for us by sampling the records. Loading JSON data is more expensive than loading many data sources, since Spark needs to read some of the records to determine the schema information. If the schema between records varies widely (or the number of records is very small), you can increase the percentage of records read to determine the schema by setting `samplingRatio` to a higher value, as in Example 3-33 where we set the sample ratio to 100%.

Example 3-33. Load JSON data, using all (100%) of records to determine the schema

```
val df2 = session.read.format("json")
  .option("samplingRatio", "1.0").load(path)
```

Spark's schema inference can be a compelling reason to use Spark for processing JSON data, even if the data size could be handled on a single node.

Since our input may contain some invalid JSON records we may wish to filter out, we can also take in an RDD of strings. This allows us to load the input as a standard text file, filter out our invalid records, and then load the data into JSON. This is done by using the built-in `json` function on the `DataFrameReader`, which takes RDDs or paths and is shown in Example 3-34. Methods for converting RDDs of regular objects are covered in "RDDs" on page 57.

Example 3-34. jsonRDD load

```
val rdd: RDD[String] = input.filter(_.contains("panda"))
val df = session.read.json(rdd)
```

JDBC

The JDBC data source represents a natural Spark SQL data source, one that supports many of the same operations. Since different database vendors have slightly different JDBC implementations, you need to add the JAR for your JDBC data sources. Since SQL field types vary as well, Spark uses `JdbcDialects` with built-in dialects for DB2, Derby, MsSQL, MySQL, Oracle, and Postgres.[5]

While Spark supports many different JDBC sources, it does not ship with the JARs required to talk to all of these databases. If you are submitting your Spark job with `spark-submit` you can download the required JARs to the host you are launching and include them by specifying `--jars` or supply the Maven coordinates to `--packages`. Since the Spark Shell is also launched this way, the same syntax works and you can use it to include the MySQL JDBC JAR in Example 3-35.

Example 3-35. Include MySQL JDBC JAR

```
spark-submit --jars ./resources/mysql-connector-java-5.1.38.jar $ASSEMBLY_JAR $CLASS
```

 In earlier versions of Spark `--jars` does not include the JAR in the driver's class path. If this is the case for your cluster you must also specify the same JAR to `--driver-class-path`.

JdbcDialects (*https://github.com/apache/spark/blob/master/sql/core/src/main/ scala/org/apache/spark/sql/jdbc/JdbcDialects.scala*) allow Spark to correctly map the JDBC types to the corresponding Spark SQL types. If there isn't a `JdbcDialect` for your database vendor, the default dialect will be used, which will likely work for many of the types. The dialect is automatically chosen based on the JDBC URL used.

---

5 Some types may not be correctly implemented for all databases.

If you find yourself needing to customize the JdbcDialect for your database vendor, you can look for a package or spark-packages or extend the JdbcDialect class and register your own dialect.

As with the other built-in data sources, there exists a convenience wrapper for specifying the properties required to load JDBC data, illustrated in Example 3-36. The convenience wrapper JDBC accepts the URL, table, and a java.util.Properties object for connection properties (such as authentication information). The properties object is merged with the properties that are set on the reader/writer itself. While the properties object is required, an empty properties object can be provided and properties instead specified on the reader/writer.

Example 3-36. Create a DataFrame from a JDBC data source

```
session.read.jdbc("jdbc:dialect:serverName;user=user;password=pass",
  "table", new Properties)

session.read.format("jdbc")
  .option("url", "jdbc:dialect:serverName")
  .option("dbtable", "table").load()
```

The API for saving a DataFrame is very similar to the API used for loading. The save() function needs no path since the information is already specified, as illustrated in Example 3-37, just as with loading.

Example 3-37. Write a DataFrame to a JDBC data source

```
df.write.jdbc("jdbc:dialect:serverName;user=user;password=pass",
  "table", new Properties)

df.write.format("jdbc")
  .option("url", "jdbc:dialect:serverName")
  .option("user", "user")
  .option("password", "pass")
  .option("dbtable", "table").save()
```

In addition to reading and writing JDBC data sources, Spark SQL can also run its own JDBC server (covered in "JDBC/ODBC Server" on page 71).

Parquet

Apache Parquet files are a common format directly supported in Spark SQL, and they are incredibly space-efficient and popular. Apache Parquet's popularity comes from a number of features, including the ability to easily split across multiple files, compression, nested types, and many others discussed in the Parquet documentation (*https://*

parquet.apache.org/documentation/latest/). Since Parquet is such a popular format, there are some additional options available in Spark for the reading and writing of Parquet files. These options are listed in Table 3-10. Unlike third-party data sources, these options are mostly configured on the `SQLContext`, although some can be configured on either the `SQLContext` or `DataFrameReader/Writer`.

Table 3-10. Parquet data source options

SQLConf	DataFrameReader/Writer option	Default	Purpose
spark.sql.parquet .mergeSchema	mergeSchema	False	Control if schema should be merged between partitions when reading. Can be expensive, so disabled by default in 1.5.0.
spark.sql.parquet .binaryAsString	N/A	False	Treat binary data as strings. Old versions of Spark wrote strings as binary data.
spark.sql.parquet .cacheMetadata	N/A	True	Cache Parquet metadata, normally safe unless underlying data is being modified by another process.
spark.sql.parquet .compression.codec	N/A	Gzip	Specify the compression codec for use with Parquet data. Valid options are uncompressed, snappy, gzip, or lzo.
spark.sql.parquet .filterPushdown	N/A	True	Push down filters to Parquet (when possible).[a]
spark.sql.parquet .writeLegacyFormat	N/A	False	Write in Parquet metadata in the legacy format.
spark.sql.parquet .output.commit ter.class	N/A	org.apache.par quet.hadoop.Par quetOutput Committer	Output committer used by Parquet. If writing to S3 you may wish to try org.apache.spark.sql.par quet.DirectParquetOutputCom mitter.

[a] Pushdown means evaluate at the storage, so with Parquet this can often mean skipping reading unnecessary rows or files.

Reading Parquet from an old version of Spark requires some special options, as shown in Example 3-38.

Example 3-38. Read Parquet file written by an old version of Spark

```
def loadParquet(path: String): DataFrame = {
  // Configure Spark to read binary data as string,
  // note: must be configured on session.
  session.conf.set("spark.sql.parquet.binaryAsString", "true")

  // Load parquet data using merge schema (configured through option)
  session.read
    .option("mergeSchema", "true")
    .format("parquet")
```

```
    .load(path)
  }
```

Writing parquet with the default options is quite simple, as shown in Example 3-39.

Example 3-39. Write Parquet file with default options

```
def writeParquet(df: DataFrame, path: String) = {
  df.write.format("parquet").save(path)
}
```

Hive tables

Interacting with Hive tables adds another option beyond the other formats. As covered in "Plain Old SQL Queries and Interacting with Hive Data" on page 49, one option for bringing in data from a Hive table is writing a SQL query against it and having the result as a DataFrame. The DataFrame's reader and writer interfaces can also be used with Hive tables, as with the rest of the data sources, as illustrated in Example 3-40.

Example 3-40. Load a Hive table

```
def loadHiveTable(): DataFrame = {
  session.read.table("pandas")
}
```

 When loading a Hive table Spark SQL will convert the metadata and cache the result. If the underlying metadata has changed you can use sqlContext.refreshTable("tablename") to update the metadata, or the caching can be disabled by setting spark.sql.par quet.cacheMetadata to false.

Saving a managed table is a bit different, and is illustrated in Example 3-41.

Example 3-41. Write managed table

```
def saveManagedTable(df: DataFrame): Unit = {
  df.write.saveAsTable("pandas")
}
```

 Unless specific conditions are met, the result saved to a Hive managed table will be saved in a Spark-specific format that other tools may not be able to understand.

RDDs

Spark SQL DataFrames can easily be converted to RDDs of Row objects, and can also be created from RDDs of Row objects as well as JavaBeans, Scala case classes, and tuples. For RDDs of strings in JSON format, you can use the methods discussed in "JSON" on page 52. Datasets of type T can also easily be converted to RDDs of type T, which can provide a useful bridge for DataFrames to RDDs of concrete case classes instead of Row objects. RDDs are a special-case data source, since when going to/from RDDs, the data remains inside of Spark without writing out to or reading from an external system.

Converting a DataFrame to an RDD is a transformation (not an action); however, converting an RDD to a DataFrame or Dataset may involve computing (or sampling some of) the input RDD.

Creating a DataFrame from an RDD is not free in the general case. The data must be converted into Spark SQL's internal format.

When you create a DataFrame from an RDD, Spark SQL needs to add schema information. If you are creating the DataFrame from an RDD of case classes or plain old Java objects (POJOs), Spark SQL is able to use reflection to automatically determine the schema, as shown in Example 3-42. You can also manually specify the schema for your data using the structure discussed in "Basics of Schemas" on page 33. This can be especially useful if some of your fields are not nullable. You must specify the schema yourself if Spark SQL is unable to determine the schema through reflection, such as an RDD of Row objects (perhaps from calling .rdd on a DataFrame to use a functional transformation, as shown in Example 3-42).

Example 3-42. Creating DataFrames from RDDs

```
def createFromCaseClassRDD(input: RDD[PandaPlace]) = {
  // Create DataFrame explicitly using session and schema inference
  val df1 = session.createDataFrame(input)

  // Create DataFrame using session implicits and schema inference
  val df2 = input.toDF()

  // Create a Row RDD from our RDD of case classes
  val rowRDD = input.map(pm => Row(pm.name,
    pm.pandas.map(pi => Row(pi.id, pi.zip, pi.happy, pi.attributes))))
```

```
    val pandasType = ArrayType(StructType(List(
      StructField("id", LongType, true),
      StructField("zip", StringType, true),
      StructField("happy", BooleanType, true),
      StructField("attributes", ArrayType(FloatType), true))))

    // Create DataFrame explicitly with specified schema
    val schema = StructType(List(StructField("name", StringType, true),
      StructField("pandas", pandasType)))

    val df3 = session.createDataFrame(rowRDD, schema)
  }
```

 Case classes or JavaBeans defined inside another class can sometimes cause problems. If your RDD conversion is failing, make sure
the case class being used isn't defined inside another class.

Converting a DataFrame to an RDD is incredibly simple; however, you get an RDD of
Row objects, as shown in Example 3-43. Since a row can contain anything, you need to
specify the type (or cast the result) as you fetch the values for each column in the row.
With Datasets you can directly get back an RDD templated on the same type, which
can make the conversion back to a useful RDD much simpler.

 While Scala has many implicit conversions for different numeric
types, these do not generally apply in Spark SQL; instead, we use
explicit casting.

Example 3-43. Convert a DataFrame

```
def toRDD(input: DataFrame): RDD[RawPanda] = {
  val rdd: RDD[Row] = input.rdd
  rdd.map(row => RawPanda(row.getAs[Long](0), row.getAs[String](1),
    row.getAs[String](2), row.getAs[Boolean](3), row.getAs[Array[Double]](4)))
}
```

 If you know that the schema of your DataFrame matches that of
another, you can use the existing schema when constructing your
new DataFrame. One common place where this occurs is when an
input DataFrame has been converted to an RDD for functional filtering and then back.

Local collections

Much like with RDDs, you can also create `DataFrames` from local collections and bring them back as local collections, as illustrated in Example 3-44. The same memory requirements apply; namely, the entire contents of the `DataFrame` will be in-memory in the driver program. As such, distributing local collections is normally limited to unit tests, or joining small datasets with larger distributed datasets.

Example 3-44. Creating from a local collection

```
def createFromLocal(input: Seq[PandaPlace]) = {
  session.createDataFrame(input)
}
```

The `LocalRelation`'s API we used here allows us to specify a schema in the same manner as when we are converting an RDD to a `DataFrame`.

In pre-1.6 versions of PySpark, schema inference only looked at the first record.

Collecting data back as a local collection is more common and often done post aggregations or filtering on the data. For example, with ML pipelines collecting the coefficents or (as discussed in our Goldilocks example in Chapter 6) collecting the quantiles to the driver. Example 3-45 shows how to collect a `DataFrame` back locally. For larger datasets, saving to an external storage system (such as a database or HDFS) is recommended.

Just as with RDDs, do not collect large `DataFrames` back to the driver. For Python users, it is important to remember that toPan das() collects the data locally.

Example 3-45. Collecting the result locally

```
def collectDF(df: DataFrame) = {
  val result: Array[Row] = df.collect()
  result
}
```

Additional formats

As with core Spark, the data formats that ship directly with Spark only begin to scratch the surface of the types of systems with which you can interact. Some vendors publish their own implementations, and many are published on Spark Packages (*http://spark-packages.org/*). As of this writing there are over twenty formats listed on the Data Source's page (*http://spark-packages.org/?q=tags%3A%22Data%20Sources%22*) with the most popular being Avro (*http://spark-packages.org/package/data bricks/spark-avro*), Redshift (*http://spark-packages.org/package/databricks/spark-redshift*), CSV (*http://spark-packages.org/package/databricks/spark-csv*),[6] and a unified wrapper around 6+ databases called deep-spark (*http://spark-packages.org/package/Stratio/deep-spark*).

Spark packages can be included in your application in a few different ways. During the exploration phase (e.g., using the shell) you can include them by specifying --packages on the command line, as in Example 3-46. The same approach can be used when submitting your application with spark-submit, but this only includes the package at runtime, not at compile time. For including at compile time you can add the Maven coordinates to your builds, or, if building with sbt, the sbt-spark-package (*https://github.com/databricks/sbt-spark-package*) plug-in simplifies package dependencies with spDependencies. Otherwise, manually listing them as in Example 3-47 works quite well.

 Spark CSV is now included as part of Spark 2.0+, so you only need to include this for earlier versions of Spark.

Example 3-46. Starting Spark shell with CSV support

```
./bin/spark-shell --packages com.databricks:spark-csv_2.11:1.5.0
```

Example 3-47. Include spark-csv as an sbt dependency

```
"com.databricks" % "spark-csv_2.11" % "1.5.0"
```

Once you've included the package with your Spark job you need to specify the format, as you did with the Spark provided ones. The name should be mentioned in the package's documentation. For spark-csv you would specify a format string of com.databricks.spark.csv. For the built-in CSV format (in Spark 2.0+) you would instead just use csv (or the full name org.apache.spark.sql.csv).

---

6 spark-csv is now included as part of Spark 2.0.

There are a few options if the data format you are looking for isn't directly supported in either Spark or one of the libraries. Since many formats are available as Hadoop input formats, you can try to load your data as a Hadoop input format and convert the resulting RDD as discussed in "RDDs" on page 57. This approach is relatively simple, but means Spark SQL is unable to push down operations to our data store.[7]

For a deeper integration you can implement your data source using the Data Source API (*https://databricks.com/blog/2015/01/09/spark-sql-data-sources-api-unified-data-access-for-the-spark-platform.html*). Depending on which operations you wish to support operator push-down for, in your base relation you will need to implement additional traits from the `org.apache.spark.sql.sources` package. The details of implementing a new Spark SQL data source are beyond the scope of this book, but if you are interested the Scaladoc for `org.apache.spark.sql.sources` (*http://spark.apache.org/docs/latest/api/scala/index.html#org.apache.spark.sql.sources.pack age*) and `spark-csv`'s CsvRelation (*https://github.com/databricks/spark-csv/blob/master/src/main/scala/com/databricks/spark/csv/CsvRelation.scala*) can be good ways to get started.

Save Modes

In core Spark, saving RDDs always requires that the target directory does not exist, which can make appending to existing tables challenging. With Spark SQL, you can specify the desired behavior when writing out to a path that may already have data. The default behavior is `SaveMode.ErrorIfExists`; matching the behavior of RDDs, Spark will throw an exception if the target already exists. The different save modes and their behaviors are listed in Table 3-11. Example 3-48 illustrates how to configure an alternative save mode.

Table 3-11. Save modes

Save Mode	Behavior
ErrorIfExists	Throws an exception if the target already exists. If target doesn't exist write the data out.
Append	If target already exists, append the data to it. If the data doesn't exist write the data out.
Overwrite	If the target already exists, delete the target. Write the data out.
Ignore	If the target already exists, silently skip writing out. Otherwise write out the data.

Example 3-48. Specify save mode of append

```
def writeAppend(input: DataFrame): Unit = {
  input.write.mode(SaveMode.Append).save("output/")
}
```

---

7 For example, only reading the required partitions when a filter matches one of our partitioning schemes.

Partitions (Discovery and Writing)

Partition data is an important part of Spark SQL since it powers one of the key optimizations to allow reading only the required data, discussed more in "Logical and Physical Plans" on page 69. If you know how your downstream consumers may access your data (e.g., reading data based on zip code), when you write your data it is beneficial to use that information to partition your output. When reading the data, it's useful to understand how partition discovery functions, so you can have a better understanding of whether your filter can be pushed down.

 Filter push-down can make a huge difference when working with large datasets by allowing Spark to only access the subset of data required for your computation instead of doing effectively a full table scan.

When reading partitioned data, you point Spark to the root path of your data, and it will automatically discover the different partitions. Not all data types can be used as partition keys; currently only strings and numeric data are the supported types.

If your data is all in a single DataFrame, the DataFrameWriter API makes it easy to specify the partition information while you are writing the data out. The parti tionBy function takes a list of columns to partition the output on, as shown in Example 3-49. You can also manually save out separate DataFrames (say if you are writing from different jobs) with individual save calls.

Example 3-49. Save partitioned by zip code

```
def writeOutByZip(input: DataFrame): Unit = {
  input.write.partitionBy("zipcode").format("json").save("output/")
}
```

In addition to splitting the data by a partition key, it can be useful to make sure the resulting file sizes are reasonable, especially if the results will be used downstream by another Spark job.

Datasets

Datasets are an exciting extension of Spark SQL that provide additional compile-time type checking. Starting in Spark 2.0, DataFrames are now a specialized version of Datasets that operate on generic Row objects and therefore lack the normal compile-time type checking of Datasets. Datasets can be used when your data can be encoded for Spark SQL and you know the type information at compile time. The Dataset API is a strongly typed collection with a mixture of relational (DataFrame) and func-

---

tional (RDD) transformations. Like `DataFrames`, `Datasets` are represented by a logical plan the Catalyst optimizer (see "Query Optimizer" on page 69) can work with, and when cached the data is stored in Spark SQL's internal encoding format.

The Dataset API is new in Spark 1.6 and will change in future versions. Users of the Dataset API are advised to treat it as a "preview." Up-to-date documentation on the Dataset API can be found in the Scaladoc (*http://spark.apache.org/docs/latest/api/scala/index.html#org.apache.spark.sql.Dataset*).

Interoperability with RDDs, DataFrames, and Local Collections

`Datasets` can be easily converted to/from `DataFrames` and RDDs, but in the initial version they do not directly extend either. Converting to/from RDDs involves encoding/decoding the data into a different form. Converting to/from `DataFrames` is almost "free" in that the underlying data does not need to be changed; only extra compile-time type information is added/removed.

In Spark 2.0 the `DataFrame` type has been replaced with a type alias to `Dataset[Row]`.

The type alias for `DataFrame` is not visible in Java for Spark 2.0, so updating Java code will require changing from `DataFrame` to `Dataset<Row>`.

To convert a `DataFrame` to a `Dataset` you can use the `as[ElementType]` function on the `DataFrame` to get a `Dataset[ElementType]` back as shown in Example 3-50. The `ElementType` must be a case class, or similar such as tuple, consisting of types Spark SQL can represent (see "Basics of Schemas" on page 33). To create `Datasets` from local collections, `createDataSet(...)` on the `SQLContext` and the `toDS()` implicit function are provided on Seqs in the same manner as `createDataFrame(...)` and `toDF()`. For converting from RDD to `Dataset` you can first convert from RDD to `DataFrame` and then convert it to a `Dataset`.

For loading data into a Dataset, unless a special API is provided by your data source, you can first load your data into a DataFrame and then convert it to a Dataset. Since the conversion to the Dataset simply adds information, you do not have the problem of eagerly evaluating, and future filters and similar operations can still be pushed down to the data store.

Example 3-50. Create a Dataset from a DataFrame

```
def fromDF(df: DataFrame): Dataset[RawPanda] = {
  df.as[RawPanda]
}
```

Converting from a Dataset back to an RDD or DataFrame can be done in similar ways as when converting DataFrames, and both are shown in Example 3-51. The toDF simply copies the logical plan used in the Dataset into a DataFrame—so you don't need to do any schema inference or conversion as you do when converting from RDDs. Converting a Dataset of type T to an RDD of type T can be done by calling .rdd, which unlike calling toDF, does involve converting the data from the internal SQL format to the regular types.

Example 3-51. Convert Dataset to DataFrame and RDD

```
/**
 * Illustrate converting a Dataset to an RDD
 */
def toRDD(ds: Dataset[RawPanda]): RDD[RawPanda] = {
  ds.rdd
}

/**
 * Illustrate converting a Dataset to a DataFrame
 */
def toDF(ds: Dataset[RawPanda]): DataFrame = {
  ds.toDF()
}
```

Compile-Time Strong Typing

One of the reasons to use Datasets over traditional DataFrames is their compile-time strong typing. DataFrames have runtime schema information but lack compile-time information about the schema. This strong typing is especially useful when making libraries, because you can more clearly specify the requirements of your inputs and your return types.

Easier Functional (RDD "like") Transformations

One of the key advantages of the Dataset API is easier integration with custom Scala and Java code. `Datasets` expose `filter`, `map`, `mapPartitions`, and `flatMap` with similar function signatures as RDDs, with the notable requirement that your return `Ele mentType` also be understandable by Spark SQL (such as tuple or case class of types discussed in "Basics of Schemas" on page 33). Example 3-52 illustrates this using a simple `map` function.

Example 3-52. Functional query on Dataset

```
def funMap(ds: Dataset[RawPanda]): Dataset[Double] = {
  ds.map{rp => rp.attributes.filter(_ > 0).sum}
}
```

Beyond functional transformations, such as `map` and `filter`, you can also intermix relational and grouped/aggregate operations.

Relational Transformations

`Datasets` introduce a typed version of `select` for relational-style transformations. When specifying an expression for this you need to include the type information, as shown in Example 3-53. You can add this information by calling `as[ReturnType]` on the expression/column.

Example 3-53. Simple relational select on Dataset

```
def squishyPandas(ds: Dataset[RawPanda]): Dataset[(Long, Boolean)] = {
  ds.select($"id".as[Long], ($"attributes"(0) > 0.5).as[Boolean])
}
```

> Some operations, such as `select`, have both typed and untyped implementations. If you supply a `Column` rather than a `TypedCol umn` you will get a `DataFrame` back instead of a `Dataset`.

Multi-Dataset Relational Transformations

In addition to single `Dataset` transformations, there are also transformations for working with multiple `Datasets`. The standard set operations, namely `intersect`, `union`, and `subtract`, are all available with the same standard caveats as discussed in Table 3-9. Joining `Datasets` is also supported, but to make the type information easier to work with, the return structure is a bit different than traditional SQL joins.

Grouped Operations on Datasets

Similar to grouped operations on DataFrames (described in "Aggregates and groupBy" on page 43), groupBy on Datasets prior to Spark 2.0 returns a GroupedDataset (*http://bit.ly/2pyMplR*) or a KeyValueGroupedDataset (*http://bit.ly/2oZ67oX*) when grouped with an arbitrary function, and a RelationalGroupedDataset (*http://bit.ly/2pySePV*) when grouped with a relational/Dataset DSL expression. You can specify your aggregate functions on all of these, along with a functional mapGroups API. As with the expression in "Relational Transformations" on page 65, you need to use typed expressions so the result can also be a Dataset.

Taking our previous example of computing the maximum panda size by zip in Example 3-23, you would rewrite it to be as shown in Example 3-54.

 The convenience functions found on GroupedData (e.g., min, max, etc.) are missing, so all of our aggregate expressions need to be specified through agg.

Example 3-54. Compute the max panda size per zip code typed

```
def maxPandaSizePerZip(ds: Dataset[RawPanda]): Dataset[(String, Double)] = {
  ds.map(rp => MiniPandaInfo(rp.zip, rp.attributes(2)))
    .groupByKey(mp => mp.zip).agg(max("size").as[Double])
}
```

Beyond applying typed SQL expressions to aggregated columns, you can also easily use arbitrary Scala code with mapGroups on grouped data as shown in Example 3-55. This can save us from having to write custom user-defined aggregate functions (UDAFs) (discussed in "Extending with User-Defined Functions and Aggregate Functions (UDFs, UDAFs)" on page 67). While custom UDAFs can be painful to write, they may be able to give better performance than mapGroups and can also be used on DataFrames.

Example 3-55. Compute the max panda size per zip code using map groups

```
def maxPandaSizePerZipScala(ds: Dataset[RawPanda]): Dataset[(String, Double)] = {
  ds.groupByKey(rp => rp.zip).mapGroups{ case (g, iter) =>
    (g, iter.map(_.attributes(2)).reduceLeft(Math.max(_, _)))
  }
}
```

Extending with User-Defined Functions and Aggregate Functions (UDFs, UDAFs)

User-defined functions and user-defined aggregate functions provide you with ways to extend the DataFrame and SQL APIs with your own custom code while keeping the Catalyst optimizer. The Dataset API (see "Datasets" on page 62) is another performant option for much of what you can do with UDFs and UDAFs. This is quite useful for performance, since otherwise you would need to convert the data to an RDD (and potentially back again) to perform arbitrary functions, which is quite expensive. UDFs and UDAFs can also be accessed from inside of regular SQL expressions, making them accessible to analysts or others more comfortable with SQL.

When using UDFs or UDAFs written in non-JVM languages, such as Python, it is important to note that you lose much of the performance benefit, as the data must still be transferred out of the JVM.

If most of your work is in Python but you want to access some UDFs without the performance penalty, you can write your UDFs in Scala and register them for use in Python (as done in Sparkling Pandas (*http://sparklingpandas.com/*)).[8]

Writing nonaggregate UDFs for Spark SQL is incredibly simple: you simply write a regular function and register it using `sqlContext.udf().register`. A simple string length UDF is shown in Example 3-56. If you are registering a Java or Python UDF you also need to specify your return type.

Example 3-56. String length UDF

```
def setupUDFs(sqlCtx: SQLContext) = {
  sqlCtx.udf.register("strLen", (s: String) => s.length())
}
```

Even with JVM languages UDFs are generally slower than the equivalent SQL expression would be if it exists. Some early work is being done in SPARK-14083 (*https://issues.apache.org/jira/browse/SPARK-14083*) to parse JVM byte code and generate SQL expressions.

---

8 As of this writing, the Sparkling Pandas project development is on hold but early releases still contain some interesting examples of using JVM code from Python.

Aggregate functions (or UDAFs) are somewhat trickier to write. Instead of writing a regular Scala function, you extend the UserDefinedAggregateFunction and implement a number of different functions, similar to the functions one might write for aggregateByKey on an RDD, except working with different data structures. While they can be complex to write, UDAFs can be quite performant compared with options like mapGroups on Datasets or even simply written aggregateByKey on RDDs. You can then either use the UDAF directly on columns or add it to the function registry as you did for the nonaggregate UDF.

Example 3-57 is a simple UDAF for computing the average, although you will likely want to use Spark's built in avg in real life.

Example 3-57. UDAF for computing the average

```
def setupUDAFs(sqlCtx: SQLContext) = {
  class Avg extends UserDefinedAggregateFunction {
    // Input type
    def inputSchema: org.apache.spark.sql.types.StructType =
      StructType(StructField("value", DoubleType) :: Nil)

    def bufferSchema: StructType = StructType(
      StructField("count", LongType) ::
      StructField("sum", DoubleType) :: Nil
    )

    // Return type
    def dataType: DataType = DoubleType

    def deterministic: Boolean = true

    def initialize(buffer: MutableAggregationBuffer): Unit = {
      buffer(0) = 0L
      buffer(1) = 0.0
    }

    def update(buffer: MutableAggregationBuffer,input: Row): Unit = {
      buffer(0) = buffer.getAs[Long](0) + 1
      buffer(1) = buffer.getAs[Double](1) + input.getAs[Double](0)
    }

    def merge(buffer1: MutableAggregationBuffer, buffer2: Row): Unit = {
      buffer1(0) = buffer1.getAs[Long](0) + buffer2.getAs[Long](0)
      buffer1(1) = buffer1.getAs[Double](1) + buffer2.getAs[Double](1)
    }

    def evaluate(buffer: Row): Any = {
      buffer.getDouble(1) / buffer.getLong(0)
    }
  }
}
```

```
  // Optionally register
  val avg = new Avg
  sqlCtx.udf.register("ourAvg", avg)
}
```

This is a little more complicated than our regular UDF, so let's take a look at what the different parts do. You start by specifying what the input type is, then you specify the schema of the buffer you will use for storing the in-progress work. These schemas are specified in the same way as `DataFrame` and `Dataset` schemas, discussed in "Basics of Schemas" on page 33.

From there the rest of the functions are implementing the same functions you use when writing `aggregateByKey` on an RDD, but instead of taking arbitrary Scala objects you work with `Row` and `MutableAggregationBuffer`. The final `evaluate` function takes the `Row` representing the aggregation data and returns the final result.

UDFs, UDAFs, and `Datasets` all provide ways to intermix arbitrary code with Spark SQL.

Query Optimizer

Catalyst is the Spark SQL query optimizer, which is used to take the query plan and transform it into an execution plan that Spark can run. Much as our transformations on RDDs build up a DAG, as we apply relational and functional transformations on `DataFrames/Datasets`, Spark SQL builds up a tree representing our query plan, called a logical plan. Spark is able to apply a number of optimizations on the logical plan and can also choose between multiple physical plans for the same logical plan using a cost-based model.

Logical and Physical Plans

The logical plan you construct through transformations on `DataFrames/Datasets` (or SQL queries) starts out as an unresolved logical plan. Much like a compiler, the Spark optimizer is multiphased and before any optimizations can be performed, it needs to resolve the references and types of the expressions.

This resolved plan is referred to as the logical plan, and Spark applies a number of simplifications directly on the logical plan, producing an optimized logical plan.

These simplifications can be written using pattern matching on the tree, such as the rule for simplifying additions between two literals. The optimizer is not limited to pattern matching, and rules can also include arbitrary Scala code.

Once the logical plan has been optimized, Spark will produce a physical plan. The physical plan stage has both rule-based and cost-based optimizations to produce the optimal physical plan. One of the most important optimizations at this stage is predicate pushdown to the data source level.

Code Generation

As a final step, Spark may also apply code generation for the components. Code generation is done using Janino to compile Java code. Earlier versions used Scala's Quasi Quotes,[9] but the overhead was too high to enable code generation for small datasets. In some TPCDS queries, code generation can result in >10× improvement in performance.

In some early versions of Spark for complex queries, code generation can cause failures. If you are on an old version of Spark and run into an unexpected failure, it can be worth disabling codegen by setting `spark.sql.codegen` or `spark.sql.tungsten.enabled` to false (depending on version).

Large Query Plans and Iterative Algorithms

While the Catalyst optimizer is quite powerful, one of the cases where it currently runs into challenges is with very large query plans. These query plans tend to be the result of iterative algorithms, like graph algorithms or machine learning algorithms. One simple workaround for this is converting the data to an RDD and back to `Data Frame`/`Dataset` at the end of each iteration, as shown in Example 3-58. Although if you're in Python, be sure to use the underlying Java RDD rather than round-tripping through Python (see Example 7-5 for how to do this). Another, somewhat more heavy option, is to write the data to storage and continue from there.

Example 3-58. Round trip through RDD to cut query plan

```
val rdd = df.rdd
rdd.cache()
sqlCtx.createDataFrame(rdd, df.schema)
```

This issue is being tracked in SPARK-13346 (*https://issues.apache.org/jira/browse/SPARK-13346*) and you can see the workaround used in GraphFrames (*http://bit.ly/2pBemeP*).

---

9 Scala Quasi Quotes are part of Scala's macro system.

Debugging Spark SQL Queries

While Spark SQL's query optimizer has access to much more information, we still sometimes need to take a peek under the hood and to make sure it's working as we expected. Similar to `toDebugString` on `RDDs`, we have `explain` and `printSchema` functions on `DataFrames`.

One thing that can make a big difference is figuring out if Spark SQL was able to push down a filter. In early versions of Spark SQL filter pushdown didn't always happen as expected, so the filter sometimes needed to be reordered to be right next to the data load. In newer versions filter pushdown is more likely to fail due to a misconfiguration of your data source.

JDBC/ODBC Server

Spark SQL provides a JDBC server to allow external tools, such as business intelligence GUIs like Tableau, to work with data accessible in Spark and to share resources. Spark SQL's JDBC server requires that Spark be built with Hive support.

> Since the server tends to be long lived and runs on a single context, it can also be a good way to share cached tables between multiple users.

Spark SQL's JDBC server is based on the HiveServer2 from Hive, and most corresponding connectors designed for HiveServer2 can be used directly with Spark SQL's JDBC server. Simba also offers specific drivers for Spark SQL (*http://www.simba.com/connectors/apache-spark-driver#documentation_content*).

The server can either be started from the command line or started using an existing HiveContext. The command-line start and stop commands are `./sbin/start-thriftserver.sh` and `./sbin/stop-thriftserver.sh`. When starting from the command line, you can configure the different Spark SQL properties by specifying `--hiveconf property=value` on the command line. Many of the rest of the command-line parameters match that of `spark-submit`. The default host and port is `localhost:10000` and can be configured with `hive.server2.thrift.port` and `hive.server2.thrift.bind.host`.

> When starting the JDBC server using an existing `HiveContext`, you can simply update the config properties on the context instead of specifying command-line parameters.

Examples 3-59 and 3-60 illustrate two different ways to configure the port used by the thrift server.

Example 3-59. Start JDBC server on a different port

```
./sbin/start-thriftserver.sh --hiveconf hive.server2.thrift.port=9090
```

Example 3-60. Start JDBC server on a different port in Scala

```
hiveContext.setConf("hive.server2.thrift.port", "9090")
HiveThriftServer2.startWithContext(hiveContext)
```

 When starting the JDBC server on an existing HiveContext, make sure to shut down the JDBC server when exiting.

Conclusion

The considerations for using DataFrames/Datasets over RDDs are complex and changing with the rapid development of Spark SQL. One of the cases where Spark SQL can be difficult to use is when the number of partitions needed for different parts of your pipeline changes, or if you otherwise wish to control the partitioner. While RDDs lack the Catalyst optimizer and relational style queries, they are able to work with a wider variety of data types and provide more direct control over certain types of operations. DataFrames and Datasets also only work with a restricted subset of data types—but when your data is in one of these supported classes the performance improvements of using the Catalyst optimizer provide a compelling case for accepting those restrictions.

DataFrames can be used when you have primarily relational transformations, which can be extended with UDFs when necessary. Compared to RDDs, DataFrames benefit from the efficient storage format of Spark SQL, the Catalyst optimizer, and the ability to perform certain operations directly on the serialized data. One drawback to working with DataFrames is that they are not strongly typed at compile time, which can lead to errors with incorrect column access and other simple mistakes.

Datasets can be used when you want a mix of functional and relational transformations while benefiting from the optimizations for DataFrames and are, therefore, a great alternative to RDDs in many cases. As with RDDs, Datasets are parameterized on the type of data contained in them, which allows for strong compile-time type checking but requires that you know your data type at compile time (although Row or other generic type can be used). The additional type safety of Datasets can be beneficial even for applications that do not need the specific functionality of `DataFrames`. One potential drawback is that the Dataset API is continuing to evolve, so updating to future versions of Spark may require code changes.

Pure RDDs work well for data that does not fit into the Catalyst optimizer. RDDs have an extensive and stable functional API, and upgrades to newer versions of Spark are unlikely to require substantial code changes. RDDs also make it easy to control partitioning, which can be very useful for many distributed algorithms. Some types of operations, such as multicolumn aggregates, complex joins, and windowed operations, can be daunting to express with the RDD API. RDDs can work with any Java or Kryo serializable data, although the serialization is more often more expensive and less space efficient than the equivalent in `DataFrames`/`Datasets`.

Now that you have a good understanding of Spark SQL, it's time to continue on to joins, for both RDDs and Spark SQL.

## CHAPTER 4

Joins (SQL and Core)

Joining data is an important part of many of our pipelines, and both Spark Core and SQL support the same fundamental types of joins. While joins are very common and powerful, they warrant special performance consideration as they may require large network transfers or even create datasets beyond our capability to handle.[1] In core Spark it can be more important to think about the ordering of operations, since the DAG optimizer, unlike the SQL optimizer, isn't able to re-order or push down filters.

Core Spark Joins

In this section we will go over the RDD type joins. Joins in general are expensive since they require that corresponding keys from each RDD are located at the same partition so that they can be combined locally. If the RDDs do not have known partitioners, they will need to be shuffled so that both RDDs share a partitioner, and data with the same keys lives in the same partitions, as shown in Figure 4-1. If they have the same partitioner, the data may be colocated, as in Figure 4-3, so as to avoid network transfer. Regardless of whether the partitioners are the same, if one (or both) of the RDDs have a known partitioner only a narrow dependency is created, as in Figure 4-2. As with most key/value operations, the cost of the join increases with the number of keys and the distance the records have to travel in order to get to their correct partition.

---

1 As the saying goes, the cross product of big data and big data is an out-of-memory exception.

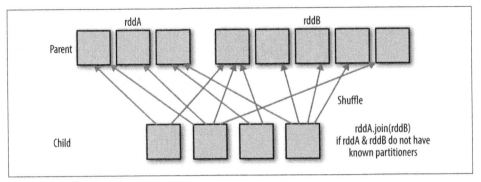

Figure 4-1. Shuffle join

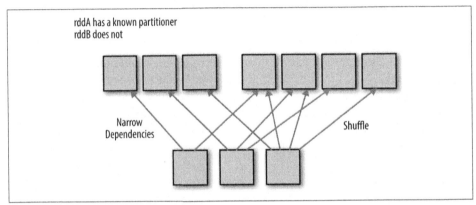

Figure 4-2. Both known partitioner join

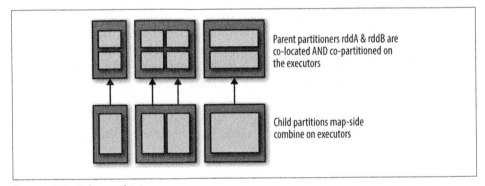

Figure 4-3. Colocated join

Two RDDs will be colocated if they have the same partitioner and were shuffled as part of the same action.

Core Spark joins are implemented using the cogroup function. We discuss cogroup in "Co-Grouping" on page 141.

Choosing a Join Type

The default join operation in Spark includes only values for keys present in both RDDs, and in the case of multiple values per key, provides all permutations of the key/value pair. The best scenario for a standard join is when both RDDs contain the same set of distinct keys. With duplicate keys, the size of the data may expand dramatically causing performance issues, and if one key is not present in both RDDs you will lose that row of data. Here are a few guidelines:

- When both RDDs have duplicate keys, the join can cause the size of the data to expand dramatically. It may be better to perform a distinct or combineByKey operation to reduce the key space or to use cogroup to handle duplicate keys instead of producing the full cross product. By using smart partitioning during the combine step, it is possible to prevent a second shuffle in the join (we will discuss this in detail later).

- If keys are not present in both RDDs you risk losing your data unexpectedly. It can be safer to use an outer join, so that you are guaranteed to keep all the data in either the left or the right RDD, then filter the data after the join.

- If one RDD has some easy-to-define subset of the keys, in the other you may be better off filtering or reducing before the join to avoid a big shuffle of data, which you will ultimately throw away anyway.

Join is one of the most expensive operations you will commonly use in Spark, so it is worth doing what you can to shrink your data before performing a join.

For example, suppose you have one RDD with some data in the form (Panda id, score) and another RDD with (Panda id, address), and you want to send each panda some mail with her best score. You could join the RDDs on id and then compute the best score for each address, as shown in Example 4-1.

Example 4-1. Basic RDD join

```
def joinScoresWithAddress1( scoreRDD : RDD[(Long, Double)],
  addressRDD : RDD[(Long, String )]) : RDD[(Long, (Double, String))]= {
  val joinedRDD = scoreRDD.join(addressRDD)
  joinedRDD.reduceByKey( (x, y) => if(x._1 > y._1) x else y )
}
```

However, this is probably not as fast as first reducing the score data, so that the first dataset contains only one row for each panda with her best score, and then joining that data with the address data (as shown in Example 4-2).

Example 4-2. Pre-filter before join

```
def joinScoresWithAddress2(scoreRDD : RDD[(Long, Double)],
  addressRDD: RDD[(Long, String)]) : RDD[(Long, (Double, String))]= {
  val bestScoreData = scoreRDD.reduceByKey((x, y) => if(x > y) x else y)
  bestScoreData.join(addressRDD)
}
```

If each Panda had 1,000 different scores then the size of the shuffle we did in the first approach was 1,000 times the size of the shuffle we did with this approach!

If we wanted to we could also perform a left outer join to keep all keys for processing even those missing in the right RDD by using leftOuterJoin in place of join, as in Example 4-3. Spark also has fullOuterJoin and rightOuterJoin depending on which records we wish to keep. Any missing values are None and present values are Some('x').

Example 4-3. Basic RDD left outer join

```
def outerJoinScoresWithAddress(scoreRDD : RDD[(Long, Double)],
  addressRDD: RDD[(Long, String)]) : RDD[(Long, (Double, Option[String]))]= {
  val joinedRDD = scoreRDD.leftOuterJoin(addressRDD)
  joinedRDD.reduceByKey( (x, y) => if(x._1 > y._1) x else y )
}
```

Choosing an Execution Plan

In order to join data, Spark needs the data that is to be joined (i.e., the data based on each key) to live on the same partition. The default implementation of a join in Spark is a *shuffled hash join*. The shuffled hash join ensures that data on each partition will contain the same keys by partitioning the second dataset with the same default partitioner as the first, so that the keys with the same hash value from both datasets are in the same partition. While this approach always works, it can be more expensive than necessary because it requires a shuffle. The shuffle can be avoided if:

1. Both RDDs have a known partitioner.
2. One of the datasets is small enough to fit in memory, in which case we can do a broadcast hash join (we will explain what this is later).

Note that if the RDDs are colocated the network transfer can be avoided, along with the shuffle.

Speeding up joins by assigning a known partitioner

If you have to do an operation before the join that requires a shuffle, such as `aggregateByKey` or `reduceByKey`, you can prevent the shuffle by adding a hash partitioner with the same number of partitions as an explicit argument to the first operation before the join. You could make the example in the previous section even faster, by using the partitioner for the address data as an argument for the `reduceByKey` step, as in Example 4-4 and Figure 4-4.

Example 4-4. Known partitioner join

```
def joinScoresWithAddress3(scoreRDD: RDD[(Long, Double)],
  addressRDD: RDD[(Long, String)]) : RDD[(Long, (Double, String))]= {
  // If addressRDD has a known partitioner we should use that,
  // otherwise it has a default hash parttioner, which we can reconstruct by
  // getting the number of partitions.
  val addressDataPartitioner = addressRDD.partitioner match {
    case (Some(p)) => p
    case (None) => new HashPartitioner(addressRDD.partitions.length)
  }
  val bestScoreData = scoreRDD.reduceByKey(addressDataPartitioner,
    (x, y) => if(x > y) x else y)
  bestScoreData.join(addressRDD)
}
```

If the RDDs sharing the same partitioner are materialized by the same action, they will end up being co-located (which can even reduce network traffic).

(Almost) always persist after repartitioning.

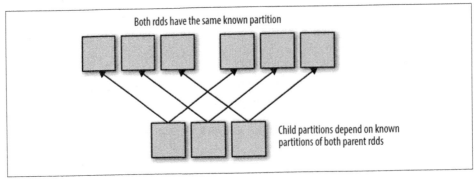

Figure 4-4. Both known partitioner join

Speeding up joins using a broadcast hash join

A broadcast hash join pushes one of the RDDs (the smaller one) to each of the worker nodes. Then it does a map-side combine with each partition of the larger RDD. If one of your RDDs can fit in memory or can be made to fit in memory it is always beneficial to do a broadcast hash join, since it doesn't require a shuffle. Sometimes (but not always) Spark SQL will be smart enough to configure the broadcast join itself; in Spark SQL this is controlled with `spark.sql.autoBroadcastJoinThres hold` and `spark.sql.broadcastTimeout`. This is illustrated in Figure 4-5.

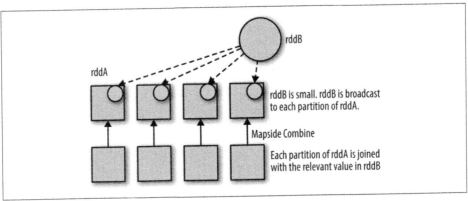

Figure 4-5. Broadcast hash join

Spark Core does not have an implementation of the broadcast hash join. Instead, we can manually implement a version of the broadcast hash join by collecting the smaller RDD to the driver as a map, then broadcasting the result, and using `mapParti tions` to combine the elements.

Example 4-5 is a general function that could be used to join a larger and smaller RDD. Its behavior mirrors the default "join" operation in Spark. We exclude elements whose keys do not appear in both RDDs.

Example 4-5. Manual broadcast hash join

```
def manualBroadCastHashJoin[K : Ordering : ClassTag, V1 : ClassTag,
V2 : ClassTag](bigRDD : RDD[(K, V1)],
 smallRDD : RDD[(K, V2)])= {
 val smallRDDLocal: Map[K, V2] = smallRDD.collectAsMap()
 val smallRDDLocalBcast = bigRDD.sparkContext.broadcast(smallRDDLocal)
 bigRDD.mapPartitions(iter => {
  iter.flatMap{
   case (k,v1 ) =>
    smallRDDLocalBcast.value.get(k) match {
     case None => Seq.empty[(K, (V1, V2))]
     case Some(v2) => Seq((k, (v1, v2)))
    }
  }
 }, preservesPartitioning = true)
}
//end:coreBroadCast[]
}
```

Partial manual broadcast hash join

Sometimes not all of our smaller RDD will fit into memory, but some keys are so overrepresented in the large dataset that you want to broadcast just the most common keys. This is especially useful if one key is so large that it can't fit on a single partition. In this case you can use countByKeyApprox[2] on the large RDD to get an approximate idea of which keys would most benefit from a broadcast. You then filter the smaller RDD for only these keys, collecting the result locally in a HashMap. Using sc.broadcast you can broadcast the HashMap so that each worker only has one copy and manually perform the join against the HashMap. Using the same HashMap you can then filter your large RDD down to not include the large number of duplicate keys and perform your standard join, unioning it with the result of your manual join. This approach is quite convoluted but may allow you to handle highly skewed data you couldn't otherwise process.

Spark SQL Joins

Spark SQL supports the same basic join types as core Spark, but the optimizer is able to do more of the heavy lifting for you—although you also give up some of your control. For example, Spark SQL can sometimes push down or reorder operations to make your joins more efficient. On the other hand, you don't control the partitioner for DataFrames or Datasets, so you can't manually avoid shuffles as you did with core Spark joins.

---

2 If the number of distinct keys is too high, you can also use reduceByKey, sort on the value, and take the top k.

DataFrame Joins

Joining data between `DataFrames` is one of the most common multi-`DataFrame` transformations. The standard SQL join types are all supported and can be specified as the `joinType` in `df.join(otherDf, sqlCondition, joinType)` when performing a join. As with joins between RDDs, joining with nonunique keys will result in the cross product (so if the left table has R1 and R2 with key1 and the right table has R3 and R5 with key1 you will get (R1, R3), (R1, R5), (R2, R3), (R2, R5)) in the output. While we explore Spark SQL joins we will use two example tables of pandas, Tables 4-1 and 4-2.

 While self joins are supported, you must alias the fields you are interested in to different names beforehand, so they can be accessed.

Table 4-1. Table of pandas and sizes (our left DataFrame)

Name	Size
Happy	1.0
Sad	0.9
Happy	1.5
Coffee	3.0

Table 4-2. Table of pandas and zip codes (our right DataFrame)

Name	Zip
Happy	94110
Happy	94103
Coffee	10504
Tea	07012

Spark's supported join types are "inner," "left_outer" (aliased as "outer"), "left_anti," "right_outer," "full_outer," and "left_semi."[3] With the exception of "left_semi" these join types all join the two tables, but they behave differently when handling rows that do not have keys in both tables.

---

3 The quotes are optional and can be left out. We use them in our examples because we think it is easier to read with the quotes present.

The "inner" join is both the default and likely what you think of when you think of joining tables. It requires that the key be present in both tables, or the result is dropped as shown in Example 4-6 and Table 4-3.

Example 4-6. Simple inner join

```
// Inner join implicit
df1.join(df2, df1("name") === df2("name"))
// Inner join explicit
df1.join(df2, df1("name") === df2("name"), "inner")
```

Table 4-3. Inner join of df1, df2 on name

Name	Size	Name	Zip
Coffee	3.0	Coffee	10504
Happy	1.5	Happy	94110
Happy	1.5	Happy	94103
Happy	1.0	Happy	94110
Happy	1.0	Happy	94103

Left outer joins will produce a table with all of the keys from the left table, and any rows without matching keys in the right table will have null values in the fields that would be populated by the right table. Right outer joins are the same, but with the requirements reversed. A sample left outer join is in Example 4-7, and the result is shown in Table 4-4.

Example 4-7. Left outer join

```
// Left outer join explicit
df1.join(df2, df1("name") === df2("name"), "left_outer")
```

Table 4-4. Left outer join df1, df2 on name

Name	Size	Name	Zip
Sad	0.9	null	null
Coffee	3.0	Coffee	10504
Happy	1.0	Happy	94110
Happy	1.0	Happy	94103
Happy	1.5	Happy	94110
Happy	1.5	Happy	94103

A sample right outer join is in Example 4-8, and the result is shown in Table 4-5.

Example 4-8. Right outer join

```
// Right outer join explicit
df1.join(df2, df1("name") === df2("name"), "right_outer")
```

Table 4-5. Right outer join df1, df2 on name

Name	Size	Name	Zip
Coffee	3.0	Coffee	10504
Happy	1.0	Happy	94110
Happy	1.0	Happy	94103
Happy	1.5	Happy	94110
Happy	1.5	Happy	94103
null	null	Tea	07012

To keep all records from both tables you can use the full outer join, which results in Table 4-6.

Table 4-6. Full outer join df1, df2 on name

Name	Size	Name	Zip
Sad	0.9	null	null
Coffee	3.0	Coffee	10504
Happy	1.0	Happy	94110
Happy	1.0	Happy	94103
Happy	1.5	Happy	94110
Happy	1.5	Happy	94103
null	null	Tea	07012

Left semi joins (as in Example 4-9 and Table 4-7) and left anti joins (as in Table 4-8) are the only kinds of joins that only have values from the left table. A left semi join is the same as filtering the left table for only rows with keys present in the right table. The left anti join also only returns data from the left table, but instead only returns records that are not present in the right table.

Example 4-9. Left semi join

```
// Left semi join explicit
df1.join(df2, df1("name") === df2("name"), "left_semi")
```

Table 4-7. Left semi join

Name	Size
Coffee	3.0
Happy	1.0
Happy	1.5

Table 4-8. Left anti join

Name	Size
Sad	0.9

Self joins

Self joins are supported on `DataFrames`, but we end up with duplicated columns names. So that you can access the results, you need to alias the `DataFrames` to different names—otherwise you will be unable to select the columns due to name collision (see Example 4-10). Once you've aliased each `DataFrame`, in the result you can access the individual columns for each `DataFrame` with `dfName.colName`.

Example 4-10. Self join

```
val joined = df.as("a").join(df.as("b")).where($"a.name" === $"b.name")
```

Broadcast hash joins

In Spark SQL you can see the type of join being performed by calling `queryExecu tion.executedPlan`. As with core Spark, if one of the tables is much smaller than the other you may want a broadcast hash join. You can hint to Spark SQL that a given DF should be broadcast for join by calling `broadcast` on the `DataFrame` before joining it (e.g., `df1.join(broadcast(df2), "key")`). Spark also automatically uses the `spark.sql.conf.autoBroadcastJoinThreshold` to determine if a table should be broadcast.

Dataset Joins

Joining `Datasets` is done with `joinWith`, and this behaves similarly to a regular relational join, except the result is a tuple of the different record types as shown in Example 4-11. This is somewhat more awkward to work with after the join, but also does make self joins, as shown in Example 4-12, much easier, as you don't need to alias the columns first.

Example 4-11. Joining two Datasets

```
val result: Dataset[(RawPanda, CoffeeShop)] = pandas.joinWith(coffeeShops,
  $"zip" === $"zip")
```

Example 4-12. Self join a Dataset

```
val result: Dataset[(RawPanda, RawPanda)] = pandas.joinWith(pandas,
  $"zip" === $"zip")
```

 Using a self join and a lit(true), you can produce the cartesian product of your Dataset, which can be useful but also illustrates how joins (especially self joins) can easily result in unworkable data sizes.

As with DataFrames you can specify the type of join desired (e.g., inner, left_outer, right_outer, left_semi), changing how records present only in one Dataset are handled. Missing records are represented by null values, so be careful.

Conclusion

Now that you have explored joins, it's time to focus on transformations and the performance considerations associated with them.

## CHAPTER 5

Effective Transformations

Most commonly, Spark programs are structured on RDDs: they involve reading data from stable storage into the RDD format, performing a number of computations and data transformations on the RDD, and writing the result RDD to stable storage or collecting to the driver. Thus, most of the power of Spark comes from its transformations: operations that are defined on RDDs and return RDDs.

At present, Spark contains specialized functionality for about a half-dozen types of RDDs, each with its own properties and scores of different transformation functions. In this section, we hope to give you the tools to think about how your RDD transformation, or series of transformations, will be evaluated. In particular: what kinds of RDDs these transformations return, whether persisting or checkpointing RDDs between transformations will make your computation more efficient, and how a given series of transformations could be executed in the most performant way possible.

The transformations in this section are those associated with the RDD object used in Spark Core (and MLlib). RDDs are also used inside of DStreams with Spark Streaming, but they have different functionality and performance properties. Likewise, most of the functions discussed in this chapter are not yet supported in Data Frames. Since Spark SQL has a different optimizer, not all of the conceptual lessons of this chapter will carry over to the Spark SQL world.

As Spark moves forward, more RDD transformations will become available on Datasets, which can be used in Spark SQL, and which are discussed in "Datasets" on page 62.

Narrow Versus Wide Transformations

In Chapter 2, we introduced one important distinction between types of transformations: those with *wide dependencies* and those with *narrow dependencies*. This distinction is important because it has strong implications for how transformations are evaluated and, consequently, for their performance. In this subsection, we will more precisely define the wide and narrow transformations, demonstrate how to determine whether a transformation is wide or narrow, and explain why this distinction matters for evaluation and performance.

 Recall that Spark is lazily evaluated, meaning that a transformation is not executed until an action that depends on that transformation is called. This, as we discussed in detail in "Lazy Evaluation" on page 11, has important consequences for fault tolerance, performance, and debugging. If the information in this tip is confusing, please refer back to Chapter 2, which will give you the basic understanding of the Spark execution engine needed for this chapter.

To summarize what we covered in Chapter 2: wide transformations are those that require a shuffle, while narrow transformations are those that do not. In "Wide Versus Narrow Dependencies" on page 17 we explained that in narrow transformations, the child partitions (the partitions in the resulting RDD) depend on a known subset of the parent partitions. While this definition is correct, it is less precise than the formal definition of narrow transformations.

The 2012 paper that first presented the evaluation semantics for Spark (*http://www-bcf.usc.edu/~minlanyu/teach/csci599-fall12/papers/nsdi_spark.pdf*) defines transformations with narrow dependencies as those in which "each partition of the parent RDD is used by at most one partition of the child RDD." The creators define transformations with wide dependencies as transformations in which "multiple child partitions may depend on [each partition in the parent]." This definition states the analogue of what we explained in Chapter 2, in which we defined narrow and wide dependencies in relation to the child RDD's dependencies. In contrast, the creators' definition defined narrow and wide dependencies in terms of the dependencies on the parent RDD, rather than those on the child RDD.

We think the definition presented in Chapter 2 is easier to conceptualize since one usually designs a program by thinking from the input data (parent RDD) to the output data (child RDD). However, the Spark evaluation engine (the "DAG") builds an execution plan in reverse: from the output (the last action) to the input RDD. Thus, the Spark creators' definition mirrors the way that Spark is evaluated and consequently it is more precise in two important ways. First, the founders' definition rules out the case of one parent partition having multiple children in a narrow dependency. It explains why coalesce is only a narrow transformation when it is reducing rather than increasing the number of partitions. Second, the founders' definition clarifies why the number of tasks used to complete a computation corresponds to each *output partition* rather than each *input partition*—when RDDs are evaluated; the tasks needed to compute a transformation are computed on the child partitions.

Figure 5-1 shows dependencies between parent and child partitions for narrow and wide transformations for the Spark program in Example 5-1. Assume RDD1 is an RDD of integers.

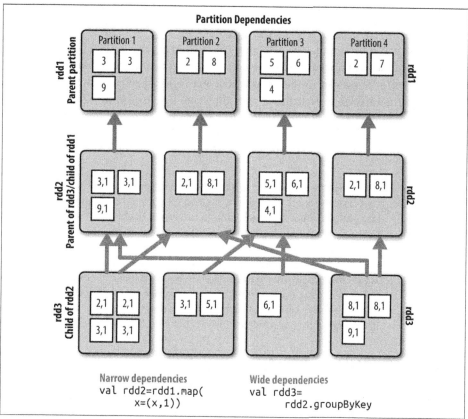

Figure 5-1. Narrow versus wide dependencies between partitions

Example 5-1. Narrow versus wide example

```
//Narrow dependency. Map the rdd to tuples  of (x, 1)
val rdd2 = rdd1.map(x => (x, 1))
//Wide dependency groupByKey
val rdd3 = rdd2.groupByKey()
```

We use the same structure as the diagrams presented in Figures 2-2 and 2-3. Arrows represent partition dependencies. Each child partition has arrows pointing to the parent partitions upon which it depends; if an arrow points from partition y to partition x, that means that x depends on y. Blue arrows represent narrow dependencies and red arrows represent wide dependencies.

We assume the RDD has four partitions. Unlike the diagrams presented in Chapter 2, here we will show how actual records in a very small RDD might be distributed amongst the partitions. In this case we show how RDD1, RDD2, and RDD3 would be partitioned if RDD1 was an RDD of the integers 3, 3, 9, 2, 8, 5, 6, 7.

As you can see, to compute the map step, each child partition depends on just one parent, since the data doesn't need to be moved between partitions for the operation to be computed. However, in the groupByKey step, Spark needs to move an arbitrary number of the records so that those with the same key are in the same partition in order to combine records corresponding to a single key into one iterator (recall that iterator is a local, rather than a distributed collection). Thus, the child partitions depend on many partitions in the parent RDD.

> This diagram is intended to show how partitions, an abstract concept used in Spark evaluation, depend on each other, rather than any physical data movement across machines. Each line of squares in the diagram represents the same executors at different points in time. The arrows denote dependencies between partitions. In fact repartitioning data does not necessarily require data movement across machines, since partitions may reside on the same executor. When changing the partition of a record does require data movement between executors, the records have to be passed through the driver rather than transferred directly between the executors.

Implications for Performance

In "Wide Versus Narrow Dependencies" on page 17 we asserted that transformations with narrow dependencies are faster to execute partly because narrow transformations can be combined and executed in one pass of the data. In this section we hope to explain why this is from an evaluation perspective.

Narrow dependencies do not require data to be moved across partitions. Consequently narrow transformations don't require communication with the driver node, and an arbitrary number of narrow transformations can be executed on any subset of the records (any partition) given one set of instructions from the driver. In Spark terminology, we say that each series of narrow transformations can be computed in the same "stage" of the query execution plan.

In contrast, as we stated in "The Anatomy of a Spark Job" on page 22, a shuffle associated with a wide dependency marks a new stage in the RDD's evaluation. Because tasks must be computed on a single partition and the data needed to compute each partition of a wide dependency may be spread across machines, transformations with wide dependencies may require data to be moved across partitions. Thus, the downstream computations cannot be computed before the shuffle finishes.

For example, it should be intuitive that sorting cannot be accomplished with narrow transformations because sorting requires an order to be defined on all of the records —not just within each partition. Indeed, the sortByKey function has wide dependencies. It requires the data to be partitioned, so all the keys within a certain range live on the same partition. That way, sorting the data on each partition leads to a sorted result. Any narrow transformations following the sort cannot be done until after the shuffle completes because the records on each partition may change.

Stage boundaries have important performance consequences. Except in the case of multiple RDD operations like join, the stages associated with one RDD must be executed in sequence (see Chapter 4). Thus, not only are shuffles expensive since they require data movement and potential disk I/O (for the shuffle files), they also limit parallelization.

Implications for Fault Tolerance

The cost of failure for a partition with wide dependencies is much higher than for one with narrow dependencies, since it requires more partitions to be recomputed. If one partition in the parent of a mappedRDD (the resulting RDD type of a map operations) fails, for example, only one of its children must be recomputed, and the tasks needed to recompute that child partition can be distributed across the executors to make this recomputation faster. In contrast, if the parent of the sorted RDD loses a partition, it is possible (in the worst case) that all the child partitions will need to be recomputed. For this reason, the cost of recomputing a partition in the case of failure for a partition with wide dependencies is much higher than for a partition with narrow dependencies.

Chaining together transformations with wide dependencies only increases the risk of a very expensive recomputation particularly if any of the wide transformations have a high probability of causing memory errors. In some instances, the cost of recomputation may be high enough that it is worth checkpointing an RDD, so the intermediate results are saved. We will discuss checkpointing in detail in "Reusing RDDs" on page 114.

The Special Case of coalesce

The `coalesce` operation is used to change the number of partitions in an RDD. As shown by the diagram in Figure 2-2 in Chapter 2, when `coalesce` reduces the number of output partitions, each parent partition is used in exactly one child partition since the child partitions are the union of several parents. Thus, according to our definition of narrow dependencies, `coalesce` is a narrow transformation even though it changes the number of partitions in the RDD. Since tasks are executed on the child partition, the number of tasks executed in a stage that includes a `coalesce` operation is equivalent to the number of partitions in the result RDD of the `coalesce` transformation.

Using `coalesce`, the number of partitions can decrease in one stage without causing a shuffle. However, `coalesce` causes the upstream partitions in the entire stage to execute with the level of parallelism assigned by `coalesce`, which may be undesirable in some cases. Avoid this behavior at the cost of a shuffle by setting the shuffle argument of `coalesce` to `true` or by using the `repartition` function instead.

However, when `coalesce` increases the number of partitions, each parent partition necessarily depends on several child partitions. Thus, according the more precise definition of wide dependencies presented in "Narrow Versus Wide Transformations" on page 88, using `coalesce` to increase the number of partitions is a wide transformation. The `coalesce` function prioritizes evenly distributing the data across the child partitions. Consequently, the location of records in the output cannot be determined at design time because it depends on how many records are stored on each input partition, and the number of records on each partition of course cannot be determined without reading the data and evaluating the upstream transformations. Ergo, increasing the number of partitions with either a `coalesce` or `repartition` call requires a shuffle.

What Type of RDD Does Your Transformation Return?

RDDs are an abstracted concept in two ways: they can be of almost any arbitrary type of record (e.g., `String`, `Row`, `Tuple`), and they can also be members of one of several implementations of the RDD interface with varying properties. Both distinctions are important for performance and evaluation. The first is important, because some transformations can only be applied to RDDs with certain record types. The second is important because each transformation returns one of the several implementations of the RDD interface, and therefore the same transformation called on two different RDD implementations (such as a `mappedRDD` versus a `GoGroupedRDD`) may be evalu-

---

ated differently. In particular, some RDD implementations retain information about the ordering or locality of the records in the RDD from previous transformations. Understanding the data locality and partitioning information associated with the resulting RDD of a transformation can help avoid unnecessary shuffles. We will save a more detailed discussion of this for "Preserving Partitioning Information Across Transformations" on page 146 since it is most relevant to Pair RDDs. In this section we will discuss preserving record type information because it can be important for performance and surprisingly difficult as Spark programs get complicated.

The RDD is a collection type which, much like collection types in Scala, Java, and most other strongly typed languages, is instantiated with a type parameter indicating the type of the members in the collection.

 In Scala, the syntax for a type parameter is brackets; e.g., List[String], which indicates a sequence of String objects. It is equivalent to the Java syntax < > (e.g., List<String>).

RDDs are similarly typed. For example, if you use sc.textfile to read in your RDD, you will end up with an RDD of String type (denoted RDD[String] in Scala and RDD<String> in Java).

The RDD's record type information is important because many transformations are only defined on RDDs that are of a particular type, so trying to use methods on an RDD of generic type will return compile-time or runtime errors. For example, if an RDD of tuples has lost its type information and is interpreted by the compiler to be of type RDD[Any] or even RDD[(Any, Int)], calling sortByKey will not compile. The compilation error occurs because sortByKey can only be called on RDDs of key/value pairs where the keys have some implicit ordering. Similarly, numeric functions such as max, min, and sum can only be called on RDDs of Long, Int, or Double.

Record type information is one of many places in the Spark API where implicit conversions are likely to cause difficulties. If you are writing subroutines to be used in RDD transformation, it is often best to specify the helper function's input and return types concretely and avoid writing them on a generic type.

One instance that often leads to problems losing type information is when working with DataFrames as RDDs. DataFrames can be implicitly converted to RDDs of Rows. However, since the Spark SQL Row object is not strongly typed (it can be created from sequences of any value type), the Scala compiler cannot "remember" the type of value used to create the row. Indexing a row will return a value of type Any, which must be cast to a more specific type, such as a String or an Int, to perform most calculations. The type information for the rows is stored in the schema. However, converting to an

RDD throws away a `DataFrame`'s schema information, so it is important to bind the `DataFrame` schema to a variable. One of the advantages of the Dataset API is that it is strongly typed, so the values in each row will retain their type information even after conversion to an RDD.

Minimizing Object Creation

"Garbage collection" is the process of freeing up the memory allocated for an object once that object is no longer needed. Since Spark runs in the JVM, which has automatic memory management and large data structures, garbage collection can quickly become an expensive part of our Spark job. Garbage collection or "GC" errors are a common cause of failure. Even if garbage collection overhead doesn't prohibit a job from running, garbage collection creates additional serialization time, which can significantly slow it down. We can minimize the GC cost by reducing the number of objects and the size of those objects. We can reduce the size and number of our objects by reusing existing objects and by using data structures (such as primitive types) that take up less space in memory.

Reusing Existing Objects

Some RDD transformations allow us to modify the parameters in the lambda expression rather than returning a new object. For example, in the sequence function of the aggregation function for `aggregateByKey` and `aggregate`, we can modify the original accumulator argument and define the combine function in such a way that the combination is created by modifying the first of the two accumulators. A common and effective paradigm for complicated aggregations is to define a Scala class with sequence and combine operations that return the existing object using the `this.type` annotations.

For example, suppose that we wanted to do some custom aggregation that is not already defined in Spark. Let's say that we have an RDD of key/value pairs where the keys are the panda's instructors and the values are the pupils' panda report cards. For each instructor we want to know the length of the longest word used, the average number of words used per report card, and the number of instances of the word "happy." One valid, easy-to-read approach would be to use the `aggregateByKey` function, which takes three arguments: a zero value that represents an empty accumulator, a sequence function that takes the accumulator and a value and adds the value to the accumulator, and a combine operator that defines how the accumulators should be combined. In this instance we could define our accumulator to be an object with four fields: the total count of all the words, the total number of reports, the longest word seen so far, and the total number of mentions of the word "happy."

For clarity we can define this as its own object with methods for sequence and combine. We have named this object `MetricsCalculator`, and it might be coded as shown in Example 5-2.

Example 5-2. Custom aggregation object

```scala
class MetricsCalculator(
  val totalWords : Int,
  val longestWord: Int,
  val happyMentions : Int,
  val numberReportCards: Int) extends Serializable {

  def sequenceOp(reportCardContent : String) : MetricsCalculator = {
    val words = reportCardContent.split(" ")
    val tW = words.length
    val lW = words.map( w => w.length).max
    val hM = words.count(w => w.toLowerCase.equals("happy"))

    new MetricsCalculator(
      tW + totalWords,
      Math.max(longestWord, lW),
      hM + happyMentions,
      numberReportCards + 1)
  }

  def compOp(other : MetricsCalculator) : MetricsCalculator = {
    new MetricsCalculator(
      this.totalWords + other.totalWords,
      Math.max(this.longestWord, other.longestWord),
      this.happyMentions + other.happyMentions,
      this.numberReportCards + other.numberReportCards)
  }

  def toReportCardMetrics =
    ReportCardMetrics(
      longestWord,
      happyMentions,
      totalWords.toDouble/numberReportCards)
}
```

We could then use this object in the arguments to our aggregation function, as shown in Example 5-4, in a routine that maps the RDD of instructors, and report text to a case class with the three metrics we care about in Example 5-3.

Example 5-3. Case class for aggregations

```scala
case class ReportCardMetrics(
  longestWord : Int,
  happyMentions : Int,
  averageWords : Double)
```

Example 5-4. Aggregation example without object reuse

```
/**
 * Given an RDD of (PandaInstructor, ReportCardText) aggregate by instructor
 * to an RDD of distinct keys of (PandaInstructor, ReportCardStatistics)
 * where ReportCardMetrics is a case class with
 *
 * longestWord -> The longest word in all of the reports written by this instructor
 * happyMentions -> The number of times this intructor mentioned the word happy
 * averageWords -> The average number of words per report card for this instructor
 */
def calculateReportCardStatistics(rdd : RDD[(String, String)]
): RDD[(String, ReportCardMetrics)] ={

  rdd.aggregateByKey(new MetricsCalculator(totalWords = 0,
    longestWord = 0, happyMentions = 0, numberReportCards = 0))(
      seqOp = ((reportCardMetrics, reportCardText) =>
        reportCardMetrics.sequenceOp(reportCardText)),
      combOp = (x, y) => x.compOp(y))
    .mapValues(_.toReportCardMetrics)
}
```

This method is superior to using a two `map` and one `reduceByKey` method. The aggregate function combines each partition locally, then does a shuffle to perform the cross-partition reduction. However, it has the disadvantage of creating a new instance of our custom object for each record in the dataset and for each combine step. A very simple way to reduce the cost of object creation would be to modify our `MetricsCalculator` to use Scala's `this.type` design paradigm so that the sequence operation modifies the original accumulator and the combine operation modifies the first accumulator rather than returning a new one, as shown in Example 5-5.

Example 5-5. Aggregation example with object reuse

```
class MetricsCalculatorReuseObjects(
  var totalWords : Int,
  var longestWord: Int,
  var happyMentions : Int,
  var numberReportCards: Int) extends Serializable {

  def sequenceOp(reportCardContent : String) : this.type = {
    val words = reportCardContent.split(" ")
    totalWords += words.length
    longestWord = Math.max(longestWord, words.map( w => w.length).max)
    happyMentions += words.count(w => w.toLowerCase.equals("happy"))
    numberReportCards +=1
    this
  }
```

```scala
def compOp(other : MetricsCalculatorReuseObjects) : this.type = {
  totalWords += other.totalWords
  longestWord = Math.max(this.longestWord, other.longestWord)
  happyMentions += other.happyMentions
  numberReportCards += other.numberReportCards
  this
}

def toReportCardMetrics =
  ReportCardMetrics(
    longestWord,
    happyMentions,
    totalWords.toDouble/numberReportCards)
}
```

Our aggregation routine will remain the same.

 It should be obvious that the Scala code within the sequence operator is slower than it needs to be. Rather than performing three different functional calls on the words array we ought to go through
the string as a string buffer, counting the words, keeping track of
the longest word, and counting the occurrence of the word "happy"
(or at least use a while loop to parse the words array rather than
three recursive calls). We have left this solution since we think it is
easier to read and the primary intention of the example is to show
how to optimize the aggregateByKey Spark routine.

Reduce (which calls aggregate) and the fold operations (foldLeft, fold, foldRight)
can also benefit from object reuse. However, these aggregation functions are unique.
It is best to avoid mutable data structures in Spark code (and Scala code in general)
because they can lead to serialization errors and may have inaccurate results. For
many other RDD functions, particularly narrow transformations, modifying the first
value of the argument is not safe because the transformations may be chained
together with lazy evaluation and may be evaluated multiple times. For example, if
you have an RDD of mutable objects, modifying the arrays with a map function may
lead to inaccurate results since the objects may be reused more times than you expect
—especially if the RDD is recomputed.

Using Smaller Data Structures

Spark can be a memory hog. An important way to optimize Spark jobs for both time
and space is to stick to primitive types rather than custom classes. Although it may
make code less readable, using arrays rather than case classes or tuples can reduce GC
overhead. Scala arrays, which are exactly Java arrays under the hood, are the most
memory-efficient of the Scala collection types. Scala tuples are objects, so in some
instances it might be better to use a two- or three-element array rather than a tuple

for expensive operations. The Scala collection types in general incur a higher GC overhead than arrays.

Notice that our `ReportCardMetrics` object is just a wrapper for a few numeric values. Although it is less readable and less object-oriented, it is more space-efficient to use a four-element array of integers. We can maintain the same readable code paradigm by using a Scala `object` instead of a `class` and defining the sequence, and combine operations as functions on strings and arrays as shown in Example 5-6.

Example 5-6. Using an array as the aggregation object

```scala
object MetricsCalculator_Arrays extends Serializable {
  val totalWordIndex = 0
  val longestWordIndex = 1
  val happyMentionsIndex = 2
  val numberReportCardsIndex = 3

  def sequenceOp(reportCardMetrics : Array[Int],
    reportCardContent : String) : Array[Int] = {

    val words = reportCardContent.split(" ")
    //modify each of the elements in the array
    reportCardMetrics(totalWordIndex) += words.length
    reportCardMetrics(longestWordIndex) = Math.max(
      reportCardMetrics(longestWordIndex),
      words.map(w => w.length).max)
    reportCardMetrics(happyMentionsIndex) += words.count(
      w => w.toLowerCase.equals("happy"))
    reportCardMetrics(numberReportCardsIndex) +=1
    reportCardMetrics
  }

  def compOp(x : Array[Int], y : Array[Int]) : Array[Int] = {
    //combine the first and second arrays by modifying the elements
    // in the first array
    x(totalWordIndex)  += y(totalWordIndex)
    x(longestWordIndex) = Math.max(x(longestWordIndex), y(longestWordIndex))
    x(happyMentionsIndex) += y(happyMentionsIndex)
    x(numberReportCardsIndex) += y(numberReportCardsIndex)
    x
  }

  def toReportCardMetrics(ar : Array[Int]) : ReportCardMetrics =
    ReportCardMetrics(
      ar(longestWordIndex),
      ar(happyMentionsIndex),
      ar(totalWordIndex)/ar(numberReportCardsIndex)
    )
}
```

We would then need to modify our aggregation code slightly. We are not using the same custom aggregation object, and the zero value has changed. This is shown in Example 5-7.

Example 5-7. Aggregation with arrays to minimize expensive object creation

```
def calculateReportCardStatisticsWithArrays(rdd : RDD[(String, String)]
): RDD[(String, ReportCardMetrics)] = {

  rdd.aggregateByKey(
    //the zero value is a four element array of zeros
    Array.fill[Int](4)(0)
  )(
  //seqOp adds the relevant values to the array
    seqOp = (reportCardMetrics, reportCardText) =>
      MetricsCalculator_Arrays.sequenceOp(reportCardMetrics, reportCardText),
  //combo defines how the arrays should be combined
    combOp = (x, y) => MetricsCalculator_Arrays.compOp(x, y))
  .mapValues(MetricsCalculator_Arrays.toReportCardMetrics)
}
```

Within a function, it is often beneficial to avoid intermediate object creation. It is important to remember that converting between types (such as between different flavors of Scala collections) creates intermediate objects. This is yet another place in which implicit conversions may have unfortunate performance implications.

For example, suppose that observing our note in the previous section, you wanted to speed up the sequence function of the `MetricsCalculator_ReuseObjects` object. Then, you realized that your coworker had written a general-purpose utility that finds the instances of the word "happy" and the longest word in a collection of strings (shown in Example 5-8).

Example 5-8. Function with implicit sequence conversions

```
def findWordMetrics[T <:Seq[String]](collection : T ): (Int, Int)={
  val iterator = collection.toIterator
  var mentionsOfHappy = 0
  var longestWordSoFar = 0
  while(iterator.hasNext){
    val n = iterator.next()
    if(n.toLowerCase == "happy"){
      mentionsOfHappy +=1
    }
    val length = n.length
    if(length> longestWordSoFar) {
      longestWordSoFar = length
    }

  }
```

```
    (longestWordSoFar, mentionsOfHappy)
  }
```

Your coworker helpfully defined her function on any type that extends a Scala Tra
versable index. Thus, you won't need to convert the array of words at all and can
happily write the code shown in Example 5-9.

Example 5-9. Aggregation with bad implicit conversions

```
val totalWordIndex = 0
val longestWordIndex = 1
val happyMentionsIndex = 2
val numberReportCardsIndex = 3
def fasterSeqOp(reportCardMetrics : Array[Int], content  : String): Array[Int] = {
  val words: Seq[String] = content.split(" ")
  val (longestWord, happyMentions) = CollectionRoutines.findWordMetrics(words)
  reportCardMetrics(totalWordIndex) += words.length
  reportCardMetrics(longestWordIndex) = longestWord
  reportCardMetrics(happyMentionsIndex) += happyMentions
  reportCardMetrics(numberReportCardsIndex) +=1
  reportCardMetrics
}
```

Unfortunately, in terms of object creation, this new implementation is actually worse
than the previous one. It creates two extra objects containing the collection with the
words each time a sequence operation is called! First when you call the findWordMet
rics routine, since the input array has to be implicitly converted to a Traversable
object (creating a new object of the same size), and again when your coworker's code
casts the Traversable object to an Iterator.

Modifying a value passed into your transformation is not always
safe, so double-check the documentation for the function you are
using.

Beyond reducing the objects that are directly allocated, Scala's
implicit conversions can sometimes cause additional allocations in
the process of converting.

Iterator-to-Iterator Transformations with mapPartitions

The RDD mapPartitions function takes as its argument a function from an itera
tor of records (representing the records on one partition) to another iterator of
records (representing the output partition).

The `mapPartitions` transformation is one of the most powerful in Spark since it lets the user define an arbitrary routine on one partition of data. The `mapPartitions` transformation can be used for very simple data transformations like string parsing, but it can also be used for complex, expensive data-processing work to solve problems such as secondary sort or highly custom aggregations. Many of Spark's other transformations, like `filter`, `map`, and `flatMap`, can be built using `mapPartitions`. Optimizing the `mapPartitions` routines is an important part of writing complicated and performant Spark code, as we will see in Chapter 6. To allow Spark the flexibility to spill some records to disk, it is important to represent your functions inside of `mapPartitions` in such a way that your functions do not force loading the entire partition in-memory (e.g., implicitly converting to a list). Iterators have many methods we can use to write functional-style transformations. You may also construct your own custom iterator extending the `Iterator` interface. When a transformation directly takes and returns an iterator without forcing it through another collection, we call it an *iterator-to-iterator* transformation.

What Is an Iterator-to-Iterator Transformation?

A Scala `iterator` object is not actually a collection, but a function that defines a process of accessing the elements in a collection one-by-one. Not only are iterators immutable, but the same element in an iterator can only be accessed one time. In other words, iterators can only be traversed once, and they extend the Scala interface `TraversableOnce`. Iterators have some of the same methods defined on them as other immutable Scala collections, such as mappings (`map` and `flatMap`), additions (`++`), folds (`foldLeft`, `reduceRight`, `reduce`), element conditions (`forall` and `exists`), and traversals (`next` and `foreach`). In some instances, these methods behave differently than other Scala collections. Since the iterator can only be traversed once, any of the iterator methods that require looking at all the elements in the iterator will leave the original iterator empty.

Java has its own implementation of iterators, `java.util.Iterator`, which have the same benefits as Scala iterators for Spark's evaluation.

Beware of your function calls. It is easy to accidentally consume an iterator by calling an object that traverses through the iterator such as `size`, or to trigger an implicit conversion. Iterators can be converted to any other Scala collection type. However, converting them requires accessing each of the elements. Thus, after it has been converted to a new collection type, an iterator will be at its last element (empty).

In some ways it can be helpful to conceptualize iterator methods as we would RDD methods—as either *transformations* or *actions*—because like an RDD, an iterator is actually a set of evaluation instructions rather than a stored state. Some iterator methods, like `next`, `size`, and `foreach`, traverse the iterator and evaluate it (more like an action). Others, like `map` and `flatMap`, return a new iterator—which is really a set of evaluation instructions—much like RDD transformations return a new RDD. However, in contrast to Spark transformations, iterator transformations are executed linearly, one element at at time, rather than in parallel. This makes iterators slower but much easier to use than if they could be executed in parallel. For example, if we needed to store some information about the records we have seen, we can do that in a `filter` or a `map` function on the iterator, since the map/filter routine will be applied to each element sequentially. (See Example 5-12 at the end of this section.) One-to-one functions are also not chained together in iterator operations so using three `map` calls still requires looking at each element in the iterator three times.

By "iterator-to-iterator transformation" we mean using one of these iterator "transformations" to return a new iterator rather than a) converting the iterator to a different collection or b) evaluating the iterator with one of the iterator "actions" and building a new collection. To reiterate: using a while loop to traverse the elements of an iterator and build a new collection (even a new iterator) *does not* qualify as an iterator-to-iterator transformation. Converting an iterator to a more intuitive collection type, manipulating it, and converting back to an iterator is not an iterator-to-iterator transformation. Indeed, converting the iterator argument in `mapPartitions` to a collection object eliminates all the benefits of iterator-to-iterator transformations.

Space and Time Advantages

The primary advantage of using iterator-to-iterator transformations in Spark routines is that their transformations allow Spark to selectively spill data to disk. Conceptually, an iterator-to-iterator transformation means defining a process for evaluating elements one at a time. Thus, Spark can apply that procedure to batches of records rather than reading an entire partition into memory or creating a collection with all of the output records in-memory and then returning it. Consequently, iterator-to-iterator transformations allow Spark to manipulate partitions that are too large to fit in memory on a single executor without out memory errors.

Furthermore, keeping the partition as an iterator allows Spark to use disk space more selectively. Rather than spilling an entire partition when it doesn't fit in memory, the iterator-to-iterator transformation allows Spark to spill only those records that do not fit in memory, thereby saving disk I/O and the cost of recomputation. Lastly, using methods defined on iterators avoids defining intermediary data structures. Reducing the number of large intermediate data structures is a way to avoid unnecessary object creation, which can slow down garbage collection as we talked about in "Minimizing Object Creation" on page 94.

 Unfortunately the Spark Streaming mapPartitions API is one of relatively few places where the Scala API decisively outperforms its Java counterpart. Prior to Spark 1.6, mapPartitions in Spark Streaming was defined on objects of type Java Iterable rather than Java Iterator and thus automatically reads the entire collection into memory. In the Spark Core, the Java API still uses Iterable rather than iterators as the grouped result of groupByKey, thus eliminating the possibility of using an iterator-to-iterator transformation after a groupByKey call.

An Example

For all their advantages, iterators can be a much harder abstraction to conceptualize and use than collection types such as arrays and hash maps, with which users may be more familiar from other languages. Here we provide an example of a complicated mapPartitions routine, which given a sorted RDD of (value, columnIndex), count) tuples and a list of rank statistics on this partition, returns the (value, columnIndex) pairs that represent ranks statistics, shown in Example 5-10. This method is part of the optimal solution to the "Goldilocks problem," which is presented in full in "Goldilocks Version 4: Reduce to Distinct on Each Partition" on page 167 and introduced in "The Goldilocks Example" on page 129.

Example 5-10. Example mapPartitions

```
private def findTargetRanksIteratively(
        sortedAggregatedValueColumnPairs : RDD[((Double, Int), Long)],
        ranksLocations : Array[(Int, List[(Int, Long)])]): RDD[(Int, Double)] = {

  sortedAggregatedValueColumnPairs.mapPartitionsWithIndex((partitionIndex : Int,
    aggregatedValueColumnPairs : Iterator[((Double, Int), Long)]) => {

   val targetsInThisPart: List[(Int, Long)] = ranksLocations(partitionIndex)._2
   if (targetsInThisPart.nonEmpty) {
     FindTargetsSubRoutine.asIteratorToIteratorTransformation(
       aggregatedValueColumnPairs,
       targetsInThisPart)
   } else {
     Iterator.empty
   }
 })
}
```

This routine is a good example of a place where we are likely to see performance gains from an iterator-to-iterator transformation, since it is a complicated routine performed on partitions that we anticipate will be too large to fit in memory. However, it is an instance where using iterators is, from a design perspective, a non-obvious choice because we have to keep a map of running totals with the number of elements for each column we have seen so far. A more straightforward way to design this routine would be as follows: loop through the iterator, store the running totals in a hashMap, and build a new collection of the elements we want to keep using an array buffer—then convert the array buffer to an iterator, shown in Example 5-11.

Example 5-11. MapPartitions example without an iterator-to-iterator transformation

```scala
def withArrayBuffer(valueColumnPairsIter : Iterator[((Double, Int), Long)],
  targetsInThisPart: List[(Int, Long)] ): Iterator[(Int, Double)] = {

    val columnsRelativeIndex: Predef.Map[Int, List[Long]] =
      targetsInThisPart.groupBy(_._1).mapValues(_.map(_._2))

    // The column indices of the pairs that are desired rank statistics that live in
    // this partition.
      val columnsInThisPart: List[Int] = targetsInThisPart.map(_._1).distinct

    // A HashMap with the running totals of each column index. As we loop through
    // the iterator, we will update the hashmap as we see elements of each
    // column index.
      val runningTotals : mutable.HashMap[Int, Long]= new mutable.HashMap()
      runningTotals ++= columnsInThisPart.map(columnIndex => (columnIndex, 0L)).toMap

  //we use an array buffer to build the resulting iterator
      val result: ArrayBuffer[(Int, Double)] =
      new scala.collection.mutable.ArrayBuffer()

    valueColumnPairsIter.foreach {
      case ((value, colIndex), count) =>

        if (columnsInThisPart contains colIndex) {

          val total = runningTotals(colIndex)
          //the ranks that are contained by this element of the input iterator.
          //get by filtering the
          val ranksPresent = columnsRelativeIndex(colIndex)
            .filter(index => (index <= count + total) && (index > total))
          ranksPresent.foreach(r => result += ((colIndex, value)))
          //update the running totals.
          runningTotals.update(colIndex, total + count)
      }
    }
    //convert
```

```
    result.toIterator
  }
```

At first this looks like an okay solution since we are estimating that the number of elements we are returning is small, and because array buffers are usually a relatively performant way to build up Scala collections. However, if the input data is very large relative to the cluster size, we still see out-of-memory errors and failures in this step. A more efficient solution would be to use an iterator-to-iterator transformation. We can convert this subroutine to an iterator-to-iterator transformation although our routine is not parallelizable (it requires keeping a list of running totals). We can do this because the subroutine we need can be completed on one element of the iterator without any information about the other elements. The final solution uses the `filter` function of iterators—to eliminate any elements that are not in the final data—and a `flatMap` to build the new iterator of elements in the resulting partitions, as shown in Example 5-12.

Example 5-12. MapPartitions with iterator-to-iterator transformations

```
def asIteratorToIteratorTransformation(
  valueColumnPairsIter : Iterator[((Double, Int), Long)],
  targetsInThisPart: List[(Int, Long)] ): Iterator[(Int, Double)] = {

  val columnsRelativeIndex = targetsInThisPart.groupBy(_._1).mapValues(_.map(_._2))
  val columnsInThisPart = targetsInThisPart.map(_._1).distinct

  val runningTotals : mutable.HashMap[Int, Long]= new mutable.HashMap()
   runningTotals ++= columnsInThisPart.map(columnIndex => (columnIndex, 0L)).toMap

  //filter out the pairs that don't have a column index that is in this part
  val pairsWithRanksInThisPart = valueColumnPairsIter.filter{
    case (((value, colIndex), count)) =>
      columnsInThisPart contains colIndex
  }

  // map the valueColumn pairs to a list of (colIndex, value) pairs that correspond
  // to one of the desired rank statistics on this partition.
  pairsWithRanksInThisPart.flatMap{

    case (((value, colIndex), count)) =>

        val total = runningTotals(colIndex)
        val ranksPresent: List[Long] = columnsRelativeIndex(colIndex)
                                    .filter(index => (index <= count + total)
                                      && (index > total))

        val nextElems: Iterator[(Int, Double)] =
          ranksPresent.map(r => (colIndex, value)).toIterator

        //update the running totals
```

```
        runningTotals.update(colIndex, total + count)
        nextElems
    }
  }
```

This approach allows the function to spill to disk selectively by working with each element in the iterator one at a time. This implementation saves space by incrementally building the result rather than storing the new collection type in memory as an array buffer. It saves a penny on garbage collection by not creating the array buffer as an intermediate step.

 If you are using an `ArrayBuffer` to build a new collection for `map Partitions`, it is always possible (and likely more performant) to use a `map` or `flatMap` on the iterator to incrementally add new elements.

Set Operations

Spark has a variety of set-like operations, some of which are expensive and some of which have different behavior than the mathematical definitions of the equivalent operations. In this section we hope to explain how to use these operations safely and effectively.

Since RDDs aren't distinct, they mainly differ from mathematical set operations in how they handle duplicates. For example, `union` merely combines its arguments, so the result of union will always have the size of both RDDs combined. `intersection` and `subtract` are defined similarly to their set-theoretic counterparts, but since the input RDDs (unlikely mathematical sets) can have duplicates the results may be unexpected. Subtracting will remove all of the elements in the first RDD that have a key present in the second RDD. Thus it is possible that by subtracting, the result will be smaller than the size of the first RDD minus the size of the second, breaking one of the laws of set theory.

For example, the simple unit test in Example 5-13 will pass.

Example 5-13. Subtract example

```
val a = Array(1, 2, 3, 4, 4, 4, 4)
val b = Array(3, 4)
val rddA = sc.parallelize(a)
val rddB = sc.parallelize(b)
val rddC = rddA.subtract(rddB)
assert(rddC.count() < rddA.count() - rddB.count())
```

In Spark, `intersection` co-groups the argument RDDs using their values as keys and filters out those elements that don't appear in both. Consequently the result of RDD `intersection` contains no duplicates. Although this is the expected behavior for `intersection`, using several set operations on RDDs containing duplicates can lead to unexpected behavior. The union of the two RDDs in Example 5-13 is an RDD containing two elements, 1 and 2. Thus, as the unit test in Example 5-14 demonstrates, we cannot always "re-create" `rddA` as the union of the intersection and the subtraction.[1]

Example 5-14. Intersection example

```
val a = Array(1, 2, 3, 4, 4, 4, 4)
val b = Array(3, 4)
val rddA = sc.parallelize(a)
val rddB = sc.parallelize(b)
val intersection = rddA.intersection(rddB)
val subtraction = rddA.subtract(rddB)
val union = intersection.union(subtraction)
assert(!rddA.collect().sorted.sameElements(union.collect().sorted))
```

 To make an RDD more like a set, you can use `distinct` prior to computing any set operations. However, calling `distinct` will cause a shuffle, and if the data is not already partitioned this can be expensive.

Reducing Setup Overhead

Some operations require setup work per-worker or per-partition, like creating a database connection or setting up a random number generator. For transformations you can use `mapPartitions`, do the setup work per partition in the map function, and then perform your desired transformation on the iterator for the partition. We will illustrate doing this with a pseudorandom number generator in Example 5-15.

Example 5-15. Create one random number generator per partition using broadcast variable

```
rdd.mapPartitions{itr =>
  // Only create once RNG per partitions
  val r = new Random()
```

---

[1] If A and B are sets, $(A - B) \cup (B \cap A) = A$ in all cases. This is not true in Spark. If `rddA` or `rddB` have duplicate keys or if `rddA` and `rddB` have overlapping keys, then $(A - B) \cup (B \cap A)$ is a *subset* of A.

```
    itr.filter(x => r.nextInt(10) == 0)
}
```

 It is important to remember to use an iterator-to-iterator transformation to allow spilling to disk selectively, as discussed in "Iterator-to-Iterator Transformations with mapPartitions" on page 100.

Beyond using this pattern to reduce setup overhead in transformations, another common pattern is to create a connection inside of an action to save the data. If your work is writing out the data you can use the same pattern as with `mapPartitions` except with `foreachPartition`.

If the setup work can be serialized, a broadcast variable can distribute the object that we cover next. If the setup work can't be serialized, a broadcast variable with a `transient lazy val` can be used as well. See Example 5-17 in the next section.

Shared Variables

Spark has two types of shared variables—broadcast variables and accumulators—each of which can only be written in one context (driver or worker, respectively) and read in the other. Broadcast variables can be written in the driver program and read on the executors, whereas accumulators are written onto the executors and read on the driver.

Broadcast Variables

Broadcast variables give us a way to take a local value on the driver and distribute a read-only copy to each machine rather than shipping a new copy with each task. Broadcast variables might not seem especially useful, since we can just capture a local variable in our closure to transfer data from the driver to the workers; however, the savings of only sending one copy per machine versus sending one copy per task can make a huge difference, especially when the same broadcast variable is used in additional transformations. Two common examples of using broadcast variables are a) broadcasting a small table to join against and b) broadcasting a machine learning model to be able to run the predictions on our data.

Creating a broadcast variable is done by calling `broadcast` on the `SparkContext`. This distributes the value to the workers and gives us back a wrapper that allows us to access the value on the workers by calling `value`, as shown in Examples 5-16 and 5-17. If a `broadcast` variable is created with a variable input, the input should not be modified after the variable has been created since existing workers will not see the updates and new workers may see the new value.

Example 5-16. Sample broadcast of a hashset of invalid panda locations to filter out

```
val invalid = HashSet() ++ invalidPandas
val invalidBroadcast = sc.broadcast(invalid)
input.filter{panda => !invalidBroadcast.value.contains(panda.id)}
```

Example 5-17. Create one random number generator per worker

```
class LazyPrng {
  @transient lazy val r = new Random()
}
def customSampleBroadcast[T: ClassTag](sc: SparkContext, rdd: RDD[T]): RDD[T]= {
  val bcastprng = sc.broadcast(new LazyPrng())
  rdd.filter(x => bcastprng.value.r.nextInt(10) == 0)
}
```

The value for a broadcast variable must be a local, serializable value: no RDDs or other distributed data structures.

Internally, Spark uses broadcast variables for the Hadoop job configuration objects and large blocks of Python code for UDFs. If a broadcast variable is no longer needed, you can explicitly remove it by calling unpersist() on the broadcast variable.

Accumulators

Accumulators are the second type of Spark's shared variables, allowing us to collect by-product information from a transformation or action on the workers and then bring the result back to the driver. With Spark's execution model, Spark adds to accumulators only once the computation has been triggered (e.g., by an action). If the computation happens multiple times, Spark will update the accumulator each time. This multiple counting can be desirable for process-level information, like computing the entire time spent parsing records. However, it can be disastrous for data-related information like counting the number of invalid records.

Spark accumulators have had an API update for 2.0—these examples are updated for the 2.X API, although 1.X examples are still available in the examples repo (*https://github.com/high-performance-spark/high-performance-spark-examples/blob/master/src/main/scala/com/high-performance-spark-examples/trans formations/Accumulators.scala*).

Accumulators can be unpredictable. In their current state, they are best used where potential multiple counting is the desired behavior.

Accumulators have a number of built-in types that make it easy to create an accumulator for common use cases. Accumulators are not intended for collecting large amounts of information, so if you find yourself adding a large number of elements to a collection or appending to a string you may wish to consider a separate action instead of an accumulator. The default operation for numeric accumulators is the + operation, so we could use this to sum the fuzzyness of all of the pandas as shown in Example 5-18.

Example 5-18. Compute fuzzyness of pandas with accumulators

```
def computeTotalFuzzyNess(sc: SparkContext, rdd: RDD[RawPanda]):
    (RDD[(String, Long)], Double) = {
  // Create a named accumulator for doubles
  val acc = sc.doubleAccumulator("fuzzyNess")
  val transformed = rdd.map{x => acc.add(x.attributes(0)); (x.zip, x.id)}
  // accumulator still has zero value
  // Note: This example is dangerous since the transformation may be
  // evaluated multiple times.
  transformed.count() // force evaluation
  (transformed, acc.value)
}
```

Additionally, accumulators support a wide variety of data types provided the operation is associative, but some are easier to get in trouble with than others. To use an accumulator of a different type, you need to implement the AccumulatorV2[Input Type, ValueType] interface and provide reset, copy, isZero, value, merge, and add methods. You are responsible for the specifics of the class that keeps track of the accumulated values. In general, a simple var or two will do the trick. In addition to the required method, override resetAndCopy to improve performance in certain cases.

Generally the reset and copy methods are used together with the resetAndCopy method, which can often be more efficiently implemented to avoid the copy stage (as is done in both of the custom accumulator examples, Examples 5-19 and 5-20). The reset method resets the value of the current accumulator back to "zero" so that isZero, if called, will return true. The copy method needs to create a copy of the provided accumulator, with the new accumulator having the same value as the current accumulator. This is called when copying the value to the workers so that Spark can avoid the expense (and confusion) of copying any of the previously accumulated work to the drivers.

The type parameters of the `AccumulatorV2` interface specify the type being accumulated over (`add`) and the final return type (`value`). Importantly, this does *not* constrain or specify the type used to hold the accumulation itself. A single variable is used to keep track of values in the following examples. However, you need not limit yourself to one variable. Inside of many of Spark's numeric accumulators, two `var`s are used.

The `merge` method for the accumulator API's type signature takes the same base `AccumulatorV2` type. Since the `AccumulatorV2` trait doesn't specify anything about how workers should keep track of the values as they are evaluated, you will need to cast the accumulator you receive to the expected type so you can access your own internal accumulation field(s). A basic implementation of this is shown in Example 5-19.

Example 5-19. Compute maximum panda id

```
def computeMaxFuzzyNess(sc: SparkContext, rdd: RDD[RawPanda]):
    (RDD[(String, Long)], Option[Double]) = {
  class MaxDoubleAccumulator extends AccumulatorV2[Double, Option[Double]] {
    // Here is the var we will accumulate our value in to.
    var currentVal: Option[Double] = None
    override def isZero = currentVal.isEmpty

    // Reset the current accumulator to zero - used when sending over the wire
    // to the workers.
    override def reset() = {
      currentVal = None
    }

    // Copy the current accumulator - this is only really used in context of
    // copy and reset - but since it's part of the public API let's be safe.
    def copy() = {
      val newCopy = new MaxDoubleAccumulator()
      newCopy.currentVal = currentVal
      newCopy
    }

    // We override copy and reset for "speed" - no need to copy the value if
    // we are going to zero it right away. This doesn't make much difference
    // for Option[Double] but for something like Array[X] could be huge.

    override def copyAndReset() = {
      new MaxDoubleAccumulator()
    }

    // Add a new value (called on the worker side)
    override def add(value: Double) = {
      currentVal = Some(
        // If the value is present compare it to the new value - otherwise
        // just store the new value as the current max.
        currentVal.map(acc => Math.max(acc, value)).getOrElse(value))
```

```
  }

    override def merge(other: AccumulatorV2[Double, Option[Double]]) = {
      other match {
        case otherFuzzy: MaxDoubleAccumulator =>
          // If the other accumulator has the option set merge it in with
          // the standard add procedure. If the other accumulator isn't set
          // do nothing.
          otherFuzzy.currentVal.foreach(value => add(value))
        case _ =>
          // This should never happen, Spark will only call merge with
          // the correct type - but that won't stop someone else from calling
          // merge so throw an exception just in case.
          throw new Exception("Unexpected merge with unsupported type" + other)
      }
    }
    // Return the accumulated value.
    override def value = currentVal
  }
  // Create a new custom accumulator
  val acc = new MaxDoubleAccumulator()
  sc.register(acc)
  val transformed = rdd.map{x => acc.add(x.attributes(0)); (x.zip, x.id)}
  // accumulator still has None value.
  // Note: This example is dangerous since the transformation may be
  // evaluated multiple times.
  transformed.count() // force evaluation
  (transformed, acc.value)
}
```

This still requires that the result is the same as the type we are accumulating. If we wanted to collect all of the distinct elements, we would likely want to collect a set and the types would be different. This is shown in Example 5-20.

Example 5-20. Compute unique panda ids

```
def uniquePandas(sc: SparkContext, rdd: RDD[RawPanda]): HashSet[Long] = {
  class UniqParam extends AccumulatorV2[Long, HashSet[Long]] {
    var accValue: HashSet[Long] = new HashSet[Long]()

    def value = accValue

    override def copy() = {
      val newCopy = new UniqParam()
      newCopy.accValue = accValue.clone
      newCopy
    }
    override def reset() = {
      this.accValue = new HashSet[Long]()
    }
    override def isZero() = {
```

```scala
      accValue.isEmpty
    }

    // We override copy and reset for speed - no need to copy the value if
    // we care going to zero it right away.
    override def copyAndReset() = {
      new UniqParam()
    }
    // For adding new values
    override def add(value: Long) = {
      accValue += value
    }
    // For merging accumulators
    override def merge(other: AccumulatorV2[Long, HashSet[Long]]) = {
      other match {
        case otherUniq: UniqParam =>
          accValue = accValue ++ otherUniq.accValue
        case _ =>
          throw new Exception("only support merging with same type")
      }
    }
  }
  // Create an accumulator for keeping track of unique values
  val acc = new UniqParam()
  // Register with a name
  sc.register(acc, "Unique values")
  val transformed = rdd.map{x => acc.add(x.id); (x.zip, x.id)}
  // accumulator still has Double.MinValue
  transformed.count() // force evaluation
  acc.value
}
```

The value function can perform complex work and return a different type than the input type or internal accumulated value. For example, if you were computing the average, you might have a value function that divides two longs returning a double.

You may provide a name for accumulators in Scala so they show up in the web UI. Simply add a name as the second param. This does involve calling toString on the accumulator, though—so if that is an expensive operation, leave your accumulator unnamed.

When working with cached data our accumulators can seem almost consistent, but as discussed in "Interaction with Accumulators" on page 125 this is not the case.

There is a proposal to add data property (or "consistent") accumulators in Spark 2.1.[2] Property accumulators would avoid double counting—but this remains unmerged. You can follow its progress in this pull request (*https://github.com/apache/spark/pull/11105*).

Internally, beginning in Spark 2.0, Spark uses accumulators to keep track of task metrics.

Reusing RDDs

Spark offers several options for RDD reuse, including persisting, caching, and checkpointing. However, Spark does not perform any of these automatically[3] because storing RDD for reuse breaks some pipelining, which can be a waste if the RDD is only used once or if the transformation is inexpensive to recompute. All kinds of persistence (of which caching is one type) and checkpointing have some cost and are unlikely to improve performance for operations that are performed only once. Furthermore, on large datasets the cost of persisting or checkpointing can be so high that recomputing is more desirable. However, for some specific kinds of Spark programs, reusing an RDD can lead to huge performance gains, both in the terms of speed and reducing failures.

Cases for Reuse

In this section we cover some instances when persisting or checkpointing RDDs may foster performance gains. Broadly speaking, the most important cases for reuse are using an RDD many times; performing multiple actions on the same RDD; and for long chains of (or very expensive) transformations.

Iterative computations

For transformations that use the same parent RDD multiple times, reusing an RDD forces evaluation of that RDD and so can help avoid repeated computations. For example, if you were performing a loop of joins to the same dataset, persisting that dataset could lead to huge performance improvements since it ensures that the partitions of that RDD will be available in-memory to do each join.

In Example 5-21 we are computing the root mean squared error (RMSE) on a number of different RDDs representing predictions from different models. To do this we have to join each RDD of predictions to an RDD of the data in the validation set.

---

2 Originally planned for 2.0.

3 Some notable exceptions are inside of certain ML algorithms, which if passed in an unpersisted RDD will automatically persist and unpersist the RDD.

In this example we use `persist()`, which persists the RDD in memory. As we will explain in "Types of Reuse: Cache, Persist, Checkpoint, Shuffle Files" on page 118, `cache()` is equivalent to `per sist()`, which is equivalent to `persist("MEMORY_ONLY")`.

Example 5-21. A function with iterative computations

```
val testSet: Array[RDD[(Double, Int)]] =
  Array(
    validationSet.mapValues(_ + 1),
    validationSet.mapValues(_ + 2),
    validationSet)
validationSet.persist() //persist since we are using this RDD several times
val errors = testSet.map( rdd => {
    rmse(rdd.join(validationSet).values)
})
```

Without persisting, Spark would have to reload and repartition the training dataset RDD to complete the `join`. However, with persistence, the training RDD will stay loaded in memory on the executors with each run of the algorithm. We discuss performance considerations with different kinds of joins in detail in "Core Spark Joins" on page 75.

Checkpointing, another form of RDD reuse that writes an RDD to external storage, will also break the RDD's lineage. However, checkpointing will keep the partitions loaded on the executors.

Multiple actions on the same RDD

If you do not reuse an RDD, each action called on an RDD will launch its own Spark job with the full lineage of RDD transformations. Persisting and checkpointing breaks the RDD's lineage, so the same series of transformations preceding the `per sist` or `checkpoint` call will be executed only once. Because persisting or checkpointing an RDD lasts for the duration of a Spark application (although it *may* be evicted by subsequent cached/persisted data), an RDD persisted during one Spark job will be available in a subsequent job executed with the same `SparkContext`. For example, suppose that we wanted to collect the first 10% of the records in an RDD. We could use the code in Example 5-22, which calls `sortByKey`, then `count`, then `take`.

Example 5-22. An example of two actions without a persist step

```
val sorted = rddA.sortByKey()
val count = sorted.count() // sorted Action 1
val sample: Long = count / 10
val sampled = sorted.take(sample.toInt) // sorted Action 2
```

The sortByKey (and presumably the read operation) needed to create the RDD, sorted, will occur twice if we do not store the RDD: once in the job called by count and again in the job called by take. We can't test this element of the execution programmatically, but if you were to run this application and view the web UI you would see that this code launches two jobs and each one includes a sort stage. However, if we add a persist or checkpoint call before the actions (as shown in Example 5-23), the transformation will only be executed once, since Spark builds a lineage graph from either an RDD's creation or a persisted/checkpointed RDD.

Example 5-23. Two actions with a persist step

```
val sorted = rddA.sortByKey()
sorted.persist()
val count = sorted.count() // sorted Action 1
val sample: Long = count / 10
val sampled = sorted.take(sample.toInt) // sorted Action 2
```

 Persisted RDDs only survive for the duration of a Spark application. To reuse data between Spark applications, use checkpointing with the same directory.

If the cost to compute each partition is very high

Even if a program does not use the same RDD multiple times, persisting and checkpointing can speed up a routine and reduce the cost of failures by storing intermediary results. Persisting or checkpointing can be particularly useful if the cost of computing one partition is very high because they ensure that the entire expensive operation will not need to be recomputed in the case of downstream failures.

For example, if your program requires a long series of one-to-one transformations, those transformations will all be combined into very computationally intensive tasks. While this is good so long as the tasks succeed and fit in memory, it does mean that if one of the downstream transformations fails, then the cost to recompute a single partition may be enormous. If all of the narrow transformations together create more GC overhead or memory strain than your cluster's executors can handle, then checkpointing or persisting off_heap can be particularly useful. Both persisting off_heap and checkpointing allow the RDD to be stored outside of the Spark executor memory, leaving space to compute. These options are also the only way to prevent recomputation if the entire Spark worker fails. Sometimes breaking up a long lineage graph for its own sake can help a job succeed since it means each of the tasks will be smaller.

Narrow transformations are generally faster than wide ones. However, some individual narrow transformations, such as training a model per partition or working with very wide rows, can be expensive. In these cases, reusing an RDD after the expensive computation so it is not recomputed may improve performance.

Deciding if Recompute Is Inexpensive Enough

Although persisting in memory is a flagship feature of Spark, it is not free. It is space intensive to store data in memory and will take time to serialize and deserialize. As we will discuss in "Dividing the Space Within One Executor" on page 283, persisting in memory and in-memory computations are both done in the Spark executor JVM. Thus, persisting in memory may take space that could be used for downstream computations or increase the risk or memory failures. Caching with Java-based memory structures (any of Spark's options besides using off_heap storage options) will incur a much higher garbage collecting cost than will recomputing.

Persisting to disk or *checkpointing* (writing the RDD to an external filesystem) has the disadvantages of MapReduce, causing expensive write and read operations. If the RDD is checkpointed or persisted to disk we must factor in not only the disk space used on the cluster to write the RDD, but also the computational cost on the Spark executors of the additional disk I/O. In most cases, checkpointing a large RDD can be used to reduce failures in high-traffic clusters but rarely leads to performance improvements, even if the RDD has to be recomputed due to the high cost of checkpointing.

Our experience has been that it is easy to underestimate just how expensive storing and reading an RDD is relative to recomputing. We have also found that for relatively simple operations the cost of the read operation needed to load the RDD far outweighs the others, so persisting is most useful when it prevents triggering another read operation or in the case of many iterative computations.

Furthermore, breaking an RDD's lineage by forcing evaluation through persisting or checkpointing prevents transformations with narrow dependencies from being combined into a single task. Consequently, we lose some of the narrow transformations cannot be combined and executed in one task. For instance, persisting or checkpointing between a simple map and filter step will break pipelining so that the previously intermediate data can be persisted, causing Spark to do two passes through the data rather than just one, since the transformation has to be evaluated in order to materialize the RDD after the map. Breaking lineage between narrow transformations is only desirable in the most extreme cases.

The preceding guidelines are good heuristics for when reuse will provide significant benefits. In general, it is worth reusing an RDD rather than recomputing it if the computation is large relative to your cluster and the rest of your job. The best way to tell if you need to reuse your RDDs is to run a job. If your job runs very slowly, see if persisting the RDDs may help before attempting to rewrite the program since persisting and checkpointing will help reduce the cost of recomputing data in the case of a failure or eliminate it altogether. If a job is failing with GC or out-of-memory errors, checkpointing or persisting off_heap may allow the job to complete, particularly if the cluster is noisy. On the other hand, if you were already persisting with the options that use in-memory persistence consider removing the persist call or switching to checkpointing or off_heap persistence.

> If you are testing some code before putting it into production, consider creating the persistence level with a variable so that you can pass in a persistence level to try as a command-line argument. The function presented in Example 5-24 uses this paradigm; it contains a storageLevel argument (which could be NONE).

Types of Reuse: Cache, Persist, Checkpoint, Shuffle Files

If you decide that you need to reuse your RDD, Spark provides a multitude of options for how to store the RDD. Thus it is important to understand when to use the various types of persistence. There are three primary operations that you can use to store your RDD: cache, persist, and checkpoint. In general, caching (equivalent to persisting with the in-memory storage) and persisting are most useful to avoid recomputation during one Spark job or to break RDDs with long lineages, since they keep an RDD on the executors during a Spark job. Checkpointing is most useful to prevent failures and a high cost of recomputation by saving intermediate results. Like persisting, checkpointing helps avoid computation, thus minimizing the cost of failure, and avoids recomputation by breaking the lineage graph.

Persist and cache

Persisting an RDD means materializing an RDD (usually by storing it in-memory on the executors), for reuse *during the current job*. Spark remembers a persisted RDD's lineage so that it can recompute it for the duration of a Spark job if one of the persisted partitions is lost. After the job ends, the persist function takes a StorageLevel argument that specifies how the RDD should be stored. Spark provides a number of different storage levels as constants, but each one is created based on five attributes of how to store the RDD: useDisk, useMemory, useOfHeap, deserialized, and replication. Calling toString on a storage level will reveal what options it contains. The Spark documentation about persistence (*http://spark.apache.org/docs/latest/programming-guide.html#rdd-persistence*) includes a fairly comprehensive list of the out-of-the-box storage options that are exposed to you.

Still, we think it may useful to provide some more information about each of the five properties that compose each storage option. This should give you a deeper understanding of which option to choose:

`useDisk`

If set, partitions that do not fit in memory will be written to disk.

The storage-level flags containing `DISK` (such as `MEMORY_AND_DISK`) enable this. By default, if partitions do not fit in memory, they will simply be evicted and will need to be recomputed when the persisted RDD is used (see "LRU Caching" on page 123). Therefore, persisting to disk can ensure that recomputation of those additional large partitions is avoided. However, reading from disk can be time-intensive, so persistence to disk is only important if the cost of recomputation is particularly high.

 It may be beneficial to allow writing to disk if you expect that an RDD cannot fit in memory. However, if the cost of recomputing the partitions is not high (they are simple mappings and don't reduce the size of the data) it may actually be faster to recompute some partitions rather than read from disk.

`useMemory`

If set, the RDD will be stored in-memory or be directly written to disk.

The `DISK_ONLY` storage levels are the only options that mark this as false. Most of the speed benefits of caching come from keeping RDDs in memory, so if the motivation for reuse is fast access for repeated computations, it is probably a good idea to choose a storage option that stores partitions in memory. However, there are some cases where disk-only persistence makes sense, e.g., when the computation is more expensive than reading in local disk or the network filesystem is especially slow (such as with certain object stores).

`useOfHeap`

If set, the RDD will be stored outside of the Spark executor in an external system such as Tachyon.

The storage option `off_heap` enables this property. If memory is a serious issue, or a cluster is noisy and partitions are evicted, this option may be compelling. We will talk more about the benefits of Tachyon in "Alluxio (nee Tachyon)" on page 122.

`deserialized`

If set, the RDD will be stored as deserialized Java objects.

As we will discuss in "Kryo" on page 290, this can make storing RDDs more space efficient, especially when using a faster serializer—but incurs some performance overhead. Storage options that include the "`_SER`" suffix such as `MEMORY_ONLY_SER` enable serialization.

If your RDD is too large to persist in-memory, first try to serialize it with the MEMORY_ONLY_SER option. This will keep the RDD fast to access, but will decrease the memory needed to store it.

`replication`

Replication is an integer that controls the number of copies of the persisted data to be stored in the cluster.

By default this is set to 1; however, serialization options that end in _2 such as DISK_ONLY_2 replicate each partition across two nodes. Use this option to ensure faster fault tolerance. However, be aware that persistence with replication incurs double the space and speed costs of persistence without replication. Replication is usually only necessary in an instance of a noisy cluster or bad connection where failures are unusually likely. It might also be useful if you do not have time to recompute in case of failure, such as when serving a live web application.

The RDD operation cache() is equivalent to the persist operation with no storage level argument, i.e., persist(). Both cache() and persist() persist the RDD with the default storage-level MEM ORY_ONLY, which is equivalent to StorageLevel(false, true, false, true), which stores RDDs in-memory as deserialized Java objects, does not write to disk as partitions get evicted, and doesn't replicate partitions.

Checkpointing

Checkpointing writes the RDD to an external storage system such as HDFS or S3, and—in contrast to persisting—forgets the RDD's lineage. Since checkpointing requires writing the RDD outside of Spark, checkpointed information survives beyond the duration of a single Spark application and forces evaluation of an RDD. Checkpointing takes up more space in external storage and may be slower than persisting since it requires potentially costly write operations. However, it does not use any Spark memory and will not incur recomputation if a Spark worker fails.

Figure 5-2 illustrates the difference between in-memory persistence and checkpointing and RDD. Persisting stores the RDD's partitions in-memory or on disk in the caching layer of each executor. Checkpointing writes each partition to some external system.

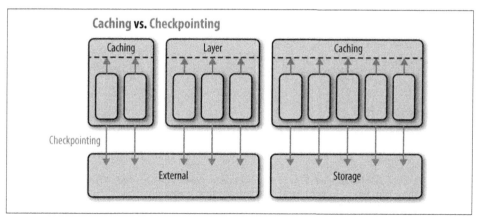

Figure 5-2. Caching versus checkpointing

It is best to use checkpointing when the cost of failure and recomputation is of more concern than additional space in external storage. Broadly speaking, we advise persisting when jobs are slow and checkpointing when they are failing. If a Spark job is failing due to out-of-memory errors, checkpointing will reduce the cost and likelihood of failure without using up memory on the executors. If your jobs are failing due to network errors or preemption on a noisy cluster, checkpointing can reduce the likelihood of failure by breaking up a long-running job into smaller segments. To call checkpoint, call setCheckpointDir(directory: String) from the SparkContext object and pass in a path to a location on HDFS to write the intermediate results. Then, in the Spark job, call .checkpoint() from the RDD.

Checkpointing example

Example 5-24 makes use of custom storage level and checkpointing options. The function is used in the Goldilocks example, which we describe in detail in "Goldilocks Version 4: Reduce to Distinct on Each Partition" on page 167, that makes use of custom storage level and checkpointing options. In this case we are doing several very expensive transformations: first a sort and then two very substantial map partitions routines. When running on a noisy cluster, we found it advantageous to checkpoint this function after the sort. The value of the directory parameter is the checkpoint directory. The sorted value is a sorted RDD or key/value pairs.

Example 5-24. Checkpoint example

```
def findQuantilesWithCustomStorage(valPairs: RDD[((Double, Int), Long)],
  colIndexList: List[Int],
  targetRanks: List[Long],
  storageLevel: StorageLevel = StorageLevel.MEMORY_AND_DISK,
  checkPoint : Boolean, directory : String = ""): Map[Int, Iterable[Double]] = {
```

```
  val n = colIndexList.last + 1
  val sorted  = valPairs.sortByKey()
  if (storageLevel != StorageLevel.NONE) {
    sorted.persist(storageLevel)
  }

  if (checkPoint) {
    sorted.sparkContext.setCheckpointDir(directory)
    sorted.checkpoint()
  }

  val partitionColumnsFreq = getColumnsFreqPerPartition(sorted, n)
  val ranksLocations  = getRanksLocationsWithinEachPart(
    targetRanks, partitionColumnsFreq, n)
  val targetRanksValues = findTargetRanksIteratively(sorted, ranksLocations)
  targetRanksValues.groupByKey().collectAsMap()
}
```

 Spark includes a *Local Checkpointing* option that truncates the RDD's lineage graph but doesn't persist to stable storage. This is not suitable for clusters that may experience failures, preemption, or dynamic scale-downs during the time the RDD may be referenced.

Alluxio (nee Tachyon)

Tachyon is a distributed, in-memory storage system that is developed separately from Spark. It sits above a storage system, such as S3 or HDFS, and can be used on its own or with an external computational framework such as Spark or MapReduce. Like Spark, Tachyon can be used in a standalone cluster mode, or with Mesos or YARN. Read more about Tachyon's architecture and how to integrate it with Spark in the Tachyon documentation (*http://www.alluxio.org*).

Tachyon can be used as an input or output source for Spark applications (data stored with Tachyon can be used to create RDDs) or for off_heap persistence during a Spark application. Using Tachyon for persistence has several advantages. First, it reduces garbage collection overhead, since data is not stored as Java objects. Second, it allows multiple executors to share the same external memory pool in Tachyon. Third, since the data is stored in memory outside of Spark, it is not lost if individual executors crash. It can be particularly useful if you want to reuse an RDD but are running out of memory or seeing garbage collection errors. It is also the best way to reuse a very large RDD between multiple applications.

Tachyon's developer and user communities are very strong in China, so part of its documentation may be stronger in Mandarin than in English.

LRU Caching

RDDs that are stored in memory and/or on disk in Spark are not automatically un-persisted when they are no longer going to be used downstream. Instead, RDDs stay in memory for the duration of a Spark application, until the driver program calls the function `unpersist`, or memory/storage pressure causes their eviction. Spark uses *Least Recently Used* or LRU caching, to determine which partitions to evict if the executors begin to run out of memory.

LRU caching dictates that the data structure that was least recently accessed will be evicted. However, because of lazy evaluation it may be a bit tricky to predict which partitions will be evicted first. Generally, Spark evicts the oldest partitions; those that were created or used in the earliest Spark job or in the earliest stage within a given job. (See "Dividing the Space Within One Executor" on page 283 for a more detailed explanation of memory management and partitions.) LRU caching behaves differently for different persistence options. For memory-only persistence operations configured with LRU caching, Spark will recompute the evicted partition each time it is needed. For memory and disk options, LRU caching will write the evicted partition to disk. If you want to take a persisted RDD out of memory to free up space, use `unpersist`.

Shuffle files

Regardless of a `persist` or `checkpoint` call, Spark does write some data to disk during a shuffle. These files are called "shuffle files" and they usually contain all of the records in each input partition sorted by mapper. Usually shuffle files remain in the local directory on the workers for the duration of an application. Thus if the driver program reuses an RDD that has already been shuffled, Spark may be able to avoid recomputing that RDD up to the point of shuffle by using the shuffle files on the mapper.

Unlike the other caches, we can't determine if a given RDD still has its shuffle files present; e.g., there is no equivalent of the `isCheckPointed` command, which returns true if that RDD has been checkpointed. In general, though, shuffle files aren't explicitly cleaned up until an RDD goes out of scope. However the web UI can be helpful in determining if stages are being skipped this way, as shown in Figure 5-3.

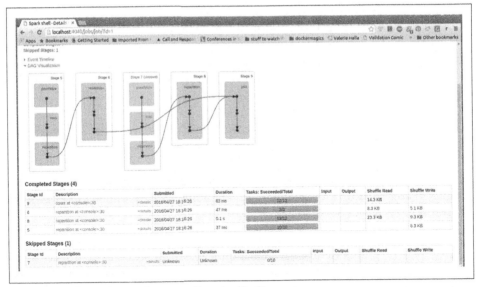

Figure 5-3. Skipped stage from reading shuffle files

The performance of reusing shuffle files is similar to the performance of an RDD that is cached at the level of disk only.

 Shuffle files can be large, and Spark has no explicit cache management for them. Keeping references to RDDs depending on shuffled output can lead to out-of-disk errors if the RDDs are not garbage collected on the driver.

Out-of-disk-space errors can be unexpected, but in clusters with small amounts of disk space they are surprisingly common. Disk space errors can be caused by long-running shell environments in which RDDs created at the top scope are never garbage collected. Spark writes the output of its shuffle operations to files on the disk of the workers in the Spark local dir. These files are only cleaned up when an RDD is garbage collected, which if the amount of memory assigned to the driver program is large, can occur infrequently. One solution is to explicitly trigger garbage collection (assuming the RDDs have gone out of scope)—if the DAG is getting too long, check-pointing can help make the RDDs available for garbage collection.

Noisy Cluster Considerations

Noisy clusters, or those with a high volume of unpredictable traffic, pose a funda-mental challenge to Spark's evaluation. By default, Spark doesn't save most inter-mediate results (besides in a shuffle step). Thus, in the case of preemptions, Spark will have to recompute the calculation in the job up to the point of failure. In a noisy cluster, where long-running jobs are often interrupted, this poses a huge challenge. Checkpointing can be especially helpful to get jobs to run at all. Checkpointing breaks an RDD's lineage, therefore reducing the cost to recompute downstream transformations. Checkpointing also persists to external storage, so that unexpected failures do not lead to data loss. If failures are common but not fatal, it may be worth configuring your job to persist to multiple machines using a storage option like MEM ORY_AND_DISK_2, which replicates data on two machines. That way, failures on one node will not require a recompute. This can be especially important with wide transformations, which are very expensive.

By default, Spark uses a first in, first out (FIFO) paradigm to queue jobs within a system. This means that the first job submitted will run in its entirety, getting priority on all the available resources. However, if a job doesn't need the whole cluster, the next job may start. FIFO scheduling can be useful to ensure that space-intensive jobs are able to use the resources that they need. However, if you launch a job a few seconds behind a many-hour process, the FIFO strategy can be frustrating. Spark offers a fair scheduler, modeled after the Hadoop fair scheduler, to allow high-traffic clusters to share resources more evenly. The fair scheduler allocates the tasks from different jobs to the executors in a "round-robin fashion" (i.e., parsing out a few tasks to the executors from each job). With the fair scheduler, a short, small job can be launched before an earlier long-running job is completed.

The fair scheduler also supports putting jobs into pools and allocating different priority (weight) to those pools. Jobs within a pool are allocated the same number of resources, and the pools are allocated resources according to their weight. Using pools can be a good way to ensure that high-priority jobs or very expensive jobs are completed. The fair scheduler also ensures that users are allocated resources evenly regardless of how many jobs they submit. You can read more about using and configuring a fair scheduler in the the Spark job scheduling documentation (*https:// spark.apache.org/docs/latest/job-scheduling.html*).

Interaction with Accumulators

The interaction of caching and accumulators can make reasoning about accumulators more difficult. As we mentioned, if part of an RDD has to be recomputed, Spark may continue to add values to the accumulator as it recomputes; causing the values in the recomputed part to be double counted. Furthermore, not all computations will always compute the entirety of a partition. Surprisingly, caching does not prevent either double counting or problems that arise from partially evaluated partitions. Cached partitions may be evicted, so double counting may still arise if the machine with the cached data fails or if the partition is evicted to make space for a more recently cached partition. Unfortunately, caching with accumulators may cause a job that appears to compute the correct value on small data to later compute the incorrect value on large data.

Conclusion

Now that you have explored how to get the most out of your standard RDD transformations, as well as joins, it's time to explore the concerns associated with the most important and complicated subset of RDD transformations, key/value pair operations. Not all of the techniques you will have learned need to be applied in every Spark program, and some of the takeaways from this chapter are more about when certain tools are not a good fit (see "Accumulators" on page 109). Many of the same techniques and considerations for standard RDD transformations apply when working with key/value data: if your transformation doesn't depend on the key, the techniques from this chapter may even be more relevant.

## CHAPTER 6

Working with Key/Value Data

Like any good distributed computing tool, Spark relies heavily on the key/value pair paradigm to define and parallelize operations, particularly wide transformations that require the data to be redistributed between machines. Anytime we want to perform grouped operations in parallel or change the ordering of records amongst machines —be it computing an aggregation statistic or merging customer records—the key/ value functionality of Spark is useful as it allows us to easily parallelize our work. Spark has its own `PairRDDFunctions` class containing operations defined on RDDs of tuples. The `PairRDDFunctions` class, made available through implicit conversion, contains most of Spark's methods for joins, and custom aggregations. The `Order edRDDFunctions` class contains the methods for sorting. The `OrderedRDDFunctions` are available to RDDs of tuples in which the first element (the key) has an implicit ordering.

Similar operations are available on `Datasets` as discussed in "Grouped Operations on Datasets" on page 66.

Despite their utility, key/value operations can lead to a number of performance issues. In fact, most expensive operations in Spark fit into the key/value pair paradigm because most wide transformations are key/value transformations, and most require some fine tuning and care to be performant. These performance considerations will be the focus of this chapter. We hope to provide not just a guide to using the functions in the `PairRDDFunctions` and `OrderedRDDFunctions` classes, but to build on the architecture lessons of Chapters 2 and 5 to present a thorough guide to thinking about how Spark evaluates wide transformations and how to redesign the logic of a program to make tasks that require ordering data most efficient.

In particular, operations on key/value pairs can cause:

- Out-of-memory errors in the driver
- Out-of-memory errors on the executor nodes
- Shuffle failures
- "Straggler tasks" or partitions, which are especially slow to compute

The first problem, memory errors in the driver, is usually caused by actions. We will discuss the performance problems associated with actions on key/value pairs in "Actions on Key/Value Pairs" on page 133. The last three performance issues—out of memory on the executors, shuffles, and straggler tasks—are all most often caused by shuffles associated with the wide transformations in the `PairRDDFunctions` and `OrderedRDDFunctions` classes. Throughout this chapter, we will focus on two primary techniques to avoid performance problems associated with shuffles, which we call "shuffle less" and "shuffle better":

Shuffle less often
We will provide techniques to minimize the number of shuffles needed to complete a complex computation. One way to minimize the number of shuffles in a computation that requires several transformations is to make sure to preserve partitioning across narrow transformations to avoid reshuffling data (see "Preserving Partitioning Information Across Transformations" on page 146). In some instances, we can use the same partitioner on a sequence of wide transformations. This can be particularly useful to avoid shuffles during joins and to reduce the number of shuffles required to compute a sequence of wide transformations (see "Co-Grouping" on page 141 and "Leveraging Co-Located and Co-Partitioned RDDs" on page 146). We will also discuss leveraging custom partitioners (see "Custom Partitioning" on page 145) to distribute the data most effectively for downstream computations as well as how to push computational work into the shuffle stage to make a complicated computation more efficient (see "Secondary Sort and repartitionAndSortWithinPartitions" on page 151).

Shuffle better
Sometimes, computation cannot be completed without a shuffle. However, not all wide transformations and not all shuffles are equally expensive or prone to failure. By using wide transformations such as `reduceByKey` and `aggregateByKey` that can preform map-side reductions and that do not require loading all the records for one key into memory, you can prevent memory errors on the executors and speed up wide transformations, particularly for aggregation operations (see "What's So Dangerous About the groupByKey Function" on page 134 and "Preventing out-of-memory errors with aggregation operations" on page 140). Lastly, shuffling data in which records are distributed evenly throughout the

keys, and which contain a high number of distinct keys, prevents out-of-memory errors on the executors and "straggler tasks" (see "Straggler Detection and Unbalanced Data" on page 165).

The Goldilocks Example

Throughout this chapter, we will refer to a project that the authors worked on that required finding arbitrary rank statistics in high-dimensionality and high-volume data as an example of a complex key/value transformation.

The client—we will call her Goldilocks—had data representing thousands of different metrics for hundreds of millions of pandas. Her data looked something like Table 6-1.

Table 6-1. Goldilocks example data

Panda name	Happiness	Niceness	Softness	Sweetness
Mama Panda	15.0	0.25	2467.0	0.0
Papa Panda	2.0	1000	35.4	0.0
Baby Panda	10.0	2.0	50.0	0.0
Baby Panda's toy Panda	3.0	8.5	0.2	98.0

The attributes for each panda are represented as a doubles.

Goldilocks wanted us to design an application that would let her input an arbitrary list of integers n1...nk and return the nth best element in each column. For example, if Goldilocks input 8, 1000, and 20 million, our function would need to return the 8th, 1000th, and 20 millionth best-ranking panda for each attribute column.

To illustrate this example, suppose that Goldilocks wanted to find the 2nd and 4th element from Table 6-1. We would want our function to return something like Table 6-2.

Table 6-2. Goldilocks example result

Column name	Column index	Rank statistics
happiness	1	List(3.0, 15.0)
niceness	2	List(2.0, 1000.0)
softness	3	List(35.4, 2467.0)
sweetness	4	List(0.0, 98.0)

We call this candidate "Goldilocks" because she was very picky and her house (i.e., in-house cluster) was crowded with other users (bears). In this case, Goldilocks would not accept approximate quantile boundaries, but required the output of our function to be values in the original dataset. Thus, this task is inherently expensive since it requires sorting all the values in each column in some way.

Because the data is columnar, we could consider Spark SQL to solve this problem. However, early Spark SQL did not have any support for rank statistics. It may be possible to write a UDF/UDAF to solve the problem, but it would be quite cumbersome because our use case is complicated and cannot be computed on each row. Thus, our solution has to leverage Spark Core.[1]

Goldilocks Version 0: Iterative Solution

One intuitive solution to the Goldilocks problem is to loop through each column, mapping each row to a single value, then use Spark's sortBy and zipWithIndex function on each column, and then filter for the indices that correspond to the desired rank statistics.

For simplicity, we will assume that the columnar data was read in from stable storage as a DataFrame, that the rows are all well formed, and that the string column with each panda's name was dropped. Consequently, our function takes a DataFrame of all double columns (representing the panda data) and a list of long types representing the positions of the elements to find for each column (e.g., 1st, 100th). The function should return a map from the column index to a list of the rank statistics in that column.

Example 6-1 is an implementation of this first solution to the Goldilocks problem in which we loop through each column and sort each one using Spark's distributed sort.

Example 6-1. Goldilocks version 0, iterative solution

```
def findRankStatistics(
  dataFrame: DataFrame,
  ranks: List[Long]): Map[Int, Iterable[Double]] = {
  require(ranks.forall(_ > 0))
  val numberOfColumns = dataFrame.schema.length
  var i = 0
  var  result = Map[Int, Iterable[Double]]()

  while(i < numberOfColumns){
```

---

1 As we hope to demonstrate in this chapter, even in cases where out-of-the-box functionality in Spark SQL may cover your use case, the creative control offered by Spark Core can often allow us to develop a better routine for a very specific use case. Indeed the final solution we present in this chapter is able to do some clever reductions that probably make it faster than even a well-implemented rank statistics implementation in Spark SQL.

```
    val col = dataFrame.rdd.map(row => row.getDouble(i))
    val sortedCol : RDD[(Double, Long)] = col.sortBy(v => v).zipWithIndex()
    val ranksOnly = sortedCol.filter{
      //rank statistics are indexed from one. e.g. first element is 0
      case (colValue, index) =>  ranks.contains(index + 1)
    }.keys
    val list = ranksOnly.collect()
     result += (i -> list)
     i+=1
  }
  result
}
```

This solution works and is relatively robust, but it is very slow since it has to sort the data once for each column and does so iteratively. In other words, if we have 8,000 columns we have to do 8,000 sorts!

So how can we do better?

Since each sort can be done without knowledge of the other sorts, our intuition should be that it is possible to parallelize this computation using each column as the unit of parallelization. We can represent the data as one long list of key/value pairs where the keys represent the column indices. Then, we can perform our computation in parallel for each key.

We would map the data in Table 6-1 to the following list of key/value pairs:

(key, value)
(1, 15.0)
(2, 0.25)
(3, 2467.0)
(4, 0.0)
(1, 2.0)
(2, 1000.0)
(3, 35.4)
(4, 0.0)
(1, 10.0)
(2, 2.0)
(3, 50.0)
(4, 0.0)
(1, 3.0)
(2, 8.5)
(3, 0.2)
(4, 98.0)

If we read in our data as a `DataFrame`, we can do this mapping with a simple function like the one shown in Example 6-2.

Example 6-2. Goldilocks version 1, mapping to column index/value pairs

```
def mapToKeyValuePairs(dataFrame: DataFrame): RDD[(Int, Double)] = {
  val rowLength = dataFrame.schema.length
  dataFrame.rdd.flatMap(
    row => Range(0, rowLength).map(i => (i, row.getDouble(i)))
  )
}
```

 Spark's `flatMap` operation mimics the behavior of the `flatMap` operation that is defined on iterators and collections in Scala. `flatMap` is a very versatile narrow transformation, but for those new to Scala it can be a bit confusing. `flatMap` lets the user define a mapping from each record to a collection of elements and then combines the resulting collections together. In this case the mapping is defined from a Spark SQL `Row` object to a sequence of elements, in this case (`columnIndex`, `value`) pairs. The resulting RDD will have more records than the previous RDD, and each will be of (`columnIndex`, `value`) pairs. Increasing the total number of records is not a requirement for the `flatMap` operation. In fact, `flatMap` can be particularly useful because unlike `map` it allows us to return an empty collection for one of the records. Thus, the operator can be used to both filter and transform the elements in one pass. In other words, a `map` and `filter` on the same RDD or collection can always be combined into one `flatMap` step.

After applying this function, we can perform this computation in parallel by column index (in this case column index is the key for each record). Framed in this way, the Goldilocks problem is a key/value pair problem. Specifically:

Design a function that takes an input RDD of integer/double pairs and a list of longs, n1 ... nk and returns a map of key to a list of k doubles that are the n1th, n2th .. nkth elements for that column index (key).

How to Use PairRDDFunctions and OrderedRDDFunctions

If you have been using Spark for a while, you are probably familiar with the `PairRDD Functions` and `OrderedRDDFunctions` classes. However, we will still provide a brief introduction about how to use them. If you are new to these functions, "Chapter 4: Working with Key/Value Pairs" in *Learning Spark* provides a very good introduction. The Spark RDD class makes use of Scala implicits, and the `PairRDDFunctions` will be available on any RDD of type (K,V). For `PairRDDFunctions`, K and V can be of any type, but for the `OrderedRDDFunctions` (`sortByKey`, `repartitionAndSortWithinPar titions`, `filterByRange`) K must have some implicit ordering. Most common types, like the numeric types or strings, have their ordering already defined in Scala. To use a custom type, you may have to define the ordering yourself. Spark uses implicit conversion to convert an RDD that meets the `PairRDD` or `OrderedRDD` requirements from a generic type to the `PairRDD` or `OrderedRDD` type. This implicit conversion requires that the correct library already be imported. Thus, to use Spark's `pairRDDFunctions`, you need to have imported the `SparkContext`; i.e., imports must include `import org.apache.spark.SparkContext._`.

When writing a function that uses `OrderedRDDFunctions` of generic key type, you may need to include code defining an implicit val of type `ordering`. In the secondary sort example, which we will discuss in "Secondary Sort and repartitionAndSortWithin-Partitions" on page 151, we define an ordering of an object called "Panda Keys" as shown in Example 6-3.

Example 6-3. Defining an implicit ordering to work with OrderedRDDFunctions

```
implicit def orderByLocationAndName[A <: PandaKey]: Ordering[A] = {
  Ordering.by(pandaKey => (pandaKey.city, pandaKey.zip, pandaKey.name))
}

implicit val ordering: Ordering[(K, S)] = Ordering.Tuple2
```

Actions on Key/Value Pairs

In "Functions on RDDs: Transformations Versus Actions" on page 17, we discussed how transformations are computed on the Spark executors when an action is called. We also explained that actions usually move data out of the Spark executors either by collecting it to the driver or by writing to stable storage. In general, we advised you to be very cautious about actions that return unbounded data to the driver as they can cause out-of-memory errors in the driver. Most key/value actions (including `countBy Key`, `countByValue`, `lookUp`, and `collectAsMap`) return data to the driver. In most instances they return unbounded data since the number of keys and the number of values are unknown. For example, `countByKey` returns a data point for each key, and thus it may cause memory errors if there are more distinct keys than fit in memory on the driver. Conversely, `lookUp` returns all the values for each key, so it will cause memory problems if one key has more data than will fit in memory on the driver.

The lookUp operation is also expensive because it triggers a shuffle if the RDD doesn't have a known partitioner.

In addition to number of records, the size of each record is an important factor in causing memory errors. For example, if each record is a custom object or a collection type, an action that succeeded in collecting the same number of records in an RDD of bytes may still fail. In general, we want to try to design key/value problems so that the keys fit into memory on the driver. The values should be at least well distributed by key and at best distributed so that each key has no more records than can fit in memory on each executor. We will discuss the effects of bad key distribution in "Straggler Detection and Unbalanced Data" on page 165, and will provide some suggestions for working around skewed data. As with all Spark programs, we should try to perform transformations that reduce the size of the data before calling actions that move results to the driver.

Key/value transformations can also cause memory errors, most often in the executors, if they require all the data associated with one key to be kept in memory on one partition. Avoiding memory errors and optimizing transformations for fewer shuffles is a bit more complicated than avoiding problems with actions. Thus, key/value transformations will be the focus of the rest of this chapter.

What's So Dangerous About the groupByKey Function

Many sources—including the Spark documentation—warn against the scalability of the groupByKey function, which returns an iterator of each element by key. This section attempts to explain the cases in which groupByKey causes problems at scale. We also hope to offer and some advice about alternatives to using groupByKey. First, we want to revisit the Goldilocks case, because our first solution to the Goldilocks problem was to use groupByKey.

Goldilocks Version 1: groupByKey Solution

One simple solution to the Goldilocks problem is to use groupByKey to group the element in each column. GroupByKey returns an iterator of elements by each key, so to sort the elements by key we have to convert the iterator to an array and then sort the array.[2] After converting the iterator to an array, we can sort the array and filter for the elements that correspond to our rank statistics.

Example 6-4 is an implementation of the groupByKey solution. For consistency, this function also takes a DataFrame and a list of element positions as long values. It calls the function that creates key/value pairs that we described in Example 6-2.

Example 6-4. Goldilocks version 1, GroupByKey solution

```
def findRankStatistics(
  dataFrame: DataFrame,
  ranks: List[Long]): Map[Int, Iterable[Double]] = {
  require(ranks.forall(_ > 0))
  //Map to column index, value pairs
  val pairRDD: RDD[(Int, Double)] = mapToKeyValuePairs(dataFrame)

  val groupColumns: RDD[(Int, Iterable[Double])] = pairRDD.groupByKey()
  groupColumns.mapValues(
    iter => {
      //convert to an array and sort
      val sortedIter = iter.toArray.sorted

      sortedIter.toIterable.zipWithIndex.flatMap({
      case (colValue, index) =>
          if (ranks.contains(index + 1)) {
            Iterator(colValue)
          } else {
            Iterator.empty
          }
    })
  }).collectAsMap()
}

def findRankStatistics(
  pairRDD: RDD[(Int, Double)],
  ranks: List[Long]): Map[Int, Iterable[Double]] = {
  assert(ranks.forall(_ > 0))
  pairRDD.groupByKey().mapValues(iter => {
    val sortedIter = iter.toArray.sorted
    sortedIter.zipWithIndex.flatMap(
      {
      case (colValue, index) =>
          if (ranks.contains(index + 1)) {
            //this is one of the desired rank statistics
```

---

2 Iterators can only be traversed once. Thus, iterators cannot be used without conversion because sorting requires multiple passes through the data. They must be converted to another data structure first. For more about the iterator type, and its advantages and limitations, see "Iterator-to-Iterator Transformations with mapPartitions" on page 100.

```
            Iterator(colValue)
        } else {
            Iterator.empty
        }
    }
    ).toIterable //convert to more generic iterable type to match out spec
}).collectAsMap()
}
```

This solution has several advantages. First, it gives the correct answer. Second, it is very short and easy to understand. It leverages out-of-the-box Spark and Scala functions and so it introduces few edge cases and is relatively easy to test. On small data, particularly if the input data has many columns but few records, it is actually relatively efficient because it only requires one shuffle in the groupByKey step and because the sorting step can be computed as a narrow transformation on the executors.

 In this function, we do use collectAsMap, which can have the same issues as collect that we warned you about earlier. In this instance, however, the danger of memory errors is minimal because at the point of collecting, we know the number of keys and the number of values per each key. The number of keys is exactly the number of columns, which we have assumed to be no larger than a few thousand. The number of values is equal to the length of the rank statistics list we used as input for the function, which was not originally stored in a distributed way. However, it might be good practice to add a limit to the size of the input list to prevent failures in the collect step.

In the environment that we were using and on data with 10,000 rows and a few thousand columns, this solution was orders of magnitude faster than the one presented in "The Goldilocks Example" on page 129 in which we looped through the columns iteratively and sorted each one. However, on data with a few million rows, we found that the solution failed consistently with memory exceptions even on a many-node cluster.

Why GroupByKey fails

If you have read *Learning Spark* or spent much time working with Spark at scale, the results of the groupByKey approach to solving the Goldilocks problem shouldn't surprise you as groupByKey is known to cause memory errors at scale. The reason is that the "groups" created by groupByKey are always iterators, which can't be distributed. This causes an expensive "shuffled read" step in which Spark has to read all of the shuffled data from disk and into memory.

Figure 6-1 is a screenshot taken from the Spark web UI that illustrates the high cost of groupByKey.

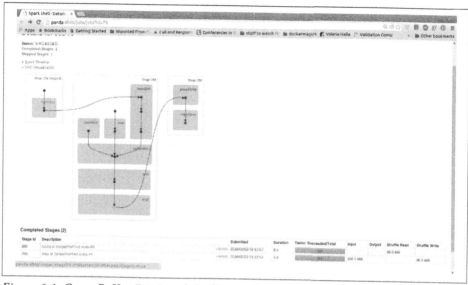

Figure 6-1. GroupByKey DAG and shuffled read

Notice that in this computation, the shuffled read is 86 MB even though the input data is about 200 MB. In other words, Spark has to read almost all of the shuffled data into memory.

As a consequence of partitioning by the hash value of the keys and pulling the result into memory to group as iterators, groupByKey often leads to out-of-memory errors on the executors if there are many duplicate records per key. Each record whose key has the same hash value must live in memory on a single machine. Thus, if just one of your keys contains too many records to fit in memory on one executor, the entire operation will fail.

Figure 6-2 illustrates a groupByKey operation of data about handlebar mustaches. As you can see, there are more records corresponding to the 94110 zip code, which is the zip code for the Mission District in San Francisco. Even if the records fit on the executors when evenly distributed, all the records associated with the 94110 zip code will not fit on a single executor after the groupByKey step.

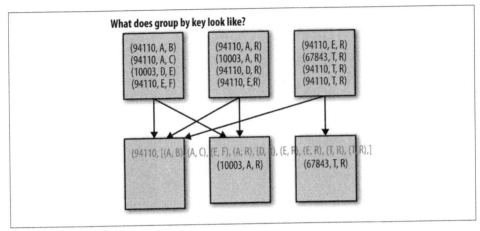

Figure 6-2. GroupByKey tip over

In general it is better to choose aggregation operations that can do some map-side reduction to decrease the number of records by key before shuffling (e.g., aggregate ByKey or reduceByKey). If this is not possible, using a wide transformation that does not require all the values associated with one key to be kept in-memory as we discuss in "Secondary Sort and repartitionAndSortWithinPartitions" on page 151 is a good alternative to groupByKey. If you must use groupByKey, it is best if the next operation is an iterator-to-iterator transformation as discussed in "Iterator-to-Iterator Transformations with mapPartitions" on page 100.

Choosing an Aggregation Operation

Shuffling the records to combine those with the same key is a common use case for key/value Spark operations, and Spark provides a number of such aggregation operations. Most of them are built atop the generic combineByKey operation, but they differ widely in performance. In this section we will detail these operations and some of the performance considerations associated with them.

Dictionary of Aggregation Operations with Performance Considerations

Aggregation operations have specific performance considerations, which we summarize in Table 6-3.

Table 6-3. A dictionary of Spark's key/value aggregation operations

Function	Purpose	Key restriction	Runs out of memory when	Slow when	Output partitioner
groupBy Key	Group values with the same key into a single iterator.	Cannot have array keys with the default Hash Partitioner. To use array keys, use a custom partitioner.	If all of the records associated with any single key take up too much space in-memory to be read from disk on one executor.	If there is not a known partitioner, this causes a shuffle. The shuffle gets more expensive as the number of distinct keys increases, the number of records per key increases, or the records are not evenly distributed across the keys.	HashParti tioner by default, but supports custom partitioning.
combine ByKey	Combine values with the same key using a different result type.	Same as above.	The "combine by" routine uses too much memory or creates too much garbage collection overhead, or the accumulator for one key becomes too large (this is the problem in group ByKey).	Same as above, but *can* be faster than groupByKey if the combine operation is a reduction.	Same as above.
aggrega teByKey	Same as combineBy Key, but uses one zero value for all accumulators.	Same as above.	Same as above, but if implemented well less likely to cause garbage collection errors (see "Minimizing Object Creation" on page 94).	See above, but generally faster than combineByKey since it will perform the merging map-side before sending to a combiner.	Same as above.
reduce ByKey	Combine values with the same key. Reduction must be to same type as original values	See above, but often less expensive than combineBy Key since aggregateBy Key supports reusing the accumulator object to avoid object creation.	See above, but the type restriction makes memory errors unlikely. So long as the combine is not to a collection type, the function is probably reducing. Garbage collection is less than aggregateByKey since no additional accumulator object is created.	Same as aggrega teByKey.	Same as above.

Function	Purpose	Key restriction	Runs out of memory when	Slow when	Output partitioner
foldBy Key	Combine values with the same key using an associative combine function and a zero value, which can be added to the result an arbitrary number of times. Use instead of reduceByKey when a natural 0 exists.	See above.	See above.	See above. Performance is nearly identical to reduceByKey.	See above.

 To avoid memory allocation in aggregateByKey, modify the accumulator rather than return a new one. See "Minimizing Object Creation" on page 94.

Preventing out-of-memory errors with aggregation operations

CombineByKey and all of the aggregation operators built on top of it (reduceByKey, foldLeft, foldRight, aggregateByKey) are no better than groupByKey in terms of memory errors *if* they cause the accumulator to become too large for one key. In fact, if you look up the implementation of groupByKey, you can see that it is actually implemented using combineByKey where the accumulator is an iterator with all the data. Thus, the accumulator is the size of all the data for that key. In other words, these operations are unlikely to cause memory errors as long as the combining steps make the data smaller. However, if the accumulator gets larger with the addition of each new record, it will eventually cause memory errors if there are many records associated with one key.

Imagine doing a back-of-the-envelope memory calculation on your sequence and combine operators:

Given the sequence operation:

```
SeqOp(acc, v) => acc'
```

...and the combine operation:

```
combOp(acc1, acc2) = acc3.
```

Calculate whether:

```
memory(acc') < memory(acc) + memory(v)
and memory(acc3) < memory(acc1) + memory(acc2).
```

If so, the function is likely a reduction. If not, as is the case in groupByKey, you may need to consider a different strategy.

Beyond being less likely to run out of memory than groupByKey, the following four functions—reduceByKey, treeAggregate, aggregateByKey, and foldByKey—are implemented to use map-side combinations, meaning that records with the same key are combined before they are shuffled. This can greatly reduce the shuffled read. Compare the shuffled read in our original groupByKey (Figure 6-1) to the amount in reduceByKey in Figure 6-3. Recall that in the groupByKey case, our shuffled read was close to the size input. However, applying reduceByKey to the same input data reduces that number to a few hundred kilobytes!

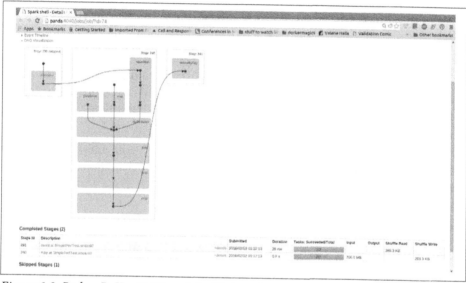

Figure 6-3. ReduceByKey DAG and shuffled read

Multiple RDD Operations

Some transformations can operate on multiple RDD inputs. The most obvious of these are join type operations, but they are far from the only ones.

Co-Grouping

Much in the same way all of the accumulator operations (reduceByKey, aggregateBy Key, foldByKey) are implemented using combineByKey, all of the join operations are implemented using the cogroup function, which uses the CoGroupedRDD type. A CoGroupedRDD is created from a sequence of key/value RDDs, each with the same key type. cogroup shuffles each of the RDDs so that the items with the same value from each of the RDDs will end up on the same partition and into a single RDD by key.

The `PairRDDFunctions` class provides several signatures for cogroup. cogroup and its alias `groupWith` can take one, two, or three RDDs, with the same key type as arguments (regardless of value type), return an RDD with each key, and then return a tuple of `Iterable` objects where each `Iterable` is all the values of the RDDs for that key.

Suppose, for example, that we had two datasets of information about each panda: one with the scores in a series of games, and one with their favorite foods. We could use cogroup to associate each panda's ID with an iterator of their scores and another iterator of their favorite foods, as in Example 6-5.

Example 6-5. Cogroup example

```
val cogroupedRDD: RDD[(Long, (Iterable[Double], Iterable[String]))] =
  scoreRDD.cogroup(foodRDD)
```

cogroup can be useful as an alternative to join when joining with multiple RDDs. Rather than doing joins on multiple RDDs with one RDD it is more performant to co-partition the RDDs since that will prevent Spark from shuffling the RDD being repeatedly joined.

For example, if we needed to join the panda score data with both address and favorite foods, it would be better to use cogroup than two join operations, as shown in Example 6-6.

Example 6-6. Cogroup to avoid multiple joins on the same RDD

```
val addressScoreFood = addressRDD.cogroup(scoreRDD, foodRDD)
```

Despite its advantages, cogroup will cause memory errors for the same reason as groupByKeys if one key in either RDD or both combined is associated with more data than will fit on a single partition. In particular, cogroup requires that all the records in all of the co-grouped RDDs for one key be able to fit on one partition. For more information on joins, see Chapter 4.

Partitioners and Key/Value Data

As we covered in Chapter 2, a partition in Spark represents a unit of parallel execution that corresponds to one task. An RDD without a known partitioner will assign data to partitions according only to the data size and partition size.[3] The partitioner object defines a mapping from the records in an RDD to a partition index. By assigning a partitioner to an RDD, we can guarantee something about the records on each partition—for example, that it falls within a given range (range partitioner) or includes only elements whose keys have the same hash code (hash partitioner).

There are three methods that exist exclusively to change the way an RDD is partitioned. For RDDs of a generic record type, `repartition` and `coalesce` can be used to simply change the number of partitions that the RDD uses, irrespective of the value of the records in the RDD. As we discussed in "The Special Case of coalesce" on page 92, `repartition` shuffles the RDD with a hash partitioner and the given number of partitions. (We will explain in more detail how hash partitioning works in "Hash Partitioning" on page 144.) `coalesce`, on the other hand, is an optimized version of `repartition` that avoids a full shuffle if the desired number of partitions is less than the current number of partitions. Recall that when `coalesce` reduces the number of partitions, it does so by merely combining partitions—and thus `coalesce` is not a wide transformation since the partition can be determined at design time. When `coalesce` increases the number of partitions it has the same behavior as `repartition`. For RDDs of key/value pairs, we can use a function called `partitionBy`, which takes a partition object rather than a number of partitions and shuffles the RDD with the new partitioner. `PartitionBy` allows for much more control in the way that the records are partitioned since the partitioner supports defining a function that assigns a partition to a record based on the value of that key.

In all cases, `repartition` and `coalesce` do not assign a known partitioner to the RDD. In contrast, using `partitionBy` (and most other key/value functions that cause a shuffle) results in an RDD with a known partitioner. In some instances, when an RDD has a known partitioner, Spark can rely on the information about data locality provided by the partitioner to avoid doing a shuffle even if the transformation has wide dependencies. The rest of the sections in this chapter will be about ways to leverage knowledge about partitioning or use custom partitioning to "shuffle less" and "shuffle better." Specifically, we aim to use this information to minimize the number of times a program causes a shuffle, the distance the data has to travel in a shuffle, and the likelihood that a disproportionate amount of the data will be sent to one partition, thus causing out-of-memory errors or straggler tasks.

---

3 Often RDDs without known partitioners can be RDDs loaded from storage. In this case the RDD's data is most often effectively partitioned in the same way as the underlying storage (e.g., the Splits in Hadoop). However, once the data is read into Spark, Spark does not know what the underlying partitioning is and consequently cannot take advantage of this information. This is one way in which checkpointing is different from simply saving an RDD to stable storage and then reading it manually. In the checkpointing case, Spark saves some metadata about the RDD including, if applicable, its partitioner.

Using the Spark Partitioner Object

Conceptually, the partitioner defines how records will be distributed and thus which records will be completed by each task. Practically, a partitioner is actually an interface with two methods—numPartitions and getPartition. numPartitions defines the number of partitions in the RDD after partitioning. getPartition defines a mapping from a key to the integer index of the partition where records with that key should be sent. There are two implementations for the partitioner object provided by Spark: the HashPartitioner and RangePartitioner. If neither of these suit your needs, it is possible to define a custom partitioner.

Hash Partitioning

The default partitioner for pair RDD operations (not ordered RDD operations) is a HashPartitioner. A HashPartitioner determines the index of the child partition based on the hash value of the key. The hash partitioner requires a partitions parameter, which determines the number of partitions in the output RDD and the number of bins used in the hashing function. If unspecified, Spark uses the value of the spark.default.parallelism value in the SparkConf to determine the number of partitions. If the default parallelism value is unset, Spark defaults to the largest number of partitions that the RDD has had in its lineage. In wide transformations that use hash partitioning, such as aggregateByKey, the optional number of partitions parameter is used as an argument to the hash partitioner. See "Number and Size of Partitions" on page 287 for information and advice about setting the spark.default.parallelism value and choosing the number of partitions.

Range Partitioning

Range partitioning assigns records whose keys are in the same range to a given partition. Range partitioning is required for sorting since it ensures that by sorting records within a given partition, the entire RDD will be sorted. The range partitioner first determines the range bounds for each partition by sampling: optimizing for an equal distribution of records across partitions. Then, each record in the RDD will be shuffled to the partition whose range bounds include the key. Highly unbalanced data (i.e., lots of values for some keys and not others, and if the distribution of the keys is not uniform) makes the sampling less accurate—and, as we have discussed, uneven partitioning may cause downstream tasks to be slower than others, causing "straggler" tasks. If there are too many duplicate keys for all the records associated with one key to fit on one executor, then range partitioning, like hash partitioning, may cause memory errors. Performance problems associated with sorting are usually caused by these problems with the range partitioning step.

Creating a `RangePartitioner` with Spark requires not only a number of partitions, but also the actual RDD to sample. The RDD must be a tuple and the keys must have an ordering defined.

Sampling actually requires partially evaluating the RDD, causing a break in the execution graph. Thus range partitioning is actually both a transformation and an action. The cost of sampling means that, in general, range partitioning is more expensive than hash partitioning. The requirement that keys be ordered means that range partitioning cannot be done on all RDDs of tuples. Therefore, key/value operations (such as aggregations), which require records with each key to be on the same machine but not ordered in a particular way, use a `HashPartitioner` as the default. However, these methods can also be performed with a custom partitioner or range partitioner.

Custom Partitioning

To define a unique function for partitioning the data other than by the key's hash-value or ordering, Spark allows the user to define a custom partitioner. In order to define a partitioner, you must implement the following methods:

numPartitions
> A method that returns an integer number of partitions. Expect that this number is greater than zero.

getPartition
> A method that takes a key (of the same type as the RDD being partitioned) and returns an integer representing the index of the partition that specifies where records with that key belong. The integer must be between zero and the number of partitions (defined in the numPartitions method).

equals
> An (optional) method to define equality between partitioners. The equality method for a `HashPartitioner` returns true if the number of partitions are equal. The range partitioner does so only if the range bounds are equal. The equality of partitioners can be particularly important for joins and cogrouping, because in some instances if an RDD is already partitioned according to a partitioner, Spark is smart enough not to shuffle again with the same partitioner. We will discuss this in more detail in "Leveraging Co-Located and Co-Partitioned RDDs" on page 146.

hashcode
> This method is required only if the equals method has been overridden. The hashcode of a `HashPartitioner` is simply its number of partitions. The hashcode of a `RangePartitioner` is a hash function derived from the range bounds.

Preserving Partitioning Information Across Transformations

Some wide transformations change the partitioning of an RDD, as will be shown in Table 6-4. Spark remembers this information by updating the partitioner property of the RDD. When doing a series of transformations, it is important to understand how an RDD is partitioned, because in some instances we can use this information to avoid doing future shuffles.

Using narrow transformations that preserve partitioning

Some narrow transformations, such as `mapValues`, preserve the partitioning of an RDD if it exists. Unless a transformation is known to only change the value part of the key/value pair in Spark, the resulting RDD will not have a known partitioner (even if the partitioning has not changed). It's important to note that common transformations like `map` and `flatMap` can change the key, so even if your function does not change the key, the resulting RDD will not have a known partitioner. Instead, if we don't want to modify the keys, we can call the `mapValues` function (defined only on pair RDDs) because it keeps the keys, and therefore the partitioner, exactly the same. The `mapPartitions` function will also preserve the partition if the `preserves Partitioning` flag is set to true. Assuming we have some RDD `data` of type `RDD[(Double, Int)]`, we could write the test in Example 6-7 to illustrate this property.

Example 6-7. Maintaining partitioning information with `mapValues`

```
val sortedData = data.sortByKey()
val mapValues: RDD[(Double, String)] = sortedData.mapValues(_.toString)
assert(mapValues.partitioner.isDefined,
  "Using Map Values preserves partitioning")

val map = sortedData.map( pair => (pair._1, pair._2.toString))
assert(map.partitioner.isEmpty, "Using map does not preserve partitioning")
```

Leveraging Co-Located and Co-Partitioned RDDs

Co-located RDDs are RDDs with the same partitioner that reside in the same physical location in memory. Co-location is important because all of the `CoGroupedRDD` functions—a category which includes the `cogroup` operations and all of the join operations—require the RDDs being grouped to have all of their partitions co-located. RDDs can only be combined without any network transfer if they have the same partitioner and if each of the corresponding partitions in-memory are on the same executor. Partitions will be in-memory on the same executor if they were partitioned in the lineage associated with the same job.

Co-partitioning is related to but distinct from partition co-location. We say that multiple RDDs are *co-partitioned* if they are partitioned by the same known partitioner.

We say that partitions are *co-located* if they are both loaded into memory on the same machine. RDDs are only guaranteed to be co-located if they are put into memory by the same job and the same partitioner: if one action contains the partitioning of both RDDs in its lineage. RDDs will be co-partitioned if their partitioner objects are equal, but if the corresponding partitions for each RDD are not in the same physical location. Recall that "same partitioner" means the partitioner objects are equal according to the equality function defined in the partitioner class.

In Example 6-8, both `rddA` and `rddB` will be co-located.

Example 6-8. An example of co-located RDDs

```
val rddA = a.partitionBy(partitionerX)
rddA.cache()
val rddB = b.partitionBy(partitionerY)
rddB.cache()
val rddC = a.cogroup(b)
rddC.count()
```

Before Spark evaluates `RDDC.count()`, neither RDD is actually loaded into memory due to Spark's lazily evaluated nature. When Spark launches the associated `RDDC.count()` job, both RDDs are pulled into memory since their lineages are merged by the `cogroup` operation. In this case the join won't cause any network traffic because both RDDs are loaded into memory in the same location.

In contrast, if we were to call an action on `rddA` and `rddB` before the action on the co-grouped RDD, the `cogroup` may cause some network traffic since the RDDs are not co-located (Example 6-9).

Example 6-9. RDDs co-partitioned but not co-located

```
val rddA = a.partitionBy(partitionerX)
rddA.cache()
val rddB = b.partitionBy(partitionerY)
rddB.cache()
val rddC = a.cogroup(b)
rddA.count()
rddB.count()
rddC.count()
```

In this case, `rddA` and `rddB` are loaded into memory from different actions. They are co-partitioned, but there is no guarantee that their partitions will all be co-located. Thus, although the repartition calls prevent the join operator from triggering shuffles in both RDDs, there may still be some network traffic to line up the partitions and load both RDDs into memory. Although the design of your program may require calling actions in this order, it is often worth thinking about the lineage of an RDD before calling an action on it, so as to minimize network traffic.

Dictionary of Mapping and Partitioning Functions PairRDDFunctions

The performance of the different mapping and partitioning functions available on PairRDDs is shown in Table 6-4.

Table 6-4. Dictionary of mapping and sampling operations for RDDs or key/value pairs

Function	Purpose	Key restriction	Runs out of memory when	Slow when	Output partitioner
mapVal ues	Apply a mapping function to each value of a pair RDD without changing the key.	None	Almost never	Slow when the mapping operation is very complicated or expands the size of each record.	In contrast to map, this preserves the partitioning of the data for use in future operations. If the input RDD has a known partitioner, the output RDD will have the same partitioner. If you can perform your mapping on just the values it is almost always beneficial to do so.
flatMap Values	Perform the flatMap function on just the values of a key/value RDD. See our discussion of the flatMap paradigm near the end of "Goldilocks Version 0: Iterative Solution" on page 130.	None	Unlikely unless the function applied to each value is very expensive or the result iterator is very large, causing a dramatic expansion of the number of records for each key.	Slow when the mapping routine is very complicated, creates many new objects, or dramatically increases the number of records (such as tokenization).	Preserves partitioner associated with the input RDD. However, the distribution of duplicate values in the keys may change. If many duplicated values are created, this may slow down downstream shuffles.
keys	Return an RDD of just the keys (not distinct).	None	Almost never	Essentially free	Preserves the partitioning.
values	Return an RDD of just the values.	None	Almost never	Essentially free	Does not preserve partitioning. Future wide transformations will cause a shuffle even if they have the same partitioner as the input RDD.

Function	Purpose	Key restriction	Runs out of memory when	Slow when	Output partitioner
sample ByKey	Given a map from the keys to the percent of each key to sample, returns a stratified sample of the input RDD. The function is implemented with `mapPartitions` and uses a random number to determine whether each record will be kept. Thus, the size of the resulting sample may not exactly correspond to the percentage specified.	None	Almost never, unless the key map is too large to be broadcast to one of the worker nodes.	Same as `mapPartitions`, the function completes one pass through the data and does not require a shuffle.	Preserves partitioning of the input data.

In addition to sampling and mapping operations specific to PairRDDs, Table 6-5 shows the partitioning functions.

Table 6-5. Partitioning functions

Function	Purpose	Key restriction	Runs out of memory when	Slow when	Output partitioner
parti tionBy	Takes a partitioner object and partitions the RDD accordingly. The partitioner object defines target partition index for records based on key.	Depends on which partitioner is used. See "Using the Spark Partitioner Object" on page 144.	When there are many duplicate values for each key, regardless of partitioner.	Always causes a shuffle. Range partitioners are generally slower than hash partitioners since they require the data to be partially evaluated in order to sample it.	Partitioned according to the partition argument.

The PairRDDFunctions class also includes all of the multiple RDD operations including join and cogroup, which we covered in detail in Chapter 4.

Dictionary of OrderedRDDOperations

In addition to special functions for RDDs of key/value pairs, RDDs with an ordering on the key have even more functions, summarized in Table 6-6.

Table 6-6. Dictionary of operations in the OrderedRDDFunctions class

Function	Purpose	Key restriction	Runs out of memory when	Slow when	Output partitioner
sortByKey	Return an RDD sorted by the key.	Key must have implicit ordering.	When data is very unevenly distributed both in terms of repeated keys and distribution of keys. In particular, if the data associated with one key can't fit in memory.	Slows down with many duplicate keys. If the keys are not uniformly distributed, the data won't be partitioned evenly, which can also cause straggler tasks. Note: One of the few nonpure transformations requires an action to sample the input to create the range partitioner.	Range partitioner. Default number of partitions is the same as the input RDD.
repartitionAndSortWithinPartitions	Takes a partitioner and an implicit ordering. Partitions the RDD according to the partitioner and then sorts all the records on each partition according to the implicit ordering.	Key must have implicit ordering.	Depends on the partitioner. See partitionBy.	Slow with key skew because partitioner creates straggler tasks and because sorting each key will be more expensive. However, this is much faster than partitioning using partitionBy and then sorting within each key using map Partitions because the sort is pushed into the shuffle step. See "Secondary Sort and repartitionAndSortWithinPartitions" on page 151.	Same as partitioner argument.
filterByRange	Takes a lower and an upper bound for the keys and returns an RDD of just the records whose key falls in that range.	See above.	Almost never.	When the RDD has already been partitioned by a range partitioner this is cheaper than a generic filter because it scans only the partitions whose keys are in the desired range. Otherwise performance is the same as the generic filter operation.	Preserves partitioning.

Sorting by Two Keys with SortByKey

Spark's `sortByKey` does allow sorting by tuples of keys for tuples with two elements. Thus, it is relatively easy to sort by two values in Spark by making use of Scala's implicit tuple ordering, then sort by a composite key described by (`Key1`, `Key2`). For example, suppose that rather than finding the `nth` item, Goldilocks just wanted us to create a directory of (`columnIndex`, `value`) pairs sorted first by column index then by value. Assuming an RDD `indexValuePairs` of type `RDD[(Int, Double)]`, we could solve this problem with:

```
indexValuePairs.map((_, null)).sortByKey()
```

Then `sortByKey` will use the implicit ordering on an (`Int`, `Double`) tuple, which simply compares the first value and then compares the second.

> SortByKey does not support implicit ordering on product types other than `Tuple2`.

Secondary Sort and repartitionAndSortWithinPartitions

Sorting in Spark could be implemented by partitioning an RDD with a `RangeParti tioner` and then sorting within each partition using `mapPartitions`, much as we did in Example 6-4. However, this approach to sorting is slower than Spark's actual implementation of `sortByKey`. Instead of partitioning and then sorting, Spark leverages a technique called *secondary sort*, which pushes some of the work of sorting on the individual machine into the shuffle stage.

> Secondary sort is a performant way of ordering data both amongst machines and within a single machine. The term comes from the MapReduce paradigm and describes a technique by which the programmer maps with one function, but defines a different order for the elements to be used in the reduce call. The effect of this in Spark is that some of the sorting work that must be done locally can be accomplished during the shuffle stage rather than in the next stage, after the shuffle has completed.

Spark has a built-in function to perform secondary sort called `repartitionAndSort WithinPartitions`. The `repartitionAndSortWithinPartitions` function is a wide transformation that takes a partitioner—defined on the argument RDD—and an implicit ordering, which must be defined on the keys of the RDD. The function partitions the data according to the partitioner argument and then sorts the records on each partition according to the ordering.

 We do not need to directly pass an implicit ordering to the `reparti tionAndSortWithinPartitions` function. If the function is called on an RDD whose keys have an ordering, Spark can infer that ordering and will sort accordingly. To use `repartitionAndSortWi thinPartitions` to order on types that either do not have an implicit ordering or have an ordering other than the one we want, we need to define the implicit ordering on the keys of the RDD in our program before calling the `repartitionAndSortWithinParti tions` function. See Example 6-12.

If we look up the implementation of `sortByKey`, we can see that it calls the `reparti tionAndSortWithinPartitions` function with a `RangePartitioner` and uses implicit ordering defined on the keys. As we discussed in "Range Partitioning" on page 144, the `RangePartitioner` will sample the data and assign a range of values for each partition based on the inferred distribution of the keys (for example, keys with values between 0 and 10 shall be placed on partition index two). Then `repartitionAndSort WithinPartitions` will sort the values on each partition (each range of data) and thus the entire result will be sorted by key. The secondary sort paradigm and the `reparti tionAndSortWithinPartitions` can be used not only to do a performant sort on one key, but also to define two kinds of ordering on the data: one that governs partitioning and another that governs the ordering of elements on the child partitions. The rest of this section will focus on the second use case, in which we want to organize the data first by one ordering and next by another.

Leveraging repartitionAndSortWithinPartitions for a Group by Key and Sort Values Function

The best way to order data with two orderings is to use the `repartitionAndSortWi thinPartitions` function. One common use case for this is to a define a function, which we might call "group by key and sort values," that returns an RDD grouped by key with the values in each group sorted. Unlike sorting by tuple keys, which we discussed in "Sorting by Two Keys with SortByKey" on page 151, this approach could be generalized to any partitioning defined on any key type and any custom ordering. We use `repartitionAndSortWithinPartitions` to repartition the RDD by one ordering on the keys and then define an implicit ordering for the records on a given partition.

With a little searching you can find numerous `groupByKeyAndSortValues` functions, although none of them have been merged into Spark. Sandy Ryza's presentation in *Advanced Analytics with Spark* is particularly good, and the following implementation closely mirrors his. This `groupByKeyAndSortValues` function assumes data in the form ((k, s), v), where s is the secondary key (perhaps derived from the value). It partitions the RDD by the first part of the key, then sorts by the second part of the key. Then, it then combines all the values associated with one key into a sorted iterator.

The function has four steps:

1. Define a custom partitioner that partitions records according to the first element of the key.

2. Define an implicit ordering on the values. This is only necessary because the function is generic. The implicit ordering on tuples is first value, second value. We just have to tell Spark to use that tuple ordering.

3. Use `repartitionAndSortWithinPartitions` on the input RDD with the custom partitioner defined in step 1.

4. Coalesce the items using a `mapPartitions` routine. We can leverage the fact that items with the same first key are on the same partition and that the elements within each partition are sorted first by the first ordering and then by the second ordering.

 Because we are using hash partitioning, this function does not actually sort values by the first key. Rather, it groups keys with the same hash value on the same machine. Thus, if we run the function of the values one through five and use four partitions, the first partition will contain one and five. To force the keys to appear in true sorted order, we would need to define a range partitioner. However, using the hash value is good enough if our goal is simply to group like keys.

Example 6-10 is the code for the custom partitioner. As you can see we order only on the first part of the key. If we define the ordering on both parts of the key, the partitioner will group by the hash value of the entire tuple key. Consequently the function may put elements with the same primary key, but different secondary keys on two different partitions.

Example 6-10. Step 1 of secondary sort: defining a custom partitioner

```
class PrimaryKeyPartitioner[K, S](partitions: Int) extends Partitioner {
  /**
   * We create a hash partitioner and use it with the first set of keys.
   */
  val delegatePartitioner = new HashPartitioner(partitions)

  override def numPartitions = delegatePartitioner.numPartitions
```

```
/**
 * Partition according to the hash value of the first key
 */
override def getPartition(key: Any): Int = {
  val k = key.asInstanceOf[(K, S)]
  delegatePartitioner.getPartition(k._1)
}
}
```

Next, we define the implicit ordering, as shown in Example 6-11. Recall from the specification of the function, that both parts of the key already have an ordering defined. Spark already has an ordering for tuples of two elements with orderings so we can simply tell Spark to use the generic Tuple2 ordering.

Example 6-11. Step 2 of secondary sort: define the implicit ordering

```
implicit def orderByLocationAndName[A <: PandaKey]: Ordering[A] = {
  Ordering.by(pandaKey => (pandaKey.city, pandaKey.zip, pandaKey.name))
}

implicit val ordering: Ordering[(K, S)] = Ordering.Tuple2
```

Now, incorporating these two subroutines, we can define a function groupByKeyAnd SortBySecondaryKey, as in Example 6-12. The new function will partition according to the partitioner defined in step 1, sort by the order defined in step 2, and then use a groupSorted function to combine the elements with the same first key into a single iterator.

Example 6-12. A general example of a "group by key and sort by secondary key" function

```
def groupByKeyAndSortBySecondaryKey[K : Ordering : ClassTag,
  S : Ordering : ClassTag,
  V : ClassTag]
  (pairRDD : RDD[((K, S), V)], partitions : Int):
    RDD[(K, List[(S, V)])] = {
  //Create an instance of our custom partitioner
  val colValuePartitioner = new PrimaryKeyPartitioner[Double, Int](partitions)

  //define an implicit ordering, to order by the second key the ordering will
  //be used even though not explicitly called
  implicit val ordering: Ordering[(K, S)] = Ordering.Tuple2

  //use repartitionAndSortWithinPartitions
  val sortedWithinParts =
    pairRDD.repartitionAndSortWithinPartitions(colValuePartitioner)

  sortedWithinParts.mapPartitions( iter => groupSorted[K, S, V](iter) )
```

```
}

def groupSorted[K,S,V](
  it: Iterator[((K, S), V)]): Iterator[(K, List[(S, V)])] = {
  val res = List[(K, ArrayBuffer[(S, V)])]()
  it.foldLeft(res)((list, next) => list match {
    case Nil =>
      val ((firstKey, secondKey), value) = next
      List((firstKey, ArrayBuffer((secondKey, value))))

    case head :: rest =>
      val (curKey, valueBuf) = head
      val ((firstKey, secondKey), value) = next
      if (!firstKey.equals(curKey) ) {
        (firstKey, ArrayBuffer((secondKey, value))) :: list
      } else {
        valueBuf.append((secondKey, value))
        list
      }

  }).map { case (key, buf) => (key, buf.toList) }.iterator
}
```

When developing a function like this one that relies heavily on par‐
titioning, make sure that your unit tests are for data that spans
more than one partition. Make sure to test on different numbers of
partitions and different data, because there is some randomness in
partitioning (especially range partitioning). See Chapter 8 for more
about running good distributed tests.

How Not to Sort by Two Orderings

It's important to note that several other seemingly obvious approaches to this prob‐
lem are not guaranteed to give the correct result. For example, even regardless of per‐
formance issues, using groupByKey does not maintain the order of the values within
the groups. Thus the following implementation may not give the correct results:

```
indexValuePairs.sortByKey().groupByKey()
```

Spark sorting is also not guaranteed to be stable (preserve the original order of ele‐
ments with the same value). Hence, repeated sorting is not a viable option:

```
indexValuePairs.sortByKey.map(_.swap()).sortByKey
```

In this case, the second sortByKey may not preserve the ordering generated in the
first sort.

Goldilocks Version 2: Secondary Sort

The logic of secondary sort generalizes well beyond simply ordering data. It applies to any use case that requires the records to be arranged according to two different keys. The original Goldilocks example is related to secondary sort since it requires us to shuffle on one key (the column index) and then order the data within each key by value (by the value in the cells). Thus, rather than using groupByKey to ensure that the values associated with each key are coalesced and then sorting the elements associated with each key as a separate step, we can use repartitionAndSortWithinPartitions. Using repartitionAndSortWithinPartitions we can partition on the column index and sort on the value in each column. We are then guaranteed that all the values associated with each column will be on one partition and that they will be in sorted order of the value. We can simply loop through the elements on each partition, filter for the desired rank statistics in one pass through the data, and use the groupSorted function to combine the rank statistics associated with our column.

Defining the custom partitioner

The ordering and partition in repartitionAndSortWithinPartitions must be defined on the keys of the RDD, and thus we need to use the (column index, value) pairs as keys. We can map to a dummy value (like 1 or null) so that Spark will interpret the RDD as key/value pairs where the keys are a tuple of (column index, value). We will then need to define a custom partitioner that partitions the keys based on the hash value of the first part of the key (the column index), as shown in Example 6-13.

Example 6-13. Goldilocks version 2, defining a custom partitioner to partition on column index

```
class ColumnIndexPartition(override val numPartitions: Int)
  extends Partitioner {
  require(numPartitions >= 0, s"Number of partitions " +
    s"($numPartitions) cannot be negative.")

  override def getPartition(key: Any): Int = {
    val k = key.asInstanceOf[(Int, Double)]
    Math.abs(k._1) % numPartitions //hashcode of column index
  }
}
```

Filtering on each partition

On each partition, we want the elements to be ordered first by column index, and second by value. The former ensures that all the records associated with one key are on the same partition. The latter ensures that the elements that are adjacent will be

---

those with the same column indices and will be sorted so that we can find the rank statistics.

Ordering by the first value of a tuple and then the second is the existing implicit ordering on tuples. Thus, we do not have to specify an ordering for our data. After the repartitionAndSortWithinPartitions call, we know that the data will be partitioned according to column index and sorted by column index and value. For example, suppose that we were using the DataFrame described in Table 6-1 and that we were using three partitions. The first partition would contain the following values:

((1, 2.0), 1)

((1, 3.0), 1)

((1, 10.0), 1)

((1, 15.0), 1)

((4, 0.0), 1)

((4, 0.0), 1)

((4, 0.0), 1)

((4, 98.0), 1)

We can use the filter operation to loop through the elements of the iterator even though the filter requires us to keep track of global data. Recall from our discussion of iterator-to-iterator transformations in "Iterator-to-Iterator Transformations with mapPartitions" on page 100 that the map, filter, and flatMap operations defined on iterators transform the elements in the iterator in order. Thus, because the elements are sorted and grouped by key, we can keep track of a running total for the column index. If the element is one of the ones that corresponds to the target ranks statistic, then we can keep it. We then have to map the iterator to the first half of the tuple to remove the 1 dummy value. Note that we could combine these map and filter steps into one flatMap operation. We have chosen to present them separately in Example 6-14 since we think that the filter operation is easier to interpret.

Example 6-14. Goldilocks version 2, leveraging repartitionAndSortWithinPartitions

```
def findRankStatistics(dataFrame: DataFrame,
  targetRanks: List[Long], partitions: Int) = {

  val pairRDD: RDD[((Int, Double), Int)] =
    GoldilocksGroupByKey.mapToKeyValuePairs(dataFrame).map((_, 1))

  val partitioner = new ColumnIndexPartition(partitions)
  //sort by the existing implicit ordering on tuples first key, second key
  val sorted = pairRDD.repartitionAndSortWithinPartitions(partitioner)

  //filter for target ranks
```

```
val filterForTargetIndex: RDD[(Int, Double)] =
  sorted.mapPartitions(iter => {
    var currentColumnIndex = -1
    var runningTotal = 0
    iter.filter({
      case (((colIndex, value), _)) =>
        if (colIndex != currentColumnIndex) {
          currentColumnIndex = colIndex //reset to the new column index
          runningTotal = 1
        } else {
          runningTotal += 1
        }
        //if the running total corresponds to one of the rank statistics.
        //keep this ((colIndex, value)) pair.
        targetRanks.contains(runningTotal)
    })
  }.map(_._1), preservesPartitioning = true)
  groupSorted(filterForTargetIndex.collect())
}
```

Combine the elements associated with one key

After the `mapPartitions` step, we have to do one last local transformation to group
the elements associated with one column index into a map. The code for the `group
Sorted` function is presented in Example 6-15.

Example 6-15. Goldilocks version 2, group the elements associated with one key

```
private def groupSorted(
  it: Array[(Int, Double)]): Map[Int, Iterable[Double]] = {
  val res = List[(Int, ArrayBuffer[Double])]()
  it.foldLeft(res)((list, next) => list match {
    case Nil =>
      val (firstKey, value) = next
      List((firstKey, ArrayBuffer(value)))
    case head :: rest =>
      val (curKey, valueBuf) = head
      val (firstKey, value) = next
      if (!firstKey.equals(curKey)) {
        (firstKey, ArrayBuffer(value)) :: list
      } else {
        valueBuf.append(value)
        list
      }
  }).map { case (key, buf) => (key, buf.toIterable) }.toMap
}
```

Notice that this code is very similar to the grouping function presented in
Example 6-12.

Performance

This solution is considerably faster than the version 1 `groupByKey` solution on any shape of data. By using `repartitionAndSortWithinPartitions`, we are able to push the work to sort each column into the shuffle stage. Since the elements are sorted after the shuffle, we are able to use iterator-to-iterator transformations to filter the data and avoid forcing all the values associated with one partition into memory.

However, if the columns are relatively long, the `repartitionAndSortWithinParti` `tions` step may still lead to failures since it still requires one executor to be able to store all of the values associated with all of the columns that have the same hash value. Indeed, in our case we still saw failures in the shuffle stage using this approach at scale. In fact, a viable solution to the Goldilocks problem required taking an entirely different approach.

A Different Approach to Goldilocks

Unfortunately, none of the existing key/value transformations provided a magic bullet for the Goldilocks problem. None of the other aggregation operations that we might use as alternative to `groupByKey` help us since the operation that we want to perform for each key—a sort—won't reduce the size of the data by key. As we discussed in the previous section, even rewriting our `groupByKey` approach using sophisticated secondary sort techniques was leading to failures. In the end, the secondary sort approach still required partitioning by the column index, which was not granular enough for the size of our data and the resources we had available. Instead, a performant solution to this problem required entirely rethinking how we parallelized the computational work.

Before we dive into the solution, let's review some of the methods we have learned to make transformations more performant:

- Narrow transformations on key/value data are quick and easy to parallelize relative to wide transformations that cause a shuffle.

- Partition locality can be retained across some narrow transformations following a shuffle. This applies to `mapPartitions` if we use `preservePartitioning=true`, or `mapValues`.

- Wide transformations are best with many unique keys. This prevents shuffles from directing a large proportion of the data to reside on one executor.

- `SortByKey` is a particularly good way to partition data and sort within partitions since it pushes the ordering of data on local machines into the shuffle stage.

- Using iterator-to-iterator transforms in `mapPartitions` prevents whole partitions from being loaded into memory.

- We can sometimes rely on shuffle files to prevent recomputation of wide transformations even if we call several actions on the same RDD.

Using these insights, we were able to construct a solution to the Goldilocks problem using only one sortByKey and three mapPartitions operations. The critical insight is that the unit of parallelization for this problem does not need to be the columns. We can essentially solve the problem for each range of values. If the cell values are sorted and we know how many elements are on each partition from each column (which is easy to calculate using a performant mapPartitions routine), then we can determine the location of the nth element.

Our solution can be enumerated in five steps:

1. Map the rows of data to pairs of (cell value, index).

2. Perform a sortByKey operation on all tuples defined in step 1.

3. Using mapPartitions, determine how many elements in each column are on each partition and collect that information to the driver.

4. Perform a local computation on the result of step 3 to determine the location of each desired rank statistic. For example, suppose that we are looking for the 13th element. Suppose also that in step 3 we determined that the first partition had 10 elements from column six. In this case, we can conclude that the 13th element will be the third largest element in column six on the second partition.

5. Using the result of step 4, use another mapPartitions transformation to filter for the elements that correspond to the desired rank statistics. Collect this information back to the driver.

Map to (cell value, column index) pairs

Example 6-16 is the code for step 1 of our solution: mapping to the (cell value, column index) pairs. We use Spark's flatMap function to transform each row into a sequence of tuples.

Example 6-16. Goldilocks algorithm version 3, map to (cell value, column index) pairs

```
private def getValueColumnPairs(dataFrame : DataFrame): RDD[(Double, Int)] = {
  dataFrame.rdd.flatMap{
    row: Row => row.toSeq.zipWithIndex
                  .map{
                    case (v, index) => (v.toString.toDouble, index)}
  }
}
```

Sort and count values on each partition

Once we have mapped the rows so that they are keyed on cell value, use sortByKey. After the sort, we will have calculated the number of elements on each partition. Example 6-17 is a function that takes a sorted RDD of (double, column index) pairs and the number of columns in the original DataFrame, then returns an array where each element corresponds to a partition. Each element of the array contains the partition index and an array of the counts of elements on that partition each column. The length of each subarray will correspond to the number of columns in the original dataset.

Example 6-17. Goldilocks algorithm version 3, count values by column on each partition

```scala
private def getColumnsFreqPerPartition(sortedValueColumnPairs: RDD[(Double, Int)],
  numOfColumns : Int):
  Array[(Int, Array[Long])] = {

  val zero = Array.fill[Long](numOfColumns)(0)

  def aggregateColumnFrequencies (partitionIndex : Int,
    valueColumnPairs : Iterator[(Double, Int)]) = {
    val columnsFreq : Array[Long] = valueColumnPairs.aggregate(zero)(
      (a : Array[Long], v : (Double, Int)) => {
        val (value, colIndex) = v
        //increment the cell in the zero array corresponding to this column index
        a(colIndex) = a(colIndex) + 1L
        a
      },
      (a : Array[Long], b : Array[Long]) => {
        a.zip(b).map{ case(aVal, bVal) => aVal + bVal}
      })

    Iterator((partitionIndex, columnsFreq))
  }

  sortedValueColumnPairs.mapPartitionsWithIndex(
    aggregateColumnFrequencies).collect()
}
```

The subfunction aggregateColumnFrequencies is applied to the records on each partition. It uses the aggregate operation defined on iterators. The zero value is an array the length of the original column of zeros. For each pair in the iterator, the sequence operation of the aggregation operation increments the cell that corresponds to that column index in the zero array. The combine operation adds the values in two of these arrays. Thus, the result is an array of the counts for the corresponding column index. For example, assume that there were three columns and the first two partitions contained the following key/value pairs:

```
Partition 1: (1.5, 0) (1.25, 1) (2.0, 2) (5.25, 0)
Partition 2: (7.5, 1) (9.5, 2)
```

The output would be:

```
[(0, [2, 1, 1]), (1, [0, 1, 1])]
```

We expect this step to be a relatively inexpensive operation. The mapPartitions step is a narrow transformation since it requires traversing the iterator just once. Thus this operation will not incur a shuffle and can spill to disk selectively. We use arrays to aggregate because as we discussed in "Using Smaller Data Structures" on page 97, they should create the least garbage collection overhead. After this mapPartitions step, we collect the results into an array.

> We are not using the result of this mapPartitions operation in a distributed way since we are collecting it to the driver. Thus, we actually do not need to set the preserves partitioning function to false.

Determine location of rank statistics on each partition

Once we have the results of the getColumnsFreqPerPartition function, we have to use that information to determine where the rank statistics are on each partition, as shown in Example 6-18. This computation is done locally with the results of the previous function. In order to determine the location of each rank statistic, we loop through the (sorted) result of the previous function while keeping a running total of the elements in each column across the partitions. If, for any of the columns a rank statistic is between the previous and updated value of the running total, we know that the rank statistics can be found on that partition. If this is the case, we increment the relevantIndexList with the column index and the rank statistic—the previous running total. We can then return an array, where each element is the partition index, and a list object of pairs. Each pair represents a column index for that rank statistic and the index of that rank statistics in that column.

For example, if the inputs to the function were:

```
targetRanks: [5]
partitionColumnsFreq: [(0, [2, 3]), (1, [4, 1]), (2, [5, 2])]
numOfColumns: 2
```

The output will be:

```
(0, []), (1, [(0, 3)]), (2, [(1, 1)])
```

Example 6-18. Goldilocks algorithm version 3, determine location of rank statistics on each partition.

```
private def getRanksLocationsWithinEachPart(targetRanks : List[Long],
        partitionColumnsFreq : Array[(Int, Array[Long])],
        numOfColumns : Int) : Array[(Int, List[(Int, Long)])] = {

  val runningTotal = Array.fill[Long](numOfColumns)(0)
  // The partition indices are not necessarily in sorted order, so we need
  // to sort the partitionsColumnsFreq array by the partition index (the
  // first value in the tuple).
  partitionColumnsFreq.sortBy(_._1).map { case (partitionIndex, columnsFreq) =>
    val relevantIndexList = new MutableList[(Int, Long)]()

    columnsFreq.zipWithIndex.foreach{ case (colCount, colIndex)  =>
      val runningTotalCol = runningTotal(colIndex)
      val ranksHere: List[Long] = targetRanks.filter(rank =>
        runningTotalCol < rank && runningTotalCol + colCount >= rank)

      // For each of the rank statistics present add this column index and the
      // index it will be at on this partition (the rank - the running total).
      relevantIndexList ++= ranksHere.map(
        rank => (colIndex, rank - runningTotalCol))

      runningTotal(colIndex) += colCount
    }

    (partitionIndex, relevantIndexList.toList)
  }
}
```

Filter for rank statistics

Now, armed with the location (partition index and position within each partition) of the rank statistics for each column, we have to pass through the sorted data again to filter for the correct rank statistics. This task is accomplished with the function in Example 6-19, called `findTargetRanksIteratively`, which uses the original sorted tuples of (`value`, `column index`) pairs and the results of the previous function. We use an iterator-to-iterator transformation with a `filter` and a `map` step. (Note that these could be replaced by `flatMap`). This produces the final result, an RDD of (`col umnIndex`, `rank statistic`) pairs, which we can then collect back to the driver.

Example 6-19. Goldilocks algorithm version 3, filter for the desired rank statistics

```
private def findTargetRanksIteratively(
  sortedValueColumnPairs : RDD[(Double, Int)],
  ranksLocations : Array[(Int, List[(Int, Long)])]):
    RDD[(Int, Double)] = {
```

```
sortedValueColumnPairs.mapPartitionsWithIndex(
  (partitionIndex : Int, valueColumnPairs : Iterator[(Double, Int)]) => {
    val targetsInThisPart: List[(Int, Long)] = ranksLocations(partitionIndex)._2
    if (targetsInThisPart.nonEmpty) {
      val columnsRelativeIndex: Map[Int, List[Long]] =
      targetsInThisPart.groupBy(_._1).mapValues(_.map(_._2))
      val columnsInThisPart = targetsInThisPart.map(_._1).distinct

      val runningTotals : mutable.HashMap[Int, Long]=  new mutable.HashMap()
      runningTotals ++= columnsInThisPart.map(
        columnIndex => (columnIndex, 0L)).toMap

//filter this iterator, so that it contains only those (value, columnIndex)
//that are the ranks statistics on this partition
//Keep track of the number of elements we have seen for each columnIndex using the
//running total hashMap.
      valueColumnPairs.filter{
        case(value, colIndex) =>
          lazy val thisPairIsTheRankStatistic: Boolean = {
            val total = runningTotals(colIndex) + 1L
            runningTotals.update(colIndex, total)
            columnsRelativeIndex(colIndex).contains(total)
          }
          (runningTotals contains colIndex) && thisPairIsTheRankStatistic
      }.map(_.swap)
    }
    else {
      Iterator.empty
    }
  })
}
```

Goldilocks Version 3: Sort on Cell Values

Combining all of these functions, we get a full solution to the Goldilocks problem
(Example 6-20).

Example 6-20. Goldilocks version 3, sort on values

```
def findRankStatistics(dataFrame: DataFrame, targetRanks: List[Long]):
  Map[Int, Iterable[Double]] = {

  val valueColumnPairs: RDD[(Double, Int)] = getValueColumnPairs(dataFrame)
  val sortedValueColumnPairs = valueColumnPairs.sortByKey()
  sortedValueColumnPairs.persist(StorageLevel.MEMORY_AND_DISK)

  val numOfColumns = dataFrame.schema.length
  val partitionColumnsFreq =
    getColumnsFreqPerPartition(sortedValueColumnPairs, numOfColumns)
  val ranksLocations = getRanksLocationsWithinEachPart(
    targetRanks, partitionColumnsFreq, numOfColumns)
```

```
val targetRanksValues = findTargetRanksIteratively(
  sortedValueColumnPairs, ranksLocations)
targetRanksValues.groupByKey().collectAsMap()
}
```

From a code readability perspective, this solution is ugly. It requires dozens of lines of code and four passes through the data. However, we expect that it will avoid memory errors on the executors and complete faster than the `groupByKey` or secondary sort solutions. This is because the data on each column should be mostly distinct doubles, and thus the shuffle should be fairly efficient. The final two `mapPartitions` routines involve reducing the data and can be achieved through iterator-to-iterator transformations, so we expect them to scale well. Indeed, on randomly distributed test data with many records, this solution outperforms the other implementations of the Goldilocks problem by orders of magnitude.

Straggler Detection and Unbalanced Data

"Stragglers" are those tasks within a stage that take much longer to execute than the other tasks in that stage. Recall from our discussion in "Spark Job Scheduling" on page 19 that a new stage begins after each wide transformation. When wide transformations are called on the same RDD, stages must usually be executed in sequence, so straggler tasks may hold up an entire job. Stragglers occur when Spark has not allocated resources correctly, and in particular if the data has not been partitioned evenly. Stragglers are a good indication of unbalanced keys because the distribution of tasks depends on partitioning, which in turn depends on the keys. The Spark Web UI allows you to monitor tasks as they are executed in real time.

If during a wide transformation you notice that some partitions take much longer than others or show more retries, it is likely that the data is not being partitioned evenly. This usually happens because some keys have many more values than others. In this case, it will speed up shuffle operations to either use something else as keys, or add random "noise" to your keys to create more distinct keys. Sometimes, you can even perform a map-side reduction to combine or filter records with duplicates on each partition before shuffling all the data.

 While `sortByKey` is less likely to cause memory errors at scale than `groupByKey`, it is still quite possible. Think back to Figure 6-2 and see how we can still tip over with a `sortByKey` in Figure 6-4.

One workaround to unbalanced keys can be adding "junk" to the end of the key, such as a random number. That way, Spark can recognize the keys as distinct and spread them across partitions. In our case, this could mean spreading the zeros across machines, which should not affect the accuracy.

The following images are meant to illustrate an imbalanced sortByKey (Figure 6-4), and a balanced sortByKey (Figure 6-5).

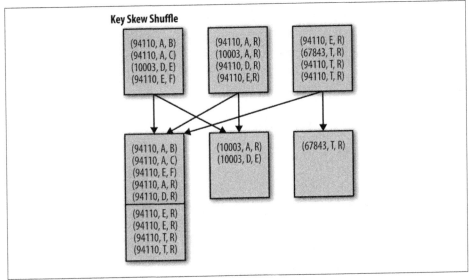

Figure 6-4. SortByKey memory errors

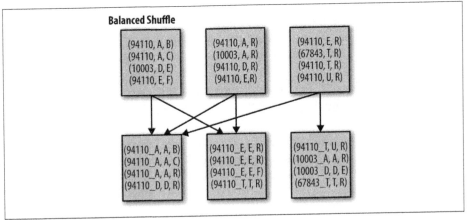

Figure 6-5. SortByKey balanced shuffle

Back to Goldilocks (Again)

Goldilocks has told us that her data was evenly distributed and that all the columns had "lots" of distinct values. However, when she tried to run the algorithm on her data, it failed. When we observed the algorithm running in the web UI, we noticed that some partitions were running much slower than the others, and sometimes running out of memory. This indicated that we had too many duplicate keys. This was surprising because in our implementation, the keys were the values of the data (doubles). However, further analysis revealed that in most of the columns, about twenty-five percent of the values were zeros. Thus, nearly one in four keys in our sort was a zero value. This meant that 1/4 of the records in the RDD we were sorting clustered around zero. Consequently, no matter how many partitions we used, a quarter of the records were being shuffled to the first few partitions.

Goldilocks Version 4: Reduce to Distinct on Each Partition

Rather than trying to partition those pairs differently, we realized that the last four steps of the algorithm could be modified to work on input of tuples of ((cell value, column index), count). Then, in the first step, rather than mapping the records on each partition to (cell value, column index) pairs, we could map each partition to distinct pairs, keeping track of the number of times each ((cell value, column index)) pair appeared on that partition. By mapping to distinct on each partition, we reduce the number of duplicate keys without incurring a shuffle (as would a distributed distinct call on the entire RDD).

After creating these ((value, columnIndex), count) tuples, we know that although we might have some repeated keys, we introduce a theoretical limit on the number of duplicate keys. Specifically, if the same value is present in a column on each partition, the maximum number of duplicate keys is (the number of columns * the number of partitions).[4] Not only does this input step balance the data so it can be partitioned more effectively, it also dramatically reduces the total number of records to be shuffled. In the Goldilocks case, where 25% of the rows were zero, we now have roughly 75% the number of tuples to sort as the previous iteration of our solution.

Aggregate to ((cell value, column index), count) on each partition

Example 6-21 is the code for this first step. Rather than mapping to (cell_value, column_index) pairs, we mapped to ((cell value, column index), count) on each partition. We were transforming the columnar data into pairs by using a mapPartitions step. Now, rather than doing a flatMap of each row in the original data, we

---

4 Using a distributed reduceByKey could have reduced this to simply the number of columns at the cost of a shuffle.

update a HashMap whose keys are the (value, index) pairs and whose values are the number of times that (cell value, column index) pair appears in that partition. Even if each column on a given partition has all unique values, we expect that this solution will not cause out-of-memory errors. We are making the HashMap on each partition, and so the size of the HashMap should still be smaller than the iterator of all the records. However, if we did have all distinct values, this might not be the case, because a hash map is a much less memory-efficient data structure than an iterator.

Example 6-21. Goldilocks version 4, aggregate on each partition

```
def getAggregatedValueColumnPairs(dataFrame: DataFrame):
    RDD[((Double, Int), Long)] = {

  val aggregatedValueColumnRDD = dataFrame.rdd.mapPartitions(rows => {
    val valueColumnMap = new mutable.HashMap[(Double, Int), Long]()
    rows.foreach(row => {
      row.toSeq.zipWithIndex.foreach{ case (value, columnIndex) =>
        val key = (value.toString.toDouble, columnIndex)
        val count = valueColumnMap.getOrElseUpdate(key, 0)
        valueColumnMap.update(key, count + 1)
      }
    })

    valueColumnMap.toIterator
  })

  aggregatedValueColumnRDD
}
```

Sort and find rank statistics

The rest of the function is similar to the original version. We simply adjust for keeping track of the number of times the pair appears rather than assuming that each pair in the sorted RDD occurred once. The updated code is shown in Examples 6-22, 6-23, 6-24, and 6-25, with Example 6-26 bringing everything together.

Example 6-22. Goldilocks version 4, count values per column on each partition

```
private def getColumnsFreqPerPartition(
    sortedAggregatedValueColumnPairs: RDD[((Double, Int), Long)],
    numOfColumns : Int): Array[(Int, Array[Long])] = {

  val zero = Array.fill[Long](numOfColumns)(0)

  def aggregateColumnFrequencies(
      partitionIndex : Int, pairs : Iterator[((Double, Int), Long)]) = {
    val columnsFreq : Array[Long] = pairs.aggregate(zero)(
      (a : Array[Long], v : ((Double, Int), Long)) => {
```

```
        val ((value, colIndex), count) = v
        a(colIndex) = a(colIndex) + count
        a},
      (a : Array[Long], b : Array[Long]) => {
        a.zip(b).map{ case(aVal, bVal) => aVal + bVal}
      })

    Iterator((partitionIndex, columnsFreq))
  }

  sortedAggregatedValueColumnPairs.mapPartitionsWithIndex(
    aggregateColumnFrequencies).collect()
}
```

Example 6-23. Goldilocks version 4, determine locations of rank statistics on each partition

```
private def getRanksLocationsWithinEachPart(targetRanks : List[Long],
      partitionColumnsFreq : Array[(Int, Array[Long])],
      numOfColumns : Int) : Array[(Int, List[(Int, Long)])]  = {

  val runningTotal = Array.fill[Long](numOfColumns)(0)

  partitionColumnsFreq.sortBy(_._1).map { case (partitionIndex, columnsFreq)=>
    val relevantIndexList = new mutable.MutableList[(Int, Long)]()

    columnsFreq.zipWithIndex.foreach{ case (colCount, colIndex)  =>
      val runningTotalCol = runningTotal(colIndex)

      val ranksHere: List[Long] = targetRanks.filter(rank =>
        runningTotalCol < rank && runningTotalCol + colCount >= rank)
      relevantIndexList ++= ranksHere.map(
        rank => (colIndex, rank - runningTotalCol))

      runningTotal(colIndex) += colCount
    }

    (partitionIndex, relevantIndexList.toList)
  }
}
```

Example 6-24. Goldilocks version 4, filter for rank statistics

```
private def findTargetRanksIteratively(
      sortedAggregatedValueColumnPairs : RDD[((Double, Int), Long)],
      ranksLocations : Array[(Int, List[(Int, Long)])]): RDD[(Int, Double)] = {

  sortedAggregatedValueColumnPairs.mapPartitionsWithIndex((partitionIndex : Int,
    aggregatedValueColumnPairs : Iterator[((Double, Int), Long)]) => {

    val targetsInThisPart: List[(Int, Long)] = ranksLocations(partitionIndex)._2
```

```
    if (targetsInThisPart.nonEmpty) {
      FindTargetsSubRoutine.asIteratorToIteratorTransformation(
        aggregatedValueColumnPairs,
        targetsInThisPart)
    } else {
      Iterator.empty
    }
  })
}
```

Example 6-25. Goldilocks version 4, iterator-to-iterator transformation to filter for the rank statistics

```
def asIteratorToIteratorTransformation(
  valueColumnPairsIter : Iterator[((Double, Int), Long)],
  targetsInThisPart: List[(Int, Long)] ): Iterator[(Int, Double)] = {

  val columnsRelativeIndex = targetsInThisPart.groupBy(_._1).mapValues(_.map(_._2))
  val columnsInThisPart = targetsInThisPart.map(_._1).distinct

  val runningTotals : mutable.HashMap[Int, Long]= new mutable.HashMap()
   runningTotals ++= columnsInThisPart.map(columnIndex => (columnIndex, 0L)).toMap

  //filter out the pairs that don't have a column index that is in this part
  val pairsWithRanksInThisPart = valueColumnPairsIter.filter{
    case (((value, colIndex), count)) =>
      columnsInThisPart contains colIndex
  }

  // map the valueColumn pairs to a list of (colIndex, value) pairs that correspond
  // to one of the desired rank statistics on this partition.
  pairsWithRanksInThisPart.flatMap{

    case (((value, colIndex), count)) =>

        val total = runningTotals(colIndex)
        val ranksPresent: List[Long] = columnsRelativeIndex(colIndex)
                                        .filter(index => (index <= count + total)
                                          && (index > total))

        val nextElems: Iterator[(Int, Double)] =
          ranksPresent.map(r => (colIndex, value)).toIterator

        //update the running totals
        runningTotals.update(colIndex, total + count)
        nextElems
  }
}
```

Putting all the code together, we have a final solution to the Goldilocks problem (Example 6-26).

Example 6-26. Goldilocks with hash map

```
def findRankStatistics(dataFrame: DataFrame, targetRanks: List[Long]):
Map[Int, Iterable[Double]] = {

  val aggregatedValueColumnPairs: RDD[((Double, Int), Long)] =
    getAggregatedValueColumnPairs(dataFrame)
  val sortedAggregatedValueColumnPairs = aggregatedValueColumnPairs.sortByKey()
  sortedAggregatedValueColumnPairs.persist(StorageLevel.MEMORY_AND_DISK)

  val numOfColumns = dataFrame.schema.length
  val partitionColumnsFreq =
    getColumnsFreqPerPartition(sortedAggregatedValueColumnPairs, numOfColumns)
  val ranksLocations  =
    getRanksLocationsWithinEachPart(targetRanks,
      partitionColumnsFreq, numOfColumns)

  val targetRanksValues =
    findTargetRanksIteratively(sortedAggregatedValueColumnPairs, ranksLocations)
  targetRanksValues.groupByKey().collectAsMap()
}
```

As expected, this solution led to a 4× to 5× speed up of an empty cluster.

Goldilocks postmortem

Given the task of finding an arbitrary number of rank statistics by group (column), we have presented five solutions:

- "Goldilocks Version 0: Iterative Solution" on page 130. Our first solution iteratively looped through each group and performed a distributed sort, resulting in one stage and one expensive distributed sort per group.

- "Goldilocks Version 1: groupByKey Solution" on page 134. The next solution used groupByKey shuffle records associated with the same group onto the same partition. Then we were able to sort each group in one stage by using mapParti tions to sort the values in each group.

- "Goldilocks Version 2: Secondary Sort" on page 156. Using the secondary sort technique, we improved our groupByKey solution by replacing the groupByKey and sorting steps with the repartitionAndSortWithinPartitions function to push the work of sorting each group into the shuffle stage.

- "Goldilocks Version 3: Sort on Cell Values" on page 164. Next, we realized that it was possible to solve the problem using only one sort on the value of each record, rather than the group. We developed a solution that keyed the records by value (rather than by group/column index), sorted all the records, and then performed a series of narrow transformations to collect the results. We expected the new sorting keys (the values in the columns) to contain fewer duplicates than the the size of each group, which we used as a key in version 2.

- "Goldilocks Version 4: Reduce to Distinct on Each Partition" on page 167. Finally, upon realizing that we had a high number of duplicate records in each group, we modified the previous solution to perform a map-side reduction before sorting the data. This solution had better results with our client's skewed data.

We found that performance was dependent mostly on three characteristics of the input data: 1) the number of original records, 2) the number of groups (columns in this case) to compute the metrics on, and 3) the percentage of duplicate records by group. Note that these metrics are all relative to the size and shape of the hardware you are computing on. A small number of records really means that the records fit comfortably in the computational memory of all of the executors.

"Goldilocks Version 4: Reduce to Distinct on Each Partition" on page 167 is not the best solution for all input data. The only one of these five solutions that is always "bad" is the groupByKey solution (version 1). We would expect that version 1 should perform worse than the repartitionAndSortWithinPartitions (version 2) solution in all cases due to the limitations of groupByKey and the advantages of secondary sort (see "Secondary Sort and repartitionAndSortWithinPartitions" on page 151). The remaining four versions are all desirable in some cases.

Version 0 uses the value in each group to sort (as do solutions 3 and 4). Thus it is optimal there is only one group, because it doesn't require extra passes through the data.

Version 2 partitions by group. Thus it is optimal if there are many groups, and each group fits easily in memory on one executor. If the groups are sufficiently small, it would outperform versions 3 and 4, which sort on value and require three narrow transformations to determine the correct results, because this solution requires fewer passes through the data. With enough groups and rank statistics this solution may also be more likely to succeed than versions 3 and 4, both of which require keeping a hash map of rank statistics for each group in memory.

Version 3 partitions by values across all groups. Thus it is optimal if each group is very large, and there are few duplicate values across the columns. Unlike version 2, only the records with duplicate values need to be on one partition. Assuming that the number of duplicate values is less than the maximum group size this will lead to better parallelization.

Version 4 uses a narrow transformation to aggregate distinct values by group on the input partitions, then partitions by distinct values (like solution 3). Solution 4 is better than 3 only when there are many duplicate values in the columns. However, if all values are unique, this operation provides no benefit and risks causing memory errors by creating a hash map of all the values on each partition.

In our use case, we had input data containing several thousand groups with 300 million records each. In each column (group) we saw that about 25% of records were identical. Versions 0, 1, and 2 did not complete on a 10-node, crowded cluster. Version 3 did complete, but version 4 led to a 4× improvement in production over version 3.

Conclusion

In this chapter, we have seen how to use functions in the `PairRDDFunctions` and `OrderedRDDFunctions` classes in ways that are more likely to succeed at scale. Much of the chapter has focused on specific techniques for working with wide transformations. We focused on some of the causes of memory errors during the shuffle stage such as avoiding aggregation operations like `groupByKey` that do not reduce the space needed to store all the records associated with each key. We have learned about partitioning: how thinking ahead toward the next key/value transformation and doing smart partitioning can reduce the number of shuffles we need. We have focused on some strategies to do fewer shuffles: using smart partitioning, maintaining partition information with narrow transformations, and leveraging co-location for joins. When shuffles are required, we have covered some techniques for reducing the cost of those shuffles. In particular, we have shown that unbalanced data, particularly a high number of duplicate values per key, is likely to slow down shuffles and cause memory errors.

We hope that in addition to presenting some tricks for improving the performance of RDD transformations, this chapter provides some tools for reconceptualizing problem solving with Spark. By focusing on the Goldilocks use case, we have tried to show that writing performant Spark code sometimes requires a new kind of thinking. Simply stringing together the set of API calls that most obviously describe what you are trying to do often leads to a solution such as the one presented in "Goldilocks Version 1: groupByKey Solution" on page 134: an implementation that succeeds on relatively small, clean inputs and fails in the wild west of real-world data. Instead, we hope to show that despite the relative simplicity of writing distributed code with Spark, the best results can be achieved only with a close eye to how those distributed computations will be performed. We hope to encourage you to think of keys in Spark not as the index or category for the records, but as the axis of parallelization for the computational load. We encourage you wherever possible to design Spark routines with as much knowledge as possible about the size, distribution, and complexity of the data they are processing. Philosophically, we want to demonstrate how high-performance code often requires big rather than small changes—and that the most performant code is not always the cleanest.

## CHAPTER 7

Going Beyond Scala

Working in Spark doesn't mean limiting yourself to Scala, or even limiting yourself to the JVM, or languages that Spark explicitly supports. Spark has first-party APIs for writing driver programs and worker code in R,[1] Python, Scala, and Java with third-party bindings[2] for additional languages including JavaScript, Julia, C#, and F#. Spark's language interoperability can be thought of in two tiers: one is the worker code inside of your transformations (e.g., the lambda's inside of your maps) and the second is being able to specify the transformations on RDDs/Datasets (e.g., the driver program). This chapter will discuss the performance considerations of using other languages in Spark, and how to effectively work with existing libraries.

Often the language you will choose to specify the code inside of your transformations will be the same as the language for writing the driver program, but when working with specialized libraries or tools (such as CUDA[3]) specifying our entire program in one language would be a hassle, even if it was possible. Spark supports a range of languages for use on the driver, and an even wider range of languages can be used inside of our transformations on the workers. While the APIs are similar between the languages, the performance characteristics between the different languages are quite different once they need to execute outside of the JVM. We will discuss the design behind language support and how the performance difference can impact your work.

---

1 There are multiple competing R APIs, but for the purposes of performance they share the same underlying design.

2 Just because support is first party does not mean it will be fast; in some cases third-party bindings have taken interesting work to minimize overhead that has not been implemented in the first-party languages.

3 CUDA is a specialized language for parallel GPU programming from NVIDIA.

Generally the non-JVM language binding calls the Java interface for Spark using an RPC mechanism, such as Py4J, passing along a serialized representation of the code to be executed on the worker. Regardless of the language used to specify the driver program, the Spark workers will execute in the JVM and if necessary call the language-specific worker program. If the language you're looking for doesn't have Spark driver binding available, remember you can write your transformations to call another language on the workers.

On the worker side, the Spark worker is always running in the JVM, and if necessary will start another process for the target and copy the required data and result. This copying is expensive, but Spark's dependency DAG and clever pipelining minimize the number of times the copying needs to occur. The techniques that the different language APIs use for interfacing their worker code are similar to the same techniques you can use to call your custom code regardless of the language of your driver.

There are many ways to go outside the JVM, ranging from Java Native Interface (JNI), Unix pipes, or interfacing with long-running companion servers over sockets. These are the same techniques used inside of Spark's internals when interfacing with other languages. For example, JNI is used for calling some linear algebra libraries and Unix pipes are used for interfacing with Python code on the workers. The most efficient solution often depends on whether there are multiple transformations that will need to be evaluated, environment and language setup cost, and the computational complexity of the transformations. Regardless of which specific approach you choose to integrate other languages outside the JVM, these all currently require copying your data from the JVM to the runtime of your target language. Work on both Tungsten and Arrow integration means that in the future it will be easier to work with data from Spark outside of the JVM.

Not all languages require going outside of the JVM, and using these languages with Spark can avoid the expensive copy of the data from the Spark worker to the target language. Some languages take a mixed approach, like the Eclair JS project (see "How Eclair JS Works" on page 192), which executes the worker inside of the JVM but leaves the driver program outside of the JVM. While there is, of course, some overhead in having the driver program outside of the JVM, the amount of data that needs to be passed between the Scala driver and target driver is much smaller compared to the amount of data processed by even just one of the workers.

Beyond Scala within the JVM

This section will look at how to access the Spark APIs from different languages within the JVM and some of the performance considerations of going outside of Scala. Even if you are going outside of the JVM, it is useful to understand this section since the non-JVM languages often depend on the Java APIs rather than the Scala APIs.

Working in other languages doesn't always mean having to move beyond the JVM, and staying within the JVM can have many performance benefits—mostly from not having to copy data. While you don't necessarily need special bindings or wrappers to access Spark outside of Scala, calling Scala code can be difficult from other languages. Spark supports Java 8 lambdas for use within transformations, and users with older versions of the JDK can implement the corresponding interface from `org.apache.spark.api.java.function`. Even when data doesn't need to be copied, working in a different language can have small, yet important, performance considerations.

The difficulty with accessing the Scala APIs is especially true for accessing functions with class tags or using functionality provided through implicit conversions (such as all of the `Double` and `Tuple` specific functionality on RDDs). For functionality that depends on implicit conversions, equivalent classes are often provided along with explicit transformations to these concrete classes. For functions that depend on class tags, "fake" class tags (e.g., `AnyRef`) can be supplied (and are automatically supplied often by wrappers). Using the concrete class instead of the implicit conversion generally doesn't add any overhead, but the fake class tags can limit some of the compiler optimizations.

The Java API is kept quite close to the Scala API in terms of features, with only the occasional functionality or Developer API not being available. Support for other JVM languages, like Clojure with Flambo (*https://github.com/yieldbot/flambo*) and sparkling (*https://github.com/gorillalabs/sparkling/*), is done using the Java APIs instead of calling the Scala APIs directly. Since most of the language bindings, even non-JVM languages like Python and R, go through the Java APIs, it is useful to understand the Java APIs (*http://bit.ly/2qx9vbA*).

The Java APIs closely resemble the Scala APIs, while avoiding depending on class tags or implicit conversions. The lack of implicit conversions means that rather than automatically converting RDDs containing `Tuples` or `doubles` to special classes with additional functions, explicit function conversions must be used (such as `mapToDouble` and `mapToPair`). These functions are only defined on Java RDDs; thankfully, for interoperability, these special types are simply wrappers of Scala RDDs. These special functions also return different types, such as `JavaDoubleRDD` and `JavaPairRDD`, which have the functionality that is provided by the implicit conversions in Scala.

Let's revisit the canonical word count example using the Java APIs (Example 7-1). Since it can sometimes be convoluted to call the Scala API from Java, Spark's Java APIs are mostly implemented in Scala while hiding class tags and implicit conversions. This allows the Java wrappers to be a very thin layer, consisting of only a few lines on average, with very little reimplementation required.

Example 7-1. Java Word count example

```
import scala.Tuple2;

import org.apache.spark.api.java.JavaRDD;
import org.apache.spark.api.java.JavaPairRDD;
import org.apache.spark.api.java.JavaSparkContext;

import java.util.regex.Pattern;
import java.util.Arrays;

public final class WordCount {
  private static final Pattern pattern = Pattern.compile(" ");

  public static void main(String[] args) throws Exception {
    JavaSparkContext jsc = new JavaSparkContext();
    JavaRDD<String> lines = jsc.textFile(args[0]);
    JavaRDD<String> words = lines.flatMap(e -> Arrays.asList(
                                       pattern.split(e)).iterator());
    JavaPairRDD<String, Integer> wordsIntial = words.mapToPair(
      e -> new Tuple2<String, Integer>(e, 1));
  }
}
```

 Spark supports Java 8 lambdas for most transformations. If you are working with an earlier version of Java you will need to create instances from org.apache.spark.api.java.function.package (*http:// bit.ly/2oYVMJs*). The function names are generally similar to the name of the transformation (e.g., FlatMapFunction and Double Function).

Sometimes you may want to convert your Java RDDs to Scala RDDs or vice versa. Most commonly this is for libraries that require or return Scala RDDs, but sometimes core Spark functionality may not yet be available in the Java API and converting your RDD to a Scala RDD is an easy way to access the new functionality.

If you have a Java RDD you want to pass to a Scala library expecting a regular Spark RDD, you can access the underlying Scala RDD with rdd(). Most often this is sufficient to pass the resulting RDD to whichever Scala library you need to call; some notable exceptions are Scala libraries that depend on implicit conversions of the contents of the RDD or class tag information. In this case writing a small wrapper in Scala can be the simplest way to access the implicit conversions. If a Scala shim is out of the question, explicitly calling the corresponding function on the JavaConverters (*http://www.scala-lang.org/api/2.12.0/scala/collection/JavaConverters$.html*) object, construct a fake class tag.

To construct a fake class tag you can use `scala.reflect.ClassTag$.MODULE$.Any Ref()` or get the actual class tag with `scala.reflect.ClassTag$.MODULE $.apply(CLASS)` as illustrated in Examples 7-2 and 7-3.

Going from a Scala RDD to a Java RDD often requires class tag information more than most Spark libraries. This is because, while the different JavaRDDs expose public constructors that take Scala RDDs as arguments, these are intended to be called from within Scala and therefore expect class tag information.

> If you are in a mixed language project or library, consider constructing the Java RDD in the Scala where the class tag information is more easily available.

Fake class tags are most commonly used in generic or templated code in which you don't know the exact types at compile time. Using fake class tags often work, although some specialization may be lost in the Scala side; very occasionally the Scala code depends on correct class tag information. In this case you *must* use a real class tag. In most cases, using a real class tag is not substantially more effort and can offer performance advantages, so use them when possible.

Example 7-2. Java/Scala RDD interoperability with fake class tag

```
public static JavaPairRDD wrapPairRDDFakeCt(
  RDD<Tuple2<String, Object>> rdd) {
  // Construct the class tags by casting AnyRef - this would be more commonly done
  // with generic or templated code where we can't explicitly construct the correct
  // class tag as using fake class tags may result in degraded performance.
  ClassTag<Object> fake = ClassTag$.MODULE$.AnyRef();
  return new JavaPairRDD(rdd, fake, fake);
}
```

Example 7-3. Java/Scala RDD interoperability

```
public static JavaPairRDD wrapPairRDD(
  RDD<Tuple2<String, Object>> rdd) {
  // Construct the class tags
  ClassTag<String> strCt = ClassTag$.MODULE$.apply(String.class);
  ClassTag<Long> longCt = ClassTag$.MODULE$.apply(scala.Long.class);
  return new JavaPairRDD(rdd, strCt, longCt);
}
```

Both the Spark SQL and the ML pipeline APIs are mostly unified between Scala and Java. There are still Java-specific helper functions in which the equivalent Scala function is difficult to call. Some examples of this are the various numeric functions, like plus minus, etc., on `Column` as the overloaded `Scala` equivalents (+, -) cannot be easily accessed. Rather than having `JavaDataFrame` and a `JavaSQLContext`, the methods required for Java access are available on the regular `DataFrame` and `SQLContext`. This can be somewhat confusing, as some of the methods that will appear in the Java-Doc may not be usable from Java, but in those cases similarly named functions will be provided to be called from Java.

Java UDFs, and by extension most other non-Scala languages, require specifying the return type of your function as it can't be inferred in the same way it is done in Scala (Example 7-4).

Example 7-4. Sample Java UDF

```
sqlContext.udf()
   .register("strlen",
            (String s) -> s.length(), DataTypes.StringType);
```

While the types required by the Scala and Java APIs are different, for the most part, the Java collection types can be wrapped without requiring an extra copy. For iterators, the wrap conversion can be done lazily as the elements are accessed, allowing Spark to spill the data as needed (as discussed in "Iterator-to-Iterator Transformations with mapPartitions" on page 100). This is especially important since for many simple operations the cost of copying the data can quickly dominate the actual computation required.

 In earlier versions of Spark, the Java API mistakenly required `Iterable` rather than `Iterator`, which limited the ability to create iterator-to-iterator transformations in Java.

Beyond Scala, and Beyond the JVM

Going beyond the JVM greatly opens up the scope of different languages available for you to work in. However, in its current architecture, going outside of the JVM in Spark—especially on the workers—can involve a substantial performance cost of copying data on worker nodes between the JVM and the target language. For complex operations the cost of copying the data is relatively low, but for simpler operations the cost of copying the data can easily double the computation cost.

The first non-JVM language to be directly supported inside of Spark is Python, and its API and interface have become a model that other non-JVM languages have based their implementations on.

How PySpark Works

PySpark connects to JVM Spark using a mixture of pipes on the workers and Py4J, a specialized library for Python/Java interoperability, on the driver. This relatively simple architecture hides a large number of complexities involved in making PySpark work, as Figure 7-1 shows. One of the bigger challenges is that even once the data has been copied from the Python worker to the JVM, it isn't in a form the JVM can easily parse. This requires special handling on both the Python worker and Java to ensure sufficient information for things like partitioning is available in the JVM.

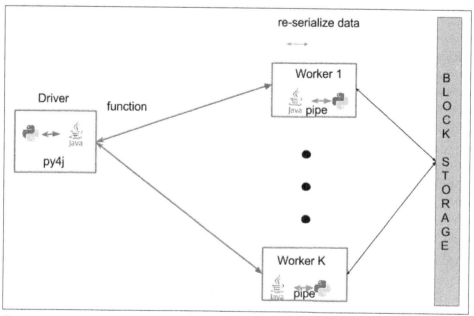

Figure 7-1. PySpark diagram

 After the initial reading from persistent storage (like HDFs or S3) and between any shuffle, the data on the workers needs to be passed between the JVM and Python.

 Is IPython your jam? In Spark 2.0+ the old syntax to get an IPython notebook has changed from `IPYTHON_OPTS="notebook"` to `PYSPARK_DRIVER_PYTHON="ipython"` `PYSPARK_DRIVER_ PYTHON_ OPTS="notebook"`.

PySpark RDDs

Transferring the data to and from the JVM and starting the Python executor has significant overhead. Using the DataFrame/Dataset API avoids many of the performance challenges with the PySpark RDD API by keeping the data inside the JVM for as long as possible.

Copying the data from the JVM to Python is done using sockets and pickled bytes. A more general version of this, for talking to programs in other languages, is available through the PipedRDD interface illustrated in "Using Pipe and Friends" on page 193.

Since piping the data back and forth for each transformation would be expensive, PySpark pipelines Python transformations inside of the Python interpreter when possible, so a filter then a map will be chained together on the iterator of Python objects using a specialized PipelinedRDD. Even when the data has to be shuffled and PySpark is unable to chain our transformations inside of a single worker VM, the Python interpreter is capable of being reused so the interpreter startup overhead doesn't further slow us down.

This is only part of the puzzle. Normal PipedRDDs work on Strings, which can't easily be shuffled since there is no inherent key. The approach taken in PySpark, and mirrored in many other language bindings, is a special PairwiseRDD in which the key must be a long and the key only is deserialized with custom Scala code to parse the Python value. This deserialization is not overly expensive, but does serve to illustrate that for the most part, Spark Scala treats the results of Python as opaque bytes arrays.

 Since there is some overhead associated with serialization and deserialization, PySpark uses a batch serializer, and this can occasionally result in unexpected effects (like when repartitioning PySpark will not split up things in the same batch).

For all its simplicity this approach to integrating works surprisingly well, with the majority of operations on Scala RDDs available in Python. Some of the more difficult places are interacting with libraries, such as MLlib, and loading and saving from different sources.

Interacting with different formats is another restriction, as much of Spark's load/save code is based on Hadoop's Java interfaces. This means that any data loaded is initially loaded into the JVM and then transferred to Python.

For interacting with MLlib, generally two approaches have been taken: either a specialized data type is used in PySpark with equivalent Scala decoders, or the algorithm is reimplemented in Python. These problems are avoided with Spark ML, which uses the DataFrame/Dataset interface that generally keeps the data stored in the JVM.

PySpark DataFrames and Datasets

`DataFrames` and `Datasets` avoid many of the performance downsides of the Python RDD API by keeping the data inside the JVM for as long as possible. The same benchmark we did to illustrate `DataFrames`' general improvement over RDDs (Figure 3-1) shows a greater difference when rerun in Python (Figure 7-2).

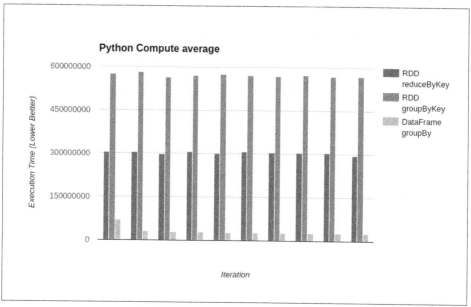

Figure 7-2. Spark SQL performance in Python

For many operations on `DataFrames` and `Datasets`, the data may never actually need to leave the JVM, although using Python UDFs, UDAFs, or lambdas naturally requires transferring some of the data to the JVM. This results in a simplified architecture diagram for many operations, which instead of Figure 7-1, looks like Figure 7-3.

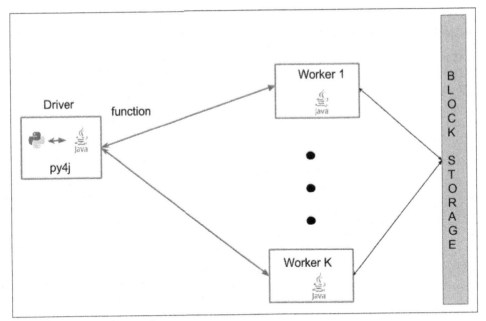

Figure 7-3. PySpark SQL diagram

PySpark doesn't use Jython because it has been found that a lot of Python users need access to libraries, like numpy, scipy, and pandas, which do not work well in Jython.

Some early work is being investigated to see if Jython can be used to accelerate Python UDFs, which don't depend on C extensions. See SPARK-15369 (*https://issues.apache.org/jira/browse/SPARK-15369*) for updates.

Accessing the backing Java objects and mixing Scala code

An important implication of the PySpark architecture is that many of Spark's Python classes simply exist as wrappers to translate your Python calls to the JVM.

If you work with Scala/Java developers and you wish to collaborate, preexisting wrappers won't exist to call your own code—but you can register Java/Scala UDFs and then use them from Python. Starting in Spark 2.1 this can be done with the register JavaFunction utility on the sqlContext.

Sometimes these wrappers don't do everything you need, and since Python doesn't have strong protections around accessing private methods, you can jump directly into the JVM. The same techniques can be used to call your own JVM code, and with a bit of work translate the results into Python objects.

 While the Py4J API is accessible, these techniques depend on implementation details of PySpark, and these implementation details may change between releases.

Thinking back to "Large Query Plans and Iterative Algorithms" on page 70, we suggested that it was important to use the JVM version of DataFrames and RDDs to cut the query plan. This is a workaround for when a query plan becomes too large for the Spark SQL optimizer to process, by putting an RDD in the middle the SQL optimizer can't see back past the point where the data is in an RDD. While you could accomplish the same thing using public Python APIs, you would lose much of the advantage of DataFrames as the entire data would need to be round-tripped through the Python workers. Instead, by using some of the internal APIs, you can cut the lineage from Python while keeping the data in the JVM (as shown in Example 7-5).

Example 7-5. Cut large DataFrame query plan with Python

```
def cutLineage(df):
    """
    Cut the lineage of a DataFrame - used for iterative algorithms

    .. Note: This uses internal members and may break between versions
    >>> df = rdd.toDF()
    >>> cutDf = cutLineage(df)
    >>> cutDf.count()
    3
    """
    jRDD = df._jdf.toJavaRDD()
    jSchema = df._jdf.schema()
    jRDD.cache()
    sqlCtx = df.sql_ctx
    try:
        javaSqlCtx = sqlCtx._jsqlContext
    except:
        javaSqlCtx = sqlCtx._ssql_ctx
    newJavaDF = javaSqlCtx.createDataFrame(jRDD, jSchema)
    newDF = DataFrame(newJavaDF, sqlCtx)
    return newDF
```

In general, the convention for most python objects is _j[shortname] to access the underlying Java version. So, for example, the SparkContext has _jsc to get at the underling Java SparkContext. This is only available on the driver program, so if any

PySpark objects are sent to the workers you won't be able to access the underlying Java component and large parts of the API will not work.

 The Python APIs generally wrap Java versions of the API rather than directly wrapping the Scala versions.

If you want to access a JVM Spark class that does not already have a Python wrapper, you can directly use the Py4J gateway on the driver. The SparkContext contains a reference to the gateway in _gateway. Arbitrary Java objects can be accessed with `sc._gateway.jvm.[fulljvmclassname]`.

 Py4J depends heavily on reflection to determine which methods to call. This is normally not a problem, but can become confusing with numeric types. Attempting to call a Scala function expecting a `Long` with an `Integer` will result in an error message about not being able to find the method, even though in Python the distinction normally would not matter.

The same technique works for your own Scala classes provided they are on the class path. You can add JARs to the class path with `spark-submit` with `--jars` or by setting the `spark.driver.extraClassPath` configuration property. Example 7-6, which we used to generate Figure 7-2, is intentionally structured to use the existing Scala code to generate the performance testing data.

Example 7-6. Calling non-Spark JVM classes with Py4J

```
sc = sqlCtx._sc
# Get the SQL Context, 2.1, 2.0 and pre-2.0 syntax - yay internals :p
try:
    try:
        javaSqlCtx = sqlCtx._jsqlContext
    except:
        javaSqlCtx = sqlCtx._ssql_ctx
except:
    javaSqlCtx = sqlCtx._jwrapped
jsc = sc._jsc
scalasc = jsc.sc()
gateway = sc._gateway
# Call a java method that gives us back an RDD of JVM Rows (Int, Double)
# While Python RDDs are wrapped Java RDDs (even of Rows) the contents are
# different, so we can't directly wrap this.
# This returns a Java RDD of Rows - normally it would better to
# return a DataFrame directly, but for illustration we will work
```

```
# with an RDD of Rows.
java_rdd = (gateway.jvm.com.highperformancespark.examples.
            tools.GenerateScalingData.
            generateMiniScaleRows(scalasc, rows, numCols))
# Schemas are serialized to JSON and sent back and forth
# Construct a Python Schema and turn it into a Java Schema
schema = StructType([
    StructField("zip", IntegerType()),
    StructField("fuzzyness", DoubleType())])
# 2.1 / pre-2.1
try:
    jschema = javaSqlCtx.parseDataType(schema.json())
except:
    jschema = sqlCtx._jsparkSession.parseDataType(schema.json())
# Convert the Java RDD to Java DataFrame
java_dataframe = javaSqlCtx.createDataFrame(java_rdd, jschema)
# Wrap the Java DataFrame into a Python DataFrame
python_dataframe = DataFrame(java_dataframe, sqlCtx)
# Convert the Python DataFrame into an RDD
pairRDD = python_dataframe.rdd.map(lambda row: (row[0], row[1]))
return (python_dataframe, pairRDD)
```

Attempting to use the Py4J bridge inside of your transformations will fail at runtime.

While many of the Python classes are simply wrappers of Java objects, not all Java objects can directly be wrapped into Python objects and then used in Spark. For example, objects in PySpark RDDs are represented as pickled strings, which can only be easily parsed in Python. Thankfully, DataFrames are standardized between the languages, so provided you can convert your data into a DataFrame, you can then wrap it in Python and use it directly as a Python DataFrame or convert the Python DataFrame to a Python RDD.

Scala UDFs and UDAFs can be used from Python without having to go through the Py4J API.

PySpark dependency management

Often a large part of the reason one wants to use a language other than Scala is for the libraries that are available with that language. In addition to language-specific libraries, you may need to include libraries for Spark itself to use, especially when working with different data formats. There are a few different options for using both Spark-specific and language-specific libraries in PySpark.

Spark Packages (*http://spark-packages.org/*) is a system that allows us to easily include JVM dependencies with Spark. A common reason for wanting additional JVM libraries in PySpark is support for additional data formats.

If you are working in the Scala shell you can use the `--packages` command-line argument to specify the Maven coordinates of a package you want in the shell. If you are building a Scala package you also add any requirements to your assembly *.jar*.

For Python, you can create a Java or Scala project with your JVM dependencies and add the *.jar* with `--jar`. If you're working in the PySpark shell command-line arguments aren't allowed, so you can instead specify the `spark.jars.packages` configuration variable.

When using Spark Packages the dependencies are automatically fetched from Maven and distributed to the cluster. If your JVM dependency is not available in Maven, you can use the same technique we discuss next for adding local Python dependencies.

Adding local dependencies with PySpark can be done at both job submission time and dynamically using the `SparkContext`. Local dependencies can be *.jar* files, for JVM requirements, or *.zip* and *.egg* for Python dependencies, which are automatically added to the PYTHONPATH.

There is currently work under way to allow Python Spark programs to specify required pip packages and have them auto installed, but the proposal has not yet been accepted. See the pull request (*https://github.com/apache/spark/pull/12398*) and SPARK-5929 (*https://issues.apache.org/jira/browse/SPARK-5929*) for the status of this proposal.

For individuals working with a CDH cluster, it is now possible to easily add packages with Anaconda. Cloudera's post Making Python on Apache Hadoop Easier (*http://blog.cloudera.com/blog/2016/02/making-python-on-apache-hadoop-easier-with-anaconda-and-cdh/*) details how to install the packages on your cluster. To make the resulting packages accessible to Apache Spark, all you need to do is set the shell environment variable PYSPARK_PYTHON to `/opt/cloudera/parcels/Anaconda/bin/python` either with export in your shell profile or in your *spark-env.sh* file.

If none of the above work for your cluster configuration there are a few remaining options, all of which are somewhat less than ideal. The simplest, but very hacky, approach is to simply have your transformations explicitly import the package and on failure, perform a pip installation. Similar approaches can be done with broadcast variables or a setup map at the start of the program. Failing that you can ask your cluster administrator to install the package systemwide with parallel-ssh or similar, as shown in Example 7-7.

Example 7-7. Parallel ssh install pip packages

```
parallel-ssh pip install -h ./conf/slaves
```

Installing PySpark

First-party languages for Spark don't require any separate installation, but as mentioned for Python packages, Python has its own mechanisms for dealing with package management.

Installation with pip was added in PySpark version 2.1, and at that point you can download the PySpark package from the Apache download mirror and run `pip install pyspark-2.1.0.tar.gz`, allowing virtualenv support as well. PySpark 2.2.0 (and forward) are directly published `PyPi` allowing for an even simpler `pip install pyspark`. Once you have PySpark pip installed you can then start your favorite Python interpreter and import `pyspark` like any other package or start the PySpark shell with `pyspark`.

It's important to note that pip installing Spark is optional. If you wish you can run PySpark from a regular Spark setup without pip installation (although then you must use `spark-submit` or pyspark from the Spark `bin` directory).

How SparkR Works

SparkR takes a similar approach to PySpark, but does not currently expose the ability to perform arbitrary R code in the workers. While a similar `PipedRDD` wrapper exists for R as it does for Python, it is kept internal and the only public interface for working with R is through `DataFrames`.

 Of the directly supported languages, SparkR is the furthest away from Scala Spark in terms of feature completeness. This gap will likely close over time, but be careful when selecting SparkR to ensure it has the features you need. The API documentation (*http://spark.apache.org/docs/latest/api/R/index.html*) will give you an idea if what you are looking for is already available.

To give you an idea of what the SparkR interface looks like, the standard word count example has been rewritten in R in Example 7-8.

Example 7-8. SparkR word count

```
library(SparkR)

# Setup SparkContext & SQLContext
sc <- sparkR.init(appName="high-performance-spark-wordcount-example")

# Initialize SQLContext
sqlContext <- sparkRSQL.init(sc)

# Load some simple data

df <- read.text(fileName)

# Split the words
words <- selectExpr(df, "split(value, \" \") as words")

# Compute the count
explodedWords <- select(words, alias(explode(words$words), "words"))
wc <- agg(groupBy(explodedWords, "words"), "words" = "count")


# Attempting to push an array back fails
# resultingSchema <- structType(structField("words", "array<string>"))
# words <- dapply(df, function(line) {
#    y <- list()
#    y[[1]] <- strsplit(line[[1]], " ")
# }, resultingSchema)
# Also attempting even the identity transformation on a DF from read.text fails
# in Spark 2.0-preview (although works fine on other DFs).

# Display the result
showDF(wc)
```

To execute your own custom R code you can use the `dapply` method on `DataFrames`
as illustrated in Example 7-9. SparkR's custom code execution support has a long way
to go, as illustrated by the difficulty of attempting to perform a word count with `dap`
`ply` in Example 7-8.

Example 7-9. SparkR arbitrary code with DataFrames

```
library(SparkR)

# Setup SparkContext & SQLContext
sc <- sparkR.init(appName="high-performance-spark-wordcount-example")

# Initialize SQLContext
sqlContext <- sparkRSQL.init(sc)
```

```
# Count the number of characters - note this fails on the text DF due to a bug.
df <- createDataFrame (sqlContext,
  list(list(1L, 1, "1"),
  list(2L, 2, "22"),
  list(3L, 3, "333")),
  c("a", "b", "c"))
resultingSchema <- structType(structField("length", "integer"))
result <- dapply(df, function(row) {
  y <- list()
  y <- cbind(y, nchar(row[[3]]))
}, resultingSchema)
showDF(result)
```

Internally `dapply` is implemented in a similar way to Python's UDF support, but since the RDD API isn't exposed it leaves more potential for future optimizations and encourages development with the more optimized `DataFrame` APIs.

As with PySpark, arbitrary non-JVM code execution is slower than traditional Scala Spark code.

SparkR isn't the only interface for running Spark and R together. Sparklyr (*http://spark.rstudio.com/*) is a 3rd party library, from R Studio, which is also quite popular. From a performance point of view, it shares the same underlying mechanisms as SparkR in interfacing with the JVM.

Spark.jl (Julia Spark)

Spark.jl (*https://github.com/dfdx/Spark.jl*) is one of the newer projects to provide bindings for Spark and as such does not yet have a fully functional subset of the API supported. Spark.jl is incredibly easy to install (see Example 7-10), and it automatically installs a supported version of Spark along side it. The general design of Spark.jl is similar to that of PySpark, with a custom implementation of the `PipedRDD` that is able to parse limited amounts of serialized data from Julia implemented inside of the JVM. The same general performance caveats of using PySpark also apply to Spark.jl.

Example 7-10. Julia Spark install

```
Pkg.clone("https://github.com/dfdx/Spark.jl")
Pkg.build("Spark")
# we also need latest master of JavaCall.jl
Pkg.checkout("JavaCall")
```

As of this writing, named Julia functions cannot be fully serialized, so functions used inside of transformations should be anonymous.

Until keyed operations are supported in Spark.jl we can't even build the simple word count example. Namely, reduceByKey is missing, which is required for shuffling, and while others like flatMap are missing it can be replaced with mapPartitions. For now Spark.jl is an early stage project that shows promise but is not ready for use.

How Eclair JS Works

Eclair JS takes a different approach than R and Python support, mostly staying inside the JVM except for the driver program. Eclair JS runs JavaScript in both the JVM and V8 JavaScript engine (*https://developers.google.com/v8/*), with the functions inside of the transformations being evaluated by the JVM using Nashorn (*http://www.oracle.com/technetwork/articles/java/jf14-nashorn-2126515.html*). The split between driver-side and worker-side evaluation allows for fast integration on the workers and NodeJS (*https://nodejs.org/en/*) bindings on the driver. See Figure 7-4 for a diagram of this.

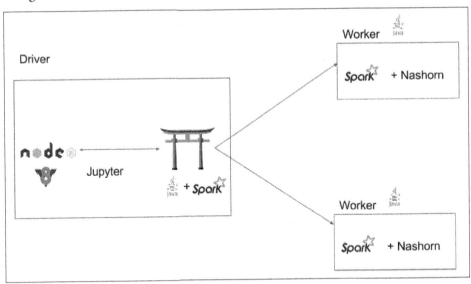

Figure 7-4. Eclair JS diagram

This somewhat unorthodox approach means that certain library functions may not be available inside of the transformations, but saves us from the double serialization problem found in PySpark and SparkR UDFs. The node driver communicates using

Apache Toree (*https://toree.incubator.apache.org/*) to send the required functions to the JVM, which then sends them to the workers.

Installing Eclair JS is easy relative to other languages as the worker side is able to run without any extra packages. The getting started guide (*https://github.com/EclairJS/ eclairjs-nashorn/wiki/Getting-Started-With-EclairJS-Nashorn*) walks you through the setup process.

 While Eclair JS presents some interesting novel ideas, it has been deprecated.

Spark on the Common Language Runtime (CLR)—C# and Friends

Microsoft's Mobius project (*https://github.com/Microsoft/Mobius*) provides C# bindings for working with Apache Spark. The general design is similar to that of PySpark, with the internals of `PythonRDD` instead communicating with the CLR. As with PySpark, RDD transformations involve copying the data from the JVM, and `Data Frame` transformations that don't use UDFs in C# don't require copying the data on the workers (or even launching the CLR). If you are curious about using Mobius you can check out the design documents (*https://github.com/Microsoft/Mobius/tree/ master/docs*) and examples (*https://github.com/Microsoft/Mobius/tree/master/exam ples*).

Calling Other Languages from Spark

In addition to using other languages to call Spark, we can *call* other languages from Spark.

Using Pipe and Friends

If there aren't existing wrappers for the language you are working with, one of the simplest options is using Spark's `pipe` interface. To use the `pipe` interface you start by converting your RDDs into a format in which they can be sent over a Unix pipe. Often simple formats like JSON or CSV are used for communicating, as lightweight libraries exist for generating and parsing these records in many languages.

Let's return to the Goldilocks example from "The Goldilocks Example" on page 129. Suppose that in addition to optimal panda porridge temperature, you also wanted to find out which pandas had been commenting on Spark PRs;[4] you might cook up a

---

4 This is somewhat of a stretch as far as the relationship to Goldilocks goes, but you know.

quick little Perl script, as in Example 7-11. Later on, if you want to use this script in Spark you can use the pipe command to call your Perl script from the workers. Since pipe only works with strings, you will need to format your inputs as a string and parse the result string back into the correct data type, as in Example 7-12.

Example 7-11. Perl script to be called from pipe

```perl
#!/usr/bin/perl
use strict;
use warnings;

use Pithub;
use Data::Dumper;

# Find all of the commentors on an issue
my $user = $ENV{'user'};
my $repo = $ENV{'repo'};
my $p = Pithub->new(user => $user, repo => $repo);
while (my $id = <>) {
    chomp ($id);
    my $issue_comments = $p->issues->comments->list(issue_id => $id);
    print $id;
    while (my $comment = $issue_comments->next) { print " ".$comment->{"user"}->{"login"};
    }
    print "\n";
}
```

Example 7-12. Using pipe (from Scala Spark) to talk to a Perl program on the workers

```scala
def lookupUserPRS(sc: SparkContext, input: RDD[Int]): RDD[(Int, List[String])] = {
  // Copy our script to the worker nodes with sc.addFile
  // Add file requires absolute paths
  val distScriptName = "ghinfo.pl"
  val userDir = System.getProperty("user.dir")
  val localScript = s"${userDir}/src/main/perl/${distScriptName}"
  val addedFile = sc.addFile(localScript)

  // Pass enviroment variables to our worker
  val enviromentVars = Map("user" -> "apache", "repo" -> "spark")
  val result = input.map(x => x.toString)
    .pipe(SparkFiles.get(distScriptName), enviromentVars)
  // Parse the results
  result.map{record =>
    val elems: Array[String] = record.split(" ")
    (elems(0).toInt, elems.slice(1, elems.size).sorted.distinct.toList)
  }
}
```

Spark will not automatically copy your script to the worker machines, so if you are calling a custom program you can use the `sc.addFile` interface as in Example 7-12. Otherwise (e.g., if you are calling a systemwide program), just skip that part.

PySpark and SparkR both use specialized version of the Piped RDDs for communication on the workers.

Make sure that you handle empty partitions, since your program will be called even for empty partitions (although this functionality may change in future versions).

JNI

The Java Native Interface (JNI) is another option for interfacing with other languages. JNI can work well for calling certain C/C++ libraries, as well as other statically compiled languages like FORTRAN. While JNI doesn't exactly suffer from double serialization in the same way calling PySpark or using `pipe` does, you still need to copy your data out of the JVM and back.

This is why some libraries, such as JBLAS (*http://jblas.org/*), implement some components inside of the JVM, since once copy cost is added, the performance benefit of native code can go away.

To illustrate how to use JNI with Spark, consider calling a very simple C function that sums all of the nonzero inputs. Its function signature is shown in Example 7-13.

Example 7-13. Simple C header

```
#ifndef _SUM_H
#define _SUM_H

int sum(int input[], int num_elem);

#endif /* _SUM_H */
```

You can write the JNI specification to call this in either Java (Example 7-14) or Scala (Example 7-15). Although the tooling for Java can be a bit simpler, there is no significant difference between them.

Example 7-14. Simple Java JNI

```
class SumJNIJava {
  public static native Integer sum(Integer[] array);
}
```

Example 7-15. Simple Scala JNI

```
class SumJNI {
  @native def sum(n: Array[Int]): Int
}
```

 Manually writing wrappers takes effort. Check out SWIG (*http://www.swig.org/*) to automatically generate parts of your bindings.

Once you have your C function and your JNI class specification, you need to generate your class files and from them generate the binder heading (see Example 7-16). The javah command will take the class files and generate headers that is then used to create a C-side wrapper.

Example 7-16. Generate header with the command-line interface

```
javah -classpath ./target/examples-0.0.1.jar \
com.highperformancespark.examples.ffi.SumJNI
```

For those of you building with SBT, Jakob Odersky's sbt-jni package makes it easy to integrate your native code with your Scala project. sbt-jni is published as an SBT plug-in like spark-packages-sbt, and is included by adding an entry to *project/ plugins.sbt* as shown in Example 7-17.

Example 7-17. Add sbt-jni plug-in to project/plugins.sbt

```
addSbtPlugin("ch.jodersky" %% "sbt-jni" % "1.0.0-RC3")
```

sbt-jni simplifies generating the header file by adding the javah target to sbt, which will generate the header files and place them in *./target/native/include/*.

Once we have our header file we need to write a wrapper in C. The generated header file shouldn't be modified, but rather imported into our shim as shown in Example 7-18.

Example 7-18. JNI C shim

```c
#include "sum.h"
#include "include/com_highperformancespark_examples_ffi_SumJNI.h"
#include <ctype.h>
#include <jni.h>

/*
 * Class:     com_highperformancespark_examples_ffi_SumJNI
 * Method:    sum
 * Signature: ([I)I
 */
JNIEXPORT jint JNICALL Java_com_highperformancespark_examples_ffi_SumJNI_sum
(JNIEnv *env, jobject obj, jintArray ja) {
  jsize size = (*env)->GetArrayLength(env, ja);
  jint *a = (*env)->GetIntArrayElements(env, ja, 0);
  return sum(a, size);
}
```

sbt-jni also simplifies building and packaging native code, adding nativeCompile, javah, and packageBin to allow you to easily build an assembly JAR with both your native files and Java artifacts. For sbt-jni to build your native code (in addition to the JVM code) as well, you need to provide a Makefile. If you are starting with a new project, nativeInit CMake target will generate a skeleton *CMakeLists.txt* file you can use as a basis for your native build.

 In our example project, we've built the native code along with the Scala code. Alternatively, especially if you plan to support multiple architectures, you may wish to create a separate package for your native code.

If your artifact is built with sbt-jni you can use the nativeLoader decorator from ch.jodersky.jni.nativeLoader to automatically load your native code as needed. In the example we've been working on, our library is called libhigh-performance-spark0 so we can have it automatically loaded by adding the decorator to our SumJNI class, as in Example 7-19.

Example 7-19. Native Loader decorator

```
@nativeLoader("high-performance-spark0")
```

If you are working in Java, or just want more control, you can use System.loadLibrary, which takes a library name and searches java.library.path or System.load with an absolute path.

Leave off the "lib" prefix, which `loadLibrary` (and `sbt-jni`) automatically append, or you will get confusing runtime linking errors.

The Oracle JNI specification (*https://docs.oracle.com/javase/8/docs/technotes/guides/jni/spec/jniTOC.html*) can be a useful reference.

If your native library likely isn't packaged in your JAR, you need to make sure the JVM running the Spark worker is able to call it. If your library is already installed on the workers you can add `-Djava.library.path=...` to your `spark.executor.extraJavaOptions`.

Java Native Access (JNA)

Java Native Access (JNA) (*https://github.com/java-native-access/jna*) is a community-driven alternative to JNI to allow calling of native code, ideally without all of the boilerplate required by JNI. Although JNA is a community package this does not mean it is low quality; it is used by a variety of mature projects and has been used by Spark application developers. We can use JNA to call our previous example in both Scala (Example 7-20) and Java.

Example 7-20. Scala simple JNA

```scala
import com.sun.jna._
object SumJNA {
  Native.register("high-performance-spark0")
  @native def sum(n: Array[Int], size: Int): Int
}
```

It's important to note that these JNA examples skip the requirement for writing the JNI wrapper (as in Example 7-18) and instead directly call the C function for us. While SWIG can do a good job of generating much of the JNI wrappers, for some this is a compelling reason to use JNA over JNI.

When using JNA, `jna.boot.library.path` allows you to add libraries to the search path *before* the system library path.

Underneath Everything Is FORTRAN

A surprising number of numeric computing libraries still have FORTRAN implementations. Thankfully many of these libraries already have Java or Python wrappers, which greatly simplify our access. These libraries often can make intelligent decisions about what operations are worth the overhead of copying our data into FORTRAN and what operations make more sense to be implemented in the host language. Not all FORTRAN code already has wrappers, and you may find yourself in a place with which you want to interface.

The general process is to first create a C/C++ wrapper that exposes the FORTRAN code for Java to call, and then link the C/C++ code together with the FORTRAN code. Continuing the sum example in FORTRAN (Example 7-21), you would create a C wrapper like Example 7-22, and then follow the existing steps for calling a C library in "JNI" on page 195.

Example 7-21. FORTRAN sum function

```
INTEGER FUNCTION SUMF(N,A) BIND(C, NAME='sumf')
INTEGER A(N)
SUMF=SUM(A)
END
```

Example 7-22. C wrapper for FORTRAN sum function

```
// Fortran routine
extern int sumf(int *, int[]);

// Call the fortran code which expects by reference size
int wrap_sum(int input[], int size) {
  return sumf(&size, input);
}
```

 If you like sbt-jni you can extend the generated CMake file to also compile your FORTRAN code.

These wrappers can also be automatically generated with programs like fortrwrap (*http://fortwrap.sourceforge.net/*), or skipped entirely with JNA. Calling the FORTRAN function with JNA is very similar to calling the C function, as shown in Example 7-23.

Example 7-23. FORTRAN SUMF through JNA

```
import com.sun.jna._
import com.sun.jna.ptr._
object SumFJNA {
  Native.register("high-performance-spark0")
  @native def sumf(n: IntByReference, a: Array[Int]): Int
  def easySum(size: Int, a: Array[Int]): Int = {
    val ns = new IntByReference(size)
    sumf(ns, a)
  }
}
```

Calling FORTRAN code from the JVM is more difficult than calling C code. If available, it's often better to use existing wrappers as they can make intelligent decisions about which components to execute in FORTRAN rather than in the JVM.

Getting to the GPU

GPUs are another great way of working with parallel, numeric computing problems. They have been shown to be particularly effective at certain types of machine learning problems. Some single-node distributed systems exist just to coordinate the work of multiple GPUs. If your problem is well suited to GPU acceleration, the performance improvement can be huge (SparkGPULR (*https://github.com/kiszk/spark-gpu/ blob/dev/examples/src/main/scala/org/apache/spark/examples/SparkGPULR.scala*) showed a 3× improvement).

The GPUEnabler (*https://github.com/IBMSparkGPU/GPUEnabler*) Spark package exists to simplify interfacing Spark with CUDA. The package simplifies the setup of JCUDA and automates converting your data into a columnar format for working on GPUs.

 Some people (*https://iamtrask.github.io/2014/11/22/spark-gpu/*) have also used aparapi (*https://github.com/aparapi/aparapi*) to automate compilation of Java code to OpenCL (*https://en.wikipe dia.org/wiki/OpenCL*), although no packages exist to simplify the integration currently.

At present there is no unified way inside of Apache Spark to perform GPU acceleration, with competing proposals from IBM (spark-gpu (*https://github.com/kiszk/ spark-gpu*)), Adobe (spark-gpu (*https://github.com/adobe-research/spark-gpu*)), and others.

For those interested you may wish to follow SPARK-12620 (*https://issues.apache.org/jira/browse/SPARK-12620*) and friends.

The Future

Tungsten has the ability to store data off-heap with Spark, but the data format is currently not stable or sufficiently documented to enable shared access from other languages. Two possibilities exist to improve this: either the standardization of Tungsten, SPARK-9697 (*https://issues.apache.org/jira/browse/SPARK-9697*), or the integration of Arrow in Python and Spark, SPARK-13534 (*https://issues.apache.org/jira/browse/SPARK-13534*). Hopefully future editions of this book will be able to report the awesomeness that these changes have enabled.

Conclusion

Writing high-performance Spark code need not be limited to Scala, let alone the JVM (although it can certainly make things easier). Spark has a wide variety of language bindings, both built-in and third party, and can interface with even more languages using JNI, JNA, pipes, or sockets. For some operations, the cost of copying the data outside of the JVM and back can be more expensive than just doing the operation in the JVM—even with specialized libraries—so it is important to consider the complexity of your transformations before going outside of the JVM. While not currently supported, Tungsten's off-heap support may eventually standardize in such a way as to better support language interoperability on the workers.

## CHAPTER 8

Testing and Validation

Automated testing in the world of Spark is often overlooked, but with long batch jobs and complex streaming setup, manually verifying functionality is time-consuming and error prone. Having effective tests allows us to develop faster and simplify when refactoring for performance.

Tests that verify performance pose some additional challenges, especially in distributed systems. However, by using Spark's counters we can get the execution time statistics from all the workers, the number of records processed, and the number of records shuffled. These counters can serve the same purpose as system timings on a single machine system.

Testing is an excellent way for catching the kinds of errors that we can conceive of. Beyond that, the real world is often able to come up with new and exciting ways to make our software fail, and sometimes it isn't as obvious as a null pointer exception. In these cases, it is important that we are able to detect the error state, in order to avoid making decisions with faulty models.

Unit Testing

Unit testing allows us to focus on testing small components of functionality with complex dependencies (such as data sources), often mocked out. Unit tests are generally faster than integration tests and are frequently used during development. If you are willing to do some refactoring, you can test a lot of your code without any special considerations related to Spark. For the rest of your code, libraries can greatly simplify the process.

General Spark Unit Testing

Depending on how our Spark job is written, the smallest components of it can be tested without any Spark dependencies. For testing the data flow of our Spark job itself, we will need a `SparkContext` to create testing RDDs or DStreams with local collections. From there we can apply our transformations, comparing the results locally with our unit testing framework of choice.

Factoring your code for testability

Since many of Spark's transformations take in functions that operate on individual elements or iterators of partitions, we can test those functions (Example 8-1) without having to create an RDD or use a `SparkContext`, unlike Example 8-2.

Example 8-1. Easy-to-test inner function

```
def tokenizeRDD(input: RDD[String]) = {
  input.flatMap(tokenize)
}

protected[tokenize] def tokenize(input: String) = {
  input.split(" ")
}
```

Example 8-2. Hard-to-test inner function

```
def difficultTokenizeRDD(input: RDD[String]) = {
  input.flatMap(_.split(" "))
}
```

Thinking back to our Goldilocks example, one of the components that retrieves the provided indexes inside of partition could be tested in this way (see Example 6-25 in Chapter 6). When your code is factored this way, you can use the normal unit testing that you are familiar with. Readability is another good reason to avoid using Scala's anonymous function syntax when your functions get too complicated.

> Even when you can factor your helper functions to test the internal logic of your transformations separately, it is still a good practice to ensure that you test with RDDs or DStreams in order to catch potential serialization errors.

Regular Spark jobs (testing with RDDs)

In addition to testing the functions that you provide to Spark's transformations, it's important that you test the logic expressed through these transformations as well. A simple way to test transformations is to create a `SparkContext`, `parallelize` the input, apply your transformations, and collect the results locally for comparison with the expected value (Example 8-3).

Example 8-3. Simple Spark unit test

```scala
class QuantileOnlyArtisanalTest extends FunSuite with BeforeAndAfterAll {
  @transient private var _sc: SparkContext = _
  def sc: SparkContext = _sc

  val conf = new SparkConf().setMaster("local[4]").setAppName("test")

  override def beforeAll() {
    _sc = new SparkContext(conf)
    super.beforeAll()
  }

  val inputList = List(GoldiLocksRow(0.0, 4.5, 7.7, 5.0),
    GoldiLocksRow(4.0, 5.5, 0.5, 8.0),
    GoldiLocksRow(1.0, 5.5, 6.7, 6.0),
    GoldiLocksRow(3.0, 5.5, 0.5, 7.0),
    GoldiLocksRow(2.0, 5.5, 1.5, 7.0)
  )

  val expectedResult = Map[Int, Set[Double]](
    0 -> Set(1.0, 2.0),
    1 -> Set(5.5, 5.5),
    2 -> Set(0.5, 1.5),
    3 -> Set(6.0, 7.0))

  test("Goldilocks naive Solution"){
    val sqlContext = new SQLContext(sc)
    val input = sqlContext.createDataFrame(inputList)
    val whileLoopSolution = GoldilocksWhileLoop.findRankStatistics(
      input, List(2L, 3L)).mapValues(_.toSet)
    val inputAsKeyValuePairs = GoldilocksGroupByKey.mapToKeyValuePairs(input)
    val groupByKeySolution = GoldilocksGroupByKey.findRankStatistics(
      inputAsKeyValuePairs, List(2L,3L)).mapValues(_.toSet)
    assert(whileLoopSolution == expectedResult)
    assert(groupByKeySolution == expectedResult)
  }

  override def afterAll() {
    // We clear the driver port so that we don't try and bind to the same port on
    // restart.
    sc.stop()
    System.clearProperty("spark.driver.port")
    _sc = null
    super.afterAll()
  }
}
```

The one unexpected bit in Example 8-3 is where we clear the port; this is done so that if we run many Spark tests in sequence, they will not bind to the same port. This will result in an exception trying to bind to a port that is already in use.

If the data has become too large to directly call collect, you can use toLocalItera tor, which only brings back a single partition at a time. If you are dealing with a process that creates a very large RDD, the techniques for comparing RDDs (introduced in "Computing RDD Difference" on page 213 and "Integration Testing" on page 216) can also be used, but this may also be a sign that your data test size has exceeded that of unit testing.

 toLocalIterator can trigger multiple evaluations so make sure to cache or persist the RDD it is called on.

Streaming

Testing Spark Streaming requires special work to create test streams, collect the data locally to verify the results are as expected, and determine test completion. If it fits your application well, the spark-testing-base library provides a wrapper that allows you to write your tests by simply specifying the input and the expected output.

Creating input streams can be done quickly with queueStream (Example 8-4). However, the resulting streams (since Spark 1.4.1) do not support operations that require checkpointing (such as windowing or updateStateByKey). For a more complete local test stream, we can create a custom InputDStream or use fileStream or rawSocket Stream, and write our input data to either the local filesystem or socket. If you are using spark-testing-base, TestInputStream works like a checkpointable version of queueStream (Example 8-5).

Example 8-4. Creating a non-checkpointable input DStream

```
def makeSimpleQueueStream(ssc: StreamingContext) = {
  val input = List(List("hi"), List("happy pandas", "sad pandas"))
    .map(sc.parallelize(_))
  val idstream = ssc.queueStream(Queue(input:_*))
}
```

Example 8-5. Creating a checkpointable input DStream using spark-testing-base

```
/**
 * Create an input stream for the provided input sequence. This is done using
 * TestInputStream as queueStreams are not checkpointable.
 */
```

```
private[holdenkarau] def createTestInputStream[T: ClassTag](
    sc: SparkContext,
    ssc_ : TestStreamingContext,
    input: Seq[Seq[T]]): TestInputStream[T] = {
  new TestInputStream(sc, ssc_, input, numInputPartitions)
}
```

Compared to creating the input data, collecting the results from streaming is quite simple. The simplest solution is to use something like an `ArrayBuffer` along with `foreachRDD` to collect the results (Example 8-6).

Example 8-6. Collect results

```
class TestOutputStream[T: ClassTag](parent: DStream[T],
  val output: ArrayBuffer[Seq[T]] = ArrayBuffer[Seq[T]]()) extends Serializable {

  parent.foreachRDD{(rdd: RDD[T], time) =>
    val collected = rdd.collect()
    output += collected
  }

}
```

Figuring out when your streaming test is over is somewhat more challenging. A simple approach is to wait for the number of collected results to match the expected value along with a timeout as a backup. However, this can lead to flaky tests if you don't choose your timeout well (Example 8-7). A custom manual clock can be used to control Spark Streaming's processing, but this solution requires extending many internals that may change between versions.

Example 8-7. Artisanal streaming test (flaky and does not support windowing or similar operations)

```
test("artisinal streaming test") {
  val ssc = new StreamingContext(sc, Seconds(1))
  val input = List(List("hi"), List("happy pandas", "sad pandas"))
    .map(sc.parallelize(_))
  // Note: does not work for windowing or checkpointing
  val idstream = ssc.queueStream(Queue(input:_*))
  val tdstream = idstream.filter(_.contains("pandas"))
  val result = ArrayBuffer[String]()
  tdstream.foreachRDD{(rdd: RDD[String], _) =>
    result ++= rdd.collect()
  }
  val startTime = System.currentTimeMillis()
  val maxWaitTime = 60 * 60 * 30
  ssc.start()
  while (result.size < 2 && System.currentTimeMillis() - startTime < maxWaitTime) {
    ssc.awaitTerminationOrTimeout(50)
```

```
  }
  ssc.stop(stopSparkContext = false)
  assert(List("happy pandas", "sad pandas") === result.toList)
}
```

For simplicity, spark-testing-base provides two streaming test base classes: `Streaming SuiteBase` for transformations and `StreamingActionBase` for actions. This allows you to write tests for transformations by specifying the expected input and output (Example 8-8). The library then takes care of interfacing with the internals.

Example 8-8. StreamingSuiteBase example test

```
test("really simple transformation") {
  val input = List(List("hi"), List("hi holden"), List("bye"))
  val expected = List(List("hi"), List("hi", "holden"), List("bye"))
  testOperation[String, String](input, tokenize _, expected, ordered = false)
}

// This is the sample function we are testing
def tokenize(f: DStream[String]): DStream[String] = {
  f.flatMap(_.split(" "))
}
```

Mocking RDDs

Testing with a `SparkContext` involves overhead: you need to create a local Spark cluster. This overhead can slow your tests down, especially when using frameworks like scalacheck that generate hundreds of tests. For tests that are focused on testing the business logic rather than the specifics of your interactions with Spark (like serializability), mock RDDs can offer the ability to run more tests faster.

While testing with mock RDDs can be a great way to quickly test your business logic, the testing is not as complete since it avoids testing the serialization and other Spark interactions. Daniel Westheide has made a library called kontextfrei (*https:// github.com/dwestheide/kontextfrei*) to support a number of operations on mock RDDs.

kontextfrei is a Scala-only library that enables to you to write the business logic and test code of your Spark application without depending on RDDs, but using the same API. To get a fast feedback loop during development, you can then execute those tests against fast Scala collections locally, and against RDDs on your CI server, to make sure you don't have any serializability issues.

Testing DataFrames

The primary additional complexity when testing with `DataFrames` is figuring out when our result matches our expected value. At its simplest, if we only have a few columns we care about, we can just extract the elements and compare them. This can quickly get tedious with complex DataFrames, so we can also compare against expected rows (Example 8-9).

Example 8-9. Check DataFrame for row equality

```
test("verify exact equality") {
  // test minHappyPandas
  val inputDF = sqlContext.createDataFrame(pandaInfoList)
  val result = HappyPandas.minHappyPandas(inputDF, 2)
  val resultRows = result.collect()

  val expectedRows = List(Row(sandiego, "red", 2, 3))
  assert(expectedRows === resultRows)
}
```

 Row equality works most of the time, but with ByteArrays simple Scala quality is insufficient. In that case, the values must be compared.

Since DataFrames often have floating-point data in them, pure equality may not be enough. We can use approxEqualDataFrames from spark-testing-base, which compares two DataFrames for approximate equality (Example 8-10), or compare individual elements as in Example 8-11.

Example 8-10. Compare two DataFrames for approximate equality

```
test("verify simple happy pandas Percentage") {
  val expectedList = List(Row(toronto, 0.5),
    Row(sandiego, 2/3.0),
    Row(virginia, 1/10.0))
  val expectedDf = createDF(expectedList, ("place", StringType),
                                          ("percentHappy", DoubleType))

  val inputDF = sqlContext.createDataFrame(pandaInfoList)
  val resultDF = HappyPandas.happyPandasPercentage(inputDF)

  assertDataFrameApproximateEquals(expectedDf, resultDF, 1E-5)
}
```

Example 8-11. Approximate equality using Scalatest +- Matcher on a row element

```
assert(expectedRows.length === resultRows.length)
expectedRows.zip(resultRows).foreach{case (r1, r2) =>
  assert(r1(0) === r2(0))
```

```
    assert(r1.getDouble(1) === (r2.getDouble(1) +- 0.001))
  }
```

Besides the different steps for equality checking, we also need to make the SQLCon text for our test suite. We can construct the SQLContext in beforeAll, as we did with the SparkContext in Example 8-3.

Getting Test Data

So far, we've focused on using small sample test data you create by hand. This can work well for basic unit testing, but many bugs in Spark require larger datasets to uncover. Without enough (varied) data you won't be able to discover unbalanced partitioning, incorrect handling of empty partitions, and other issues.

An excellent source of test data is sampling production data, although this is often not possible due to legal and privacy concerns. Sampled production data is in many ways the gold standard; you don't have to worry about generating data that isn't representative.

When you need to test on datasets too large to generate or store on a single machine, Spark's MLlib provides customizable distributed random RDD generators. With these generators it's useful to try and at least get a distribution of your real production data, so that any issues related to skew will be properly discovered during testing.

In addition to explicitly generating large datasets, another technique is property-based checkers where you specify invariants about your code, and you delegate the generation of test inputs to the property checker. These property checkers, if well constructed, can use Spark's built-in tools for random generation to generate truly large-scale data for testing.

Generating Large Datasets

Often, when tracking down performance issues, you will require large datasets for testing. Since problems often arise with key or data skew, it's important to understand the distribution of the data you are looking to generate, as discussed in Chapter 6.

Thinking back to our Goldilocks example, if we had our porridge organized by zip code (or any market data by zip code), we would end up with some zip codes having a large amount of information relative to the others.

Spark has some built-in components for generating random RDDs in the RandomRDDs (*http://bit.ly/2oZcJnf*) object in mllib. There are built-in generator functions for exponential, gamma, logNormal, normal, poisson, and uniform distributions as both RDDs of doubles and RDDs of vectors. If you have data for multiple distributions (as we do in Goldilocks), you can generate the different components and zip them together as in Example 8-12. For more complex data types, or for different distributions, we can implement our own element generator by extending `RandomDataGenerator`.

 New versions of spark-testing-base use `RandomRDDs` as their base to support generating datasets too large for your local machine. Some other property-checking libraries do not yet support this.

Example 8-12. Generate some performance scale data for our Goldilocks example

```
/**
 * Generate a Goldilocks data set all with the same id.
 * We expect the zip code to follow an exponential
 * distribution and the data its self to be normal.
 * Simplified to avoid a 3-way zip.
 *
 * Note: May generate less than number of requested rows due to
 * different distribution between partitions and zip being computed
 * per partition.
 */
def generateGoldilocks(sc: SparkContext, rows: Long, numCols: Int):
    RDD[RawPanda] = {
  val zipRDD = RandomRDDs.exponentialRDD(sc, mean = 1000,  size = rows)
    .map(_.toInt.toString)
  val valuesRDD = RandomRDDs.normalVectorRDD(
    sc, numRows = rows, numCols = numCols)
  zipRDD.zip(valuesRDD).map{case (z, v) =>
    RawPanda(1, z, "giant", v(0) > 0.5, v.toArray)
  }
}
```

The spark-sql-perf project (*https://github.com/databricks/spark-sql-perf*), from Databricks, provides another example of generating a large, scaled-out dataset for testing. If it's easier to specify with ScalaCheck you can also make a dummy test to save the data out and use it later.

Sampling

If it's available as an option to you, sampling your production data can be a great source of test data. Spark's core RDD and Pair RDD functionality both support customizable random samples. When our work depends on joins between multiple tables, it is important to join from our sampled table to make sure we have all of the records we need.

The simplest method for sampling, directly on the RDD class, is the function `sample`, which takes `withReplacement: Boolean, fraction: Double, seed: Long` (optional) (Example 8-13). This allows us to specify the percentage of data we want and creates a sample without any special considerations.

Example 8-13. Basic RDD sample

```
rdd.sample(withReplacement=false, fraction=0.1)
```

The size of the result of `sample` is specified as a fraction of the input: if you need to upsample, the fraction can be set to >1 if `with Replacement` is enabled.

Under the hood, depending on if you sample with replacement or not, `sample` constructs a `PartitionwiseSampledRDD` with two different samplers (poisson or bernoulli). If you need more control, you can directly construct a `Partition wiseSampleRDD` with your own sampler, provided it implements the `RandomSampler` trait from `org.apache.spark.util.random`.

Sampling has other uses, too, especially in machine learning. Sometimes it's useful to have a sample from X (e.g., `s` is some elements of X) and its inverse (`i` is the set of X that is not in `s`), and in that case manually constructing a `PartitionwiseSampledRDD` will allow you to use the `cloneComplement()` function on your sampler to construct an inverse `PartitionwiseSampledRDD`.

When working with data of multiple classes, it's often important to ensure that you have some representation from each class. `sampleByKeyExact` and `sampleByKey` take in a map of the percentage for each key to keep allowing you to perform stratified sampling (Example 8-14). Depending on your needs, your sample could be done to try to represent the key distribution in the input or population set, or to try to create a balanced sample of an unbalanced population (HAM/SPAM), or to look at some percentage of users from each locale to validate your handling of different locales.

Example 8-14. Stratified sample

```
// 5% of the red pandas, and 50% of the giant pandas
val stratas = Map("red" -> 0.05, "giant" -> 0.50)
rdd.sampleByKey(withReplacement=false, fractions = stratas)
```

Sometimes you will want to go beyond sampling returning a single RDD, and sample into many different RDDs at a time. The `randomSplit` function takes an array of weights and returns an array of RDDs with elements proportional to those weights.

DataFrames also have `sample` and `randomSplit` available directly on them. If you want to perform stratified sampling on `DataFrames`, you must convert them to an RDD first.

Property Checking with ScalaCheck

ScalaCheck (*https://www.scalacheck.org/*) is a property-based testing library for Scala similar to Haskell's QuickCheck (*https://hackage.haskell.org/package/QuickCheck*). Property-based testing allows you to specify invariants about your code (for example, all of the outputs should have the substring "panda") and lets the testing library generate different types of test input for you. Two libraries, sscheck (*https://github.com/juanrh/sscheck*) and spark-testing-base (*https://github.com/holdenk/spark-testing-base*), implement generators for Spark. A property-based check with spark-testing-base is shown in Example 8-15.

Example 8-15. ScalaCheck property-based test example

```
// A trivial property that the map doesn't change the number of elements
test("map should not change number of elements") {
  val property =
    forAll(RDDGenerator.genRDD[String](sc)(Arbitrary.arbitrary[String])) {
      rdd => rdd.map(_.length).count() == rdd.count()
    }

  check(property)
}
```

ScalaCheck will automatically generate a number of common edge conditions, but we can also specify inputs that we think are likely to cause trouble. This is the technique used by the generator itself to create RDDs with varying partition sizes, with a bias toward creating some empty partitions.

Computing RDD Difference

Bringing data back locally works really well if your test data is small enough to collect back to a local machine. If you are running your tests on a cluster and have a larger dataset you instead need to compute the difference between the RDDs directly—without bringing the full data back to the driver.

Most of your unit tests should be able to be done with just `parallelize` and `collect`; however, RDD equality, like general collection equality, has a few different possibilities. The two cases we will examine are order matters, and the order does not matter.

Let's start with comparing two RDDs where we expect the order to be the same (Example 8-16). This would be the case if we had called `sortByKey`, as we do in

Goldilocks after counting the unique values. If the partitioner is the same we can `zip` the two RDDs together and compare the elements directly without doing a shuffle. Otherwise, we just repartition one of the RDDs to match the other.

Example 8-16. Comparing RDDs with order

```
/**
 * Asserts two RDDs are equal (with the same order).
 * If they are equal assertion succeeds, otherwise assertion fails.
 */
def assertRDDEqualsWithOrder[T: ClassTag](
  expected: RDD[T], result: RDD[T]): Unit = {
  assertTrue(compareRDDWithOrder(expected, result).isEmpty)
}

/**
 * Compare two RDDs with order (e.g. [1,2,3] != [3,2,1])
 * If the partitioners are not the same this requires multiple passes
 * on the input.
 * If they are equal returns None, otherwise returns Some with the first mismatch.
 * If the lengths are not equal, one of the two components may be None.
 */
def compareRDDWithOrder[T: ClassTag](
  expected: RDD[T], result: RDD[T]): Option[(Option[T], Option[T])] = {
  // If there is a known partitioner just zip
  if (result.partitioner.map(_ == expected.partitioner.get).getOrElse(false)) {
    compareRDDWithOrderSamePartitioner(expected, result)
  } else {
    // Otherwise index every element
    def indexRDD[T](rdd: RDD[T]): RDD[(Long, T)] = {
      rdd.zipWithIndex.map { case (x, y) => (y, x) }
    }
    val indexedExpected = indexRDD(expected)
    val indexedResult = indexRDD(result)
    indexedExpected.cogroup(indexedResult).filter { case (_, (i1, i2)) =>
      i1.isEmpty || i2.isEmpty || i1.head != i2.head
    }.take(1).headOption.
      map { case (_, (i1, i2)) =>
        (i1.headOption, i2.headOption) }.take(1).headOption
  }
}

/**
 * Compare two RDDs. If they are equal returns None, otherwise
 * returns Some with the first mismatch. Assumes we have the same partitioner.
 */
def compareRDDWithOrderSamePartitioner[T: ClassTag](
  expected: RDD[T], result: RDD[T]): Option[(Option[T], Option[T])] = {
  // Handle mismatched lengths by converting into options and padding with Nones
  expected.zipPartitions(result) {
    (thisIter, otherIter) =>
```

```
      new Iterator[(Option[T], Option[T])] {
        def hasNext: Boolean = (thisIter.hasNext || otherIter.hasNext)

        def next(): (Option[T], Option[T]) = {
          (thisIter.hasNext, otherIter.hasNext) match {
            case (false, true) => (Option.empty[T], Some(otherIter.next()))
            case (true, false) => (Some(thisIter.next()), Option.empty[T])
            case (true, true) => (Some(thisIter.next()), Some(otherIter.next()))
            case _ => throw new Exception("next called when elements consumed")
          }
        }
      }
    }.filter { case (v1, v2) => v1 != v2 }.take(1).headOption
  }
```

If order does not matter, and the equality operator is sufficient, we can cogroup the two RDDs (along with dummy values), as shown in Example 8-17.

Example 8-17. Comparing RDDs without order

```
/**
  * Asserts two RDDs are equal (unordered).
  * If they are equal assertion succeeds, otherwise assertion fails.
  */
def assertRDDEquals[T: ClassTag](expected: RDD[T], result: RDD[T]): Unit = {
  assertTrue(compareRDD(expected, result).isEmpty)
}


/**
  * Compare two RDDs where we do not require the order to be equal.
  * If they are equal returns None, otherwise returns Some with the first mismatch.
  *
  * @return None if the two RDDs are equal, or Some containing
  *         the first mismatch information.
  *         The mismatch information will be Tuple3 of:
  *         (key, number of times this key occur in expected RDD,
  *         number of times this key occur in result RDD)
  */
def compareRDD[T: ClassTag](expected: RDD[T], result: RDD[T]):
    Option[(T, Int, Int)] = {
  // Key the values and count the number of each unique element
  val expectedKeyed = expected.map(x => (x, 1)).reduceByKey(_ + _)
  val resultKeyed = result.map(x => (x, 1)).reduceByKey(_ + _)
  // Group them together and filter for difference
  expectedKeyed.cogroup(resultKeyed).filter { case (_, (i1, i2)) =>
    i1.isEmpty || i2.isEmpty || i1.head != i2.head
  }
    .take(1).headOption.
    map { case (v, (i1, i2)) =>
      (v, i1.headOption.getOrElse(0), i2.headOption.getOrElse(0)) }
}
```

These examples may not match exactly how you need to test equality, but you should be able to generalize from them. If, for example, you are comparing RDDs of doubles you might sort them and then use a similar function like `compareWithOrder` but check within tolerance rather than exact equality.

 The same general approach works for computing `DataFrame` difference, and is implemented in spark-testing-base through `equalData Frames` and `approxEqualDataFrames`.

Integration Testing

Sometimes simply faking data sources and mocking isn't enough (or becomes too complicated) to test your system. Integration testing tends to be slower than unit testing, and the failures tend to take more time to debug, but it catches a completely different class of bugs. Integration testing can also be combined with some of our performance testing methods mentioned later, to give us an idea of not only the performance of our code but the performance of the entire system.

Choosing Your Integration Testing Environment

At some point we will reach the limit of what we can test with our unit tests. In large-scale data systems, errors in data ingestion or misunderstandings of formats can be a common source of errors, so having some tests of the integration of your systems is important—albeit more challenging.

Local mode

While we've looked at using local mode mostly in the context of unit testing (see "Unit Testing" on page 203), for small enough projects we can use many of the same techniques. Instead of mocking our data sources and using functions like `parallel ize` and `queueStream`, we can set up smaller versions of our data stores and stream sources.

Docker-based

Docker containers provide an easy way to package and distribute multiple virtual lightweight containers, which can vastly simplify automated deployments. This is especially useful for integration testing with distributed systems, like Spark, which require both workers and master node, and whatever services your data requires (e.g., HDFS, Mongo, etc.). Several sample projects exist for setting up Docker-based Spark integration environments, including @cfregley's pipeline project (*https://github.com/*

fluxcapacitor/pipeline/wiki) and Databrick's spark-perf project (*https://github.com/databricks/spark-perf*).

Yarn MiniCluster

Hadoop has built-in testing libraries to set up a local YarnCluster, which can be a lighter-weight alternative to even Docker. If you don't have the resources to set up a full test cluster, or want some medium-weight integration tests, using a Yarn Mini-Cluster can be a good option.

Yarn MiniClusters represent a middle ground and can be set up purely in the JVM. On early (pre-1.6) versions of Spark, Yarn MiniCluster–based tests cannot be easily intermixed with other tests because of persistent global state. An example of how to use Yarn MiniCluster with Spark (*https://github.com/holdenk/spark-testing-base/blob/master/src/main/1.3/scala/com/holdenkarau/spark/testing/SharedMiniCluster.scala*) is available in spark-testing-base (*https://github.com/holdenk/spark-testing-base*).

All of these options limit you to testing on a single machine, which is insufficient to test the ability of your system to scale. Thankfully, Spark's existing standard deployment modes can be used just as easily for integration testing.

> If you have an existing YARN cluster setup, yarn-client mode makes it easy to run integration tests. For users without a long-running cluster, Spark's EC2 scripts make it simple to dynamically set up a cluster as needed. Spark's deployment modes are covered in more detail in Chapter 7 of *Learning Spark*, as well as in the Spark "Cluster Mode Overview" documentation (*http://spark.apache.org/docs/latest/cluster-overview.html*).

Verifying Performance

The primary motivation for using Spark (and reading this book), is the ability to have highly performant processing of big data. Since this is an important motivation behind many people's use of Spark, it's important to verify that your specific use of Spark is performing as expected.

Spark Counters for Verifying Performance

Spark tracks a number of counters during our job, many of which can be useful for debugging performance. You have access to many of the counters in the WebUI, and can get programmatic access to them by registering a `SparkListener` (*http://spark.apache.org/docs/latest/api/scala/index.html#org.apache.spark.scheduler.SparkListener*) to collect the information. Spark uses callbacks to provide the metrics, and for performance info we can get most of what we need through `onTaskEnd`, for which

Spark gives us a `SparkListenerTaskEnd` (*http://spark.apache.org/docs/latest/api/scala/index.html#org.apache.spark.scheduler.SparkListenerTaskEnd*). We can get the bytes read, execution time, records read, and many other important metrics this way (Example 8-18).

Example 8-18. Simple SparkListener for execution time

```scala
class PerfListener extends SparkListener {
  var totalExecutorRunTime = 0L
  var jvmGCTime = 0L
  var recordsRead = 0L
  var recordsWritten = 0L
  var resultSerializationTime = 0L

  /**
   * Called when a task ends
   */
  override def onTaskEnd(taskEnd: SparkListenerTaskEnd) {
    val info = taskEnd.taskInfo
    val metrics = taskEnd.taskMetrics
    updateMetricsForTask(metrics)
  }

  private def updateMetricsForTask(metrics: TaskMetrics): Unit = {
    totalExecutorRunTime += metrics.executorRunTime
    jvmGCTime += metrics.jvmGCTime
    resultSerializationTime += metrics.resultSerializationTime
    recordsRead += metrics.inputMetrics.recordsRead
    recordsWritten += metrics.outputMetrics.recordsWritten
  }
}
```

Using this listener we can quickly validate the overall execution time (Example 8-19).

Example 8-19. Sample execution time test

```scala
test("wordcount perf") {
  val listener = new PerfListener()
  sc.addSparkListener(listener)
  doWork(sc)
  println(listener)
  assert(listener.totalExecutorRunTime > 0)
  assert(listener.totalExecutorRunTime < 10000)
}
```

Projects for Verifying Performance

There are two common projects used for verifying performance of Spark jobs. The spark-perf package (*https://github.com/databricks/spark-perf*), from Databricks, is designed for comparing different versions of Spark but can also be extended to do performance testing of our own code. Spark-perf is written in Python but is primarily used for performance testing Scala code. The Testing Spark: Best Practices (*https:// spark-summit.org/2014/wp-content/uploads/2014/06/Testing-Spark-Best-Practices-Anupama-Shetty-Neil-Marshall.pdf*) talk from Spark Summit 2014 suggests using Gatling (*http://gatling.io*) along with the Spark Jobserver (*https://github.com/spark-jobserver/spark-jobserver*), which allows you to expose Spark jobs as a rest service, for performance testing.

Job Validation

Job validation is an important part of ensuring that the results of your Spark job match your expectations before using the results. Using accumulators you can keep track of information important to your job, such as the number of valid and invalid records, or the number of users for whom you have no recommendations.

You can use some of the same information we examined in "Spark Counters for Verifying Performance" on page 217 to validate your jobs. The same listener can be used, and the results can be aggregated over all the stages.

Spark's accumulators can also be used for validating jobs. A common use case for accumulators is to track the number of invalid records when processing your data. You can use these accumulators beyond just debugging and make them part of an automated validation suite. Since, as explained in "Accumulators" on page 109, Spark accumulators can frequently (and somewhat unpredictably) double count values added to accumulators, it's important for all of your validation rules to be relative (e.g., invalid records / total records).

The spark-validator (*https://github.com/holdenk/spark-validator*) project exists to make writing these rules simple, but as of this writing it is still in its early stages. By writing out values from previous runs you can also create relative rules; for example, the number of records you read from job to job should be within some variance of the average from the previous jobs (Example 8-20).

Example 8-20. Validating a minimum % of valid records with spark-validator

```
val validationRules = List[ValidationRule](
  new AbsolutePercentageRule(
    "invalidRecords", "validRecords", Some(0.0), Some(1.0)))
val vc = new ValidationConf(tempPath, "job_7", true, validationRules)
val sqlCtx = new SQLContext(sc)
val validator = Validation(sqlCtx, vc)

val valid = sc.accumulator(0)
validator.registerAccumulator(valid, "validRecords")
```

```
val invalid = sc.accumulator(0)
validator.registerAccumulator(invalid, "invalidRecords")

runTwoCounterJob(sc, valid, invalid)
```

Conclusion

In this chapter, we have seen how to create tests for both the functionality and performance of our Spark code. We've covered a technique for writing local tests as well as for comparing RDDs and DataFrames when test data is too large. The tests you make using these techniques should let you feel confident as you refactor to apply the performance improvements from the previous chapters.

## CHAPTER 9

Spark MLlib and ML

Spark has two machine learning libraries—Spark MLlib and Spark ML—with very different APIs, but similar algorithms. These machine learning libraries inherit many of the performance considerations of the RDD and Dataset APIs they are based on, but also have their own considerations. MLlib is the first of the two libraries and is entering a maintenance/bug-fix only mode. Normally we would skip discussing Spark MLlib and focus on the new API; however, for existing algorithms not all of the functionality has been ported over to the new Spark ML API. Spark ML is the newer, scikit-learn inspired, machine learning library and is where new active development is taking place.

Choosing Between Spark MLlib and Spark ML

At first glance, the most obvious difference between MLlib and ML is the data types they work on, with MLlib supporting RDDs and ML supporting DataFrames and Datasets. The data format difference isn't all that important since they both deal with RDDs and Datasets of vectors, which are easily represented and converted between the RDD and Dataset formats.

From a design philosophy point of view, Spark's MLlib is focused on providing a core set of algorithms for people to use, while largely leaving the data pipeline, cleaning, preparation, and feature selection problems up to the user. Spark ML instead focuses on exposing a scikit-learn inspired pipeline API for everything from data preparation to model training.

Currently, if you need to do streaming or online training your only option is working with the MLlib APIs. Select algorithms in Spark MLlib support training on streaming data, using the Spark Streaming DStream API we cover in "Stream Processing with Spark" on page 257. Spark ML is still waiting for streaming support (see SPARK-16424 (*https://issues.apache.org/jira/browse/SPARK-16424*)), but as work is still actively progressing on streaming `Datasets`, it is difficult to know when streaming ML will be available.

It is important to keep the future in mind when deciding between MLlib and ML. New features will continue to be developed for Spark ML, which will not be backported to Spark MLlib as it is in a bug-fix only stage.

Spark ML's integrated pipeline API makes it easier to implement meta-algorithms, like parameter search over different components. Both APIs support regression, classification, and clustering algorithms. If you're on the fence for your project, choosing Spark ML is a reasonable default to pick as it is the primary actively developed machine learning library for Spark going forward.

Working with MLlib

Many of the same performance considerations in working with Spark Core also directly apply to working with MLlib. One of the most direct ones is with RDD reuse; many machine learning algorithms depend on iterative computation or optimization, so ensuring your inputs are persisted at the right level can make a huge difference.

Supervised algorithms in the Spark MLlib API are trained on RDDs of labeled points, with unsupervised algorithms using RDDs of vectors. These labeled points and vectors are unique to the MLlib library, and separate from both Scala's vector class and Spark ML's equivalent classes.

Getting Started with MLlib (Organization and Imports)

You can include MLlib in the same way as other Spark components. Its inclusion can be simplified using the steps discussed in "Managing Spark Dependencies" on page 31. The Maven coordinates for Spark 2.2's MLlib are `org.apache.spark:spark-mllib_2.11:2.2.0`.

The imports for MLlib are a little scattered compared to the other Spark components —see the imports used to train a simple classification model in Example 9-1.

Example 9-1. Sample MLlib imports for building a LogisticRegression model

```
import com.github.fommil.netlib.BLAS.{getInstance => blas}
import org.apache.spark.mllib.linalg.Vectors
import org.apache.spark.mllib.classification.{LogisticRegressionWithLBFGS,
  LogisticRegressionModel}
// Rename Vector to SparkVector to avoid conflicts with Scala's Vector class
import org.apache.spark.mllib.linalg.{Vector => SparkVector}
import org.apache.spark.mllib.regression.LabeledPoint
import org.apache.spark.mllib.feature._
```

The individual algorithms are organized by purpose, so regression algorithms live in `org.apache.spark.mllib.regression`, most classification algorithms in `org.apache.spark.mllib.classification`, and clustering algorithms in `org.apache.spark.mllib.clustering`. Tree algorithms (decision tree, random forest, etc.) are stored separately in `org.apache.spark.mllib.tree`. In addition to the traditional machine learning algorithms, `org.apache.spark.mllib.feature` provides a limited set of tools to help with feature preparation.

Some algorithms can be used for both classification and regression, so the same algorithm may appear in both `org.apache.spark.mllib.regression` and `org.apache.spark.mllib.classification`, with different APIs.

The `LabeledPoint` class, which is needed for all of the supervised learning algorithms in MLlib, is in the `org.apache.spark.mllib.regression` package. Vector, which is needed to construct `LabeledPoint` and used directly by clustering algorithms, is in `org.apache.spark.mllib.linalg`.

Throughout the examples in this section, we refer to Spark MLlib's Vector class as "SparkVector" so as not to conflict with Scala's vector class.

Spark's Vector name can easily collide with other packages, including Scala. This can result in confusing error messages.

MLlib Feature Encoding and Data Preparation

Feature selection and scaling require that our data is already in Spark's internal format, so before we cover those, let's look at how to encode data into the required format.

Once the data is encoded, or sometimes during the process, many machine learning data pipelines filter out data to discard invalid or malformed records, which could cause problems in any resulting model. For this step Spark's MLlib package expects you to do your filtering using Spark's RDD transformations.

For many problems, applying some of the techniques for quantiles/ outliers we examined with the Goldilocks problem in "The Goldilocks Example" on page 129 can be a good way to identify outliers and normalize features, although we encourage you to consider approximate algorithms instead.

Once you have done your initial filtering, Spark MLlib provides useful tools to help with feature selection and scaling. These feature transformers can be used to perform feature selection, feature encoding, and scaling.

Don't feel the need to restrict yourself to the feature scaling and encoding tools in MLlib; you can (and maybe should) write your own.

Working with Spark vectors

Spark's internal vector format is distinct from Scala's, and there are separate vector libraries between MLlib and ML. Rather than construct the vectors directly, Spark provides a factory object `org.apache.spark.mllib.linalg.Vector`, which can construct both dense and sparse vectors. If you have an array of features you can directly create a dense Spark vector using `Vector.dense` (Example 9-2).

Example 9-2. Create dense Spark vector

```
def toSparkVectorDense(input: Array[Double]) = {
  Vectors.dense(input)
}
```

If you have a dense vector that you know would be better represented as a sparse vector, you can call `toSparse` on it, or you can directly create a sparse vector by providing a sequence of nonzero (`index`, `value`) tuples with `Vector.sparse`.

Be careful that you are constructing the correct vector types. Import renaming, as done in Example 9-1, can help.

Preparing textual data

Not all features can be directly encoded like this; if you have textual data you need to get it into a numeric format. For encoding textual data, both `Word2Vec` and `HashingTF` are available. `HashingTF` is one of the simplest feature operators as it does not require any training, and can be directly applied to your data. `HashingTF` works on an RDD of Iterable[String], so it is up to you to tokenize your data as you see fit. For simple English text, you can encode it as shown in Example 9-3.

Example 9-3. Simple HashingTF on RDD of Strings

```
def hashingTf(rdd: RDD[String]): RDD[SparkVector] = {
  val ht = new HashingTF()
  val tokenized = rdd.map(_.split(" ").toIterable)
  ht.transform(tokenized)
}
```

 While some of Spark MLlib's encoding tools return a SparkVector, Spark requires one single input vector for all the features (rather than multiple vectors).

While the preceding approach is quite simple, it returns a SparkVector discarding everything besides the HashingTF result. Most likely you have a mix of features and label information you need to preserve, so you won't want to use this directly. Rather than directly using the transform function on RDDs during data preparation, you can use the transform function to encode string records inside of a custom map as in Example 9-4.

Example 9-4. Simple HashingTF on RDD of strings preserving the original record

```
def toVectorPerserving(rdd: RDD[RawPanda]): RDD[(RawPanda, SparkVector)] = {
  val ht = new HashingTF()
  rdd.map{panda =>
    val textField = panda.pt
    val tokenizedTextField = textField.split(" ").toIterable
    (panda, ht.transform(tokenizedTextField))
  }
}
```

 HashingTF changed default hashing algorithms from Scala's hash function to MurmurHash3 in Spark 2.0, so if you're upgrading an existing pipeline you may need to retrain.

Some of the feature transformers, like Word2Vec and normalization, require training, much as a "regular" machine learning model does. The primary difference is that you likely don't want to use their output directly. To train a Word2Vec model you need to tokenize your input, and then simply call fit on an instance of Word2Vec, which will return a Word2VecModel as in Example 9-5.

Example 9-5. Train a Word2Vec model

```
def word2vecTrain(rdd: RDD[String]): Word2VecModel = {
  // Tokenize our data
  val tokenized = rdd.map(_.split(" ").toIterable)
  // Construct our word2vec model
  val wv = new Word2Vec()
  wv.fit(tokenized)
}
```

The resulting Word2VecModel is a little different than most transformers produced by estimators. Most models generated by estimators transform or predict on the same input type, often vectors. Instead, for Word2VecModel, the training requires a field of sentences and the resulting model transforms fields of individual words, as in Example 9-6.

Example 9-6. Use a Word2Vec model

```
def word2vec(sc: SparkContext, rdd: RDD[String]): RDD[SparkVector] = {
  // Tokenize our data
  val tokenized = rdd.map(_.split(" ").toIterable)
  // Construct our word2vec model
  val wv = new Word2Vec()
  val wvm = wv.fit(tokenized)
  val wvmb = sc.broadcast(wvm)
  // WVM can now transform single words
  println(wvm.transform("panda"))
  // Vector size is 100 - we use this to build a transformer on top of WVM that
  // works on sentences.
  val vectorSize = 100
  // The transform function works on a per-word basis, but we have
  // sentences as input.
  tokenized.map{words =>
    // If there is nothing in the sentence output a null vector
    if (words.isEmpty) {
      Vectors.sparse(vectorSize, Array.empty[Int], Array.empty[Double])
    } else {
      // If there are sentences construct a running sum of the
      // vectors for each word
      val sum = Array[Double](vectorSize)
      words.foreach { word =>
        blas.daxpy(
          vectorSize, 1.0, wvmb.value.transform(word).toArray, 1, sum, 1)
      }
      // Then scale it by the number of words
      blas.dscal(sum.length, 1.0 / words.size, sum, 1)
      // And wrap it in a Spark vector
      Vectors.dense(sum)
    }
```

```
    }
  }
```

Broadcasting your model can produce a big performance improvement, especially for potentially large or complex models. In
Example 9-6 we broadcast the model so that each executor would
only have one copy.

Preparing data for supervised learning

To use algorithms on labeled data, you start with creating a `LabeledPoint` with the
label and vector of features. `LabeledPoint` requires that your labels are doubles,
much in the same way the elements in a vector must also be doubles. As with feature
encoding, if your label is numeric the conversion is easy, but for other types a custom
function or similar techniques (such as `StringIndexer`) must be used.

Revisiting our Goldilocks example, we have an array of features about the pandas as
well as a boolean feature indicating if the panda is happy. Assuming the data is
already relatively clean we could get it ready for MLlib to use as in Example 9-7.

Rather than encoding the label as the index zero feature, as in some
systems, Spark and `LabeledPoint` has the label separate.

Example 9-7. RawPanda to LabeledPoint

```
def toLabeledPointWithHashing(rdd: RDD[RawPanda]): RDD[LabeledPoint] = {
  val ht = new HashingTF()
  rdd.map{rp =>
    val hashingVec = ht.transform(rp.pt)
    val combined = hashingVec.toArray ++ rp.attributes
    LabeledPoint(booleanToDouble(rp.happy),
      Vectors.dense(combined))
  }
}
```

If you have string labels you need to work with, one of the simplest approaches to
encoding string labels is to create a map as in Example 9-8.

Example 9-8. Create label lookup

```
def createLabelLookup[T](rdd: RDD[T]): Map[T, Double] = {
  val distinctLabels: Array[T] = rdd.distinct().collect()
  distinctLabels.zipWithIndex
```

```
    .map{case (label, x) => (label, x.toDouble)}.toMap
}
```

Feature Scaling and Selection

Feature scaling and selection can lead to vastly improved results for certain algorithms and optimizers, and MLlib provides a feature transformer to help with this. You *can* skip this step if you're in a rush and just building a toy example, but we encourage you to always consider the features used in your model carefully. Like Word2Vec they need to be trained on your input data, and thankfully the resulting models can be directly used without the same complex logic we added for Word2Vec (see Example 9-9).

Example 9-9. Scale features

```
// Trains a feature scaler and returns the scaler and scaled features
def trainScaler(rdd: RDD[SparkVector]): (StandardScalerModel, RDD[SparkVector]) = {
  val scaler = new StandardScaler()
  val scalerModel = scaler.fit(rdd)
  (scalerModel, scalerModel.transform(rdd))
}
```

> If after feature scaling you find that outliers are throwing off your scaling, then you can go back to the filtering stage.

For feature selection, PCA and ChiSqSelector can be trained on the raw features, which return both transformers as well as information about which features have been selected. See Example 9-10.

Example 9-10. Select top ten features using ChiSqSelector

```
def selectTopTenFeatures(rdd: RDD[LabeledPoint]):
    (ChiSqSelectorModel, Array[Int], RDD[SparkVector]) = {
  val selector = new ChiSqSelector(10)
  val model = selector.fit(rdd)
  val topFeatures = model.selectedFeatures
  val vecs = rdd.map(_.features)
  (model, topFeatures, model.transform(vecs))
}
```

MLlib Model Training

Now that you have your features selected and scaled, it's time to train your model. Most MLlib algorithms present a run, which takes in an RDD of LabeledPoints (supervised algorithms) or Vectors (unsupervised algorithms) and returns a model. Each algorithm has specific parameters that can vastly change the performance,[1] so take the time to review the API documentation for the algorithm you are working with. While configuration provides many benefits, most of the algorithms will work without any specific configuration as shown in Example 9-11.

Example 9-11. Train simple classification model to predict panda happiness

```
def trainModel(rdd: RDD[LabeledPoint]): LogisticRegressionModel = {
  val lr = new LogisticRegressionWithLBFGS()
  val lrModel = lr.run(rdd)
  lrModel
}
```

The preceding model (Example 9-11) is trained using entirely default parameters, such as number of clusters. It is likely that when you are using MLlib in production you will need to set some specific parameters. Unlike models in Spark ML, each model has its own methods for configuration, so you will need to play close attention to Spark's API documentation for the models you are using. We can easily update the Example 9-11 to include an intercept, as in Example 9-12.

Example 9-12. Train simple classification model to predict panda happiness with an intercept

```
def trainModelWithInterept(rdd: RDD[LabeledPoint]): LogisticRegressionModel = {
  val lr = new LogisticRegressionWithLBFGS()
  lr.setIntercept(true)
  val lrModel = lr.run(rdd)
  lrModel
}
```

 One shortcoming of MLlib is that since the parameters do not follow a standard format, meta-algorithms (like parameter search) are difficult to implement, relative to Spark ML, which has a standardized format and parameter search tools.

Predicting

Once you have your model, it's time to use it to predict some results. The simplest way to use your model is to continue to use it inside of the same Spark cluster where it was trained, as this avoids needing to export and load the model. However, many use cases require lower latency than Spark's batch mechanism can support. For most

---

1 Both running time and accuracy/recall.

online prediction, using a Spark cluster is not feasible, unless a micro-batch approach works for you. Spark offers limited support for record-at-a-time prediction, but still requires a local cluster.

Most of the MLlib models have `predict` functions that work on RDDs of SparkVectors, and many also provide an individual `predict` function for use on one vector at a time. This is not true for all models; for example, `LDAModel` has a `topicDistribution` method instead of a `predict` method, so double-check the API documentation for your specific models. Continuing from Example 9-11, you can use the batch prediction API to predict which pandas are happy as in Example 9-13. Once again the batch API isn't well suited to even all batch use cases, as it does not keep the original record around—so you may find using the individual record API a better fit even in batch mode (as with Example 9-4).

Example 9-13. Predict if the pandas are happy

```
def trainModel(rdd: RDD[LabeledPoint]): LogisticRegressionModel = {
  val lr = new LogisticRegressionWithLBFGS()
  val lrModel = lr.run(rdd)
  lrModel
}
```

Some models will attempt to broadcast their internals when used in batch mode, which can reduce overhead. As with the feature transformations, if you need to use the individual predict function inside of a transformation, consider broadcasting the model as well.

Serving and Persistence

Model persistence and serving are closely related, as many deployments need to use a different set of machines for serving than for training. If your only use for your model is for batch prediction on records inside of Spark jobs, you will still likely want to persist your model so you can use it between different Spark jobs.

MLlib provides export support for two formats, a Spark internal format and PMML (Predictive Model Markup Language) (*https://en.wikipedia.org/wiki/Predictive_Model_Markup_Language*). Inside of MLlib, model saving is implemented using the `Saveable` and `PMMLExportable` traits. `Saveable` provides a Spark internal format, which can be read back into Spark easily and is implemented on a variety of models. `Saveable` is also often the more space-efficient option. `PMMLExportable` results in larger outputs than `Saveable`, and surprisingly, the models exported with PMML export cannot be loaded back into Spark. However, PMML exports have the benefit of being able to read into external systems.

Saveable (internal format)

The `Saveable` trait provides a `save` function that takes a `SparkContext` and a target path and writes the model out in a Spark internal format, as illustrated in Example 9-14. The internal format consists of JSON-formatted metadata (the type of model, number of features, and number of classes) and semi-opaque Parquet data representing the model itself. This format is not portable among systems, but is normally readable by newer versions of Spark.

Example 9-14. Exporting a model to Spark's internal format

```
// Save to internal - remote path
model.save(sc, path + "/internal")
```

To load a model stored in Spark's internal format, you call the static `load` method on a companion object of the model. Using the `load` method can be confusing, since the method doesn't always show up in the generated API docs or in your IDE's autocomplete. You can load back the *internal* model that was exported in Example 9-14 with Example 9-15.

Example 9-15. Load back an exported LogisticRegressionModel in Spark's internal format

```
def load(sc: SparkContext, path: String): LogisticRegressionModel = {
  LogisticRegressionModel.load(sc, path + "/internal")
}
```

> If you need to interact with a model outside of Spark that does not have PMML export but is saveable, you can write your own model-loading code to parse Spark's internal format.

PMML

The `PMMLExportable` trait provides a more standardized output format, although it is implemented on a smaller subset of models and cannot be loaded back into Spark directly (Example 9-16).

Example 9-16. Exporting a model to PMML formats

```
// Save to PMML - remote path
model.toPMML(sc, path + "/pmml")
// Save to PMML local path
model.toPMML(path + "/pmml")
```

While Spark provides PMML export support, since it is primarily intended for interfacing with external projects, loading PMML exported models is left up to the downstream consumers.

The JPMML evaluator project can be used to load and evaluate PMML exported models, but is AGPL licensed.

Custom

You need not limit yourself to the built-in storage formats available in Spark, although doing so will often require accessing Spark's internals. Custom exporting requires accessing internal APIs, and is discussed in the context of Spark ML in "General Serving Considerations" on page 252.

Some particularly adventurous users who don't plan to use their models between versions have also had success using Java serialization. This approach is very brittle and will break when upgrading Spark, but for Spark MLlib models without save/load support, using Java serialization can be a quick way to build a proof of concept.

For low latency serving, Spark MLlib may not a be feasible option: in its present incarnation, loading a natively exported Spark model requires using a SparkContext as well as all of the regular Spark dependencies. Some contributors to Spark's ML libraries are investigating separating out the serving code, but this is in its very early stages.

If you have an existing serving system that does not support PMML, another approach is to manually extend the model and write custom export code. This is brittle, as the internals of the way the model is represented may change between versions, but if you only need support for a limited number of models and have an existing serving system in place, it can be a good option.

Model Evaluation

Beyond prediction functionality, many models also contain accuracy information, or other summary statistics that can be interesting as a data scientist (or developer), so take a look at all of the fields of the resulting model. For example, the KMeans model (*http://spark.apache.org/docs/latest/api/scala/index.html#org.apache.spark.mllib.clustering.KMeans*) gives you access to the cluster centers, and the LogisticRegressionModel (*http://spark.apache.org/docs/latest/api/scala/*

index.html#org.apache.spark.mllib.classification.LogisticRegressionModel), that we trained to predict panda happiness in Example 9-12, contains the intercept and feature weights.

 In addition to built-in model summaries, `org.apache.spark.mllib.evaluation` contains tools for calculating a number of different metrics given the predictions and the ground truth. The `MLU tils` object provides a `kfold` function to segment your data for evaluation.

Working with Spark ML

The Spark ML API is built around the concept of a "pipeline" consisting of the different stages. Each stage performs a separate task, and stages exist for tasks ranging from data cleaning, to feature selection, through applying a machine learning algorithm. For those familiar with scikit-learn much of the design will seem familiar. These pipeline stages are grouped into estimators and transformers.

Estimators, such as NaiveBayes, require training before use, whereas transformers, like the vector encoder, can be used directly. The pipeline API makes it easy to use a variety of data preparation and cleaning tools in addition to our standard machine learning algorithms, while also supporting the ability to save the entire pipeline for later use.

Spark ML Organization and Imports

Spark ML and Spark MLlib both live in the same Spark component currently, and in Spark 2.2 its Maven coordinates are `org.apache.spark:spark-mllib_2.11:2.2.0`. Once you have added this to your build, you can start importing the parts of Spark ML relevant to your specific ML task.

The tools for constructing a machine learning pipeline live in the root at `org.apache.spark.ml`. The different algorithm families (classification, regression, recommendation, and clustering) each have their own package under the ML package (e.g., classification algorithms live under `org.apache.spark.ml.classifica tion`). In addition to traditional machine learning algorithms, there is a strong collection of feature transformers under `org.apache.spark.ml.feature` and meta-algorithms under `org.apache.spark.ml.tuning`.

The standard imports are shown in Example 9-17, although you will likely want to avoid the wildcards. In addition to these standard imports, if you need to work with Spark ML's vector class you will likely benefit from using import renaming as shown in Example 9-18.

Example 9-17. Standard imports for Spark ML

```
import org.apache.spark.ml._
import org.apache.spark.ml.feature._
import org.apache.spark.ml.classification._
```

As with Spark's MLlib, Spark ML also has a basic local linear algebra components, which are under `org.apache.spark.ml.linalg`, and starting in Spark 2.0 the linear algebra package is available as a target JAR without dependencies on the rest of Spark. The goal of this package is to eventually help with local serving.

 Throughout the examples in this section we refer to Spark ML's Vector class as "SparkVector" so as not to conflict with Scala's vector class.

Example 9-18. Renamed import for SparkVector

```
import org.apache.spark.ml.linalg.{Vector => SparkVector}
```

 It should be noted that `org.apache.spark.mllib.Vector` is not the same as `org.apache.spark.ml.Vector`.

 The `fromML` function on `org.apache.spark.mllib.linalg.Vec tors` can be used to convert from `ml` to `mllib` format.

Pipeline Stages

Pipeline stages are the core building block of Spark ML. Both data preparation tasks and classic model training are available as pipeline stages. Pipeline stages can be either *transformers*, which don't require fitting on the data before use, or *estimators*, which require fitting before they can be used.

While you will normally use pipeline stages in the context of a full pipeline, which we will introduce later, it can be useful to debug them one at a time. When used in a pipeline, the differences between how transformers and estimators work isn't visible; however, when used outside of a pipeline, the API differences become visible. By working with transformers and estimators outside of a pipeline first, you can get a better understanding of how they differ and work.

A transformer is the simplest pipeline stage, and an estimator when fit returns a transformer. For transformer pipeline stages, you can directly call the `transform` method, which takes an input `DataFrame`. The `transform` method returns a new `Data Frame` with the result transformed; normally this will be purely additive (e.g., adds new columns created from old columns). For estimators, you can fit the estimator to a particular input `DataFrame` using `fit`. Fit returns a transformer pipeline stage that you can then call `transform` on.

Almost all pipeline stages have some basic parameters that need to be set before they can be used (such as the column of the `DataFrame` they should apply their transformation to), so before we go too far we need to understand how parameters work.

Pipeline stages share a common method for specifying the parameters, which is the basis for meta algorithms like parameter search. The parameters are grouped together in a "Parameters" section of the Javadocs for each stage with the getters and setters grouped under "Parameter getters" and "Parameter setters," respectively. To start with you can configure your machine learning algorithms with the parameter setters, and the getters will come in handy later on. Some parameters have default values, although these are often chosen for backward compatibility rather than optimal performance.

Even though the defaults are often chosen for backward compatibility, they do sometimes change between releases—so for better reproducibility explicitly setting even the default values you wish to use can be beneficial.

Python users working with Spark ML may find the documentation on the default values of the different parameters missing; in those cases, refer to the Scala version of the documentation. However, differences may exist between languages so explicitly setting equivalent values to the defaults is still a best practice.

Explain Params

If you are working in the shell, `explainParams()` will list all of the params of the stage, the documentation associated with it, and the current value. Use `explain param("paramName")` for a single parameter. Example 9-19 is a sample of the `Binar izer` pipeline stage without any of the values overridden.

Example 9-19. Explain Params output on a Binarizer pipeline stage

```
inputCol: input column name (undefined)
outputCol: output column name (default: binarizer_8b03ca79966b__output)
threshold: threshold used to binarize continuous features (default: 0.0)
```

Most stages will perform additional validation on the values that have been set (e.g., check for a nonzero scaling factor) at the time they need to transform the schema of the input `DataFrame` (e.g., `transform` or `fit` on a `DataFrame`).

As you can see, in Example 9-19 the input column is not set and lacks a default value. Thus, to use the stage, you would first need to set it to a specific value. This can be done through `setParameterName([value])` on the pipeline stage (in this case `setInputCol("inputCol")`). The setters update the pipeline stage they are called on, and also return the stage to make it easier to chain multiple setter operations. It's important to note that the setter does not copy the stage; rather it modifies the stage it is called on and returns that stage.

 While fitting/training a transformer/model, the parameter values are copied from the estimator to the transformer.[2]

The parameters can often be updated on the model: for example, if you have one column you use for training and another in "live" serving you can change the input column on the resulting model with the same setter methods used on the estimator. Be careful when changing parameters on the model, because occasionally parameters can be changed on the model but will not actually have any impact (e.g., changing regularization).

Now that you understand the basics of how to configure pipeline stages, you can use Spark ML's data preparation tools.

Data Encoding

Despite taking in a `Dataset[_]`, most of Spark's ML models require that your data is encoded in a specific format. The features are required to be represented in a column of the `Vector` type. If training a supervised algorithm, the labels are required to be of `Double` type with the features as a separate `Vector`.

 Some algorithms in Spark assume that the label column is zero indexed, and may behave suboptimally (in training time or prediction quality) if the input label column is not zero indexed. The `StringIndexer` feature transformer we discuss later on in this section can help solve this problem.

---

2 This doesn't happen in Python currently, but there is an open PR to resolve this issue.

Thankfully, Spark ML has a wide range of pipeline options for data preparation. These live under the `org.apache.spark.ml.feature` package, and at the time of the writing, include 35+ algorithms covering everything from `Binarizer` and `PCA`, to `Word2Vec`. Data preparation stages can exist as both estimators (like `Word2Vec` or `StringIndexer`) or transformers (like `HashingTF`).

The most common feature transformer is the `VectorAssembler`, which is used to get your inputs into a format that Spark ML's machine learning models can work with. If your data is already available as numeric types, using the `VectorAssembler` is simply a matter of specifying the input columns and desired output column for the assembled feature vector as in Example 9-20.

Example 9-20. Simple vector assembler

```
val assembler = new VectorAssembler()
assembler.setInputCols(Array("size", "zipcode"))
```

If you have textual inputs, Spark's ML pipeline has the basic text-encoding functions like `Word2Vec`, `StopWordsRemover`, `NGram`, `IDF`, `HashingTF`, and a simple `Tokenizer`. By using `Tokenizer` together with `HashingTF` you can convert an input text column into a numeric feature that can be used by Spark. In Example 9-21 we illustrate how to do this by hand, but using a pipeline (covered in "Putting It All Together in a Pipeline" on page 240) will make this process much simpler.

Example 9-21. Construct a tokenizer and use its output for HashingTF

```
val tokenizer = new Tokenizer()
tokenizer.setInputCol("name")
tokenizer.setOutputCol("tokenized_name")
val tokenizedData = tokenizer.transform(df)
val hashingTF = new HashingTF()
hashingTF.setInputCol("tokenized_name")
hashingTF.setOutputCol("name_tf")
hashingTF.transform(tokenizedData)
```

If you find yourself wanting more powerful NLP tools in Spark, you can look at the spark-packages community website or consider extending Spark's pipeline with your own custom code, as covered in "Extending Spark ML Pipelines with Your Own Algorithms" on page 244.

Once you have your features in a `Vector` for Spark to train on, it's time to get your labels encoded as well. As the name implies, `StringIndexer` can be used to convert strings to indexes, and is a common way to handle text-labeled data. The `StringIndexer` can also be used on categorical numeric input types; this is useful for working with a categorical label column that may not already be zero indexed. `StringIndexer` is an estimator, as it aims to provide the most commonly occurring labels with the lowest string index with zero collisions. To be able to sort the strings by how frequently they occur, the StringIndexer needs to see the most common strings. When you've fit a string indexer it returns a StringIndexerModel (as shown in Example 9-22), which can be used to transform the data.

Example 9-22. Handling string labels with StringIndexer

```
// Construct a simple string indexer
val sb = new StringIndexer()
sb.setInputCol("name")
sb.setOutputCol("indexed_name")
// Construct the model based on the input
val sbModel = sb.fit(df)
```

StringIndexerModel also has an important counterpoint transformer called IndexTo String, which can be used to convert predictions back to the original labels. In theory, it can function using metadata that is encoded in the DataFrames schema (as in Example 9-23), but many estimators do not copy the metadata from the label column to the prediction column.

Example 9-23. IndexToString requiring metadata

```
// Construct the inverse of the model to go from
// index-to-string after prediction.
val sbInverseMD = new IndexToString()
sbInverseMD.setInputCol("prediction")
```

When the metadata is missing on the output column, to recover the original labels, you will need to construct the IndexToString object manually as shown in Example 9-24.

Example 9-24. IndexToString without metadata

```
// Construct the inverse of the model to go from index-to-string
// after prediction.
val sbInverse = new IndexToString()
sbInverse.setInputCol("prediction")
sbInverse.setLabels(sbModel.labels)
```

 If new values are encountered, say because one of the labels was missing during k-fold training, StringIndexerModel can either throw an exception or skip the record. You can control this behavior with the handleInvalid param (which defaults to "error").

Data Cleaning

Beyond the basics of simply getting your data into a format that Spark is capable of working with, additional feature engineering can make a huge difference in the performance of your models. You can use `Binarizer` to threshold a specific feature, and `PCA` to reduce the dimension of your data. When you are training models that work better with normalized features, you can use `Normalizer` (entire feature vector), as shown in Example 9-25, or `MinMaxScaler` (individual column) to easily add normalization of your features to an existing pipeline.

Example 9-25. Constructing a normalizer

```
val normalizer = new Normalizer()
normalizer.setInputCol("features")
normalizer.setOutputCol("normalized_features")
```

Now that you've done a first pass at prepairing your dataset for training, it's time to jump into Spark ML's algorithms for machine learning.

Spark ML Models

Spark has a wide variety of machine learning algorithms, ranging from classification, regression, and clustering. Each model has tuning parameters, which are described in the Scala/Javadoc. All of the supervised algorithms have at least `labelCol`, `features Col`, and `predictionCol`.

The different machine learning algorithms are organized by usage. Since each family of machine learning algorithms (classification (*http://spark.apache.org/docs/latest/api/scala/index.html#org.apache.spark.ml.classification.package*), regression (*http://spark.apache.org/docs/latest/api/scala/index.html#org.apache.spark.ml.regres sion.package*), recommendation (*http://spark.apache.org/docs/latest/api/scala/index.html#org.apache.spark.ml.recommendation.package*), and clustering (*http://spark.apache.org/docs/latest/api/scala/index.html#org.apache.spark.ml.clustering.pack age*)) are grouped by package, you can view your algorithm options by browsing to the corresponding package. In addition to the models that ship directly with Spark, you can extend the pipeline stages for your own algorithm—see "Extending Spark ML Pipelines with Your Own Algorithms" on page 244, or look at the community provided algorithms (see "Using Community Packages and Libraries" on page 271).

Constructing and configuring a machine learning stage is the same as configuring other estimators, like the `StringIndexer`. The machine learning estimators often have more parameters available for configuration than the data preperation estimators, and often take longer to fit. Most of these parameters have default values, so constructing a machine learning estimator need not involve much configuration, as in Example 9-26.

Example 9-26. Construct Naive Bayes stage with minimal configuration

```
val nb = new NaiveBayes()
nb.setLabelCol("happy")
nb.setFeaturesCol("features")
nb.setPredictionCol("prediction")
val nbModel = nb.fit(df)
```

 When working in the Spark shell or notebook, the same general techniques that we discussed in "Explain Params" on page 235 continue to work on ML stages.

As with the other estimators, you can directly call the fit method, but using the machine learning stage inside of a pipeline will be much easier than manually chaining the stages with your own code.

Putting It All Together in a Pipeline

Spark's ML pipeline interface gives you a way to chain together your data preparation and model training steps. This is especially useful for saving your pipeline or when running meta-algorithms (like parameter search) over multiple components of your pipeline. Even without the benefits of simplified persistence or meta-algorithms, chaining together transformers and estimators in a unified pipeline can simplify your model training code compared to manually stringing together fit and transform calls.

Now that you know how to construct the individual pipeline stages, putting them together in a pipeline is straightforward. The same parameter mechanism used for configuring the pipeline stages is used to configure pipelines themselves, and a pipeline is also an estimator (one could make a pipeline of pipelines, but there is very little benefit to doing so).

To build a pipeline all you need to do is create an instance of org.apache.spark .ml.Pipeline and call setStages with an array of the stages in your pipeline. You can compile the stages from the previous examples together into a single pipeline, saving the effort of manually transforming your DataFrame as shown in Example 9-27.

Example 9-27. Constructing a simple pipeline

```
val tokenizer = new Tokenizer()
tokenizer.setInputCol("name")
tokenizer.setOutputCol("tokenized_name")
val hashingTF = new HashingTF()
```

```
hashingTF.setInputCol("tokenized_name")
hashingTF.setOutputCol("name_tf")
val assembler = new VectorAssembler()
assembler.setInputCols(Array("size", "zipcode", "name_tf",
  "attributes"))
val nb = new NaiveBayes()
nb.setLabelCol("happy")
nb.setFeaturesCol("features")
nb.setPredictionCol("prediction")
val pipeline = new Pipeline()
pipeline.setStages(Array(tokenizer, hashingTF, assembler, nb))
```

A great thing about pipelines is that new stages can be easily added, such as adding a normalizer to Example 9-27 in Example 9-28.

Example 9-28. Pipeline with normalizer

```
val normalizer = new Normalizer()
normalizer.setInputCol("features")
normalizer.setOutputCol("normalized_features")
nb.setFeaturesCol("normalized_features")
pipeline.setStages(Array(tokenizer, hashingTF, assembler, normalizer, nb))
val normalizedPipelineModel = pipelineModel.transform(df)
```

Training a Pipeline

Since the pipeline is simply a special type of estimator, one that may contain other estimators, you can use it in much the same way. Calling `fit()` with a specified Data set will fit the pipeline stages in order (skipping `transformers`) returning a pipeline consisting of entirely trained transformers ready to be used to predict inputs.

Accessing Individual Stages

You may find yourself wanting to access the individual stages in the pipeline, either for debugging information or for manually persisting one component. The root `Pipe line` class contains a `stages` param consisting of an array of the pipeline stages. After training, the resulting `PipelineModel` has an array called `stages`, consisting of all of the pipeline stages after fitting. Accessing the stages in Scala normally requires casting it to the explicit type, as shown in Example 9-29.

Example 9-29. Accessing selected stages of a ML pipeline

```
val tokenizer2 = pipelineModel.stages(0).asInstanceOf[Tokenizer]
val nbFit = pipelineModel.stages.last.asInstanceOf[NaiveBayesModel]
```

Most commonly you will want to access the last stage of your pipeline to get information about the performance of your model. Another common reason is to construct an inverse to the `StringIndexerModel` by getting its labels to construct an `IndexTo` `String` stage.

Data Persistence and Spark ML

It may seem counterintuitive, but *not* explicitly caching your data when working with Spark's machine learning algorithms can sometimes be faster than explicitly caching your input. If your data is not reused outside of the machine learning algorithm, many iterative algorithms will handle their own caching, or allow you to configure the persistence level with the `intermediateStorageLevel` property. Often one of the first steps inside of each model transforms the input into a more usable internal format, and any internal persistence is applied on this internal format. As such, letting the model handle its own persistence can cache more efficiently—provided the pipeline stage handles persistence.

> Not all pipeline stages intelligently support persistence. If there is no persistence parameter and the Scaladoc does not mention persistence, that can be a good sign you should look at the Spark UI and see if manually persisting the input to your pipeline would be beneficial.

Regardless of whether you explicitly cache your inputs, or leave it up to the algorithm to cache the prepared version of your data, all of the same considerations in "Types of Reuse: Cache, Persist, Checkpoint, Shuffle Files" on page 118 apply for selecting the storage level.

Automated model selection (parameter search)

Model tuning represents a challenging problem, especially for engineers with less of a machine learning background. Thankfully, Spark ML's standardized approach to model parameters simplifies parameter search, allowing you to specify the parameters you wish to search over along with a method of evaluating those parameters.

> For those new to machine learning or parameter search, remember that when using automated model selection (or any hand tuning) to keep a separate train, test, and validation sets. This will help you get to get a more accurate measurement of model effectiveness.

Spark can then search across the different parameters to automatically select the best parameters, and the model from it. Using our pipeline example in Example 9-27, you can construct a parameter grid to search for the best smoothing parameter as in Example 9-30.

Example 9-30. Specify simple single parameter search

```
// ParamGridBuilder constructs an Array of parameter combinations.
val paramGrid: Array[ParamMap] = new ParamGridBuilder()
  .addGrid(nb.smoothing, Array(0.1, 0.5, 1.0, 2.0))
  .build()
```

 While the training and evaluation for each given configuration is done in parallel, the search through the different configurations is done linearly and no optimization is used to narrow the provided search space. So, the amount of time required can quickly grow with the number of options given.

Spark currently provides two tools for splitting the data for model evaluation: cross-validation and train-validation split. Both these automatically cache the training and validation sets at in-memory storage level, so if your input training set is too large to be cached in-memory on your workers, consider sampling it for parameter search.

In addition to choosing how to run the trials, you can also configure the evaluation metric used to select the best model. For our running example data we have binary classification input, so Example 9-31 uses a `BinaryClassificationEvaluator`, and for other data types `RegressionEvaluator` and `MulticlassClassificationEvaluator` are available.

Example 9-31. Running a parameter search with cross-validation

```
val cv = new CrossValidator()
  .setEstimator(pipeline)
  .setEstimatorParamMaps(paramGrid)
val cvModel = cv.fit(df)
val bestModel = cvModel.bestModel
```

Just as with pipeline stages, you can configure your evaluator. The most common one to change is the metric being evaluated, which all of the built-in evaluators expose with a `metricName` parameter. The `BinaryClassificationEvaluator` supports `areaUnderROC` and `areaUnderPR`. The other evaluators also support a number of different metrics, which can be explored in their Java/Scala docs.

 You can also implement your own evaluator by following the `org.apache.spark.ml.evaluation.Evaluator` class.

The parameters you search over need not be limited to those on a single stage either. If you want to search for parameters in different stages in the same pipeline, all you need to do is add extra parameters to the `ParamGridBuilder`. Returning to the example, you can easily search the `hashingTF numFeatures`, binary encoding, and normalizer p-norm parameter configurations as shown in Example 9-32.

Example 9-32. All stages parameter search

```
val complexParamGrid: Array[ParamMap] = new ParamGridBuilder()
  .addGrid(nb.smoothing, Array(0.1, 0.5, 1.0, 2.0))
  .addGrid(hashingTF.numFeatures, Array(1 << 18, 1 << 20))
  .addGrid(hashingTF.binary, Array(true, false))
  .addGrid(normalizer.p, Array(1.0, 1.5, 2.0))
  .build()
```

One downside of making these large parameter searches is that the set of models to be tested quickly grows with each new parameter added to the search space. Work exists to do smarter automatic parameter searching in scikit-learn and similar systems, but this is not yet in Spark.

Early version of `RegressionEvaluator` occasionally return invalid results. If you experience `NaN` evaluation results, check out SPARK-14489   (*https://issues.apache.org/jira/browse/ SPARK-14489*).

These model evaluation tools can be used outside of parameter search to measure model effectiveness, which can be especially useful in sanity-checking new models before deploying the results to production.

Extending Spark ML Pipelines with Your Own Algorithms

While Spark ML pipelines have a wide variety of algorithms, you may want additional functionality without having to leave the pipeline model. In Spark MLlib, this isn't much of a problem—you can manually implement your algorithm with RDD transformations in the middle of using built-in functions. You can use the same approach with Spark ML pipelines, but doing so loses some of the nicely integrated properties of the pipeline, including the ability to automatically run meta-algorithms, such as cross-validation parameter search.

To add your own algorithm to a Spark pipeline, you need create either an `Estimator` or `Transformer`, both of which implement the `PipelineStage` interface. Use the `Transformer` interface for algorithms not requiring training. Use the `Estimator` interface for algorithms that *do* require training. Both of these interfaces are in the

```
    }
    // Add the return field
    schema.add(StructField($(outputCol), IntegerType, false))
  }

  override def transform(dataset: Dataset[_]): DataFrame = {
    val indexer = udf { label: String => labelToIndex(label) }
    dataset.select(col("*"),
      indexer(dataset($(inputCol)).cast(StringType)).as($(outputCol)))
  }
}
//end::SimpleIndexer[]
```

 If you are implementing an iterative algorithm you may wish to consider caching the input data automatically if not already cached or allow the user to specify a persistence level.

For many algorithms, the `org.apache.spark.ml.Predictor` or `org.apache`
`.spark.ml.classificationClassifier` helper classes are easier to work with than
directly using the `Estimator` interface.

The `Predictor` interface adds the two most common parameters (input and output
columns, as labels column, features column, and prediction column) and automatically handles the schema transformation for us.

The `Classifier` interface is similar to the `Predictor` interface. The predictor interface additionally includes a `rawPredictionColumn` in the output and provides tools to
detect the number of classes (`getNumClasses`), which are helpful for classification
problems. We can use the classifier interface to implement a simplified Naive Bayes
classifier, as shown in Example 9-38. If you want to work with a legacy MLlib-style
algorithm, it also provides tools to convert the input `DataFrame` to an RDD of `Label`
`edPoints`.

Example 9-38. Simple Naive Bayes classifier

```
// Simple Bernoulli Naive Bayes classifier - no sanity checks for brevity
// Example only - not for production use.
class SimpleNaiveBayes(val uid: String)
    extends Classifier[Vector, SimpleNaiveBayes, SimpleNaiveBayesModel] {

  def this() = this(Identifiable.randomUID("simple-naive-bayes"))

  override def train(ds: Dataset[_]): SimpleNaiveBayesModel = {
    import ds.sparkSession.implicits._
    ds.cache()
    // Note: you can use getNumClasses & extractLabeledPoints to get an RDD instead
```

```scala
// Using the RDD approach is common when integrating with legacy machine
// learning code or iterative algorithms which can create large query plans.
// Compute the number of documents
val numDocs = ds.count
// Get the number of classes.
// Note this estimator assumes they start at 0 and go to numClasses
val numClasses = getNumClasses(ds)
// Get the number of features by peaking at the first row
val numFeatures: Integer = ds.select(col($(featuresCol))).head
  .get(0).asInstanceOf[Vector].size
// Determine the number of records for each class
val groupedByLabel = ds.select(col($(labelCol)).as[Double]).groupByKey(x => x)
val classCounts = groupedByLabel.agg(count("*").as[Long])
  .sort(col("value")).collect().toMap
// Select the labels and features so we can more easily map over them.
// Note: we do this as a DataFrame using the untyped API because the Vector
// UDT is no longer public.
val df = ds.select(col($(labelCol)).cast(DoubleType), col($(featuresCol)))
// Figure out the non-zero frequency of each feature for each label and
// output label index pairs using a case class to make it easier to work with.
val labelCounts: Dataset[LabeledToken] = df.flatMap {
  case Row(label: Double, features: Vector) =>
    features.toArray.zip(Stream from 1)
      .filter{vIdx => vIdx._2 == 1.0}
      .map{case (v, idx) => LabeledToken(label, idx)}
}
// Use the typed Dataset aggregation API to count the number of non-zero
// features for each label-feature index.
val aggregatedCounts: Array[((Double, Integer), Long)] = labelCounts
  .groupByKey(x => (x.label, x.index))
  .agg(count("*").as[Long]).collect()

val theta = Array.fill(numClasses)(new Array[Double](numFeatures))

// Compute the denominator for the general priors
val piLogDenom = math.log(numDocs + numClasses)
// Compute the priors for each class
val pi = classCounts.map{case(_, cc) =>
  math.log(cc.toDouble) - piLogDenom }.toArray

// For each label/feature update the probabilities
aggregatedCounts.foreach{case ((label, featureIndex), count) =>
  // log of number of documents for this label + 2.0 (smoothing)
  val thetaLogDenom = math.log(
    classCounts.get(label).map(_.toDouble).getOrElse(0.0) + 2.0)
  theta(label.toInt)(featureIndex) = math.log(count + 1.0) - thetaLogDenom
}
// Unpersist now that we are done computing everything
ds.unpersist()
// Construct a model
val model = new SimpleNaiveBayesModel(
  uid, numClasses, numFeatures, Vectors.dense(pi),
```

```scala
    new DenseMatrix(numClasses, theta(0).length, theta.flatten, true))
    // Copy the params values to the model
    copyValues(model)
  }

  override def copy(extra: ParamMap): SimpleNaiveBayes = {
    defaultCopy(extra)
  }
}

// Simplified Naive Bayes Model
case class SimpleNaiveBayesModel(
  override val uid: String,
  override val numClasses: Int,
  override val numFeatures: Int,
  val pi: Vector,
  val theta: DenseMatrix) extends
    ClassificationModel[Vector, SimpleNaiveBayesModel] {

  override def copy(extra: ParamMap): SimpleNaiveBayesModel = {
    val copied = new SimpleNaiveBayesModel(uid, numClasses, numFeatures, pi, theta)
    copyValues(copied, extra).setParent(parent)
  }

  // We have to do some tricks here because we are using Spark's
  // Vector/DenseMatrix calculations - but for your own model don't feel
  // limited to Spark's native ones.
  val negThetaArray = theta.values.map(v => math.log(1.0 - math.exp(v)))
  val negTheta = new DenseMatrix(numClasses, numFeatures, negThetaArray, true)
  val thetaMinusNegThetaArray = theta.values.zip(negThetaArray)
    .map{case (v, nv) => v - nv}
  val thetaMinusNegTheta = new DenseMatrix(
    numClasses, numFeatures, thetaMinusNegThetaArray, true)
  val onesVec = Vectors.dense(Array.fill(theta.numCols)(1.0))
  val negThetaSum: Array[Double] = negTheta.multiply(onesVec).toArray

  // Here is the prediciton functionality you need to implement - for
  // ClassificationModels transform automatically wraps this.
  // If you might benefit from broadcasting your model or other optimizations you
  // can override transform and place your desired logic there.
  def predictRaw(features: Vector): Vector = {
    // Toy implementation - use BLAS or similar instead
    // the summing of the three vectors but the functionality isn't exposed.
    Vectors.dense(thetaMinusNegTheta.multiply(features).toArray.zip(pi.toArray)
      .map{case (x, y) => x + y}.zip(negThetaSum).map{case (x, y) => x + y}
    )
  }
}
```

If you are implementing a regression or clustering interface, there is no public base set of interfaces to use, so you will need to use the generic Estimator interface.

If you simply need to modify an existing algorithm, you can access the required internals by putting your code in the org.apache .spark package. By doing this none of the API guarantees between Spark versions necessarily apply, and you will need to be very careful updating. This is the technique we explore in "Stream Processing with Spark" on page 257 to add streaming.

If you want more examples, one of the best places to look is Spark's ML library itself (*https://github.com/apache/spark/tree/master/mllib/src/main/scala/org/apache/spark/ml*), and although most of them use some internal APIs they can be a good reference point for adding your own functions.

Now that you are ready to start extending Spark's ML pipelines, you can consider creating a Spark package to share your new tools with the community as in "Using Community Packages and Libraries" on page 271.

Model and Pipeline Persistence and Serving with Spark ML

Built-in model and pipeline persistence options with Spark ML are limited to Spark's internal format. Using a persisted pipeline requires a full SparkContext, and has a high level of overhead as the per-element predict APIs are not yet public. PMML export functionality has not yet made it from Spark MLlib to Spark ML; however, other external projects exist to provide this support.

PMML persistence is especially interesting for serving where you do not want to bring in the entire Spark dependencies, as it is supported by multiple systems. There is an external project, MLeap (*https://github.com/TrueCar/mleap*), which offers support for exporting many models in PMML format, and other projects are exploring adding PFA support. We will discuss how to use external projects like this in "Using Community Packages and Libraries" on page 271.

The Spark ML developers are considering improving the persistence options for Spark ML, including adding PMML in SPARK-11171 (*https://issues.apache.org/jira/browse/SPARK-11171*), but this will have to wait for future versions of Spark.

General Serving Considerations

Both Spark ML and MLlib have limited persistence options, which can make it difficult to use the trained model in an online environment. For users with an existing serving infrastructure in place, a common approach is to manually write a persistence layer to their custom format. This can be time-consuming as it must be done for each type of model. This is the approach taken by MLeap (*https://github.com/TrueCar/*

mleap), which offers a custom model serialization format for many Spark models with an online serving layer. For users without an existing serving system, using PMML export along with an online serving layer, like JPMML and the JPMML evaluator (*https://github.com/jpmml/jpmml-evaluator*), represents a simple, flexible option.

> JPMML has an AGPL license and may not be suitable for your organization due to licensing constraints.

One of the simplest models to persist is linear models, which consist of only a few coefficients to write out. One of these is shown in Example 9-39.

Example 9-39. Manual persistence layer for GLM

```
def exportLRToCSV(model: LogisticRegressionModel) = {
  (model.coefficients.toArray :+ model.intercept).mkString(",")
}
```

Not all models will be as easy to export as GLMs (as in Example 9-39), and you may find that not all of the information you need to persist the model is directly available. In those cases you can lie and do "evil" things, by pretending to be in `org.apache.spark` as done in some of the streaming examples (Example 10-13 and Example 10-14).

> Extending (subclassing) the models is only required if you're working in the JVM—Py4J uses reflection so you can directly (and equally unsafely) access the model's internals for export.

Conclusion

Spark's built-in machine learning libraries offer support for a number of different algorithms, but are currently primarily focused on the batch use case. Beyond building models directly with Spark, other tools exist to do machine learning on Spark—some of which have a more mature model serving options. Oryx (*http://oryx.io/*), Mahout (*http://mahout.apache.org/*), H2O's Sparkling Water (*http://www.h2o.ai/product/sparkling-water/*), Algorithmia (*https://algorithmia.com*), and others can also be used to train machine learning models using Spark. The next chapter will explore how to use Spark components and the Spark component ecosystem.

## CHAPTER 10

Spark Components and Packages

Spark has a large number of components that are designed to work together as an integrated system, and many of them are distributed as part of Spark. This is different from the Hadoop ecosystem, which has different projects or systems for each task. You've already seen how to effectively use Spark Core, SQL, and ML components, and this chapter will introduce you to Spark's Streaming components, as well as the external/community components (often referred to as packages). Having a largely integrated system gives Spark two advantages: it simplifies both deployment/cluster management and application development by having fewer dependencies and systems to keep track of.

Even early versions of Spark provided tools that traditionally would have required the coordination of multiple systems, as illustrated in Figure 10-1.

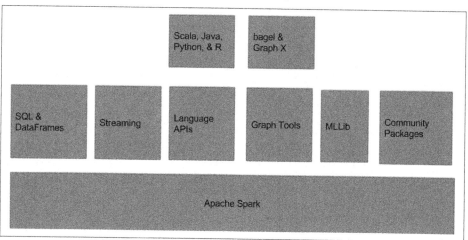

Figure 10-1. Spark components diagram

As `Datasets` and the Spark SQL engine have become a building block for other components inside of Spark, a minor reorganization illustrated in Figure 10-2 represents a more up-to-date version, including two of Spark's newest components, Spark ML and Structured Streaming. Much of your knowledge from working with core Spark and Spark SQL can be applied to the other components—although there are some unique considerations for each one.

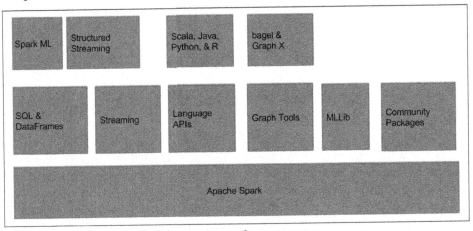

Figure 10-2. Spark 2.0+ revised components diagram

Beyond the integrated components, the community packages can add important functionality to Spark, sometimes even superseding built-in functionality—like with GraphFrames. Community packages provide a diverse set of functionality, ranging from additional data formats (mentioned in "Additional formats" on page 60) to the testing packages discussed in Chapter 8, machine learning, and graph algorithms. These community packages can sometimes become a part of Spark if their use is wide enough, as happened with the `spark-csv` package for loading CSV data in `Datasets`. This chapter will wrap up with information about how to create your own community package, so that we all can benefit from your work—not that you should feel obliged to.

If you haven't had a chance to read Chapter 3 yet, we encourage you to jump back and at least skim it, since, as Figure 10-2 illustrates, much of the new Spark development is happening on top of Spark SQL and `DataFrames`/`Datasets`.

One less directly visible benefit of this integrated approach is that each component's development can result in improvements across all of the other components. For example, Streaming required a large reduction in task creation overhead. This task overhead reduction improved Spark SQL's ability to support small queries, where the task overhead previously dominated.

Stream Processing with Spark

Spark Streaming has two APIs, one based on RDDs—called DStreams—and a second (currently in *alpha*)—called Structured Streaming—based on Spark SQL/DataFrames. Many of the performance considerations for RDD transformations and DataFrame/Dataset operations are the same in the streaming context, and many of the operations have the same names. Some operations only make sense in the context of streaming, and certain operations from the batch API aren't directly supported in the streaming API. This section will explore some considerations unique to Spark's streaming API, building on top of your knowledge from the previous chapters.

 For more information about Spark Streaming, check out the upcoming O'Reilly book *Learning Spark Streaming* by François Garillot.

One of the clearest differences between streaming and batch is with the input data sources, which can make large performance differences.

 While developing and testing streaming applications in local mode, a common problem can result from launching with local or local[1] as the master. Spark Streaming requires multiple workers to make progress, so for tests make sure to use a larger number of workers like local[4].

Sources and Sinks

Regardless of which version of the Spark Streaming API you are using, there are some special considerations for how Spark Streaming both consumes and writes out its data. Well-partitioned streaming input can make a big difference, just as having your RDD and DataFrame inputs well partitioned. Incorrectly partitioned or configured sources can result in bottlenecks reading data, as well as undesirable data loss.

Both of Spark Streaming's APIs directly support file sources that will automatically pick up new subdirectories and raw socket sources for testing. Early Kafka support exists for both structured streaming and more robust support in Spark's DStream API.

For simple testing, Spark offers in-memory streams, `QueueStreams` for `DStream` and `MemoryStream` for streaming `Datasets`. Spark's `QueueStreams` don't support many operations (like `groupByWindow`), which limits its use cases. Instead of `QueueStream`, for testing, many people use spark-testing-base as in "Streaming" on page 206.

The DStream API offers additional first-party data sources, but these are packaged as separate JARs to avoid bloat and licensing issues. These sources include Kafka, Flume, Kinesis, Twitter, ZeroMQ, and MQTT. Integration guides exist for Kafka (*http://spark.apache.org/docs/latest/streaming-kafka-integration.html*), Flume (*http:// spark.apache.org/docs/latest/streaming-flume-integration.html*), and Kinesis (*http:// spark.apache.org/docs/latest/streaming-kinesis-integration.html*). Some of these will come to structured streaming in future versions, possibly some as community packages.

Some sources have been moved out of Spark and are now provided through the Apache Bahir (*http://bahir.apache.org/*) project. This project, and other streaming sources on Spark packages, can be included using the instructions in "Using Community Packages and Libraries" on page 271.

As of this writing most Structured Streaming sources are not yet available. Additional sources will likely be made available in a similar manner to the `DStream` API in future versions and as Spark packages, which we cover in "Using Community Packages and Libraries" on page 271.

Receivers

Many of Spark's `DStream` sources depend on dedicated receiver processes to read in data from your streaming sources, with file-based and "receiverless kafka" sources being notable exceptions. In the receiver-based configuration, a certain number of workers are configured to read data from the input data streams, which—if not carefully configured—can become a bottleneck. Improper receiver configuration can severely limit the amount of streaming data that Spark can process. The details of each specific receiver depend on the data source, so make sure to read the documentation for your relevant receiver.

 Some sources have multiple options for reading in data. For example, Kafka has both a receiver-based configuration and a "direct" approach where the individual Spark executors directly read data from Kafka.

Repartitioning

As with regular RDDs and `DataFrames`, your input sources may not partitioned in a way that is optimized for processing with Spark. For receiver-based approaches, the partitioning of your `DStream` generally reflects your receiver configuration. In the direct (receiverless) approaches the initial partitioning is based on the partitioning of the input stream, much as how RDDs initial partitioning is similar to HDFS.

If your data is not ideally partitioned for processing, explicitly repartitioning as we can on RDDs is the simplest way to fix it. Repartitioning can be simpler than configuring multiple receivers and unioning them, and doing so is similar to RDDs (Example 10-1). When repartitioning keyed data, having a known partitioner can speed up many operations just as discussed in Chapter 6.

Example 10-1. DStream repartition

```
dstream.repartition(20)
```

However, if the bottleneck comes from reading, repartitioning after the initial read will not be sufficient—either you must increase the number of the partitions in the input data source (for direct) or number of receivers.

This example may look very familiar. That's because, like many operations on `DStreams`, it is implemented using `transform`. `transform` takes the RDD for each time slice and applies your transformations. If you have an RDD operation or custom function that works on RDDs you want to use on `DStreams`, `transform`'s RDD time slice view allows you to reuse it. Example 10-2 pretends `repartition` wasn't directly available on the `DStream` class and creates an alternative function.

Example 10-2. DStream repartition with transform

```
def dStreamRepartition[A: ClassTag](dstream: DStream[A]): DStream[A] = {
  dstream.transform{rdd => rdd.repartition(20)}
}
```

> Even Kafka's direct `DStream` receiver can benefit from repartitioning. If the number of Kafka partitions is not sufficient for the desired data parallelism inside of Spark, repartitioning can still be useful.

Batch Intervals

Batch intervals represent the traditional trade-off in distributed streaming systems between throughput and latency. Spark Streaming processes each batch interval completely before starting the second batch interval. As such, you should set your batch interval to be high enough for the previous batch to be processed before the next batch would be scheduled to start.

The processing time for each batch depends on your specific application, so it is difficult to provide general guidelines. Instead, it is common practice to start with a high batch interval (like 4 seconds) and work your way down until you start to encounter micro-batch processing times approaching the batch interval, and then back off the batch interval to the last safe value.

 When changing the batch interval, make sure that your window operations, discussed in "Considerations for DStreams" on page 261, are still on a multiple of your batch interval.

The interval is configured differently between the DStream and Structured Streaming APIs. In the DStream API it is configured on an application/context level, as illustrated in Example 10-3. The Structured Streaming API is configured on a per-output/query, as illustrated in Example 10-7.

Example 10-3. Creating a StreamingContext with a 1-second batch interval

```
val batchInterval = Seconds(1)
new StreamingContext(sc, batchInterval)
```

Data Checkpoint Intervals

One of Spark's biggest powers comes from the information present in the DAG (for RDDs) or query plan (for DataFrames/Datasets), and the optimizations Spark can perform with these. As with iterative algorithms, streaming operations can generate DAGs or query plans that are too large for the driver program to keep in memory. For simple operations that do not depend on previous batches, like map, filter, or join, you are not substantially more likely to run into a problem with streaming than with batch programming. For operations that depend on building a history, like streaming aggregations on Datasets and updateStateByKey on DStreams, checkpointing is required to prevent the DAG or query plan from growing too large.

 In Spark, data and operations are distributed, but the driver program must store the entire DAG or query plan. This may seem counterintuitive since Spark is a distributed system, but is key to Spark's resiliency through recomputation.

To enable checkpointing for streaming, you need to call checkpoint with a path to a persistent directory for Spark to use for checkpointing. See "Checkpointing" on page 120 for more information.

Metadata checkpointing is used to recover from failures, and is covered in "High Availability Mode (or Handling Driver Failure or Checkpointing)" on page 270.

Considerations for DStreams

Spark Streaming's DStream API is based on the RDD API, and most of its operations are simple wrappers of RDD methods with transform. These transformations have largely the same performance considerations, as we discuss in Chapter 5. Not all functions are simply wrappers of RDD operations; the most obvious function with no direct parallel to the RDD API is the window operation, which allows you to construct a sliding window of time of your input DStream, and its related friends (like reduceBy Window).

As with the Spark Scala RDD API, many functions are added through implicit conversions in Scala API. As with the Spark Java RDD API, special functions return different types to support the specific operations (e.g., JavaPairDStream for keyed/value data).

Window operations allow you to compute your data over the last K batches of data, which can be very handy for things like moving averages or Kalman filters. At their core, window operations are defined based on the windowDuration, which is the width of the window, and the slideDuration, which is how often window is computed.

One of the most important things you can do to help your window operations is to allow Spark to compute your windows incrementally by using reduceByKeyAnd Window with both a reduceFunk and an invReduceFunc. Naturally, this only works if your reduction has an inverse, which can be easily expressed (like + and -).

Output operations

The built-in options for saving DStreams are somewhat limited; built-in support exists only for saving each batch as object or text files. Example 10-4 illustrates how to save to a text file.

Object files are *not* recommended as they depend on Java serialization of objects, and are distinct from sequence files. You *may* not be able to load object files between different version of Spark.

Example 10-4. Simple output for text files

```
dstream.saveAsTextFiles(target)
```

You can save to other formats using `foreachRDD` to save on a per-batch basis using the traditional RDD APIs. `foreachRDD` works almost the same as `transform`, except it is an action rather than a transformation. Multiple versions of the `foreachRDD` API are available, depending on if you need information about the batch (like time) besides the contents (e.g., for writing out to different directories) for your action, as shown in Example 10-5.

Example 10-5. Save as sequence files with foreachRDD

```
dstream.foreachRDD{(rdd, window) =>
  rdd.saveAsSequenceFile(target + window)
}
```

Considerations for Structured Streaming

Structured Streaming introduces a new model of streaming data for Spark, more closely built on top of Spark SQL's table-like abstractions. Structured Streaming allows you to conceptually think of running SQL queries on an infinite table, which has records appended to it by the stream.[1] Unlike the RDD-based API, Structured Streaming does not introduce a new type (e.g., `DStream`) but instead keeps the existing `Dataset` type and adds a boolean `isStreaming` so that you can tell the difference between streaming and batch `Datasets`.

 Structured Streaming is new in Spark 2.0 and should not be considered production ready at the time of writing (Spark 2.2).

 Unlike `DStreams`, structured streams can be created using the regular `SparkSession`.

Streaming `Datasets` support a wide variety of operations, but not all operations implemented on batch `Datasets` are supported on streaming. The operations that are not supported do not always make logical sense—for example, in Spark 2.0 `toJson()`

---

1 It is possible to use Spark SQL with the DStream API, but it is convoluted.

(which converts a `Dataset` to a `Dataset` in JSON format) is not supported as the implementation converts the `Dataset` to an RDD. Trickily it's difficult to know if an operation is internally implemented using an RDD transformation.

> Structured Streaming is implemented by using a continuous `Data set`. However, not all of the operations supported on `Datasets` are supported on continuous `Datasets` and there is *no compile-time checking for streaming support.*

Data sources

Structured Streaming currently supports a very limited set of data sources, with more expected along the way in future versions—both internal to Spark and as packages. Loading a streaming data source is quite similar to loading regular SQL data: simply calling `readStream` instead of `read` (see Example 10-6).

Example 10-6. Simple complete mode read in

```
session.readStream.parquet(inputPath)
```

> Sampling schema inference doesn't work with streaming data, so if you want to load something like `JSON` you will have to specify the schema manually, as you would with `Datasets`.

While the current set of data sources for Structured Streaming leave something to be desired, work is progressing quickly (see SPARK-15406 (*https://issues.apache.org/jira/browse/SPARK-15406*)) to add more formats.[2] As a temporary workaround (for development only), the current `DStream` API can write to an `HDFS` store in Parquet format using `foreachRDD`, and the *parquet* directory can be used as an input to Structured Streaming.

Output operations

Structured Streaming uses a different writer class, the DataStreamWriter (*http://spark.apache.org/docs/latest/api/scala/index.html#org.apache.spark.sql.stream ing.DataStreamWriter*), than the regular `DataFrame/Dataset`, for writing to sinks. While the writer class is different, the general principles are the same. One important required configuration is the `outputMode`, which is unique and can be set to either

---

2 Indeed, between two minor releases of this book, a minor alpha release of Spark added Kafka support to Structured Streaming.

append (for new rows) or complete (for all rows). At present any streaming Dataset with aggregate operations requires complete mode, so there is no way to directly get only the aggregations that have changed (as shown in Example 10-7).

Example 10-7. Simple complete mode write out

```
val query = counts.writeStream.
  // Specify the output mode as Complete to support aggregations
  outputMode(OutputMode.Complete()).
  // Write out the result as parquet
  format("parquet").
  // Specify the interval at which new data will be picked up
  trigger(ProcessingTime(1.second)).
  queryName("pandas").start()
```

The DataStreamWriter can write collections out to other formats besides the demonstrated Parquet format. The built-in formats include console, foreach, and memory. console writes the result out to the terminal, and memory writes the result out to a local table. The foreach format is unique in that it cannot be specified with format, and instead must be set by calling foreach on the writer object so as to set up the desired function.

In Spark 2.0 console output mode collects the entire stream back locally.

Custom sinks

Beyond the standard sinks, you may wish to perform some arbitrary computation on the result of your stream beyond writing out to one of the default sinks. Since a custom sink needs to be supplied by name, it is difficult to construct it with arbitrary functions—at compile time one needs to know the function for the specified sink (e.g., it cannot vary based on user input). In Example 10-8 this is done using a function and you can specify it using the current public write API as you would for other sinks as in Example 10-9. This can be used to emulate the behavior of foreachRDD in a more general way by accessing internals, which we will examine in "Machine learning with Structured Streaming" on page 265.

The current sink APIs exposed in Structured Streaming assume microbatching, but these APIs will likely change as one of the goals of Structured Streaming is to allow the execution engine to migrate away from microbatching.

Example 10-8. Custom sink for Structured Streaming

```
/**
 * A basic custom sink to illustrate how the custom sink API is currently
 * intended to be used
 */
class BasicSinkProvider extends StreamSinkProvider {
  // Here we don't do any special work because our sink is so simple - but setup
  // work can go here.
  override def createSink(
      sqlContext: SQLContext,
      parameters: Map[String, String],
      partitionColumns: Seq[String],
      outputMode: OutputMode): BasicSink = {
    new BasicSink()
  }
}

class BasicSink extends Sink {
  /*
   * As per SPARK-16020 arbitrary transformations are not supported, but
   * converting to an RDD allows us to do magic.
   */
  override def addBatch(batchId: Long, data: DataFrame) = {
    val batchDistinctCount = data.rdd.distinct.count()
    println(s"Batch ${batchId}'s distinct count is ${batchDistinctCount}")
  }
}
```

Example 10-9. Writing to a basic custom Structured Streaming sink

```
ds.writeStream.format(
  "com.highperformancespark.examples.structuredstreaming." +
    "BasicSinkProvider")
  .queryName("customSinkDemo")
  .start()
```

In Spark 2.0, no transformations that result in changing the logical plan (e.g., no SQL/DataFrame/Dataset transformations) may be performed inside of a sink. A workaround is to convert your Data Frame into an RDD and perform your desired computation on the RDD.

Machine learning with Structured Streaming

In the first version of Structured Streaming, the machine learning APIs have not yet been integrated—however, with some creative work you can get your own machine learning algorithms working on top of Structured Streaming. Some early proof of concept work to integrate Structured Streaming and machine learning is available in this spark-structured-streaming-ml GitHub repo (*https://github.com/holdenk/spark-structured-streaming-ml*), but it is important to note this is not intended for production; rather, it serves to illustrate some interesting components.

 If you are interested in following along with the progress toward Spark's ML pipelines to support Structured Streaming, I encourage you to follow SPARK-16424 (*https://issues.apache.org/jira/browse/SPARK-16424*).

One of the simplest streaming machine learning algorithms you can implement on top of Structured Streaming is Naive Bayes, since much of the computation can be simplified to grouping and aggregating. After writing the algorithm to train the model the interesting question becomes how to collect the aggregate data in such a way that you can use it to make predictions. Spark's Structured Streaming has an in-memory table output format that you can use to store the aggregate counts, as shown in Example 10-10.

Example 10-10. Structured Streaming aggregates for Naive Bayes

```
// Compute the counts using a Dataset transformation
val counts = ds.flatMap{
  case LabeledPoint(label, vec) =>
    vec.toArray.zip(Stream from 1).map(value => LabeledToken(label, value))
}.groupBy($"label", $"value").agg(count($"value").alias("count"))
  .as[LabeledTokenCounts]
// Create a table name to store the output in
val randomId = java.util.UUID.randomUUID.toString.filter(_ != '-').toString
val tblName = "qbsnb" + randomID
// Write out the aggregate result in complete form to the in memory table
val query = counts.writeStream.outputMode(OutputMode.Complete())
  .format("memory").queryName(tblName).start()
val tbl = ds.sparkSession.table(tblName).as[LabeledTokenCounts]
val model = new QueryBasedStreamingNaiveBayesModel(tbl)
```

From here this doesn't quite include all of the data you need to make an instance of the standard Spark Naive Bayes model. You can continue to add more aggregates (for the number records, etc.), or we can start looking at a different approach.

The initial approach taken with Naive Bayes is not easily generalizable to other algorithms that cannot as easily be represented by aggregate operations on a `Dataset`. Looking back at how the early DStream-based Spark Streaming API implemented machine learning can provide some hints. Provided you can come up with an `update` mechanism on how to merge new data into your existing model, the `DStream` `fore` `achRDD` implementation allows you to access the underlying microbatch view of the data. Sadly, `foreachRDD` doesn't have a direct equivalent in Structured Streaming, but by using a custom sink you can get similar behavior (as shown in Example 10-11).

Example 10-11. Basic custom sink for training Naive Bayes

```
object SimpleStreamingNaiveBayes {
  val model = new StreamingNaiveBayes()
}

class StreamingNaiveBayesSinkprovider extends ForeachDatasetSinkProvider {
  override def func(df: DataFrame) {
    val spark = df.sparkSession
    SimpleStreamingNaiveBayes.model.update(df)
  }
}
```

As with writing `DataFrames` to customs formats, to use a third-party sink you can specify the full class name as input to the `format` function. You can use the custom sink from Example 10-11 to integrate machine learning into Structured Streaming while we are waiting for Spark ML to be updated with Structured Streaming, as done in Example 10-12.

Example 10-12. Write out to the custom sink for training Naive Bayes

```
// Train using the model inside SimpleStreamingNaiveBayes object
// - if called on multiple streams all streams will update the same model :(
// or would except if not for the hard coded query name preventing multiple
// of the same running.
def train(ds: Dataset[_]) = {
  ds.writeStream.format(
    "com.highperformancespark.examples.structuredstreaming." +
      "StreamingNaiveBayesSinkProvider")
    .queryName("trainingnaiveBayes")
    .start()
}
```

This basic custom sink needs to be fully known at compile time, since it is constructed based on the name. If you are willing to accept the difficulties in upgrading, you can access some Spark internals to construct a sink more closely to the original `fore achRDD` behavior, as shown in Example 10-13.

Example 10-13. Evil custom sink for Structured Streaming

```
/**
 * Creates a custom sink similar to the old foreachRDD. Provided function is
 * called for each time slice with the dataset representing the time slice.
 *
 * Provided func must consume the dataset (e.g. call `foreach` or `collect`).
```

```
 * As per SPARK-16020 arbitrary transformations are not supported, but converting
 * to an RDD will allow for more transformations beyond `foreach` and `collect` while
 * preserving the incremental planning.
 *
 */
abstract class ForeachDatasetSinkProvider extends StreamSinkProvider {
  def func(df: DataFrame): Unit

  def createSink(
      sqlContext: SQLContext,
      parameters: Map[String, String],
      partitionColumns: Seq[String],
      outputMode: OutputMode): ForeachDatasetSink = {
    new ForeachDatasetSink(func)
  }
}

/**
 * Custom sink similar to the old foreachRDD.
 * To use with the stream writer - do not construct directly, instead subclass
 * [[ForeachDatasetSinkProvider]] and provide to Spark's DataStreamWriter format.
 *  This can also be used directly as in StreamingNaiveBayes.scala
 */
case class ForeachDatasetSink(func: DataFrame => Unit)
    extends Sink {

  override def addBatch(batchId: Long, data: DataFrame): Unit = {
    func(data)
  }
}
```

Since the class name isn't enough to construct the sink, you need to pass the sink itself to Spark Structured Streaming. This is the part that is most likely to break in future versions of Spark.[3]

Examples 10-14 and 10-15 show how to start the query unsafely.

Example 10-14. Evil streaming query manager—allowing you to start your own queries (unsafely)

```
package org.apache.spark.sql.streaming

import scala.collection.mutable

import org.apache.spark.sql._
import org.apache.spark.sql.execution.streaming.Sink
```

---

3 Although there is a draft PR (*https://github.com/apache/spark/pull/14691*) to make something similar possible with the user-facing API.

```
/**
 * :: Experimental ::
 * A class to manage all the [[StreamingQuery]] active on a [[SparkSession]].
 *
 * @since 2.0.0
 */
case class EvilStreamingQueryManager(streamingQueryManager: StreamingQueryManager) {
  def startQuery(
    userSpecifiedName: Option[String],
    userSpecifiedCheckpointLocation: Option[String],
    df: DataFrame,
    sink: Sink,
    outputMode: OutputMode): StreamingQuery = {
    streamingQueryManager.startQuery(
      userSpecifiedName,
      userSpecifiedCheckpointLocation,
      df,
      sink,
      outputMode)
  }
}
```

Example 10-15. Using ESQM to directly starting a query with a custom sink

```
def evilTrain(df: DataFrame): StreamingQuery = {
  val sink = new ForeachDatasetSink({df: DataFrame => update(df)})
  val sparkSession = df.sparkSession
  val evilStreamingQueryManager = EvilStreamingQueryManager(sparkSession.streams)
  evilStreamingQueryManager.startQuery(
    Some(s"snb-train-$uid"),
    None,
    df,
    sink,
    OutputMode.Append())
}
```

 If you are interested in more directly supported `foreachRDD`-like support in Spark Structured Streaming—or other custom sink support—you can follow SPARK-16407 (*https://issues.apache.org/jira/browse/SPARK-16407*).

While this certainly isn't ready for use in production, you can see that the Structured Streaming API offers a number of different ways that it can be extended to support machine learning.

Stream status and debugging

One unique problem for streaming is understanding the status of your data sources and sinks. Each query is associated with at most one sink, but possible multiple sources. The status function on a StreamingQuery returns an object containing the status information for the query and all of the data sources associated with it. The toString() function returns a nicely formatted status object intended to be readable.

A common approach with RDDs is printing a small subset of the data, and Console sinks can be used to achieve the same result on streaming DataFrames. You could add a ConsoleSink for the input label points shown previously in Example 10-11, resulting in Example 10-16.

Example 10-16. Blocking Console sink

```
labeledPoints.writeStream.format("console").start().processAllAvailable()
```

 Due to a restriction in Spark 2.0, using the Console sink collects *the entire batch to the driver* so it cannot be used for large Datasets. Instead limit your data before writing to the Console sink if you may have large datasets.

High Availability Mode (or Handling Driver Failure or Checkpointing)

Most Spark applications assume that the driver program will never fail, while allowing for any number of workers/executors to fail and be recovered. For very long-running jobs, such as streaming, the assumption that the driver program will never fail may not hold true. Furthermore, simply relaunching your job is not an option with streaming as doing so may result in data loss. High availability mode works by checkpointing the driver state, and allows Spark to recover when the driver program fails. The specific restart mechanism depends on your deployment mode; however, the code changes required are the same regardless. To allow the restart to be successful, instead of creating the StreamingContext as shown in Example 10-3, you need to provide a function to handle recovery (as in Example 10-17).

Example 10-17. Metadata checkpointing/streaming context recovery

```
def createStreamingContext(): StreamingContext = {
  val batchInterval = Seconds(1)
  val ssc = new StreamingContext(sc, batchInterval)
  ssc.checkpoint(checkpointDir)
  // Then create whatever stream is required
  // And whatever mappings need to go on those streams
  ssc
}
```

```
val ssc = StreamingContext.getOrCreate(checkpointDir,
    createStreamingContext _)
// Do whatever work needs to be done regardless of state
// Start context and run
ssc.start()
```

 Accumulators and broadcast variables are not currently recovered in high availability mode. Using accumulators and broadcast variables will result in a program that seems to work, until the driver program needs to be recovered from checkpoint. You can use a singleton as a workaround, but the values won't be recovered.

GraphX

GraphX is a legacy component in Apache Spark that is no longer being updated. GraphX suffers from a number of significant performance problems; in some cases, performing iterative computation without the required checkpointing to allow Spark to clean up the DAG. As of this writing, the most promising alternative to GraphX is the community package GraphFrames (*http://graphframes.github.io/*), which we will discuss how to include in your application next.

Using Community Packages and Libraries

Beyond the components that ship in Spark, there is a whole host of community packages built for Spark. Some of the ones you have seen already in this book include spark-testing-base (*https://github.com/holdenk/spark-testing-base*), spark-csv (*https://github.com/databricks/spark-csv*), and spark-avro (*https://github.com/databricks/spark-avro*). Some other notable Spark packages include GraphFrames (*http://graphframes.github.io/*), which many people view as the successor to GraphX, and Apache Bahir (*http://bahir.apache.org/*), which provides a collection of extensions designed to work together with Apache Spark—mostly as input formats. A listing of Spark packages by area can be found on spark-packages.org (Figure 10-3).

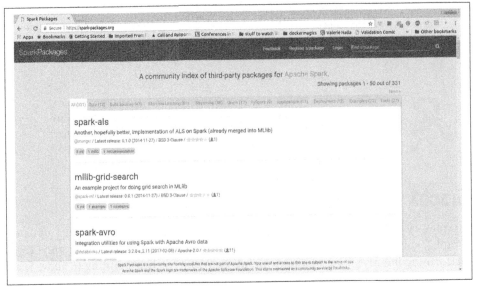

Figure 10-3. Spark packages website

Beyond public packages, if your company has internal libraries you wish to include with your Spark application or use in the Spark shell, they can be added with similar mechanisms.

Spark packages don't undergo any particular scrutiny to be released, so evaluate them yourself prior to use.

The same mechanism used to include packages from *spark-packages.org* in the shell and with `spark-submit` can be used for any artifacts published to Maven.

As you start working with a new package, you may find yourself wanting to explore it using the Spark shell. Thankfully the mechanism for including a package with `spark-submit` works just as easily with the `spark-shell`: you can just add `--packages [maven_coordinates]` to your shell launch.

In early versions of Spark, some mechanisms would result in the package only be included on the executor's class path; in that case you can manually add them to the driver class path.

To add packages that you need at compile time to Java/Scala projects, you can simply copy its Maven coordinate and include it with your build. If you're already including other libraries, you may find it useful to package all of your dependencies together in an uber JAR, but if you want to switch your package versions at runtime with spark-submit simply mark them as provided.

The Spark packages ecosystem is not limited to the JVM. However, it is more common for non-JVM languages (like Python and R) to distribute their libraries with the language-specific tools (like PyPi and CRAN). See Chapter 7 for more information on how to include custom libraries in other languages.

 Spark packages currently ship *.pyc* files for Python 2.7 and not for the 3.X line, making it less than ideal for Python users. This will hopefully change in the future. For now it means GraphFrames cannot be used from Python 3 easily.

Creating a Spark Package

Spark Packages allow people outside of the Apache Spark project to release their improvements or libraries built on top of Spark. Some Spark Packages are also created by Apache Spark contributors, like spark-testing-base or Bahir. Creating a Spark Package allows your code to be easily used by others with spark-submit or the Spark shell as well as discover it on the Spark Packages website (*https://spark-packages.org/*). All of the benefits from creating a Spark Package, except for the listing of version, can also be achieved by publishing to Maven central—which is much simpler.

The first step is signing up on the Spark Packages website (*https://spark-packages.org/*) with the GitHub account hosting your package. If you want the website to list the latest versions released, you will need to publish to both Maven central and Spark packages. The sbt-spark-package (*https://github.com/databricks/sbt-spark-package*) is the simplest way to publish and build Spark packages and also helps simplify dependency management of Spark components, as illustrated in "Managing Spark Dependencies" on page 31. To add the plug-in to your SBT build, you need to create a *project/plugins.sbt* file and make sure it contains the code in Example 10-18.

Example 10-18. Including sbt-spark-package in project/plugins.sbt

```
resolvers += ["Spark Package Main Repo" at
  "https://dl.bintray.com/spark-packages/maven"]

addSbtPlugin("org.spark-packages" % "sbt-spark-package" % "0.2.5")
```

Once you have the plug-in added to your build there are a few things you need to configure to be able to publish a new package. spName needs to be set to the GitHub project name, `sparkVersion` needs to be set to the target version of Spark, and `spark Components` to a list of the components used. A sample configuration, based on a simplified build file of spark-testing-base, is shown in Example 10-19.

Example 10-19. Sample sbt-spark-package configuration

```
sparkVersion := "2.2.0"
sparkComponents ++= Seq("core")
spName := "holdenk/spark-testing-base"
```

> If your package depends on Spark internals, it can be necessary to cross-build for different versions of Spark. There is no built-in support for this from `sbt-spark-packages`—but some packages have their own approaches, including spark-testing-base (*https:// github.com/holdenk/spark-testing-base*), which can serve as a base for your own cross-building requirements.

Conclusion

After reading this chapter you should have a basic understanding of Spark's machine learning and streaming libraries, as well as how to go out and access community packages when Spark itself isn't enough. If machine learning or streaming is a key part of your work, we recommend following this book up with some more focused resources; see suggestions in "Supporting Books and Materials" on page x.

> We hope you have found this book useful and remind you that it can make an excellent holiday gift[4] for everyone in your family, co-workers, and even pets.[5]

More seriously, if you've noticed things that can be improved about this book (either mistakes or missing content), we encourage you to get in touch with us using the information in "First Edition Notes" on page x. Now that you've finished reading you should be ready to take your Apache Spark knowledge to the next level and handle large-scale data problems with relative ease. Thank you for including us in your journey with Apache Spark and we wish you all the best—may your code be relatively bug free and cluster stable.

---

4 Not holiday time? No problem, it also makes an excellent birthday gift, or un-birthday gift.

5 We find pets tend to enjoy the box it comes in more than the book itself.

Tuning, Debugging, and Other Things Developers Like to Pretend Don't Exist

Spark Tuning and Cluster Sizing

Recall from our discussion of Spark internals in Chapter 2 that the SparkSession or SparkContext contains the Spark configuration, which specifies how an application will be launched. Most Spark settings can only be adjusted at the application level. These configurations can have a large impact on a job's speed and chance of completing. Spark's default settings are designed to make sure that jobs can be submitted on very small clusters, and are not recommended for production.

Most often these settings will need to be changed to utilize the resources that you have available and often to allow the job to run at all. Spark provides fairly finite control of how our environment is configured, and we can often improve the performance of a job at scale by adjusting these settings. For example, in Chapter 6, we explained that out-of-memory errors on the executors was a common cause of failure for Spark jobs. While it is best to focus on the techniques presented in the preceding chapters to prevent data skew and expensive shuffles, using fewer, larger executors may also prevent failures.

Configuring a Spark job is as much an art as a science. Choosing a configuration depends on the size and setup of the data storage solution, the size of the jobs being run (how much data is processed), and the kind of jobs. For example, jobs that cache a lot of data and perform many iterative computations have different requirements than those that contain a few very large shuffles. Tuning an application also depends on the goals of your team. In some instances, if you are using shared resources, you might want to configure the job that uses the fewest resources and still succeeds.

Other times, you may want to maximize the resources available to give applications the best possible performance.

In this section, we do not aim to give a comprehensive introduction to submitting or configuring a Spark application. Instead, we want to focus on providing some context and advice about how to leverage the settings that have a significant impact on performance. In other words, we are assuming that you already have a system in which you can submit an application, but are looking for ways to adjust that system to allow your applications to run faster or run on more data.

How to Adjust Spark Settings

The `SparkContext` object (`SparkSession` in 2.0) represents your connection to the Spark application. It contains a `SparkConf` object that defines how a Spark application should be configured on your system. The `SparkConf` contains all the configurations, defaults, and environment information that govern the behavior of the Spark application. These settings are represented as key/value pairs; e.g., setting the property, `spark.executor.instances` to 5, would mean submitting a job with five executors (Spark JVMs).

You may create a `SparkConf` with the desired parameters before beginning the Spark Context. Some of the properties, such as the name of the application, have corresponding API calls. Otherwise, set the properties of a `SparkConf` directly with the `.set()` method, which takes as its argument arbitrary key/value pairs. To configure a Spark application differently for each submit, you may simply create an empty `SparkConf` object and supply the configurations at runtime. See the Spark documentation (*http://spark.apache.org/docs/latest/configuration.html#dynamically-loading-spark-properties*).[1]

The configurations for a running job can be found in the "environment" tab of the web UI.

How to Determine the Relevant Information About Your Cluster

The primary resources that the Spark application manages are CPU (number of cores) and memory. Spark requests cannot ask for more resources than are available in the environment in which they will run. Thus, it is important to understand the CPU and memory available in the environment where the job will be run. If you set up your own cluster, the answers to these questions may be obvious. But often, we are working in a system that was set up by someone else, so it is important to know how

---

[1] This is a good option for Spark applications designed to run in a variety of different environments, or a use case such as ours, in which we have built a web application that submits Spark jobs from within the application.

to determine the resources available to you (or what questions to ask your sys-admin). The answers to these questions depend on the kind of system that you have, but generally speaking there are four primary pieces of information we have to know about our hardware:[2]

- How large can one request be? Most systems have a limit on each request, which caps the number of resources that can be made available to each executor and the driver. In *YARN cluster mode*, this is the maximum size of the YARN container. Each Spark executor and driver must "fit" within this limit. In terms of memory, the executors and driver require the amount provided, plus overhead. We cover calculating overhead in "Calculating Executor and Driver Memory Overhead" on page 279. In *YARN client mode*, the driver runs as a process on the client, so the cluster only needs to accommodate the resources required by the Spark executors and this does not apply to the driver.

- How large is each node? When determining the number of executors and the number of cores to allocate per executor, it is important to know how much memory and CPU resources there are on each node, since one executor can use resources from only one node. The memory available to each node is likely greater than or equal to one container. However, this question is still important, for determining the number of executors. For example, suppose that we have a three-node cluster with 20 GB nodes. Even if the YARN container limit is 15 GB, we can't run four executors, since the fourth executor would need to be spread across two nodes.

- How many nodes does your cluster have? How many are active? In general it is best to have at least one executor per node. Understanding how many nodes are up can also help you determine the total resources available.

- What percent of the resources are available on the system where the job will be submitted? If you are using a shared cluster environment, is the cluster busy? Will you be submitted into a queue, and how many resources does that queue have available? For a recurring job, you may have to query the YARN (or Mesos) API to determine resource burn before submitting. Often, if a Spark application requests more resources than exist in the queue into which it is submitted, but not more than exist on the whole cluster, the request will not fail, but instead will hang in a pending state. Understanding what resources are available per queue depends on what kind of scheduler your system is using. In the capacity schedu-ler case, each user can use a fixed percent of the resources available. In the fair scheduler case, the active applications must share resources equally. The behav-

---

[2] For a comprehensive answer to these questions for applications using YARN cluster mode, see this three-part post. (*http://alpinedata.com/how-to-use-the-yarn-api-to-determine-resources-available-for-spark-application-submission-part-1/*)

ior of the capacity and fair scheduler are well explained in the Spark documentation. I have also outlined how to determine that information from the YARN API in this post (*http://alpinedata.com/how-to-use-the-yarn-api-to-determine-resources-available-for-spark-application-submission-part-3*) for details.

Basic Spark Core Settings: How Many Resources to Allocate to the Spark Application?

The `SparkSession`/`SparkContext` begins JVMs for the executors (and in YARN cluster mode, the driver). Recall that the executors run each task (in order to compute each partition) with the cores available to each executor. Furthermore, some proportion of each executor is used for computation while some is used for caching. The size of the driver, size of the executors, and the number of cores associated with each executor, are configurable from the conf and static for the duration of a Spark application. All executors are required to be the same size. Without dynamic allocation (see "Allocating Cluster Resources and Dynamic Allocation" on page 281), the number of executors is static as well. With dynamic allocation, Spark may request decommissioning of executors between stages. Although discussed in detail in Chapter 2, I think it bears repeating that the size of each executor, the driver, and the number of cores in each driver remains fixed regardless the size of your query. So, although dynamic allocation allows Spark to add an additional executor to compute a job, Spark cannot give an executor more resources when computing a particularly expensive partition, or as resources on your environment are made available.

First we will go over the meaning of each setting. Then we will weigh in on how to determine the optimal solution for parsing the resources available between the drivers and executors given the resources you have available.

Spark setting name	Meaning	Default value	Restrictions	Guidelines
spark.driver.memory	The size of the Spark driver in MB	1024 MB	In YARN cluster mode no larger than the YARN container including overhead.	A higher setting may be required if collecting large RDDs to the driver or performing many local computations.
spark.executor.memory	1024 MB	The size of the each Spark worker.	One executor + overhead cannot be larger than the limit for one request (the size of one YARN container).	Larger Spark workers may prevent out-of-memory errors, particularly if jobs require unbalanced shuffles, but may be less efficient.
spark.executor.cores	1	The number of virtual cores that will be allocated to each executor.	The number of cores available in the YARN container.	Should be around five. Scale up as resources allow.

The total memory required by all of the executors (with overhead) and the driver (with overhead) cannot be larger than the amount of memory available on the cluster. In YARN client mode, the driver does not use resources on the cluster.

Calculating Executor and Driver Memory Overhead

In YARN cluster mode and YARN client mode, both the executor memory overhead and driver memory overhead can be set manually. In both modes the executor memory overhead is set with the `spark.yarn.executor.memoryOverhead` value. In YARN cluster mode the driver memory is set with `spark.yarn.driver.memoryOverhead`, but in YARN client mode that value is called `spark.yarn.am.memoryOverhead`. In either case, the following equations govern how memory overhead is handled when these values are not set:[3]

```
memory overhead =
        Max(MEMORY_OVERHEAD_FACTOR x requested memory, MEMORY_OVERHEAD_MINIMUM).

Where MEMORY_OVERHEAD_FACTOR = 0.10 and
MEMORY_OVERHEAD_MINIMUM = 384 mb.
```

How Large to Make the Spark Driver

In general, most of the computational work of a Spark query is performed by the executors, so increasing the size of the driver rarely speeds up a computation. However, jobs may fail if they collect too much data to the driver or perform large local computations. Thus, increasing the driver memory and correspondingly the value of `spark.driver.maxResultSize` may prevent the out-of-memory errors in the driver.

Regardless of driver memory the size of the results that can be returned to the driver are limited by the setting `spark.driver.max ResultSize`. This value bounds the total size of serialized results from all partitions being collected to the driver. The setting is used to force jobs that are likely to cause driver memory errors to fail earlier and more clearly. The default value for this setting is 1g, which is relatively small. If your job requires collecting large results and you are not competing for resources with other users, you may set the `maxResultSize` to "0", and Spark will disregard this limit.

In my experience, a good heuristic for setting the Spark driver memory is simply the lowest possible value that does not lead to memory errors in the driver, i.e., which gives the maximum possible resources to the executors.

---

3 See *https://www.cloudera.com/documentation/enterprise/5-6-x/topics/cdh_ig_running_spark_on_yarn.html* for a more detailed description of memory overhead and guidelines for how to configure it.

In YARN and Mesos cluster mode, the driver can be run with more cores, by setting the value of `spark.driver.cores`, and can run a multithreaded process. Otherwise, the driver requires one core.

A Few Large Executors or Many Small Executors?

We know that the total resources required by the executors and driver cannot be larger than the resources we have available, and each executor cannot request more memory or more cores than the resources allocated for one node (or container). However, this still leaves many, many options for how to allocate resources amongst the Spark workers. For example, suppose we are submitting a job to a cluster that has four 20 GB nodes with six cores each; do we create four 20 GB six-core executors, or eight 10 GB three-core executors? Good question! I spent several months trying to develop an algorithm to answer this question, and although there are some instances for which we can make an educated guess about resource allocation, finding the optimal configuration for one application on one cluster is not an exact science. Instead I hope to provide a few tips about how to recognize the consequences of either too large or too small executors in terms of either CPU or memory. Hopefully these tips will help you make an educated guess about configuring an application and help you determine how to correct a job if you see signs that it is misconfigured.

Many small executors

There are two potential downsides to using many small executors. The first has to do with the risk or running out of resources to compute a partition, as we discussed in Chapter 5. Since each partition cannot be computed on more than one executor, the size of each partition is bounded by the space they have to be computed. Thus, we risk running into memory problems, or spilling to disk if we need to shuffle, cache unbalanced data, or perform very expensive narrow transformations. If the executors have only one core, then we can run at most one task in each executor, which throws away the benefits of something like a broadcast variable, which only has to be sent to each executor (not each partition like other variables defined in the driver).

The second problem is that having too many executors may not be an efficient use of our resources. Each executor has some overhead, and there is some cost to communicating between executors even if they are on the same node. Recall from our discussion of memory overhead that the minimum overhead is just under 400 MB. Thus if we have many 1 GB executors, nearly 25 percent of the space that each executor will use on our cluster has to be used for overhead rather than computation. I think that there is a good argument to be made that if resources are available, executors should be no smaller than about four gigs, at which point overhead will be based on the memory overhead factor (a constant 10 percent of the executor).

Many large executors

Very large executors may be wasteful just because placing executors on nodes is a binning problem.[4] To use all the resources and to have the driver smaller than the size of one node, we might need to have more executors per node than one. For example, suppose that our cluster only has four very large nodes and our computation requires very little driver memory. In this case, having three very large executors and a driver that is only half the size of the executors may be wasteful, since it leaves half of the last node unused. Furthermore, very large executors may cause delays in garbage collection, since a larger heap will delay the time until a GC event is triggered and consequently GC pauses may be larger. Many cores per executor seems to lead to poor performance, due to some limitations from HDFS on handling many concurrent threads.[5] Sandy Ryza suggests that five cores per executor should be the upper limit. I have had jobs perform with a few more (6 or 7 cores), but it seems that, at the very least, assigning executors more than about seven or eight cores does not speed up performance and burns CPU resources unnecessarily. This limit on the CPU should correlate to some limitation in terms of executor memory, if you want to burn CPU and memory relatively evenly on your cluster. In other words, I have had relatively good results by determining the number of executors based on CPU resources —dividing the CPU on each node by about five—then setting memory per executor based on that number of executors.

Allocating Cluster Resources and Dynamic Allocation

Dynamic allocation is a process by which a Spark application can request and decommission executors as needed throughout the course of an application. This can lead to dramatic performance improvements especially on a busy cluster, because it allows an application to use resources as they become available and frees up those resources when jobs do not need them.

The following rules govern when Spark adds or removes executors with dynamic allocation. First, Spark requests additional executors when there are pending tasks. Second, Spark decommissions executors that have not been used to compute a job in the amount of time specified by the `spark.dynamicAllocation.executorIdleTime` out parameter (by default, sixty seconds). With the default settings, Spark does not remove executors that contain cached data, because once an executor has been decommissioned, the cached data has to be recomputed to be used. You may change

---

4 For any algorithm junkies, finding the best size and number of executors is similar to the Np-Complete knapsack problem. The executors have fixed sizes and cores and have to "fit" onto the various nodes.

5 See this post by Sandy Ryza (*http://blog.cloudera.com/blog/2015/03/how-to-tune-your-apache-spark-jobs-part-2*), and the data presented in this Stack Overflow post (*http://stackoverflow.com/questions/24622108/apache-spark-the-number-of-cores-vs-the-number-of-executors*).

this behavior by setting `spark.dynamicAllocation.cachedExecutorIdleTimeout` to something other than the default: `infinity`. In this case, executors with cached data will be decommissioned if they have not been used for some amount of time.

You may configure the number of executors that Spark should start with when an application is launched with `spark.dynamicAllocation.initialExecutors`, which by default is zero. If you know that the application will be launching expensive jobs and that cluster resources are available, I would recommend increasing this. Otherwise, leaving the value at the default zero is advantageous because it means that the application can scale up resources gradually. There are also configuration values for the minimum and maximum amount of executors used during a job. I suggest setting the maximum amount to be the resources that are available to the user submitting the application on your cluster to avoid hogging the entire cluster.

Because dynamic allocation does not allow executors to change in size you still must determine the size of each executor before starting the job. My recommendation is to size the executors as you would if you were trying to use all the resources on the cluster. This will ensure that if computations are expensive and Spark requests the maximum number of executors, those resources will be well allocated. One possible exception is in the case of a very high-traffic cluster. In this case, using small executors may allow dynamic allocation to increase the number of resources used more quickly if space becomes available on the nodes in a piecemeal way.

Restrictions on dynamic allocation

Dynamic allocation can be a bit difficult to configure. In order to get dynamic allocation to work, you must:

1. Set the configuration value `spark.dynamicAllocation.enabled` to true.
2. Configure an external shuffle service on each worker. This varies based on the cluster manager, so see the Spark documentation (*http://spark.apache.org/docs/latest/job-scheduling.html#configuration-and-setup*) for details.
3. Set `spark.shuffle.service.enabled` to `true`.
4. Do not provide a value for the `spark.executor.instances` parameter. Even if dynamic allocation is configured Spark will override that behavior and use the specified number of executors if this parameter is included in the conf.

In some instances, if the conf specifies using dynamic allocation but the shuffle service is misconfigured, the job will hang in a pending state, because the nodes do not have a mechanism to request executors. If you know the cluster has resources and see this behavior, make sure the shuffle service is configured on each worker and that the YARN conf contains the correct class path to the shuffle service.

Dividing the Space Within One Executor

In Figure 2-4, we suggested that executors were JVMs with some space set aside for caching and some for execution. While this is true, the division of memory usage within an executor is actually more complicated than the diagram might suggest, since the regions are not static. First, the JVM size set by the `spark.executor.memory` property does not include overhead, so Spark executors require more space on a cluster than this number would suggest. Within the executor memory, some of the space has to be reserved for Spark's internal metadata and user data structures (by default about 25%.) The remaining space on the executor, called M in the Spark documentation, is used for execution and storage. The execution memory is the memory required to compute a Spark transformation. The total space in the executor for both caching and execution is governed by a fixed fraction, exposed in the conf as the `spark.memory.fraction`. Out-of-memory errors during a transformation or when cached partitions are spilling to disk, is usually caused by the limitation in this combined storage and execution space. The default size of M is 0.6, so 60% of an executor is used for storage and execution. While it is possible to reduce the space used for internal metadata by increasing the size of M, doing so may be dangerous because this serves as a safeguard against out-of-memory errors caused by internal processes.

Within this `spark.memory.fraction`, which we will call M, some space is set aside for "storage," and the rest can be used for storage or execution. Storage in this case refers to Spark's in-memory storage of partitions, whether serialized or not. Rather than providing a fixed region for storage, Spark allows applications that do not cache anything in-memory to use the full memory fraction for execution. Within the execution space, Spark defines a region of the execution called R for storing cached data. The size of R is determined by a percentage of M set by the `spark.memory.storageFrac tion`. R is the space Spark will not reclaim for execution if there is cached data present. Spark enables persisting more data than fits in R, but allows the extra partitions to be evicted if a future task requires it.[6] In other words, to cache an RDD

---

6 Prior to Spark 1.6.0, the storage and execution memory were strictly separated by the `spark.memory.storage Fraction` value.

without allowing any partitions to be evicted from memory, all of the cached data must fit in R, the space determined by:

```
R = spark.executor.memory x
    spark.memory.fraction x spark.memory.storageFraction.
```

The following diagrams attempt to illustrate the relationship between M and R. Each box represents one Spark executor. The red quadrant at the bottom is R. The space below the overhead is M.

In Figure A-1, we have assumed that two different RDDs have been cached. And the partitions shown are those that are cached on this particular executor. The blue partition regardless of caching order, is the least recently used partition. Because the partitions do not take up all of the storage fraction R, a large computation (represented by the orange burst) may use the space in the storage fraction.

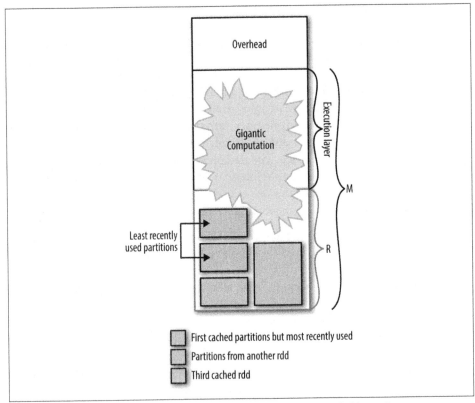

Figure A-1. A single computation may use all of the space available in the memory fraction

Next, suppose that the same application included a job that cached another partition. Now all of the cached partitions take up more space than R (see that the green boxes go above the red line). This is allowed since no computation requires this space. Suppose also that the blue partition was used in this job, making the pink partition the least recently used partition. The result is shown in Figure A-2.

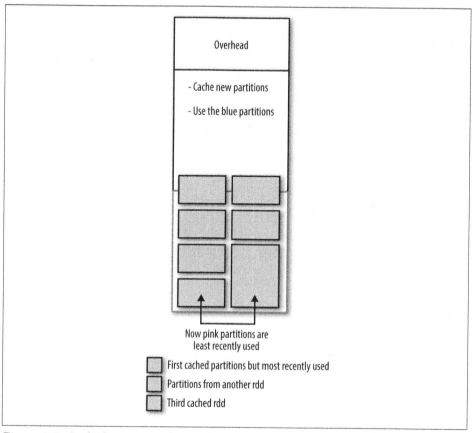

Figure A-2. Cached partitions may exceed the space allocated by spark.memory.storageFraction if no computation evicts them

Now suppose that we perform a giant computation on this executor, resulting in Figure A-3. Because the cached data takes up more space than exists in the R region, the extra partitions will be evicted to make space for the computation. The partitions that are evicted are those that were least recently used (the pink partitions), because Spark uses Least Recently Used (LRU) caching. (See "LRU Caching" on page 123 for more information about LRU caching.)

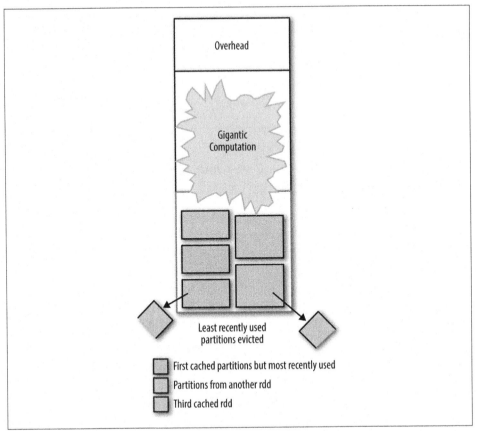

Figure A-3. A large computation may evict the cached partitions, if the storageFraction is full. The least recently used partitions are evicted first.

Adjusting the memory and storage fraction settings largely depends on the kind of computation that we want to perform. If you are not caching data, then this setting hardly matters because all of M will be reserved for computation anyway. However, if an application requires repeated access to an RDD and performance is improved by caching the RDD in memory, it may be useful to increase the size of the storage fraction to prevent the RDDs you needed cached from being evicted.

 One way to get a feel for the size of the RDD is to write a program that caches the RDD. Then, launch the job and while it is running, look at the "Storage" page of the web UI.

In Figure A-4 we see how a cached DataFrame and a cached RDD appear in the web UI. The "Size In Memory" column displaces the size of the data structure in memory.

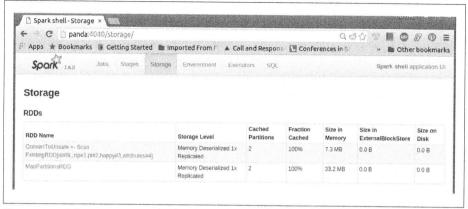

Figure A-4. The storage tab of the web UI

Number and Size of Partitions

As we discussed in Chapter 6, Spark does not have any mechanism to set the optimal number of partitions to use. By default, when an RDD is created by reading from stable storage, the number of partitions corresponds to the splits configured in that input format (usually the parts in a MapReduce file). We can explicitly change the number of partitions using coalesce, repartition, or during wide transformations such as reduceByKey or sort. If the number of partitions is not specified for the wide transformation, Spark defaults to using the number specified by the conf value of spark.default.parallelism.

> The default values of the spark.default.parallelism parameters depends on the environment that the application is running in. In YARN Cluster mode, it is the number of cores * the number of executors (in other words, the number of tasks that can be run at one time). This is the minimum value that you should use for the number of partitions, but not necessarily the optimal value.

So how many partitions should we use in a wide transformation or as the value of spark.default.parallelism?

Like most of my advice in this appendix, there is not a straight answer to this question. In general, increasing partitions improves performance until a certain point, when it simply creates too much overhead. At a minimum you should use as many partitions as total cores, because using fewer leaves some of the CPU resources idle. Increasing the number of partitions can also help reduce out-of-memory errors, since it means that Spark will operate on a smaller subset of the data for each executor. One strategy can be to determine the maximum size of a partition. That is, the largest a partition can be and still "fit" in the space allocated for one task and then work backward to determine the number of partitions to set (parts to divide the RDD into) so that each one is no larger than this size. Recall from Chapter 2 that each executor can run one task for each core and that one partition corresponds to one task. As we explained in "Dividing the Space Within One Executor" on page 283, the space that a Spark executor has available to compute is between the size of M and M – R depending on the amount of cached data. For example:

```
memory_for_compute (M)<
    (spark.executor.memory - over head) * spark.memory.fraction
```

And if there is cached data:

```
memory_for_compute (M - R) <
    (spark.executor.memory - overhead) x
    spark.memory.fraction x
    (1 - spark.memory.storage.fraction).
```

Assuming this space is divided equally between the tasks, then each task should not take more than:

```
memory_per_task =
    memory_for_compute / spark.executor.cores
```

Thus, we should set the number of partitions to:

```
number_of_partitions =
    size of shuffle stage / memory per task.
```

If partitions are larger than this size, then Spark may not be able to compute as many tasks concurrently, wasting CPU resources, since one task can use only one core. It may also increase the possibility of out-of-memory errors.

We can estimate the size of the stage using some information from the web UI. First, if you have cached the RDD in-memory and observed its size in the web UI, you can expect that a computation will require at least that much space, since presumably the computation requires loading the data first. We can also try to observe the shuffle stage to determine the memory cost of a shuffle. If we observe that during the shuffle stage the computation is not spilling to disk, then it is likely that each partition is fitting comfortably in-memory and we don't need to increase the number of partitions.

You can see if, and how much, tasks are spilling to disk with the web UI. To examine one stage, navigate to the "jobs" tab of the web UI while a job is running. Then click the stage that is running. There you will see the details for the stage. In the details for the stage, Spark lists a metric for the work done on each executor and for the tasks that are running. In the tasks table you will see the two last columns are for shuffle spill (memory) and shuffle (spill disk). If there are zero, then none of these tasks spilled to disk.[7]

If the job is spilling to disk it may be worth trying to estimate the size of the shuffle and trying to tune the number of partitions. Of course "the size of the shuffle" is not information we can determine concretely. Sandy Ryza suggests using the ratio between the amount of shuffle spill to memory (which appears in the UI as "Shuffle spill (memory)") and shuffle spill to disk (in the UI as "shuffle spill (disk)") and multipliying that ration by the size of the data on disk to approximate the size of the shuffle files.[8] We will elaborate on this procedure in the following section.

Shuffle spill (memory) is the amount of space that records took up in-memory *before* spilling to to disk. Shuffle spill (disk) is the space that the records took up *after* they had been spilled. Thus, the ratio between Shuffle spill (memory) and Shuffle spill (disk) is a measure of how much more space records take in-memory than on disk. I will call this the "rate of in memory expansion," which could be formalized with the following equation:

```
rate of in-memory expansion =
    Shuffle spill (memory) /Shuffle spill (disk)
```

In the web UI, we can see the total size of the shuffled write in the Initial Stages tab. This represents the size of the shuffle files written to disk.

Thus the size of those files in-memory is:

```
Size of shuffle in-memory =
    shuffle write * Shuffle spill (memory) /
    Shuffle spill (disk).
```

Again, for all the complexity of this method, it is really just a heuristic. It assumes incorrectly that each record will expand when read into memory at the same rate.

---

7 See *http://jason4zhu.blogspot.com/2015/06/roaming-through-spark-ui-and-tune-performance-upon-a-specific-use-case.html.*

8 This is Ryza's much cited blog post on Spark tuning and parallelism (*http://blog.cloudera.com/blog/2015/03/how-to-tune-your-apache-spark-jobs-part-2/*). It was written for an older version of Spark, so you will notice that his description of memory management differs from mine. However, most of the information, particularly the discussion of sizing partitions is still very relevant.

There is no replacement for simply increasing the number of partitions until performance stops improving.

Serialization Options

By default Spark uses Java serialization for RDDs and Tungsten-based serialization for `DataFrames`/`Datasets`. For those who can, using `DataFrames` or `Datasets` gives you access to a much more efficient serialization layer, but if working in RDDs you can also consider using Kryo serialization.

Kryo

Like the Tungsten serializer, Kryo serialization does not natively support all of the same types that are Java serializable. The details of how Kryo works with Spark and how to extend it are already covered in *Learning Spark* (and you can find public examples (*https://github.com/holdenk/learning-spark-examples/blob/master/src/main/java/com/oreilly/learningsparkexamples/java/BasicAvgWithKryo.java*) as well). One might think with Tungsten, work on Spark's Kryo integration would stop, but in fact improvement to Spark's Kryo serialization are continuing. The next version of Spark is adding support for Kryo's unsafe serializer, which can be even faster than Tungsten and can be enabled by setting `spark.kryo.unsafe` to true.

Spark settings conclusion

Adjusting Spark settings can lead to huge performance improvements. However, it is time consuming and in some case provides limited gains for hours of testing. No amount of tuning would make the unbalanced shuffle presented in "Goldilocks Version 1: groupByKey Solution" on page 134 complete on a billion rows (believe me, we tried). Because of the many variables associated with tuning an application—cluster dimensions, cluster traffic, input data size, type of computation—finding the optimal Spark configuration is difficult to do without some trial and error. However, a good understanding of what to look for in the UI, such as whether shuffles are spilling to disk or include retries, may help improve this process. Most importantly, a good knowledge of your system and the needs of your computation can help you plan the best strategy for submitting an application.

Some Additional Debugging Techniques

Debugging is an important part of the software development life cycle, and debugging with Spark has some unique considerations. The most obvious challenge of debugging Spark is that as a distributed system it can be difficult to determine which machine(s) are throwing errors, and getting access to the worker nodes may not be feasible for debugging. In addition, Spark's use of lazy evaluation can trip up developers used to more classic systems, as any logs or stack trace may at first glance point us in the wrong direction.

Debugging a system that relies on lazy evaluation requires removing the assumption that the error is necessarily directly related to the line of code that appears to trigger the error, or any of the functions it directly calls. If you are in an interactive environment, encountering an error can quickly be tracked down by adding a take(1) or count call on the parent RDDs or DataFrames to track down the issue more quickly. However, when debugging production code, the luxury of putting a take(1) or count may not be available, in part because it can substantially increase the computation time. Instead in those cases, it can be an important exercise to learn to tell the difference between two seemingly similar failures. Let us consider Examples A-1 and A-2 as well as the resulting stack traces in Examples A-3 and A-4, respectively.

Example A-1. Throw from inside an inner RDD

```
val data = sc.parallelize(List(1, 2, 3))
// Will throw an exception when forced to evaluate
val transform1 = data.map(x => x/0)
val transform2 = transform1.map(x => x + 1)
transform2.collect() // Forces evaluation
```

Example A-2. Throw from inside the topmost RDD

```
val data = sc.parallelize(List(1, 2, 3))
val transform1 = data.map(x => x + 1)
// Will throw an exception when forced to evaluate
val transform2 = transform1.map(x => x/0)
transform2.collect() // Forces evaluation
```

Example A-3. Inner failure

```
17/01/23 12:41:36 ERROR Executor: Exception in task 0.0 in stage 0.0 (TID 0)
java.lang.ArithmeticException: / by zero
    at com.highperformancespark.examples.errors.Throws$$anonfun$1
    .apply$mcII$sp(throws.scala:9)
    at com.highperformancespark.examples.errors.Throws$$anonfun$1
    .apply(throws.scala:9)
    at com.highperformancespark.examples.errors.Throws$$anonfun$1
    .apply(throws.scala:9)
    at scala.collection.Iterator$$anon$11.next(Iterator.scala:370)
    at scala.collection.Iterator$$anon$11.next(Iterator.scala:370)
    at scala.collection.Iterator$class.foreach(Iterator.scala:750)
    at scala.collection.AbstractIterator.foreach(Iterator.scala:1202)
    at scala.collection.generic.Growable$class.$plus$plus$eq(Growable.scala:59)
    at scala.collection.mutable.ArrayBuffer.$plus$plus$eq(ArrayBuffer.scala:104)
    at scala.collection.mutable.ArrayBuffer.$plus$plus$eq(ArrayBuffer.scala:48)
    at scala.collection.TraversableOnce$class.to(TraversableOnce.scala:295)
```

```
    at scala.collection.AbstractIterator.to(Iterator.scala:1202)
    at scala.collection.TraversableOnce$class.toBuffer(TraversableOnce.scala:287)
    at scala.collection.AbstractIterator.toBuffer(Iterator.scala:1202)
    at scala.collection.TraversableOnce$class.toArray(TraversableOnce.scala:274)
    at scala.collection.AbstractIterator.toArray(Iterator.scala:1202)
    at org.apache.spark.rdd.RDD$$anonfun$collect$1$$anonfun$13.
    apply(RDD.scala:935)
    at org.apache.spark.rdd.RDD$$anonfun$collect$1$$anonfun$13.
    apply(RDD.scala:935)
    at org.apache.spark.SparkContext$$anonfun$runJob$5
    .apply(SparkContext.scala:1944)
    at org.apache.spark.SparkContext$$anonfun$runJob$5
    .apply(SparkContext.scala:1944)
    at org.apache.spark.scheduler.ResultTask.runTask(ResultTask.scala:87)
    at org.apache.spark.scheduler.Task.run(Task.scala:99)
    at org.apache.spark.executor.Executor$TaskRunner.run(Executor.scala:282)
    at java.util.concurrent.ThreadPoolExecutor
    .runWorker(ThreadPoolExecutor.java:1142)
    at java.util.concurrent.ThreadPoolExecutor$Worker
    .run(ThreadPoolExecutor.java:617)
    at java.lang.Thread.run(Thread.java:745)
17/01/23 12:41:36 WARN TaskSetManager: Lost task 0.0
in stage 0.0 (TID 0, localhost, executor driver):
java.lang.ArithmeticException: / by zero
    at com.highperformancespark.examples.errors.Throws$$anonfun$1
    .apply$mcII$sp(throws.scala:9)
    at com.highperformancespark.examples.errors.Throws$$anonfun$1
    .apply(throws.scala:9)
    at com.highperformancespark.examples.errors.Throws$$anonfun$1
    .apply(throws.scala:9)
    at scala.collection.Iterator$$anon$11.next(Iterator.scala:370)
    at scala.collection.Iterator$$anon$11.next(Iterator.scala:370)
    at scala.collection.Iterator$class.foreach(Iterator.scala:750)
    at scala.collection.AbstractIterator.foreach(Iterator.scala:1202)
    at scala.collection.generic.Growable$class.$plus$plus$eq(Growable.scala:59)
    at scala.collection.mutable.ArrayBuffer.$plus$plus$eq(ArrayBuffer.scala:104)
    at scala.collection.mutable.ArrayBuffer.$plus$plus$eq(ArrayBuffer.scala:48)
    at scala.collection.TraversableOnce$class.to(TraversableOnce.scala:295)
    at scala.collection.AbstractIterator.to(Iterator.scala:1202)
    at scala.collection.TraversableOnce$class.toBuffer(TraversableOnce.scala:287)
    at scala.collection.AbstractIterator.toBuffer(Iterator.scala:1202)
    at scala.collection.TraversableOnce$class.toArray(TraversableOnce.scala:274)
    at scala.collection.AbstractIterator.toArray(Iterator.scala:1202)
    at org.apache.spark.rdd.RDD$$anonfun$collect$1$$anonfun$13
    .apply(RDD.scala:935)
    at org.apache.spark.rdd.RDD$$anonfun$collect$1$$anonfun$13
    .apply(RDD.scala:935)
    at org.apache.spark.SparkContext$$anonfun$runJob$5
    .apply(SparkContext.scala:1944)
    at org.apache.spark.SparkContext$$anonfun$runJob$5
    .apply(SparkContext.scala:1944)
    at org.apache.spark.scheduler.ResultTask.runTask(ResultTask.scala:87)
```

```
    at org.apache.spark.scheduler.Task.run(Task.scala:99)
    at org.apache.spark.executor.Executor$TaskRunner.run(Executor.scala:282)
    at java.util.concurrent.ThreadPoolExecutor
    .runWorker(ThreadPoolExecutor.java:1142)
    at java.util.concurrent.ThreadPoolExecutor$Worker
    .run(ThreadPoolExecutor.java:617)
    at java.lang.Thread.run(Thread.java:745)

17/01/23 12:41:36 ERROR TaskSetManager:
Task 0 in stage 0.0 failed 1 times; aborting job
org.apache.spark.SparkException: Job aborted due to stage failure:
Task 0 in stage 0.0 failed 1 times, most recent failure:
Lost task 0.0 in stage 0.0 (TID 0, localhost, executor driver):
java.lang.ArithmeticException: / by zero
    at com.highperformancespark.examples.errors.Throws$$anonfun$1.
    apply$mcII$sp(throws.scala:9)
    at com.highperformancespark.examples.errors.Throws$$anonfun$1.apply(throws.scala:9)
    at com.highperformancespark.examples.errors.Throws$$anonfun$1.apply(throws.scala:9)
    at scala.collection.Iterator$$anon$11.next(Iterator.scala:370)
    at scala.collection.Iterator$$anon$11.next(Iterator.scala:370)
    at scala.collection.Iterator$class.foreach(Iterator.scala:750)
    at scala.collection.AbstractIterator.foreach(Iterator.scala:1202)
    at scala.collection.generic.Growable$class.$plus$plus$eq(Growable.scala:59)
    at scala.collection.mutable.ArrayBuffer.$plus$plus$eq(ArrayBuffer.scala:104)
    at scala.collection.mutable.ArrayBuffer.$plus$plus$eq(ArrayBuffer.scala:48)
    at scala.collection.TraversableOnce$class.to(TraversableOnce.scala:295)
    at scala.collection.AbstractIterator.to(Iterator.scala:1202)
    at scala.collection.TraversableOnce$class.toBuffer(TraversableOnce.scala:287)
    at scala.collection.AbstractIterator.toBuffer(Iterator.scala:1202)
    at scala.collection.TraversableOnce$class.toArray(TraversableOnce.scala:274)
    at scala.collection.AbstractIterator.toArray(Iterator.scala:1202)
    at org.apache.spark.rdd.RDD$$anonfun$collect$1$$anonfun$13
    .apply(RDD.scala:935)
    at org.apache.spark.rdd.RDD$$anonfun$collect$1$$anonfun$13
    .apply(RDD.scala:935)
    at org.apache.spark.SparkContext$$anonfun$runJob$5
    .apply(SparkContext.scala:1944)
    at org.apache.spark.SparkContext$$anonfun$runJob$5
    .apply(SparkContext.scala:1944)
    at org.apache.spark.scheduler.ResultTask.runTask(ResultTask.scala:87)
    at org.apache.spark.scheduler.Task.run(Task.scala:99)
    at org.apache.spark.executor.Executor$TaskRunner.run(Executor.scala:282)
    at java.util.concurrent.ThreadPoolExecutor
    .runWorker(ThreadPoolExecutor.java:1142)
    at java.util.concurrent.ThreadPoolExecutor$Worker
    .run(ThreadPoolExecutor.java:617)
    at java.lang.Thread.run(Thread.java:745)

Driver stacktrace:
  at org.apache.spark.scheduler.
  DAGScheduler.org$apache$spark$scheduler$DAGScheduler$$
  failJobAndIndependentStages(DAGScheduler.scala:1435)
```

```
    at org.apache.spark.scheduler.DAGScheduler$$anonfun$abortStage$1
    .apply(DAGScheduler.scala:1423)
    at org.apache.spark.scheduler.DAGScheduler$$anonfun$abortStage$1
    .apply(DAGScheduler.scala:1422)
    at scala.collection.mutable.ResizableArray$class.foreach(ResizableArray.scala:59)
    at scala.collection.mutable.ArrayBuffer.foreach(ArrayBuffer.scala:48)
    at org.apache.spark.scheduler.DAGScheduler.abortStage(DAGScheduler.scala:1422)
    at org.apache.spark.scheduler
    .DAGScheduler$$anonfun$handleTaskSetFailed$1.apply(DAGScheduler.scala:802)
    at org.apache.spark.scheduler
    .DAGScheduler$$anonfun$handleTaskSetFailed$1.apply(DAGScheduler.scala:802)
    at scala.Option.foreach(Option.scala:257)
    at org.apache.spark.scheduler.DAGScheduler.
    handleTaskSetFailed(DAGScheduler.scala:802)
    at org.apache.spark.scheduler.DAGSchedulerEventProcessLoop.
    doOnReceive(DAGScheduler.scala:1650)
    at org.apache.spark.scheduler.DAGSchedulerEventProcessLoop
    .onReceive(DAGScheduler.scala:1605)
    at org.apache.spark.scheduler.DAGSchedulerEventProcessLoop
    .onReceive(DAGScheduler.scala:1594)
    at org.apache.spark.util.EventLoop$$anon$1.run(EventLoop.scala:48)
    at org.apache.spark.scheduler.DAGScheduler.runJob(DAGScheduler.scala:628)
    at org.apache.spark.SparkContext.runJob(SparkContext.scala:1918)
    at org.apache.spark.SparkContext.runJob(SparkContext.scala:1931)
    at org.apache.spark.SparkContext.runJob(SparkContext.scala:1944)
    at org.apache.spark.SparkContext.runJob(SparkContext.scala:1958)
    at org.apache.spark.rdd.RDD$$anonfun$collect$1.apply(RDD.scala:935)
    at org.apache.spark.rdd.RDDOperationScope$.withScope(RDDOperationScope.scala:151)
    at org.apache.spark.rdd.RDDOperationScope$.withScope(RDDOperationScope.scala:112)
    at org.apache.spark.rdd.RDD.withScope(RDD.scala:362)
    at org.apache.spark.rdd.RDD.collect(RDD.scala:934)
    at com.highperformancespark.examples.errors.Throws$.throwInner(throws.scala:11)
    ... 43 elided
Caused by: java.lang.ArithmeticException: / by zero
    at com.highperformancespark.examples.errors.Throws$$anonfun$1
    .apply$mcII$sp(throws.scala:9)
    at com.highperformancespark.examples.errors.Throws$$anonfun$1.apply(throws.scala:9)
    at com.highperformancespark.examples.errors.Throws$$anonfun$1.apply(throws.scala:9)
    at scala.collection.Iterator$$anon$11.next(Iterator.scala:370)
    at scala.collection.Iterator$$anon$11.next(Iterator.scala:370)
    at scala.collection.Iterator$class.foreach(Iterator.scala:750)
    at scala.collection.AbstractIterator.foreach(Iterator.scala:1202)
    at scala.collection.generic.Growable$class.$plus$plus$eq(Growable.scala:59)
    at scala.collection.mutable.ArrayBuffer.$plus$plus$eq(ArrayBuffer.scala:104)
    at scala.collection.mutable.ArrayBuffer.$plus$plus$eq(ArrayBuffer.scala:48)
    at scala.collection.TraversableOnce$class.to(TraversableOnce.scala:295)
    at scala.collection.AbstractIterator.to(Iterator.scala:1202)
    at scala.collection.TraversableOnce$class.toBuffer(TraversableOnce.scala:287)
    at scala.collection.AbstractIterator.toBuffer(Iterator.scala:1202)
    at scala.collection.TraversableOnce$class.toArray(TraversableOnce.scala:274)
    at scala.collection.AbstractIterator.toArray(Iterator.scala:1202)
    at org.apache.spark.rdd.RDD$$anonfun$collect$1$$anonfun$13.apply(RDD.scala:935)
```

```
    at org.apache.spark.rdd.RDD$$anonfun$collect$1$$anonfun$13.apply(RDD.scala:935)
    at org.apache.spark.SparkContext$$anonfun$runJob$5.apply(SparkContext.scala:1944)
    at org.apache.spark.SparkContext$$anonfun$runJob$5.apply(SparkContext.scala:1944)
    at org.apache.spark.scheduler.ResultTask.runTask(ResultTask.scala:87)
    at org.apache.spark.scheduler.Task.run(Task.scala:99)
    at org.apache.spark.executor.Executor$TaskRunner.run(Executor.scala:282)
    at java.util.concurrent.ThreadPoolExecutor.runWorker(ThreadPoolExecutor.java:1142)
    at java.util.concurrent.ThreadPoolExecutor$Worker.run(ThreadPoolExecutor.java:617)
    ... 1 more
```

Example A-4. Throw outer exception

```
17/01/23 12:45:27 ERROR Executor: Exception in task 0.0 in stage 1.0 (TID 1)
java.lang.ArithmeticException: / by zero
    at com.highperformancespark.examples.errors.Throws$$anonfun$4
    .apply$mcII$sp(throws.scala:17)
    at com.highperformancespark.examples.errors.Throws$$anonfun$4
    .apply(throws.scala:17)
    at com.highperformancespark.examples.errors.Throws$$anonfun$4
    .apply(throws.scala:17)
    at scala.collection.Iterator$$anon$11.next(Iterator.scala:370)
    at scala.collection.Iterator$class.foreach(Iterator.scala:750)
    at scala.collection.AbstractIterator.foreach(Iterator.scala:1202)
    at scala.collection.generic.Growable$class.$plus$plus$eq(Growable.scala:59)
    at scala.collection.mutable.ArrayBuffer.$plus$plus$eq(ArrayBuffer.scala:104)
    at scala.collection.mutable.ArrayBuffer.$plus$plus$eq(ArrayBuffer.scala:48)
    at scala.collection.TraversableOnce$class.to(TraversableOnce.scala:295)
    at scala.collection.AbstractIterator.to(Iterator.scala:1202)
    at scala.collection.TraversableOnce$class.toBuffer(TraversableOnce.scala:287)
    at scala.collection.AbstractIterator.toBuffer(Iterator.scala:1202)
    at scala.collection.TraversableOnce$class.toArray(TraversableOnce.scala:274)
    at scala.collection.AbstractIterator.toArray(Iterator.scala:1202)
    at org.apache.spark.rdd.RDD$$anonfun$collect$1$$anonfun$13
    .apply(RDD.scala:935)
    at org.apache.spark.rdd.RDD$$anonfun$collect$1$$anonfun$13
    .apply(RDD.scala:935)
    at org.apache.spark.SparkContext$$anonfun$runJob$5
    .apply(SparkContext.scala:1944)
    at org.apache.spark.SparkContext$$anonfun$runJob$5
    .apply(SparkContext.scala:1944)
    at org.apache.spark.scheduler.ResultTask.runTask(ResultTask.scala:87)
    at org.apache.spark.scheduler.Task.run(Task.scala:99)
    at org.apache.spark.executor.Executor$TaskRunner.run(Executor.scala:282)
    at java.util.concurrent.ThreadPoolExecutor
    .runWorker(ThreadPoolExecutor.java:1142)
    at java.util.concurrent.ThreadPoolExecutor$Worker
    .run(ThreadPoolExecutor.java:617)
    at java.lang.Thread.run(Thread.java:745)
17/01/23 12:45:27 WARN TaskSetManager: Lost task 0.0 in stage 1.0
(TID 1, localhost, executor driver):
java.lang.ArithmeticException: /
by zero
```

```
    at com.highperformancespark.examples.errors.Throws$$anonfun$4
    .apply$mcII$sp(throws.scala:17)
    at com.highperformancespark.examples.errors.Throws$$anonfun$4
    .apply(throws.scala:17)
    at com.highperformancespark.examples.errors.Throws$$anonfun$4
    .apply(throws.scala:17)
    at scala.collection.Iterator$$anon$11.next(Iterator.scala:370)
    at scala.collection.Iterator$class.foreach(Iterator.scala:750)
    at scala.collection.AbstractIterator.foreach(Iterator.scala:1202)
    at scala.collection.generic.Growable$class.$plus$plus$eq(Growable.scala:59)
    at scala.collection.mutable.ArrayBuffer.$plus$plus$eq(ArrayBuffer.scala:104)
    at scala.collection.mutable.ArrayBuffer.$plus$plus$eq(ArrayBuffer.scala:48)
    at scala.collection.TraversableOnce$class.to(TraversableOnce.scala:295)
    at scala.collection.AbstractIterator.to(Iterator.scala:1202)
    at scala.collection.TraversableOnce$class.toBuffer(TraversableOnce.scala:287)
    at scala.collection.AbstractIterator.toBuffer(Iterator.scala:1202)
    at scala.collection.TraversableOnce$class.toArray(TraversableOnce.scala:274)
    at scala.collection.AbstractIterator.toArray(Iterator.scala:1202)
    at org.apache.spark.rdd.RDD$$anonfun$collect$1$$anonfun$13
    .apply(RDD.scala:935)
    at org.apache.spark.rdd.RDD$$anonfun$collect$1$$anonfun$13
    .apply(RDD.scala:935)
    at org.apache.spark.SparkContext$$anonfun$runJob$5
    .apply(SparkContext.scala:1944)
    at org.apache.spark.SparkContext$$anonfun$runJob$5
    .apply(SparkContext.scala:1944)
    at org.apache.spark.scheduler.ResultTask.runTask(ResultTask.scala:87)
    at org.apache.spark.scheduler.Task.run(Task.scala:99)
    at org.apache.spark.executor.Executor$TaskRunner.run(Executor.scala:282)
    at java.util.concurrent.ThreadPoolExecutor
    .runWorker(ThreadPoolExecutor.java:1142)
    at java.util.concurrent.ThreadPoolExecutor$Worker
    .run(ThreadPoolExecutor.java:617)
    at java.lang.Thread.run(Thread.java:745)

17/01/23 12:45:27 ERROR TaskSetManager: Task 0 in stage 1.0 failed 1 times;
aborting job
org.apache.spark.SparkException: Job aborted due to stage failure:
Task 0 in stage 1.0 failed 1 times, most recent failure:
Lost task 0.0 in stage 1.0 (TID 1, localhost, executor driver):
java.lang.ArithmeticException: / by zero
    at com.highperformancespark.examples.errors.Throws$$anonfun$4
    .apply$mcII$sp(throws.scala:17)
    at com.highperformancespark.examples.errors.Throws$$anonfun$4
    .apply(throws.scala:17)
    at com.highperformancespark.examples.errors.Throws$$anonfun$4
    .apply(throws.scala:17)
    at scala.collection.Iterator$$anon$11.next(Iterator.scala:370)
    at scala.collection.Iterator$class.foreach(Iterator.scala:750)
    at scala.collection.AbstractIterator.foreach(Iterator.scala:1202)
    at scala.collection.generic.Growable$class.$plus$plus$eq(Growable.scala:59)
    at scala.collection.mutable.ArrayBuffer.$plus$plus$eq(ArrayBuffer.scala:104)
```

```
    at scala.collection.mutable.ArrayBuffer.$plus$plus$eq(ArrayBuffer.scala:48)
    at scala.collection.TraversableOnce$class.to(TraversableOnce.scala:295)
    at scala.collection.AbstractIterator.to(Iterator.scala:1202)
    at scala.collection.TraversableOnce$class.toBuffer(TraversableOnce.scala:287)
    at scala.collection.AbstractIterator.toBuffer(Iterator.scala:1202)
    at scala.collection.TraversableOnce$class.toArray(TraversableOnce.scala:274)
    at scala.collection.AbstractIterator.toArray(Iterator.scala:1202)
    at org.apache.spark.rdd.RDD$$anonfun$collect$1$$anonfun$13
    .apply(RDD.scala:935)
    at org.apache.spark.rdd.RDD$$anonfun$collect$1$$anonfun$13
    .apply(RDD.scala:935)
    at org.apache.spark.SparkContext$$anonfun$runJob$5
    .apply(SparkContext.scala:1944)
    at org.apache.spark.SparkContext$$anonfun$runJob$5
    .apply(SparkContext.scala:1944)
    at org.apache.spark.scheduler.ResultTask.runTask(ResultTask.scala:87)
    at org.apache.spark.scheduler.Task.run(Task.scala:99)
    at org.apache.spark.executor.Executor$TaskRunner.run(Executor.scala:282)
    at java.util.concurrent.ThreadPoolExecutor
    .runWorker(ThreadPoolExecutor.java:1142)
    at java.util.concurrent.ThreadPoolExecutor$Worker
    .run(ThreadPoolExecutor.java:617)
    at java.lang.Thread.run(Thread.java:745)

Driver stacktrace:
  at org.apache.spark.scheduler
  .DAGScheduler.org$apache$spark$scheduler$DAGScheduler$$failJobAndIndependentStages
  (DAGScheduler.scala:1435)
  at org.apache.spark.scheduler.DAGScheduler$$anonfun$abortStage$1
  .apply(DAGScheduler.scala:1423)
  at org.apache.spark.scheduler.DAGScheduler$$anonfun$abortStage$1
  .apply(DAGScheduler.scala:1422)
  at scala.collection.mutable.ResizableArray$class.foreach(ResizableArray.scala:59)
  at scala.collection.mutable.ArrayBuffer.foreach(ArrayBuffer.scala:48)
  at org.apache.spark.scheduler.DAGScheduler.abortStage(DAGScheduler.scala:1422)
  at org.apache.spark.scheduler.DAGScheduler$$anonfun$handleTaskSetFailed$1
  .apply(DAGScheduler.scala:802)
  at org.apache.spark.scheduler.DAGScheduler$$anonfun$handleTaskSetFailed$1
  .apply(DAGScheduler.scala:802)
  at scala.Option.foreach(Option.scala:257)
  at org.apache.spark.scheduler.DAGScheduler
  .handleTaskSetFailed(DAGScheduler.scala:802)
  at org.apache.spark.scheduler.DAGSchedulerEventProcessLoop
  .doOnReceive(DAGScheduler.scala:1650)
  at org.apache.spark.scheduler.DAGSchedulerEventProcessLoop
  .onReceive(DAGScheduler.scala:1605)
  at org.apache.spark.scheduler.DAGSchedulerEventProcessLoop
  .onReceive(DAGScheduler.scala:1594)
  at org.apache.spark.util.EventLoop$$anon$1.run(EventLoop.scala:48)
  at org.apache.spark.scheduler.DAGScheduler.runJob(DAGScheduler.scala:628)
  at org.apache.spark.SparkContext.runJob(SparkContext.scala:1918)
  at org.apache.spark.SparkContext.runJob(SparkContext.scala:1931)
```

```
      at org.apache.spark.SparkContext.runJob(SparkContext.scala:1944)
      at org.apache.spark.SparkContext.runJob(SparkContext.scala:1958)
      at org.apache.spark.rdd.RDD$$anonfun$collect$1.apply(RDD.scala:935)
      at org.apache.spark.rdd.RDDOperationScope$.withScope(RDDOperationScope.scala:151)
      at org.apache.spark.rdd.RDDOperationScope$.withScope(RDDOperationScope.scala:112)
      at org.apache.spark.rdd.RDD.withScope(RDD.scala:362)
      at org.apache.spark.rdd.RDD.collect(RDD.scala:934)
      at com.highperformancespark.examples.errors.Throws$.throwOuter(throws.scala:18)
      ... 43 elided
Caused by: java.lang.ArithmeticException: / by zero
      at com.highperformancespark.examples.errors
      .Throws$$anonfun$4.apply$mcII$sp(throws.scala:17)
      at com.highperformancespark.examples.errors
      .Throws$$anonfun$4.apply(throws.scala:17)
      at com.highperformancespark.examples.errors
      .Throws$$anonfun$4.apply(throws.scala:17)
      at scala.collection.Iterator$$anon$11.next(Iterator.scala:370)
      at scala.collection.Iterator$class.foreach(Iterator.scala:750)
      at scala.collection.AbstractIterator.foreach(Iterator.scala:1202)
      at scala.collection.generic.Growable$class.$plus$plus$eq(Growable.scala:59)
      at scala.collection.mutable.ArrayBuffer.$plus$plus$eq(ArrayBuffer.scala:104)
      at scala.collection.mutable.ArrayBuffer.$plus$plus$eq(ArrayBuffer.scala:48)
      at scala.collection.TraversableOnce$class.to(TraversableOnce.scala:295)
      at scala.collection.AbstractIterator.to(Iterator.scala:1202)
      at scala.collection.TraversableOnce$class.toBuffer(TraversableOnce.scala:287)
      at scala.collection.AbstractIterator.toBuffer(Iterator.scala:1202)
      at scala.collection.TraversableOnce$class.toArray(TraversableOnce.scala:274)
      at scala.collection.AbstractIterator.toArray(Iterator.scala:1202)
      at org.apache.spark.rdd.RDD$$anonfun$collect$1$$anonfun$13.apply(RDD.scala:935)
      at org.apache.spark.rdd.RDD$$anonfun$collect$1$$anonfun$13.apply(RDD.scala:935)
      at org.apache.spark.SparkContext$$anonfun$runJob$5.apply(SparkContext.scala:1944)
      at org.apache.spark.SparkContext$$anonfun$runJob$5.apply(SparkContext.scala:1944)
      at org.apache.spark.scheduler.ResultTask.runTask(ResultTask.scala:87)
      at org.apache.spark.scheduler.Task.run(Task.scala:99)
      at org.apache.spark.executor.Executor$TaskRunner.run(Executor.scala:282)
      at java.util.concurrent.ThreadPoolExecutor.runWorker(ThreadPoolExecutor.java:1142)
      at java.util.concurrent.ThreadPoolExecutor$Worker.run(ThreadPoolExecutor.java:617)
      ... 1 more
```

These two stack traces contain a lot of information, but most of it isn't useful to
debugging our error. Since the error is coming from inside of our worker we can
mostly ignore the information about the driver stack trace and instead look at the
exceptions reported under 17/01/23 12:41:36 ERROR Executor: Exception in
task 0.0 in stage 0.0 (TID 0).

> A common mistake is looking at the driver stack trace when the
> error is reported from the executor. In that case it can seem like the
> error is on the line of your action, whereas the root cause lies else-
> where (as in both of the preceding examples).

By looking at the error reported from the executor you can see the line number associated with the function that failed. The rest of the exception isn't normally required unless you happen to be working with `mapPartitions` and returning custom iterators, as the iterator chaining is taken care inside of Spark.

The exception is reported twice (once as a warning and then as an error) since Spark retries a partition on failures. If you had many partitions with errors this could be reported far more than twice.

You can also see these exceptions in the Spark web UI logs if your application hasn't exited.

Determining what statement threw the error can be tricky, especially with anonymous inner functions. If you instead updated Examples A-1 and A-2 to use explicit function names (e.g., Examples A-5 and A-6) you can more easily find out what's going on. The resulting stack trace now contains the function name in question (e.g., `at        com.highperformancespark.examples.errors.Throws$.divZero(throws. scala:26)`).

Example A-5. Refactored helper functions

```
def add1(x: Int): Int = {
  x + 1
}

def divZero(x: Int): Int = {
  x / 0
}
```

Example A-6. Refactored throw examples to use helper functions

```
def add1(x: Int): Int = {
  x + 1
}

def divZero(x: Int): Int = {
  x / 0
}
```

You may notice that even though the underlying "cause" of the error is a division by zero (or java.lang.ArithmeticException), the top-level exception is wrapped by org.apache.spark.SparkException. To access the underlying exception you can use getCause.

Not all exceptions will be wrapped in org.apache.spark.SparkException. When you attempt to compute an RDD backed by a nonexistent Hadoop input, you get a much simpler stack trace (as in Example A-7) directly returning the underlying exception.

Example A-7. Exception when trying to load nonexistent input

```
org.apache.hadoop.mapred.InvalidInputException:
Input path does not exist: file:/doesnotexist.txt
  at org.apache.hadoop.mapred.FileInputFormat.
  singleThreadedListStatus(FileInputFormat.java:285)
  at org.apache.hadoop.mapred.FileInputFormat.listStatus(FileInputFormat.java:228)
  at org.apache.hadoop.mapred.FileInputFormat.getSplits(FileInputFormat.java:313)
  at org.apache.spark.rdd.HadoopRDD.getPartitions(HadoopRDD.scala:202)
  at org.apache.spark.rdd.RDD$$anonfun$partitions$2.apply(RDD.scala:252)
  at org.apache.spark.rdd.RDD$$anonfun$partitions$2.apply(RDD.scala:250)
  at scala.Option.getOrElse(Option.scala:121)
  at org.apache.spark.rdd.RDD.partitions(RDD.scala:250)
  at org.apache.spark.rdd.MapPartitionsRDD.getPartitions(MapPartitionsRDD.scala:35)
  at org.apache.spark.rdd.RDD$$anonfun$partitions$2.apply(RDD.scala:252)
  at org.apache.spark.rdd.RDD$$anonfun$partitions$2.apply(RDD.scala:250)
  at scala.Option.getOrElse(Option.scala:121)
  at org.apache.spark.rdd.RDD.partitions(RDD.scala:250)
  at org.apache.spark.rdd.MapPartitionsRDD.getPartitions(MapPartitionsRDD.scala:35)
  at org.apache.spark.rdd.RDD$$anonfun$partitions$2.apply(RDD.scala:252)
  at org.apache.spark.rdd.RDD$$anonfun$partitions$2.apply(RDD.scala:250)
  at scala.Option.getOrElse(Option.scala:121)
  at org.apache.spark.rdd.RDD.partitions(RDD.scala:250)
  at org.apache.spark.rdd.MapPartitionsRDD.getPartitions(MapPartitionsRDD.scala:35)
  at org.apache.spark.rdd.RDD$$anonfun$partitions$2.apply(RDD.scala:252)
  at org.apache.spark.rdd.RDD$$anonfun$partitions$2.apply(RDD.scala:250)
  at scala.Option.getOrElse(Option.scala:121)
  at org.apache.spark.rdd.RDD.partitions(RDD.scala:250)
  at org.apache.spark.SparkContext.runJob(SparkContext.scala:1958)
  at org.apache.spark.rdd.RDD$$anonfun$collect$1.apply(RDD.scala:935)
  at org.apache.spark.rdd.RDDOperationScope$.withScope(RDDOperationScope.scala:151)
  at org.apache.spark.rdd.RDDOperationScope$.withScope(RDDOperationScope.scala:112)
  at org.apache.spark.rdd.RDD.withScope(RDD.scala:362)
  at org.apache.spark.rdd.RDD.collect(RDD.scala:934)
  at com.highperformancespark.examples.errors.Throws$
  .nonExistentInput(throws.scala:47)
  ... 43 elided
```

Debugging driver out-of-memory exceptions can be challenging, and it can be difficult to know exactly what operation caused the failure. While you should already be weary of collect statements, it is important to remember other operations like count ByKey can potentially return unbounded results to the driver program. In Spark ML and MLlib, some of the models require bringing back a large amount of data to the driver program—in that event, the easiest solution may be trying a different model.

It can be difficult to predict how much memory a driver program will use, or track down the source of high memory usage. Furthermore, the process for assigning memory to the driver program depends on how you are submitting the Spark application. When launching an application with spark-submit in "client mode" (or scripts based on it like spark-shell or pyspark), the driver JVM is started *before* the spark-defaults.conf can be parsed and before the SparkContext is created. In this case, you must set the driver memory in *spark-env.sh* or with the --driver-memory to spark-submit.

When launching Spark from Python without spark-submit or any of the helpers specifying the JVM driver size or any driver-side JVM configurations on the conf object will not be respected even though the JVM has technically not started, the JVM driver is started using the traditional spark-submit under the hood. Instead you can configure the shell environment variable PYSPARK_SUB MIT_ARGS (which defaults to pyspark-shell) as needed.

While not considered classic debugging techniques, resolving stragglers or otherwise imbalanced partitioning is very much related and discussed in Chapter 5.

Out of Disk Space Errors

Out of disk space errors can be surprising, but are common in clusters with small amounts of disk space. Sometimes disk space errors are caused by long-running shell environments where RDDs are created at the top scope and are never garbage collected. Spark writes the output of its shuffle operations to files on the disk of the workers in the Spark local dir. These files are only cleaned up when an RDD is garbage collected, which if the amount of memory assigned to the driver program is large can take quite some time. One solution is to explicitly trigger garbage collection (assuming the RDDs have gone out of scope); if the DAG is getting too long, checkpointing can help make the RDDs available for garbage collection.

Logging

Logging is an important part of debugging your application, and in a distributed system depending on `println` is probably not going to cut it. Spark uses the `log4j` through `sl4j` logging mechanism internally, so `log4j` can be a good mechanism for our application to log with as well since we can be relatively assured it is already set up.

 Early (pre-2.0) versions of Spark exposed their logging API, which is built on top of `log4j`. This is becoming private in 2.0 and beyond, and doesn't offer much functionality that isn't available directly in `log4j`, so you should instead directly use the `log4j` logger. The author herself is guilty of having accessed the internal logging APIs.[9]

You can get access to similar functionality as the internal logging used inside of Spark through typesafe's `scalalogging` package. This package offers a trait called `LazyLogging`, which uses macros to rewrite `logger.debug(xyz)` to the equivalent, but behind a guard checking the log level. A simple example of debugging logging is wanting to be able to see what elements are being filtered out. You can add logging to the previous Example 5-16 example, resulting in Example A-9. You must also include a logging library in your build (we used Example A-8).

Example A-8. Add scalalogging to build

```
"com.typesafe.scala-logging" %% "scala-logging" % "3.5.0",
```

Example A-9. Logged broadcast of a hashset of invalid panda locations to filter out

```
val invalid = HashSet() ++ invalidPandas
val invalidBroadcast = sc.broadcast(invalid)
def keepPanda(pandaId: Long) = {
  if (invalidBroadcast.value.contains(pandaId)) {
    logger.debug(s"Invalid panda ${pandaId} discovered")
    false
  } else {
    true
  }
}
input.filter{panda => keepPanda(panda.id)}
```

---

9 And she has repented for her sins in writing this warning.

Sometimes it's handy to have the logs be clearer about what RDD/partition ID/attempt number is being processed. In that case you can look to the `TaskContext` (in both JVM and Python lands) to get this information.

Configuring logging

Spark uses `log4j` for its JVM logging, and even inside of Python or R, much of the logging information is generated from inside the JVM. When running inside of the interactive shells, one of the first messages contains instructions for configuring the log level in an interactive mode:

```
To adjust logging level use sc.setLogLevel(newLevel).
For SparkR, use setLogLevel(newLevel).
```

In addition to setting the log level using the SparkContext, Spark has a *conf/log4j.properties.template* file that can be adjusted to change log level and log outputs. Simple copy *conf/log4j.properties.template* to *conf/log4j.properties* and update any required properties, e.g. if you find Spark too verbose you may wish to set the main logging to `ERROR` as done in Example A-10.

Example A-10. log4j.properties

```
log4j.logger.org.apache.spark.repl.Main=ERROR
```

You can configure log levels for different loggers to different levels (for example, the default Spark *log4j.properties.template* configures Spark logging to `WARN` and Parquet to `ERROR`. This is especially useful when your own application also uses `log4j` logging.

If *log4j.properties* doesn't suit your needs you can ship a custom *log4j.xml* file and provide it to the executors (either by including it in your JAR or with `--files`) and then add `-Dlog4j.configuration=log4j.xm` to `spark.executor.extraJavaOptions` so the executors pick it up.

Accessing logs

If your application is actively running, the Spark web UI provides an easy way to get access to the logs of the different workers. Once your application has finished, getting the logs depends more on the deployment mechanism used.

For YARN deployments with log aggregation, the `yarn logs` command can be used to fetch the logs. If you don't have log aggregation enabled, you can still access the logs by keeping them on the worker nodes for a fixed period of time with the `yarn.nodemanager.delete.debug-delay-sec` configuration property.

In addition to copying the logs back by hand, Spark has an optional "Spark History Server," which can provide a Spark UI for finished jobs.

Attaching debuggers

While log files, accumulators, and metrics can all help debug your application, sometimes what you really want is a nice IDE interface to debug with in Spark. The simplest way to do this can be running Spark in local mode and simply attaching a debugger to your local JVM. Unfortunately not all problems on real clusters can be reproduced in local mode—in that case you can set up debugging using JDWP (Java Debug Wire Protocol) (*https://docs.oracle.com/javase/8/docs/technotes/guides/jpda/jdwp-spec.html*) to debug against a remote cluster.

Using `spark.executor.extraJavaOptions` (for the executor) or `--driver-java-options` for the driver, add the JVM parameters `-agentlib: jdwp= trans port=dt_socket,server=y,address=[debugport]` to launch.

Once you have JDWP set up on the worker or driver, the rest depends on the specific IDE you are using. IBM has a guide on how to do remote debugging with eclipse (*https://www.ibm.com/developerworks/library/os-eclipse-javadebug/*) and IntelliJ is covered in this Stack Overflow answer (*http://stackoverflow.com/questions/21114066/attach-intellij-idea-debugger-to-a-running-java-process*).

Remote debugging in Python requires modifying your code to start the debugging library. Multiple options exists for this, including integrated IDE debugging with Jetbrains (*https://www.jetbrains.com/help/pycharm/2016.3/remote-debugging.html*) and Eclipse (*http://www.pydev.org/manual_adv_remote_debugger.html*), to more basic remote tracing with rpdb (*https://pypi.python.org/pypi/rpdb/*) and more listed on the Python wiki (*https://wiki.python.org/moin/PythonDebuggingTools*). Regardless of which specific option you use, you can use a broadcast variable to ensure that all of the worker nodes receive the code to start up the remote Python debugging interface.

 Adding `-mtrace` to your driver/worker Python path will not work due to hardcoded assumptions in PySpark about the arguments.

Debugging in notebooks

Depending on your notebook, logging information can be more difficult to keep track of. When working in Jupyter with an IPython kernel, the error messages reported only include the Java stack trace and often miss the important information

---

from the Python interpreter itself. In this case, you will need to look at the console from which you launched Jupyter.

Launching Spark from within a notebook can have an unexpected impact on how the configuration is handled. The biggest difference can come from handling options for the driver configurations. When working in a hosted environment, such as Databricks cloud, IBM Data Science Experience, or Microsoft's Azure hosted Spark, it's important to do the configuration through the provided mechanism.

Python debugging

PySpark has some additional considerations; the architecture introduced in Figure 7-1 means an extra level of complexity is present. The most obvious manifestation of this comes from looking at the difference between the error messages in PySpark and error messages for the same in Scala (e.g., Examples A-3 and A-13). In addition to the extra level of indirection introduced, resource contention between the different programs involved can be a source of errors as well.

Lazy evaluation in PySpark becomes even a little more complicated than in Scala. To further confuse the source of the error, evaluation of PySpark RDDs are chained together to reduce the number of round trips of the data between Python and the JVM. Let's update Examples A-1 and A-2 to Python (giving us Examples A-11 and A-12) and examine the resulting error messages in Examples A-13 and A-14.

Example A-11. Throw from inside an inner RDD (Python)

```
data = sc.parallelize(range(10))
transform1 = data.map(lambda x: x / 0)
transform2 = transform1.map(lambda x: x + 1)
transform2.count()
```

Example A-12. Throw from inside the topmost RDD (Python)

```
data = sc.parallelize(range(10))
transform1 = data.map(lambda x: x + 1)
transform2 = transform1.map(lambda x: x / 0)
transform2.count()
```

Example A-13. Inner failure error message (Python)

```
[Stage 0:>                                                          (0 + 0) /
4]17/02/28 22:28:58 ERROR Executor:
Exception in task 3.0 in stage 0.0 (TID 3)
org.apache.spark.api.python.PythonException: Traceback (most recent call last):
  File "/home/holden/repos/spark/python/lib/pyspark.zip/pyspark/worker.py",
  line 180, in main
    process()
```

```
  File "/home/holden/repos/spark/python/lib/pyspark.zip/pyspark/worker.py",
  line 175, in process
    serializer.dump_stream(func(split_index, iterator), outfile)
  File "/home/holden/repos/spark/python/pyspark/rdd.py", line 2406, in pipeline_func
    return func(split, prev_func(split, iterator))
  File "/home/holden/repos/spark/python/pyspark/rdd.py", line 2406, in pipeline_func
    return func(split, prev_func(split, iterator))
  File "/home/holden/repos/spark/python/pyspark/rdd.py", line 2406, in pipeline_func
    return func(split, prev_func(split, iterator))
  File "/home/holden/repos/spark/python/pyspark/rdd.py", line 345, in func
    return f(iterator)
  File "/home/holden/repos/spark/python/pyspark/rdd.py", line 1040, in <lambda>
    return self.mapPartitions(lambda i: [sum(1 for _ in i)]).sum()
  File "/home/holden/repos/spark/python/pyspark/rdd.py", line 1040, in <genexpr>
    return self.mapPartitions(lambda i: [sum(1 for _ in i)]).sum()
  File "high_performance_pyspark/bad_pyspark.py", line 46, in <lambda>
    transform1 = data.map(lambda x: x / 0)
ZeroDivisionError: integer division or modulo by zero

    at org.apache.spark.api.python.PythonRunner$$anon$1.
    read(PythonRDD.scala:193)
    at org.apache.spark.api.python.PythonRunner$$anon$1.
    <init>(PythonRDD.scala:234)
    at org.apache.spark.api.python.PythonRunner.compute(PythonRDD.scala:152)
    at org.apache.spark.api.python.PythonRDD.compute(PythonRDD.scala:63)
    at org.apache.spark.rdd.RDD.computeOrReadCheckpoint(RDD.scala:323)
    at org.apache.spark.rdd.RDD.iterator(RDD.scala:287)
    at org.apache.spark.scheduler.ResultTask.runTask(ResultTask.scala:87)
    at org.apache.spark.scheduler.Task.run(Task.scala:113)
    at org.apache.spark.executor.Executor$TaskRunner.run(Executor.scala:313)
    at java.util.concurrent.ThreadPoolExecutor
    .runWorker(ThreadPoolExecutor.java:1142)
    at java.util.concurrent.ThreadPoolExecutor$Worker
    .run(ThreadPoolExecutor.java:617)
    at java.lang.Thread.run(Thread.java:745)
17/02/28 22:28:58 ERROR Executor: Exception in task 2.0 in stage 0.0 (TID 2)
org.apache.spark.api.python.PythonException: Traceback (most recent call last):
  File "/home/holden/repos/spark/python/lib/pyspark.zip/pyspark/worker.py",
  line 180, in main
    process()
  File "/home/holden/repos/spark/python/lib/pyspark.zip/pyspark/worker.py",
  line 175, in process
    serializer.dump_stream(func(split_index, iterator), outfile)
  File "/home/holden/repos/spark/python/pyspark/rdd.py", line 2406, in pipeline_func
    return func(split, prev_func(split, iterator))
  File "/home/holden/repos/spark/python/pyspark/rdd.py", line 2406, in pipeline_func
    return func(split, prev_func(split, iterator))
  File "/home/holden/repos/spark/python/pyspark/rdd.py", line 2406, in pipeline_func
    return func(split, prev_func(split, iterator))
  File "/home/holden/repos/spark/python/pyspark/rdd.py", line 345, in func
    return f(iterator)
  File "/home/holden/repos/spark/python/pyspark/rdd.py", line 1040, in <lambda>
```

```
      return self.mapPartitions(lambda i: [sum(1 for _ in i)]).sum()
    File "/home/holden/repos/spark/python/pyspark/rdd.py", line 1040, in <genexpr>
      return self.mapPartitions(lambda i: [sum(1 for _ in i)]).sum()
    File "high_performance_pyspark/bad_pyspark.py", line 46, in <lambda>
      transform1 = data.map(lambda x: x / 0)
ZeroDivisionError: integer division or modulo by zero

    at org.apache.spark.api.python.PythonRunner$$anon$1.read(PythonRDD.scala:193)
    at org.apache.spark.api.python.PythonRunner$$anon$1
    .<init>(PythonRDD.scala:234)
    at org.apache.spark.api.python.PythonRunner.compute(PythonRDD.scala:152)
    at org.apache.spark.api.python.PythonRDD.compute(PythonRDD.scala:63)
    at org.apache.spark.rdd.RDD.computeOrReadCheckpoint(RDD.scala:323)
    at org.apache.spark.rdd.RDD.iterator(RDD.scala:287)
    at org.apache.spark.scheduler.ResultTask.runTask(ResultTask.scala:87)
    at org.apache.spark.scheduler.Task.run(Task.scala:113)
    at org.apache.spark.executor.Executor$TaskRunner.run(Executor.scala:313)
    at java.util.concurrent.ThreadPoolExecutor
    .runWorker(ThreadPoolExecutor.java:1142)
    at java.util.concurrent.ThreadPoolExecutor$Worker
    .run(ThreadPoolExecutor.java:617)
    at java.lang.Thread.run(Thread.java:745)
17/02/28 22:28:58 ERROR Executor: Exception in task 1.0 in stage 0.0 (TID 1)
org.apache.spark.api.python.PythonException: Traceback (most recent call last):
  File "/home/holden/repos/spark/python/lib/pyspark.zip/pyspark/worker.py",
  line 180, in main
    process()
  File "/home/holden/repos/spark/python/lib/pyspark.zip/pyspark/worker.py",
  line 175, in process
    serializer.dump_stream(func(split_index, iterator), outfile)
  File "/home/holden/repos/spark/python/pyspark/rdd.py", line 2406, in pipeline_func
    return func(split, prev_func(split, iterator))
  File "/home/holden/repos/spark/python/pyspark/rdd.py", line 2406, in pipeline_func
    return func(split, prev_func(split, iterator))
  File "/home/holden/repos/spark/python/pyspark/rdd.py", line 2406, in pipeline_func
    return func(split, prev_func(split, iterator))
  File "/home/holden/repos/spark/python/pyspark/rdd.py", line 345, in func
    return f(iterator)
  File "/home/holden/repos/spark/python/pyspark/rdd.py", line 1040, in <lambda>
    return self.mapPartitions(lambda i: [sum(1 for _ in i)]).sum()
  File "/home/holden/repos/spark/python/pyspark/rdd.py", line 1040, in <genexpr>
    return self.mapPartitions(lambda i: [sum(1 for _ in i)]).sum()
  File "high_performance_pyspark/bad_pyspark.py", line 46, in <lambda>
    transform1 = data.map(lambda x: x / 0)
ZeroDivisionError: integer division or modulo by zero

    at org.apache.spark.api.python.PythonRunner$$anon$1.read(PythonRDD.scala:193)
    at org.apache.spark.api.python.PythonRunner$$anon$1
    .<init>(PythonRDD.scala:234)
    at org.apache.spark.api.python.PythonRunner.compute(PythonRDD.scala:152)
    at org.apache.spark.api.python.PythonRDD.compute(PythonRDD.scala:63)
    at org.apache.spark.rdd.RDD.computeOrReadCheckpoint(RDD.scala:323)
```

```
    at org.apache.spark.rdd.RDD.iterator(RDD.scala:287)
    at org.apache.spark.scheduler.ResultTask.runTask(ResultTask.scala:87)
    at org.apache.spark.scheduler.Task.run(Task.scala:113)
    at org.apache.spark.executor.Executor$TaskRunner.run(Executor.scala:313)
    at java.util.concurrent.ThreadPoolExecutor
    .runWorker(ThreadPoolExecutor.java:1142)
    at java.util.concurrent.ThreadPoolExecutor$Worker
    .run(ThreadPoolExecutor.java:617)
    at java.lang.Thread.run(Thread.java:745)
17/02/28 22:28:58 ERROR Executor: Exception in task 0.0 in stage 0.0 (TID 0)
org.apache.spark.api.python.PythonException: Traceback (most recent call last):
  File "/home/holden/repos/spark/python/lib/pyspark.zip/pyspark/worker.py",
  line 180, in main
    process()
  File "/home/holden/repos/spark/python/lib/pyspark.zip/pyspark/worker.py",
  line 175, in process
    serializer.dump_stream(func(split_index, iterator), outfile)
  File "/home/holden/repos/spark/python/pyspark/rdd.py", line 2406, in pipeline_func
    return func(split, prev_func(split, iterator))
  File "/home/holden/repos/spark/python/pyspark/rdd.py", line 2406, in pipeline_func
    return func(split, prev_func(split, iterator))
  File "/home/holden/repos/spark/python/pyspark/rdd.py", line 2406, in pipeline_func
    return func(split, prev_func(split, iterator))
  File "/home/holden/repos/spark/python/pyspark/rdd.py", line 345, in func
    return f(iterator)
  File "/home/holden/repos/spark/python/pyspark/rdd.py", line 1040, in <lambda>
    return self.mapPartitions(lambda i: [sum(1 for _ in i)]).sum()
  File "/home/holden/repos/spark/python/pyspark/rdd.py", line 1040, in <genexpr>
    return self.mapPartitions(lambda i: [sum(1 for _ in i)]).sum()
  File "high_performance_pyspark/bad_pyspark.py", line 46, in <lambda>
    transform1 = data.map(lambda x: x / 0)
ZeroDivisionError: integer division or modulo by zero

    at org.apache.spark.api.python.PythonRunner$$anon$1
    .read(PythonRDD.scala:193)
    at org.apache.spark.api.python.PythonRunner$$anon$1
    .<init>(PythonRDD.scala:234)
    at org.apache.spark.api.python.PythonRunner.compute(PythonRDD.scala:152)
    at org.apache.spark.api.python.PythonRDD.compute(PythonRDD.scala:63)
    at org.apache.spark.rdd.RDD.computeOrReadCheckpoint(RDD.scala:323)
    at org.apache.spark.rdd.RDD.iterator(RDD.scala:287)
    at org.apache.spark.scheduler.ResultTask.runTask(ResultTask.scala:87)
    at org.apache.spark.scheduler.Task.run(Task.scala:113)
    at org.apache.spark.executor.Executor$TaskRunner.run(Executor.scala:313)
    at java.util.concurrent.ThreadPoolExecutor
    .runWorker(ThreadPoolExecutor.java:1142)
    at java.util.concurrent.ThreadPoolExecutor$Worker
    .run(ThreadPoolExecutor.java:617)
    at java.lang.Thread.run(Thread.java:745)
17/02/28 22:28:58 WARN TaskSetManager:
Lost task 0.0 in stage 0.0 (TID 0, localhost, executor driver):
org.apache.spark.api.python.PythonException: Traceback (most recent call last):
```

```
File "/home/holden/repos/spark/python/lib/pyspark.zip/pyspark/worker.py",
line 180, in main
  process()
File "/home/holden/repos/spark/python/lib/pyspark.zip/pyspark/worker.py",
line 175, in process
  serializer.dump_stream(func(split_index, iterator), outfile)
File "/home/holden/repos/spark/python/pyspark/rdd.py", line 2406, in pipeline_func
  return func(split, prev_func(split, iterator))
File "/home/holden/repos/spark/python/pyspark/rdd.py", line 2406, in pipeline_func
  return func(split, prev_func(split, iterator))
File "/home/holden/repos/spark/python/pyspark/rdd.py", line 2406, in pipeline_func
  return func(split, prev_func(split, iterator))
File "/home/holden/repos/spark/python/pyspark/rdd.py", line 345, in func
  return f(iterator)
File "/home/holden/repos/spark/python/pyspark/rdd.py", line 1040, in <lambda>
  return self.mapPartitions(lambda i: [sum(1 for _ in i)]).sum()
File "/home/holden/repos/spark/python/pyspark/rdd.py", line 1040, in <genexpr>
  return self.mapPartitions(lambda i: [sum(1 for _ in i)]).sum()
File "high_performance_pyspark/bad_pyspark.py", line 46, in <lambda>
  transform1 = data.map(lambda x: x / 0)
ZeroDivisionError: integer division or modulo by zero

    at org.apache.spark.api.python.PythonRunner$$anon$1.read(PythonRDD.scala:193)
    at org.apache.spark.api.python.PythonRunner$$anon$1
    .<init>(PythonRDD.scala:234)
    at org.apache.spark.api.python.PythonRunner.compute(PythonRDD.scala:152)
    at org.apache.spark.api.python.PythonRDD.compute(PythonRDD.scala:63)
    at org.apache.spark.rdd.RDD.computeOrReadCheckpoint(RDD.scala:323)
    at org.apache.spark.rdd.RDD.iterator(RDD.scala:287)
    at org.apache.spark.scheduler.ResultTask.runTask(ResultTask.scala:87)
    at org.apache.spark.scheduler.Task.run(Task.scala:113)
    at org.apache.spark.executor.Executor$TaskRunner.run(Executor.scala:313)
    at java.util.concurrent.ThreadPoolExecutor
    .runWorker(ThreadPoolExecutor.java:1142)
    at java.util.concurrent.ThreadPoolExecutor$Worker
    .run(ThreadPoolExecutor.java:617)
    at java.lang.Thread.run(Thread.java:745)

17/02/28 22:28:58 ERROR Executor: Exception in task 0.1 in stage 0.0 (TID 7)
org.apache.spark.api.python.PythonException: Traceback (most recent call last):
  File "/home/holden/repos/spark/python/lib/pyspark.zip/pyspark/worker.py",
line 180, in main
    process()
  File "/home/holden/repos/spark/python/lib/pyspark.zip/pyspark/worker.py",
line 175, in process
    serializer.dump_stream(func(split_index, iterator), outfile)
  File "/home/holden/repos/spark/python/pyspark/rdd.py", line 2406, in pipeline_func
    return func(split, prev_func(split, iterator))
  File "/home/holden/repos/spark/python/pyspark/rdd.py", line 2406, in pipeline_func
    return func(split, prev_func(split, iterator))
  File "/home/holden/repos/spark/python/pyspark/rdd.py", line 2406, in pipeline_func
    return func(split, prev_func(split, iterator))
```

```
      File "/home/holden/repos/spark/python/pyspark/rdd.py", line 345, in func
        return f(iterator)
      File "/home/holden/repos/spark/python/pyspark/rdd.py", line 1040, in <lambda>
        return self.mapPartitions(lambda i: [sum(1 for _ in i)]).sum()
      File "/home/holden/repos/spark/python/pyspark/rdd.py", line 1040, in <genexpr>
        return self.mapPartitions(lambda i: [sum(1 for _ in i)]).sum()
      File "high_performance_pyspark/bad_pyspark.py", line 46, in <lambda>
        transform1 = data.map(lambda x: x / 0)
    ZeroDivisionError: integer division or modulo by zero

        at org.apache.spark.api.python.PythonRunner$$anon$1.read(PythonRDD.scala:193)
        at org.apache.spark.api.python.PythonRunner$$anon$1
        .<init>(PythonRDD.scala:234)
        at org.apache.spark.api.python.PythonRunner.compute(PythonRDD.scala:152)
        at org.apache.spark.api.python.PythonRDD.compute(PythonRDD.scala:63)
        at org.apache.spark.rdd.RDD.computeOrReadCheckpoint(RDD.scala:323)
        at org.apache.spark.rdd.RDD.iterator(RDD.scala:287)
        at org.apache.spark.scheduler.ResultTask.runTask(ResultTask.scala:87)
        at org.apache.spark.scheduler.Task.run(Task.scala:113)
        at org.apache.spark.executor.Executor$TaskRunner.run(Executor.scala:313)
        at java.util.concurrent.ThreadPoolExecutor
        .runWorker(ThreadPoolExecutor.java:1142)
        at java.util.concurrent.ThreadPoolExecutor$Worker
        .run(ThreadPoolExecutor.java:617)
        at java.lang.Thread.run(Thread.java:745)
    17/02/28 22:28:58 ERROR TaskSetManager: Task 0 in stage 0.0 failed 2 times;
    aborting job
    17/02/28 22:28:58 ERROR Executor: Exception in task 2.1 in stage 0.0 (TID 5)
    org.apache.spark.api.python.PythonException: Traceback (most recent call last):
      File "/home/holden/repos/spark/python/lib/pyspark.zip/pyspark/worker.py",
      line 180, in main
        process()
      File "/home/holden/repos/spark/python/lib/pyspark.zip/pyspark/worker.py",
      line 175, in process
        serializer.dump_stream(func(split_index, iterator), outfile)
      File "/home/holden/repos/spark/python/pyspark/rdd.py", line 2406, in pipeline_func
        return func(split, prev_func(split, iterator))
      File "/home/holden/repos/spark/python/pyspark/rdd.py", line 2406, in pipeline_func
        return func(split, prev_func(split, iterator))
      File "/home/holden/repos/spark/python/pyspark/rdd.py", line 2406, in pipeline_func
        return func(split, prev_func(split, iterator))
      File "/home/holden/repos/spark/python/pyspark/rdd.py", line 345, in func
        return f(iterator)
      File "/home/holden/repos/spark/python/pyspark/rdd.py", line 1040, in <lambda>
        return self.mapPartitions(lambda i: [sum(1 for _ in i)]).sum()
      File "/home/holden/repos/spark/python/pyspark/rdd.py", line 1040, in <genexpr>
        return self.mapPartitions(lambda i: [sum(1 for _ in i)]).sum()
      File "high_performance_pyspark/bad_pyspark.py", line 46, in <lambda>
        transform1 = data.map(lambda x: x / 0)
    ZeroDivisionError: integer division or modulo by zero

        at org.apache.spark.api.python.PythonRunner$$anon$1.read(PythonRDD.scala:193)
```

```
    at org.apache.spark.api.python.PythonRunner$$anon$1
    .<init>(PythonRDD.scala:234)
    at org.apache.spark.api.python.PythonRunner.compute(PythonRDD.scala:152)
    at org.apache.spark.api.python.PythonRDD.compute(PythonRDD.scala:63)
    at org.apache.spark.rdd.RDD.computeOrReadCheckpoint(RDD.scala:323)
    at org.apache.spark.rdd.RDD.iterator(RDD.scala:287)
    at org.apache.spark.scheduler.ResultTask.runTask(ResultTask.scala:87)
    at org.apache.spark.scheduler.Task.run(Task.scala:113)
    at org.apache.spark.executor.Executor$TaskRunner
    .run(Executor.scala:313)
    at java.util.concurrent.ThreadPoolExecutor
    .runWorker(ThreadPoolExecutor.java:1142)
    at java.util.concurrent.ThreadPoolExecutor$Worker.run(ThreadPoolExecutor.java:617)
    at java.lang.Thread.run(Thread.java:745)
17/02/28 22:28:58 ERROR Executor: Exception in task 3.1 in stage 0.0 (TID 6)
org.apache.spark.api.python.PythonException: Traceback (most recent call last):
  File "/home/holden/repos/spark/python/lib/pyspark.zip/pyspark/worker.py",
  line 180, in main
    process()
  File "/home/holden/repos/spark/python/lib/pyspark.zip/pyspark/worker.py",
  line 175, in process
    serializer.dump_stream(func(split_index, iterator), outfile)
  File "/home/holden/repos/spark/python/pyspark/rdd.py", line 2406, in pipeline_func
    return func(split, prev_func(split, iterator))
  File "/home/holden/repos/spark/python/pyspark/rdd.py", line 2406, in pipeline_func
    return func(split, prev_func(split, iterator))
  File "/home/holden/repos/spark/python/pyspark/rdd.py", line 2406, in pipeline_func
    return func(split, prev_func(split, iterator))
  File "/home/holden/repos/spark/python/pyspark/rdd.py", line 345, in func
    return f(iterator)
  File "/home/holden/repos/spark/python/pyspark/rdd.py", line 1040, in <lambda>
    return self.mapPartitions(lambda i: [sum(1 for _ in i)]).sum()
  File "/home/holden/repos/spark/python/pyspark/rdd.py", line 1040, in <genexpr>
    return self.mapPartitions(lambda i: [sum(1 for _ in i)]).sum()
  File "high_performance_pyspark/bad_pyspark.py", line 46, in <lambda>
    transform1 = data.map(lambda x: x / 0)
ZeroDivisionError: integer division or modulo by zero

    at org.apache.spark.api.python.PythonRunner$$anon$1.read(PythonRDD.scala:193)
    at org.apache.spark.api.python.PythonRunner$$anon$1
    .<init>(PythonRDD.scala:234)
    at org.apache.spark.api.python.PythonRunner.compute(PythonRDD.scala:152)
    at org.apache.spark.api.python.PythonRDD.compute(PythonRDD.scala:63)
    at org.apache.spark.rdd.RDD.computeOrReadCheckpoint(RDD.scala:323)
    at org.apache.spark.rdd.RDD.iterator(RDD.scala:287)
    at org.apache.spark.scheduler.ResultTask.runTask(ResultTask.scala:87)
    at org.apache.spark.scheduler.Task.run(Task.scala:113)
    at org.apache.spark.executor.Executor$TaskRunner.run(Executor.scala:313)
    at java.util.concurrent.ThreadPoolExecutor
    .runWorker(ThreadPoolExecutor.java:1142)
    at java.util.concurrent.ThreadPoolExecutor$Worker
    .run(ThreadPoolExecutor.java:617)
```

```
       at java.lang.Thread.run(Thread.java:745)
17/02/28 22:28:58 ERROR Executor: Exception in task 1.1 in stage 0.0 (TID 4)
org.apache.spark.api.python.PythonException: Traceback (most recent call last):
  File "/home/holden/repos/spark/python/lib/pyspark.zip/pyspark/worker.py",
  line 180, in main
    process()
  File "/home/holden/repos/spark/python/lib/pyspark.zip/pyspark/worker.py",
  line 175, in process
    serializer.dump_stream(func(split_index, iterator), outfile)
  File "/home/holden/repos/spark/python/pyspark/rdd.py", line 2406, in pipeline_func
    return func(split, prev_func(split, iterator))
  File "/home/holden/repos/spark/python/pyspark/rdd.py", line 2406, in pipeline_func
    return func(split, prev_func(split, iterator))
  File "/home/holden/repos/spark/python/pyspark/rdd.py", line 2406, in pipeline_func
    return func(split, prev_func(split, iterator))
  File "/home/holden/repos/spark/python/pyspark/rdd.py", line 345, in func
    return f(iterator)
  File "/home/holden/repos/spark/python/pyspark/rdd.py", line 1040, in <lambda>
    return self.mapPartitions(lambda i: [sum(1 for _ in i)]).sum()
  File "/home/holden/repos/spark/python/pyspark/rdd.py", line 1040, in <genexpr>
    return self.mapPartitions(lambda i: [sum(1 for _ in i)]).sum()
  File "high_performance_pyspark/bad_pyspark.py", line 46, in <lambda>
    transform1 = data.map(lambda x: x / 0)
ZeroDivisionError: integer division or modulo by zero

       at org.apache.spark.api.python.PythonRunner$$anon$1.read(PythonRDD.scala:193)
       at org.apache.spark.api.python.PythonRunner$$anon$1
       .<init>(PythonRDD.scala:234)
       at org.apache.spark.api.python.PythonRunner.compute(PythonRDD.scala:152)
       at org.apache.spark.api.python.PythonRDD.compute(PythonRDD.scala:63)
       at org.apache.spark.rdd.RDD.computeOrReadCheckpoint(RDD.scala:323)
       at org.apache.spark.rdd.RDD.iterator(RDD.scala:287)
       at org.apache.spark.scheduler.ResultTask.runTask(ResultTask.scala:87)
       at org.apache.spark.scheduler.Task.run(Task.scala:113)
       at org.apache.spark.executor.Executor$TaskRunner.run(Executor.scala:313)
       at java.util.concurrent.ThreadPoolExecutor
       .runWorker(ThreadPoolExecutor.java:1142)
       at java.util.concurrent.ThreadPoolExecutor$Worker
       .run(ThreadPoolExecutor.java:617)
       at java.lang.Thread.run(Thread.java:745)
Traceback (most recent call last):
  File "<stdin>", line 1, in <module>
  File "high_performance_pyspark/bad_pyspark.py", line 48, in throwInner
    transform2.count()
  File "/home/holden/repos/spark/python/pyspark/rdd.py", line 1040, in count
    return self.mapPartitions(lambda i: [sum(1 for _ in i)]).sum()
  File "/home/holden/repos/spark/python/pyspark/rdd.py", line 1031, in sum
    return self.mapPartitions(lambda x: [sum(x)]).fold(0, operator.add)
  File "/home/holden/repos/spark/python/pyspark/rdd.py", line 905, in fold
    vals = self.mapPartitions(func).collect()
  File "/home/holden/repos/spark/python/pyspark/rdd.py", line 808, in collect
    port = self.ctx._jvm.PythonRDD.collectAndServe(self._jrdd.rdd())
```

```
    File "/home/holden/repos/spark/python/lib/py4j-0.10.4-src.zip/py4j/java_gateway.py",
    line 1133, in __call__
    File "/home/holden/repos/spark/python/pyspark/sql/utils.py", line 63, in deco
        return f(*a, **kw)
    File "/home/holden/repos/spark/python/lib/py4j-0.10.4-src.zip/py4j/protocol.py",
    line 319, in get_return_value
py4j.protocol.Py4JJavaError:
An error occurred while calling z:org.apache.spark.api.python.PythonRDD
.collectAndServe.
: org.apache.spark.SparkException: Job aborted due to stage failure:
Task 0 in stage 0.0 failed 2 times, most recent failure:
Lost task 0.1 in stage 0.0 (TID 7, localhost, executor driver):
org.apache.spark.api.python.PythonException: Traceback (most recent call last):
    File "/home/holden/repos/spark/python/lib/pyspark.zip/pyspark/worker.py",
    line 180, in main
        process()
    File "/home/holden/repos/spark/python/lib/pyspark.zip/pyspark/worker.py",
    line 175, in process
        serializer.dump_stream(func(split_index, iterator), outfile)
    File "/home/holden/repos/spark/python/pyspark/rdd.py", line 2406, in pipeline_func
        return func(split, prev_func(split, iterator))
    File "/home/holden/repos/spark/python/pyspark/rdd.py", line 2406, in pipeline_func
        return func(split, prev_func(split, iterator))
    File "/home/holden/repos/spark/python/pyspark/rdd.py", line 2406, in pipeline_func
        return func(split, prev_func(split, iterator))
    File "/home/holden/repos/spark/python/pyspark/rdd.py", line 345, in func
        return f(iterator)
    File "/home/holden/repos/spark/python/pyspark/rdd.py", line 1040, in <lambda>
        return self.mapPartitions(lambda i: [sum(1 for _ in i)]).sum()
    File "/home/holden/repos/spark/python/pyspark/rdd.py", line 1040, in <genexpr>
        return self.mapPartitions(lambda i: [sum(1 for _ in i)]).sum()
    File "high_performance_pyspark/bad_pyspark.py", line 46, in <lambda>
        transform1 = data.map(lambda x: x / 0)
ZeroDivisionError: integer division or modulo by zero

    at org.apache.spark.api.python.PythonRunner$$anon$1.read(PythonRDD.scala:193)
    at org.apache.spark.api.python.PythonRunner$$anon$1
    .<init>(PythonRDD.scala:234)
    at org.apache.spark.api.python.PythonRunner.compute(PythonRDD.scala:152)
    at org.apache.spark.api.python.PythonRDD.compute(PythonRDD.scala:63)
    at org.apache.spark.rdd.RDD.computeOrReadCheckpoint(RDD.scala:323)
    at org.apache.spark.rdd.RDD.iterator(RDD.scala:287)
    at org.apache.spark.scheduler.ResultTask.runTask(ResultTask.scala:87)
    at org.apache.spark.scheduler.Task.run(Task.scala:113)
    at org.apache.spark.executor.Executor$TaskRunner.run(Executor.scala:313)
    at java.util.concurrent.ThreadPoolExecutor
    .runWorker(ThreadPoolExecutor.java:1142)
    at java.util.concurrent.ThreadPoolExecutor$Worker
    .run(ThreadPoolExecutor.java:617)
    at java.lang.Thread.run(Thread.java:745)

Driver stacktrace:
```

```
at org.apache.spark.scheduler
.DAGScheduler.org$apache$$spark$scheduler$DAGScheduler$$
failJobAndIndependentStages(DAGScheduler.scala:1487)
at org.apache.spark.scheduler
.DAGScheduler$$anonfun$abortStage$1.apply(DAGScheduler.scala:1475)
at org.apache.spark.scheduler
.DAGScheduler$$anonfun$abortStage$1.apply(DAGScheduler.scala:1474)
at scala.collection.mutable.
ResizableArray$class.foreach(ResizableArray.scala:59)
at scala.collection.mutable.ArrayBuffer.foreach(ArrayBuffer.scala:48)
at org.apache.spark.scheduler.DAGScheduler
.abortStage(DAGScheduler.scala:1474)
at org.apache.spark.scheduler
.DAGScheduler$$anonfun$handleTaskSetFailed$1.apply(DAGScheduler.scala:803)
at org.apache.spark.scheduler
.DAGScheduler$$anonfun$handleTaskSetFailed$1.apply(DAGScheduler.scala:803)
at scala.Option.foreach(Option.scala:257)
at org.apache.spark.scheduler.DAGScheduler
.handleTaskSetFailed(DAGScheduler.scala:803)
at org.apache.spark.scheduler
.DAGSchedulerEventProcessLoop.doOnReceive(DAGScheduler.scala:1702)
at org.apache.spark.scheduler
.DAGSchedulerEventProcessLoop.onReceive(DAGScheduler.scala:1657)
at org.apache.spark.scheduler
.DAGSchedulerEventProcessLoop.onReceive(DAGScheduler.scala:1646)
at org.apache.spark.util.EventLoop$$anon$1.run(EventLoop.scala:48)
at org.apache.spark.scheduler.DAGScheduler.runJob(DAGScheduler.scala:628)
at org.apache.spark.SparkContext.runJob(SparkContext.scala:2011)
at org.apache.spark.SparkContext.runJob(SparkContext.scala:2032)
at org.apache.spark.SparkContext.runJob(SparkContext.scala:2051)
at org.apache.spark.SparkContext.runJob(SparkContext.scala:2076)
at org.apache.spark.rdd.RDD$$anonfun$collect$1.apply(RDD.scala:936)
at org.apache.spark.rdd.RDDOperationScope$
.withScope(RDDOperationScope.scala:151)
at org.apache.spark.rdd.RDDOperationScope$
.withScope(RDDOperationScope.scala:112)
at org.apache.spark.rdd.RDD.withScope(RDD.scala:362)
at org.apache.spark.rdd.RDD.collect(RDD.scala:935)
at org.apache.spark.api.python.PythonRDD$
.collectAndServe(PythonRDD.scala:458)
at org.apache.spark.api.python.PythonRDD
.collectAndServe(PythonRDD.scala)
at sun.reflect.NativeMethodAccessorImpl.invoke0(Native Method)
at sun.reflect.NativeMethodAccessorImpl
.invoke(NativeMethodAccessorImpl.java:62)
at sun.reflect.DelegatingMethodAccessorImpl
.invoke(DelegatingMethodAccessorImpl.java:43)
at java.lang.reflect.Method.invoke(Method.java:498)
at py4j.reflection.MethodInvoker.invoke(MethodInvoker.java:244)
at py4j.reflection.ReflectionEngine.invoke(ReflectionEngine.java:357)
at py4j.Gateway.invoke(Gateway.java:280)
at py4j.commands.AbstractCommand.invokeMethod(AbstractCommand.java:132)
```

```
      at py4j.commands.CallCommand.execute(CallCommand.java:79)
      at py4j.GatewayConnection.run(GatewayConnection.java:214)
      at java.lang.Thread.run(Thread.java:745)
Caused by: org.apache.spark.api.python.PythonException:
Traceback (most recent call last):
  File "/home/holden/repos/spark/python/lib/pyspark.zip/pyspark/worker.py",
  line 180, in main
    process()
  File "/home/holden/repos/spark/python/lib/pyspark.zip/pyspark/worker.py",
  line 175, in process
    serializer.dump_stream(func(split_index, iterator), outfile)
  File "/home/holden/repos/spark/python/pyspark/rdd.py", line 2406, in pipeline_func
    return func(split, prev_func(split, iterator))
  File "/home/holden/repos/spark/python/pyspark/rdd.py", line 2406, in pipeline_func
    return func(split, prev_func(split, iterator))
  File "/home/holden/repos/spark/python/pyspark/rdd.py", line 2406, in pipeline_func
    return func(split, prev_func(split, iterator))
  File "/home/holden/repos/spark/python/pyspark/rdd.py", line 345, in func
    return f(iterator)
  File "/home/holden/repos/spark/python/pyspark/rdd.py", line 1040, in <lambda>
    return self.mapPartitions(lambda i: [sum(1 for _ in i)]).sum()
  File "/home/holden/repos/spark/python/pyspark/rdd.py", line 1040, in <genexpr>
    return self.mapPartitions(lambda i: [sum(1 for _ in i)]).sum()
  File "high_performance_pyspark/bad_pyspark.py", line 46, in <lambda>
    transform1 = data.map(lambda x: x / 0)
ZeroDivisionError: integer division or modulo by zero

      at org.apache.spark.api.python.PythonRunner$$anon$1
      .read(PythonRDD.scala:193)
      at org.apache.spark.api.python.PythonRunner$$anon$1
      .<init>(PythonRDD.scala:234)
      at org.apache.spark.api.python.PythonRunner.compute(PythonRDD.scala:152)
      at org.apache.spark.api.python.PythonRDD.compute(PythonRDD.scala:63)
      at org.apache.spark.rdd.RDD.computeOrReadCheckpoint(RDD.scala:323)
      at org.apache.spark.rdd.RDD.iterator(RDD.scala:287)
      at org.apache.spark.scheduler.ResultTask.runTask(ResultTask.scala:87)
      at org.apache.spark.scheduler.Task.run(Task.scala:113)
      at org.apache.spark.executor.Executor$TaskRunner.run(Executor.scala:313)
      at java.util.concurrent.ThreadPoolExecutor
      .runWorker(ThreadPoolExecutor.java:1142)
      at java.util.concurrent.ThreadPoolExecutor$Worker
      .run(ThreadPoolExecutor.java:617)
      ... 1 more
```

Example A-14. Outer failure error message (Python)

```
17/02/28 22:29:21 ERROR Executor: Exception in task 1.0 in stage 1.0 (TID 9)
org.apache.spark.api.python.PythonException: Traceback (most recent call last):
  File "/home/holden/repos/spark/python/lib/pyspark.zip/pyspark/worker.py",
  line 180, in main
    process()
  File "/home/holden/repos/spark/python/lib/pyspark.zip/pyspark/worker.py",
```

```
line 175, in process
    serializer.dump_stream(func(split_index, iterator), outfile)
  File "/home/holden/repos/spark/python/pyspark/rdd.py", line 2406, in pipeline_func
    return func(split, prev_func(split, iterator))
  File "/home/holden/repos/spark/python/pyspark/rdd.py", line 2406, in pipeline_func
    return func(split, prev_func(split, iterator))
  File "/home/holden/repos/spark/python/pyspark/rdd.py", line 2406, in pipeline_func
    return func(split, prev_func(split, iterator))
  File "/home/holden/repos/spark/python/pyspark/rdd.py", line 345, in func
    return f(iterator)
  File "/home/holden/repos/spark/python/pyspark/rdd.py", line 1040, in <lambda>
    return self.mapPartitions(lambda i: [sum(1 for _ in i)]).sum()
  File "/home/holden/repos/spark/python/pyspark/rdd.py", line 1040, in <genexpr>
    return self.mapPartitions(lambda i: [sum(1 for _ in i)]).sum()
  File "high_performance_pyspark/bad_pyspark.py", line 32, in <lambda>
    transform2 = transform1.map(lambda x: x / 0)
ZeroDivisionError: integer division or modulo by zero

        at org.apache.spark.api.python.PythonRunner$$anon$1
        .read(PythonRDD.scala:193)
        at org.apache.spark.api.python.PythonRunner$$anon$1
        .<init>(PythonRDD.scala:234)
        at org.apache.spark.api.python.PythonRunner.compute(PythonRDD.scala:152)
        at org.apache.spark.api.python.PythonRDD.compute(PythonRDD.scala:63)
        at org.apache.spark.rdd.RDD.computeOrReadCheckpoint(RDD.scala:323)
        at org.apache.spark.rdd.RDD.iterator(RDD.scala:287)
        at org.apache.spark.scheduler.ResultTask.runTask(ResultTask.scala:87)
        at org.apache.spark.scheduler.Task.run(Task.scala:113)
        at org.apache.spark.executor.Executor$TaskRunner.run(Executor.scala:313)
        at java.util.concurrent.ThreadPoolExecutor
        .runWorker(ThreadPoolExecutor.java:1142)
        at java.util.concurrent.ThreadPoolExecutor$Worker
        .run(ThreadPoolExecutor.java:617)
        at java.lang.Thread.run(Thread.java:745)
17/02/28 22:29:21 WARN TaskSetManager:
Lost task 1.0 in stage 1.0 (TID 9, localhost, executor driver):
org.apache.spark.api.python.PythonException: Traceback (most recent call last):
  File "/home/holden/repos/spark/python/lib/pyspark.zip/pyspark/worker.py",
  line 180, in main
    process()
  File "/home/holden/repos/spark/python/lib/pyspark.zip/pyspark/worker.py",
  line 175, in process
    serializer.dump_stream(func(split_index, iterator), outfile)
  File "/home/holden/repos/spark/python/pyspark/rdd.py", line 2406, in pipeline_func
    return func(split, prev_func(split, iterator))
  File "/home/holden/repos/spark/python/pyspark/rdd.py", line 2406, in pipeline_func
    return func(split, prev_func(split, iterator))
  File "/home/holden/repos/spark/python/pyspark/rdd.py", line 2406, in pipeline_func
    return func(split, prev_func(split, iterator))
  File "/home/holden/repos/spark/python/pyspark/rdd.py", line 345, in func
    return f(iterator)
  File "/home/holden/repos/spark/python/pyspark/rdd.py", line 1040, in <lambda>
```

```
    return self.mapPartitions(lambda i: [sum(1 for _ in i)]).sum()
  File "/home/holden/repos/spark/python/pyspark/rdd.py", line 1040, in <genexpr>
    return self.mapPartitions(lambda i: [sum(1 for _ in i)]).sum()
  File "high_performance_pyspark/bad_pyspark.py", line 32, in <lambda>
    transform2 = transform1.map(lambda x: x / 0)
ZeroDivisionError: integer division or modulo by zero

    at org.apache.spark.api.python.PythonRunner$$anon$1.read(PythonRDD.scala:193)
    at org.apache.spark.api.python.PythonRunner$$anon$1
.<init>(PythonRDD.scala:234)
    at org.apache.spark.api.python.PythonRunner.compute(PythonRDD.scala:152)
    at org.apache.spark.api.python.PythonRDD.compute(PythonRDD.scala:63)
    at org.apache.spark.rdd.RDD.computeOrReadCheckpoint(RDD.scala:323)
    at org.apache.spark.rdd.RDD.iterator(RDD.scala:287)
    at org.apache.spark.scheduler.ResultTask.runTask(ResultTask.scala:87)
    at org.apache.spark.scheduler.Task.run(Task.scala:113)
    at org.apache.spark.executor.Executor$TaskRunner.run(Executor.scala:313)
    at java.util.concurrent.ThreadPoolExecutor
.runWorker(ThreadPoolExecutor.java:1142)
    at java.util.concurrent.ThreadPoolExecutor$Worker
.run(ThreadPoolExecutor.java:617)
    at java.lang.Thread.run(Thread.java:745)

17/02/28 22:29:21 ERROR Executor: Exception in task 0.0 in stage 1.0 (TID 8)
org.apache.spark.api.python.PythonException: Traceback (most recent call last):
  File "/home/holden/repos/spark/python/lib/pyspark.zip/pyspark/worker.py",
  line 180, in main
    process()
  File "/home/holden/repos/spark/python/lib/pyspark.zip/pyspark/worker.py",
  line 175, in process
    serializer.dump_stream(func(split_index, iterator), outfile)
  File "/home/holden/repos/spark/python/pyspark/rdd.py", line 2406, in pipeline_func
    return func(split, prev_func(split, iterator))
  File "/home/holden/repos/spark/python/pyspark/rdd.py", line 2406, in pipeline_func
    return func(split, prev_func(split, iterator))
  File "/home/holden/repos/spark/python/pyspark/rdd.py", line 2406, in pipeline_func
    return func(split, prev_func(split, iterator))
  File "/home/holden/repos/spark/python/pyspark/rdd.py", line 345, in func
    return f(iterator)
  File "/home/holden/repos/spark/python/pyspark/rdd.py", line 1040, in <lambda>
    return self.mapPartitions(lambda i: [sum(1 for _ in i)]).sum()
  File "/home/holden/repos/spark/python/pyspark/rdd.py", line 1040, in <genexpr>
    return self.mapPartitions(lambda i: [sum(1 for _ in i)]).sum()
  File "high_performance_pyspark/bad_pyspark.py", line 32, in <lambda>
    transform2 = transform1.map(lambda x: x / 0)
ZeroDivisionError: integer division or modulo by zero

    at org.apache.spark.api.python.PythonRunner$$anon$1.read(PythonRDD.scala:193)
    at org.apache.spark.api.python.PythonRunner$$anon$1
.<init>(PythonRDD.scala:234)
    at org.apache.spark.api.python.PythonRunner.compute(PythonRDD.scala:152)
    at org.apache.spark.api.python.PythonRDD.compute(PythonRDD.scala:63)
```

```
    at org.apache.spark.rdd.RDD.computeOrReadCheckpoint(RDD.scala:323)
    at org.apache.spark.rdd.RDD.iterator(RDD.scala:287)
    at org.apache.spark.scheduler.ResultTask.runTask(ResultTask.scala:87)
    at org.apache.spark.scheduler.Task.run(Task.scala:113)
    at org.apache.spark.executor.Executor$TaskRunner.run(Executor.scala:313)
    at java.util.concurrent.ThreadPoolExecutor
    .runWorker(ThreadPoolExecutor.java:1142)
    at java.util.concurrent.ThreadPoolExecutor$Worker
    .run(ThreadPoolExecutor.java:617)
    at java.lang.Thread.run(Thread.java:745)
17/02/28 22:29:21 ERROR Executor: Exception in task 3.0 in stage 1.0 (TID 11)
org.apache.spark.api.python.PythonException: Traceback (most recent call last):
  File "/home/holden/repos/spark/python/lib/pyspark.zip/pyspark/worker.py",
  line 180, in main
    process()
  File "/home/holden/repos/spark/python/lib/pyspark.zip/pyspark/worker.py",
  line 175, in process
    serializer.dump_stream(func(split_index, iterator), outfile)
  File "/home/holden/repos/spark/python/pyspark/rdd.py", line 2406, in pipeline_func
    return func(split, prev_func(split, iterator))
  File "/home/holden/repos/spark/python/pyspark/rdd.py", line 2406, in pipeline_func
    return func(split, prev_func(split, iterator))
  File "/home/holden/repos/spark/python/pyspark/rdd.py", line 2406, in pipeline_func
    return func(split, prev_func(split, iterator))
  File "/home/holden/repos/spark/python/pyspark/rdd.py", line 345, in func
    return f(iterator)
  File "/home/holden/repos/spark/python/pyspark/rdd.py", line 1040, in <lambda>
    return self.mapPartitions(lambda i: [sum(1 for _ in i)]).sum()
  File "/home/holden/repos/spark/python/pyspark/rdd.py", line 1040, in <genexpr>
    return self.mapPartitions(lambda i: [sum(1 for _ in i)]).sum()
  File "high_performance_pyspark/bad_pyspark.py", line 32, in <lambda>
    transform2 = transform1.map(lambda x: x / 0)
ZeroDivisionError: integer division or modulo by zero

    at org.apache.spark.api.python.PythonRunner$$anon$1.read(PythonRDD.scala:193)
    at org.apache.spark.api.python.PythonRunner$$anon$1
    .<init>(PythonRDD.scala:234)
    at org.apache.spark.api.python.PythonRunner.compute(PythonRDD.scala:152)
    at org.apache.spark.api.python.PythonRDD.compute(PythonRDD.scala:63)
    at org.apache.spark.rdd.RDD.computeOrReadCheckpoint(RDD.scala:323)
    at org.apache.spark.rdd.RDD.iterator(RDD.scala:287)
    at org.apache.spark.scheduler.ResultTask.runTask(ResultTask.scala:87)
    at org.apache.spark.scheduler.Task.run(Task.scala:113)
    at org.apache.spark.executor.Executor$TaskRunner.run(Executor.scala:313)
    at java.util.concurrent.ThreadPoolExecutor
    .runWorker(ThreadPoolExecutor.java:1142)
    at java.util.concurrent.ThreadPoolExecutor$Worker
    .run(ThreadPoolExecutor.java:617)
    at java.lang.Thread.run(Thread.java:745)
17/02/28 22:29:21 ERROR Executor: Exception in task 1.1 in stage 1.0 (TID 12)
org.apache.spark.api.python.PythonException: Traceback (most recent call last):
  File "/home/holden/repos/spark/python/lib/pyspark.zip/pyspark/worker.py",
```

```
line 180, in main
    process()
File "/home/holden/repos/spark/python/lib/pyspark.zip/pyspark/worker.py",
line 175, in process
    serializer.dump_stream(func(split_index, iterator), outfile)
File "/home/holden/repos/spark/python/pyspark/rdd.py", line 2406, in pipeline_func
    return func(split, prev_func(split, iterator))
File "/home/holden/repos/spark/python/pyspark/rdd.py", line 2406, in pipeline_func
    return func(split, prev_func(split, iterator))
File "/home/holden/repos/spark/python/pyspark/rdd.py", line 2406, in pipeline_func
    return func(split, prev_func(split, iterator))
File "/home/holden/repos/spark/python/pyspark/rdd.py", line 345, in func
    return f(iterator)
File "/home/holden/repos/spark/python/pyspark/rdd.py", line 1040, in <lambda>
    return self.mapPartitions(lambda i: [sum(1 for _ in i)]).sum()
File "/home/holden/repos/spark/python/pyspark/rdd.py", line 1040, in <genexpr>
    return self.mapPartitions(lambda i: [sum(1 for _ in i)]).sum()
File "high_performance_pyspark/bad_pyspark.py", line 32, in <lambda>
    transform2 = transform1.map(lambda x: x / 0)
ZeroDivisionError: integer division or modulo by zero

    at org.apache.spark.api.python.PythonRunner$$anon$1.read(PythonRDD.scala:193)
    at org.apache.spark.api.python.PythonRunner$$anon$1
    .<init>(PythonRDD.scala:234)
    at org.apache.spark.api.python.PythonRunner.compute(PythonRDD.scala:152)
    at org.apache.spark.api.python.PythonRDD.compute(PythonRDD.scala:63)
    at org.apache.spark.rdd.RDD.computeOrReadCheckpoint(RDD.scala:323)
    at org.apache.spark.rdd.RDD.iterator(RDD.scala:287)
    at org.apache.spark.scheduler.ResultTask.runTask(ResultTask.scala:87)
    at org.apache.spark.scheduler.Task.run(Task.scala:113)
    at org.apache.spark.executor.Executor$TaskRunner.run(Executor.scala:313)
    at java.util.concurrent.ThreadPoolExecutor
    .runWorker(ThreadPoolExecutor.java:1142)
    at java.util.concurrent.ThreadPoolExecutor$Worker
    .run(ThreadPoolExecutor.java:617)
    at java.lang.Thread.run(Thread.java:745)
17/02/28 22:29:21 ERROR TaskSetManager:
Task 1 in stage 1.0 failed 2 times; aborting job
17/02/28 22:29:21 ERROR Executor: Exception in task 2.0 in stage 1.0 (TID 10)
org.apache.spark.api.python.PythonException: Traceback (most recent call last):
File "/home/holden/repos/spark/python/lib/pyspark.zip/pyspark/worker.py",
line 180, in main
    process()
File "/home/holden/repos/spark/python/lib/pyspark.zip/pyspark/worker.py",
line 175, in process
    serializer.dump_stream(func(split_index, iterator), outfile)
File "/home/holden/repos/spark/python/pyspark/rdd.py", line 2406, in pipeline_func
    return func(split, prev_func(split, iterator))
File "/home/holden/repos/spark/python/pyspark/rdd.py", line 2406, in pipeline_func
    return func(split, prev_func(split, iterator))
File "/home/holden/repos/spark/python/pyspark/rdd.py", line 2406, in pipeline_func
    return func(split, prev_func(split, iterator))
```

```
  File "/home/holden/repos/spark/python/pyspark/rdd.py", line 345, in func
    return f(iterator)
  File "/home/holden/repos/spark/python/pyspark/rdd.py", line 1040, in <lambda>
    return self.mapPartitions(lambda i: [sum(1 for _ in i)]).sum()
  File "/home/holden/repos/spark/python/pyspark/rdd.py", line 1040, in <genexpr>
    return self.mapPartitions(lambda i: [sum(1 for _ in i)]).sum()
  File "high_performance_pyspark/bad_pyspark.py", line 32, in <lambda>
    transform2 = transform1.map(lambda x: x / 0)
ZeroDivisionError: integer division or modulo by zero

    at org.apache.spark.api.python.PythonRunner$$anon$1
    .read(PythonRDD.scala:193)
    at org.apache.spark.api.python.PythonRunner$$anon$1
    .<init>(PythonRDD.scala:234)
    at org.apache.spark.api.python.PythonRunner.compute(PythonRDD.scala:152)
    at org.apache.spark.api.python.PythonRDD.compute(PythonRDD.scala:63)
    at org.apache.spark.rdd.RDD.computeOrReadCheckpoint(RDD.scala:323)
    at org.apache.spark.rdd.RDD.iterator(RDD.scala:287)
    at org.apache.spark.scheduler.ResultTask.runTask(ResultTask.scala:87)
    at org.apache.spark.scheduler.Task.run(Task.scala:113)
    at org.apache.spark.executor.Executor$TaskRunner.run(Executor.scala:313)
    at java.util.concurrent.ThreadPoolExecutor
    .runWorker(ThreadPoolExecutor.java:1142)
    at java.util.concurrent.ThreadPoolExecutor$Worker
    .run(ThreadPoolExecutor.java:617)
    at java.lang.Thread.run(Thread.java:745)
17/02/28 22:29:21 WARN TaskSetManager:
Lost task 0.1 in stage 1.0 (TID 13, localhost, executor driver):
TaskKilled (killed intentionally)
17/02/28 22:29:21 WARN TaskSetManager:
Lost task 3.1 in stage 1.0 (TID 14, localhost, executor driver):
TaskKilled (killed intentionally)
Traceback (most recent call last):
  File "<stdin>", line 1, in <module>
  File "high_performance_pyspark/bad_pyspark.py", line 33, in throwOuter
    transform2.count()
  File "/home/holden/repos/spark/python/pyspark/rdd.py", line 1040, in count
    return self.mapPartitions(lambda i: [sum(1 for _ in i)]).sum()
  File "/home/holden/repos/spark/python/pyspark/rdd.py", line 1031, in sum
    return self.mapPartitions(lambda x: [sum(x)]).fold(0, operator.add)
  File "/home/holden/repos/spark/python/pyspark/rdd.py", line 905, in fold
    vals = self.mapPartitions(func).collect()
  File "/home/holden/repos/spark/python/pyspark/rdd.py", line 808, in collect
    port = self.ctx._jvm.PythonRDD.collectAndServe(self._jrdd.rdd())
  File "/home/holden/repos/spark/python/lib/py4j-0.10.4-src.zip/py4j/java_gateway.py",
  line 1133, in __call__
  File "/home/holden/repos/spark/python/pyspark/sql/utils.py", line 63, in deco
    return f(*a, **kw)
  File "/home/holden/repos/spark/python/lib/py4j-0.10.4-src.zip/py4j/protocol.py",
  line 319, in get_return_value
py4j.protocol.Py4JJavaError:
An error occurred while calling z:org.apache.spark.api.python.PythonRDD
```

```
.collectAndServe.
: org.apache.spark.SparkException:
Job aborted due to stage failure: Task 1 in stage 1.0 failed 2 times,
most recent failure: Lost task 1.1 in stage 1.0 (TID 12, localhost,
executor driver): org.apache.spark.api.python.PythonException:
Traceback (most recent call last):
  File "/home/holden/repos/spark/python/lib/pyspark.zip/pyspark/worker.py",
  line 180, in main
    process()
  File "/home/holden/repos/spark/python/lib/pyspark.zip/pyspark/worker.py",
  line 175, in process
    serializer.dump_stream(func(split_index, iterator), outfile)
  File "/home/holden/repos/spark/python/pyspark/rdd.py", line 2406, in pipeline_func
    return func(split, prev_func(split, iterator))
  File "/home/holden/repos/spark/python/pyspark/rdd.py", line 2406, in pipeline_func
    return func(split, prev_func(split, iterator))
  File "/home/holden/repos/spark/python/pyspark/rdd.py", line 2406, in pipeline_func
    return func(split, prev_func(split, iterator))
  File "/home/holden/repos/spark/python/pyspark/rdd.py", line 345, in func
    return f(iterator)
  File "/home/holden/repos/spark/python/pyspark/rdd.py", line 1040, in <lambda>
    return self.mapPartitions(lambda i: [sum(1 for _ in i)]).sum()
  File "/home/holden/repos/spark/python/pyspark/rdd.py", line 1040, in <genexpr>
    return self.mapPartitions(lambda i: [sum(1 for _ in i)]).sum()
  File "high_performance_pyspark/bad_pyspark.py", line 32, in <lambda>
    transform2 = transform1.map(lambda x: x / 0)
ZeroDivisionError: integer division or modulo by zero

    at org.apache.spark.api.python.PythonRunner$$anon$1
    .read(PythonRDD.scala:193)
    at org.apache.spark.api.python.PythonRunner$$anon$1
    .<init>(PythonRDD.scala:234)
    at org.apache.spark.api.python.PythonRunner.compute(PythonRDD.scala:152)
    at org.apache.spark.api.python.PythonRDD.compute(PythonRDD.scala:63)
    at org.apache.spark.rdd.RDD.computeOrReadCheckpoint(RDD.scala:323)
    at org.apache.spark.rdd.RDD.iterator(RDD.scala:287)
    at org.apache.spark.scheduler.ResultTask.runTask(ResultTask.scala:87)
    at org.apache.spark.scheduler.Task.run(Task.scala:113)
    at org.apache.spark.executor.Executor$TaskRunner.run(Executor.scala:313)
    at java.util.concurrent.ThreadPoolExecutor
    .runWorker(ThreadPoolExecutor.java:1142)
    at java.util.concurrent.ThreadPoolExecutor$Worker
    .run(ThreadPoolExecutor.java:617)
    at java.lang.Thread.run(Thread.java:745)

Driver stacktrace:
    at org.apache.spark.scheduler
    .DAGScheduler.org$apache$spark$scheduler$DAGScheduler$$
    failJobAndIndependentStages(DAGScheduler.scala:1487)
    at org.apache.spark.scheduler
    .DAGScheduler$$anonfun$abortStage$1.apply(DAGScheduler.scala:1475)
    at org.apache.spark.scheduler
```

```
    .DAGScheduler$$anonfun$abortStage$1.apply(DAGScheduler.scala:1474)
    at scala.collection.mutable.ResizableArray$class
    .foreach(ResizableArray.scala:59)
    at scala.collection.mutable.ArrayBuffer.foreach(ArrayBuffer.scala:48)
    at org.apache.spark.scheduler
    .DAGScheduler.abortStage(DAGScheduler.scala:1474)
    at org.apache.spark.scheduler
    .DAGScheduler$$anonfun$handleTaskSetFailed$1.apply(DAGScheduler.scala:803)
    at org.apache.spark.scheduler
    .DAGScheduler$$anonfun$handleTaskSetFailed$1.apply(DAGScheduler.scala:803)
    at scala.Option.foreach(Option.scala:257)
    at org.apache.spark.scheduler
    .DAGScheduler.handleTaskSetFailed(DAGScheduler.scala:803)
    at org.apache.spark.scheduler
    .DAGSchedulerEventProcessLoop.doOnReceive(DAGScheduler.scala:1702)
    at org.apache.spark.scheduler
    .DAGSchedulerEventProcessLoop.onReceive(DAGScheduler.scala:1657)
    at org.apache.spark.scheduler
    .DAGSchedulerEventProcessLoop.onReceive(DAGScheduler.scala:1646)
    at org.apache.spark.util.EventLoop$$anon$1.run(EventLoop.scala:48)
    at org.apache.spark.scheduler.DAGScheduler.runJob(DAGScheduler.scala:628)
    at org.apache.spark.SparkContext.runJob(SparkContext.scala:2011)
    at org.apache.spark.SparkContext.runJob(SparkContext.scala:2032)
    at org.apache.spark.SparkContext.runJob(SparkContext.scala:2051)
    at org.apache.spark.SparkContext.runJob(SparkContext.scala:2076)
    at org.apache.spark.rdd.RDD$$anonfun$collect$1
    .apply(RDD.scala:936)
    at org.apache.spark.rdd.RDDOperationScope$
    .withScope(RDDOperationScope.scala:151)
    at org.apache.spark.rdd.RDDOperationScope$.withScope(RDDOperationScope.scala:112)
    at org.apache.spark.rdd.RDD.withScope(RDD.scala:362)
    at org.apache.spark.rdd.RDD.collect(RDD.scala:935)
    at org.apache.spark.api.python.PythonRDD$
    .collectAndServe(PythonRDD.scala:458)
    at org.apache.spark.api.python.PythonRDD.collectAndServe(PythonRDD.scala)
    at sun.reflect.NativeMethodAccessorImpl.invoke0(Native Method)
    at sun.reflect.NativeMethodAccessorImpl
    .invoke(NativeMethodAccessorImpl.java:62)
    at sun.reflect.DelegatingMethodAccessorImpl
    .invoke(DelegatingMethodAccessorImpl.java:43)
    at java.lang.reflect.Method.invoke(Method.java:498)
    at py4j.reflection.MethodInvoker.invoke(MethodInvoker.java:244)
    at py4j.reflection.ReflectionEngine.invoke(ReflectionEngine.java:357)
    at py4j.Gateway.invoke(Gateway.java:280)
    at py4j.commands.AbstractCommand.invokeMethod(AbstractCommand.java:132)
    at py4j.commands.CallCommand.execute(CallCommand.java:79)
    at py4j.GatewayConnection.run(GatewayConnection.java:214)
    at java.lang.Thread.run(Thread.java:745)
Caused by: org.apache.spark.api.python.PythonException:
Traceback (most recent call last):
  File "/home/holden/repos/spark/python/lib/pyspark.zip/pyspark/worker.py",
  line 180, in main process()
```

```
File "/home/holden/repos/spark/python/lib/pyspark.zip/pyspark/worker.py",
line 175, in process
  serializer.dump_stream(func(split_index, iterator), outfile)
File "/home/holden/repos/spark/python/pyspark/rdd.py", line 2406, in pipeline_func
  return func(split, prev_func(split, iterator))
File "/home/holden/repos/spark/python/pyspark/rdd.py", line 2406, in pipeline_func
  return func(split, prev_func(split, iterator))
File "/home/holden/repos/spark/python/pyspark/rdd.py", line 2406, in pipeline_func
  return func(split, prev_func(split, iterator))
File "/home/holden/repos/spark/python/pyspark/rdd.py", line 345, in func
  return f(iterator)
File "/home/holden/repos/spark/python/pyspark/rdd.py", line 1040, in <lambda>
  return self.mapPartitions(lambda i: [sum(1 for _ in i)]).sum()
File "/home/holden/repos/spark/python/pyspark/rdd.py", line 1040, in <genexpr>
  return self.mapPartitions(lambda i: [sum(1 for _ in i)]).sum()
File "high_performance_pyspark/bad_pyspark.py", line 32, in <lambda>
  transform2 = transform1.map(lambda x: x / 0)
ZeroDivisionError: integer division or modulo by zero

    at org.apache.spark.api.python.PythonRunner$$anon$1
    .read(PythonRDD.scala:193)
    at org.apache.spark.api.python.PythonRunner$$anon$1
    .<init>(PythonRDD.scala:234)
    at org.apache.spark.api.python.PythonRunner.compute(PythonRDD.scala:152)
    at org.apache.spark.api.python.PythonRDD.compute(PythonRDD.scala:63)
    at org.apache.spark.rdd.RDD.computeOrReadCheckpoint(RDD.scala:323)
    at org.apache.spark.rdd.RDD.iterator(RDD.scala:287)
    at org.apache.spark.scheduler.ResultTask.runTask(ResultTask.scala:87)
    at org.apache.spark.scheduler.Task.run(Task.scala:113)
    at org.apache.spark.executor.Executor$TaskRunner.run(Executor.scala:313)
    at java.util.concurrent.ThreadPoolExecutor
    .runWorker(ThreadPoolExecutor.java:1142)
    at java.util.concurrent.ThreadPoolExecutor$Worker
    .run(ThreadPoolExecutor.java:617)
    ... 1 more
```

Logging is always important, and unlike JVM Spark applications we can't access the log4j logger to do our work for us.[10] For Python logging the simplest option is printing to stdout, which will end up in the stderr of the logs of the worker—however, this makes it difficult to tune logging levels. Instead, use a library like the standard logging library with stdout/stderr append functions.

---

10 Technically you can access it on the driver program using Py4J, but the gateway isn't set up on workers, which is often where logging is most important.

For YARN users you can instead have the logging library write to a file under the LOG_DIRS environment variable, which will then be picked up as part of log aggregation later.

Debugging RDD skew in PySpark can become more challanging thanks to an often overlooked feature known as "batch serialization." This feature isn't normally given a lot of discussion as at large enough datasets, the impact of batch serializations tends to have minimal effects. This can quickly become confusing when following the standard debugging practice of sampling your data down to a small manageable set and trying to reproduce cluster behavior locally.

Using Python with YARN may result in memory overhead errors that appear as out-of-memory errors. In the first part of this appendix we introduced memory overhead as some extra space required (see Figure A-1), but when running Python our entire Python process needs to fit inside of this "overhead" space. These can be difficult to debug as the error messages are the same for a few different situations.

The first possible cause of memory errors is unbalanced or otherwise large partitions. If the partitions are too large there may not be enough room for the Python workers to load the data. The web UI is one of the simpler places to check the partition sizes. If the partitions are unbalanced, a simple repartitioning can often do the trick, although the issues of key skew discussed in Chapter 6 can come into play.

The second possibility is simply not having enough overhead allocated for Python. The name "memory overhead" can be somewhat confusing but the Python worker is only able to use the "overhead" space left over in the container after the JVM has used the rest of the space. The default configuration of spark.yarn.executor.memoryOver head is only 384 MB or 10% of the entire container (whichever is larger), which for PySpark users is often not a reasonable value. The related configuration variables for application master (AM) and driver (depending on your deployment mode) are spark.yarn.am.memoryOverhead and spark.yarn.driver.memoryOverhead.

Debugging conclusion

While debugging in Spark does indeed have some unique challenges, it's important to remember some of its many benefits for debugging. One of the strongest is that its local mode allows us to quickly create a "fake" cluster for testing or debugging without having to go through a long setup process. The other is that our jobs often run faster than traditional distributed systems, so we can often quickly experiment (either in local mode or our test cluster) to narrow down the source of the error. Echoing the conclusion in Chapter 10, may you need to apply the debugging section of this book as little as possible and may your adventures in Apache Spark be fun.

Index

Symbols

! (negation) operator, 37
!== (not equal) operator, 38
$ operator, using for column lookup, 37
=== (equality) operator, 38

A

accumulators, 109
    interaction with caching, 125
    streaming high availability mode, 271
    using for job validation, 219
AccumulatorV2 interface, 110
actions, 11
    architecture implications, 20, 22
    on key/value pairs, 133
    streaming test base class, StreamActionBase, 208
    versus transformations on RDDs, 17
add function, 110
agg API, 44, 66
aggregateByKey function, 79
    avoiding memory allocation in, 140
    map-side combinations, 141
    optimizing, 94
    performance considerations, 139
aggregateColumnFrequencies function, 161
aggregations
    aggregates and groupBy, 43
    choosing aggregation operation for key/value data, 138-141
        dictionary of operations with performance issues, 138
        preventing out-of-memory errors, 140
    computing aggregates over a window, 47

extending Spark SQL with user-defined aggregate functions, 67
on each partition in Goldilocks final example, 167
on grouped data in Datasets, 66
optimizing, using array as aggregation object, 98
reducing number of records by key, 138
reusing existing objects in, 94
speeding up wide transformations in, 128
Structured Streaming aggregates for Naive Bayes, 266
with bad implicit conversions (example), 100
alias operator, 41
Anaconda, using to add packages on CDH clusters, 188
Apache Bahir project, 258
Apache Parquet (see Parquet files)
Apache Toree, 193
Append (save mode), 61
applications (Spark), 20
    application tree, 22
ArrayBuffer, using a map or flatMap instead of, 106
arrays
    Spark SQL, functions for, 41
    using for memory efficiency, 97
as operator, 41, 63

B

Bahir project, 258
batch intervals, 259
batch predictions, 230

batch serialization, 324
big data ecosystem, Spark's place in, 8
Binarizer pipeline stage, explain params, 235
broadcast hash joins, 80
    in Spark SQL, 85
    partial manual join, 81
broadcast variables, 108
    high availability mode and, 271
broadcasting training models, 227
builds, adding Spark SQL and Hive components to regular sbt build, 31

C

C#, using with Spark, 193
C/C++
    calling from Spark, using JNI, 195
    wrapper for FORTRAN code, 199
cache function, 120
caching
    checkpointing versus, 120
    in Spark ML, 242
    interaction with accumulators, 125
    LRU, 123
case classes, 33
    aggregation case class, 95
    RDDs composed of, converting to DataFrames, 57
Catalyst query optimizer, 63, 69-71
    code generation, 70
    large query plans and iterative algorithms, 70
    logical and physical plans, 69
CDH clusters, adding packages with Anaconda, 188
checkpoint function, 121
checkpointing
    costs of, 114
    data checkpoint intervals, 260
    of driver state and streaming context recovery, 270
    of RDDs, 115, 120
        caching versus, 120
        disadvantage of, 117
        example, 121
        in wide transformations, 91
        when cost for computing each partition is high, 116
    use in noisy clusters, 125
ChiSqSelector, 228

class tags
    constructing fake class tags for Scala RDD to Java RDD conversions, 178
    functions depending on, 177
classification algorithms
    ML library, 233, 239
    MLlib, 223
classification model, training in MLlib, 229
Classifier class, 249
Clojure, 177
cloneComplement function, 212
cluster managers, 8
clustering algorithms
    ML library, 233, 239
    MLlib, 223
clusters
    allocating resources for, 281
    determining relevant information about, 276
    noisy, 124
co-located RDDs, 146
co-partitioned RDDs, 146
coalesce function, 18, 143
    narrow transformation, 92
code examples from this book
    GitHub repository, 33
    ported to Java or Python, 5
code generation, by query optimizer, 70
cogroup function, 77, 141, 146
CoGroupedRDD, 141, 146
collect action, 17
collectAsMap action, 17, 136
    returning data to the driver, 133
collections
    converting local collections to/from DataFrames, 59
    higher GC overhead than arrays, 98
    interoperability of local collections with Datasets, 63
    types of members in, 93
colocated joins, 75
column operators (Spark SQL), 38
combineByKey function, 77, 138
    performance considerations, 139
Common Language Runtime (CLR), 193
components and packages, 255-274
    GraphX, 271
    Spark 2.0 components diagram, 256
    Spark Streaming, 257-271

using community packages and libraries, 271-274
configuration settings, 275-290
  basic Spark Core settings, resource allocation to applications, 278-290
  determining relevant information about clusters, 276
  how to adjust, 276
  performance and, 290
  serialization options, 290
console sink (blocking), 270
copartition joins, 75
copy function, 110
  implementation in custom transformers, 245
count function, 17
countByKey function, 133
countByKeyApprox function, 81
countByValue function, 133
counters, verifying performance with, 217
CSV (comma-separated values), 193
  specifying as data format for loading/saving in Spark SQL, 60
  starting Spark shell with CSV support, 60
CUDA, 175
  interfacing Spark with, 200

D

DAGs (directed acyclic graphs), 11
  DAG Scheduler for Spark jobs, 22
data cleaning (ML library), 239
data encoding (ML library), 236-239
data formats (see formats for reading/writing data)
data loading and saving operations, 118
  (see also persistence)
  checkpointing, 120-122
  in Spark SQL, 51-62
    data formats, 52-61
    partitions, 62
    save modes, 61
  models in MLlib, 230
  persistence in Spark ML, 242-244
  saving DStreams, 261
data property accumulators, 114
Data Source API, 51
  implementing Spark SQL data source via, 61
data sources
  in Structured Streaming, 263

Spark Streaming, 257
data structures, smaller, using to enhance performance, 97
DataFrameReader, 51
  format function, 52
DataFrames, 27
  computing difference between, 216
  converting to/from Datasets, 63
  converting to/from RDDs, 57
  creating from JDBC data sources, 54
  creating from local collections, 59
  data representation in, 49-51
  DataFrame API, 36-49
    transformation, multi-DataFrame, 48
    transformations, simple, 36-48
  Goldilocks data (example), 130
  inspecting the schema, 33
  joins, 82
    broadcast hash joins, 85
    self joins, 85
  PySpark, 183
    cutting large query plans with Python, 185
  RDD transformations, 87
  RDDs versus, 28
  registering/saving as Hive tables to perform SQL queries against, 49
  sample and randomSplit functions, 213
  Structured Streaming based on, 257
  testing, 208
  working with as RDDs, loss of type information, 93
  working with C#, 193
  working with R language, 189
DataFrameWriter, 51
  format function, 52
  specifying partition information, 62
Dataset API, 63
  (see also Datasets)
  up to date documentation on, 63
Datasets, 27, 62-67
  compile-time strong typing, 64
  converting to RDDs, 57
  data representation in, 49
  easier functional transformations, 65
  grouping operations on, 66
  interoperability with RDDs, DataFrames, and local collections, 63
  joins, 85

multi-Dataset relational transformations, 65
PySpark, 183
RDD transformations, 87
relational transformations, 65
streaming aggregations on, 260
use in Structured Streaming, 262
versus RDDs, 28
DataStreamWriter, 263
debugging
  additional techniques for, 290-324
    attaching debuggers, 304
    logging, 301-304
    Python debugging, 305-324
    using notebooks, 304
  lazy evaluation and, 13
  of Spark SQL queries, 71
  stream status and, 270
defaultCopy function, 245
dense vectors, creating, 224
dependencies
  in Spark execution, 23
  narrow versus wide, in transformations, 17,
    88-92
  PySpark dependency management, 187
  Spark SQL, 30
    avoiding Hive JARs, 32
    managing dependencies with sbt-spark-
     package plug-in, 31
dependencies function, 15
describe function, 43
deserialized (storage level), 119
directed acyclic graphs (DAGs), 11
  DAG Scheduler for Spark jobs, 22
disk space errors, 124, 301
distinct function, 77, 107
distinct, reducing to on each partition (Goldilocks example), 167
Docker-based Spark integration environments,
  216
driver, 19, 21
  actions returning unbounded data to, 133
  calculating memory overhead for, 279
  deciding how large to make it, 279
  handling driver failure, 270
dropDuplicates function, 42
DryadLINQ, 7
DStreams, 257
  batch intervals, 260
  considerations for, 261

output operations, 261
data sources, 257
  receivers for, 258
repartitioning, 259
updateStateByKey, checkpointing required
  for, 260
writing to HDFS store in Parquet format,
  263
dynamic resource allocation, 20, 278
  (see also configuration settings)
  executors, 281
  restrictions on, 282

E

Eclair JS, 176
  how it works, 192
enableHiveSupport function, 29
equality tests, 38
  for DataFrame rows, 209
  for RDDs, 214
equals function, 145
ErrorIfExists (save mode), 61
Estimator interface, 244, 251
estimators, 233, 234
  constructing with minimal configuration in
   ML library, 239
  creating custom estimators, 247
  data preparation stages, 237
evaluation, machine learning models
  in ML library, 243
  in MLlib, 232
Evaluator class, 243
executors, 20
  calculating memory overhead for, 279
  deciding between a few large and many
   small executors, 280
  dividing space within, 283
  dynamic allocation of, 281
  many large executors, 281
  number of cores in, 25
explain params (ML pipeline stages), 235
explicit conversions
  functions defined on Java RDDs, 177
  in Spark SQL, 58
explode function, 41

F

fair scheduler, 21, 125
fake class tags, 177

Java/Scala RDD interoperability with, 179
fault tolerance
    implications of narrow versus wide depen-
        dencies, 91
    in Spark, 11
    lazy evaluation and, 13
feature selection and scaling
    MLlib feature encoding and data prepara-
        tion, 223
        preparing data for supervised learning,
            227
        preparing textual data, 224
        working with Spark vectors, 224
    performing in MLlib, 228
feature transformers (ML library), 233
features
    ML library, 237
    preparation tools in MLlib, 223
FIFO scheduler, 21, 125
file sources in Spark Streaming, 257
filter function, 3
    DataFrame, accepting SQL expressions, 37
        more complex filter, 38
filter pushdown in Spark SQL, 71
filterByRange function, 150
filtering
    pre-filtering before RDD join, 78
    using flatMap, 132, 156
fit function, 236, 241
    calling on estimators, 235
    calling on StringIndexer, 238
    calling on Word2Vec, 225
    implementation in custom transformers,
        245
Flambo, 177
flatMap function, 3, 132, 160
flatMapValues function, 148
Flume, 258
fold function, 3
fold operations, object reuse with, 97
foldByKey function
    map-side combinations, 141
    performance considerations, 140
foreach function, 17
foreachPartition function, 108
foreachRDD function, 262
formats for reading/writing data, 52-61
    for pipe interface, 193
    Hive tables, 56

JDBC, 53
JSON, 52
local collections, 59
other formats, 60
Parquet files, 54
PySpark interactions with Spark formats,
    182
RDDs, 57
FORTRAN, 199
    interacting with from Spark, using JNI, 195
fromML function, 234
full outer joins, 78, 82
    sample join in Spark SQL, 84
functions
    DataFrame, accepting SQL expressions, 37
    defined on RDDs, transformations versus
        actions, 17
    intermediate object creation in, avoiding, 99
    RDD function classes, 16
    Spark SQL aggregate functions, 44
    Spark SQL standard functions, 40

G

garbage collection (GC)
    cutting costs of by minimizing object cre-
        ation, 94
    shuffle files and, 124
getOrCreate function, 29
getPartition function, 145
GLM (generalized linear model), persisting,
    253
Goldilocks example, 129-133
    review of all solutions, 171
    using PairRDDFunctions and Order-
        edRDDFunctions, 132
    Version 0, iterative solution, 130
    Version 1, groupByKey solution, 134
        why it fails, 136
    Version 2, using secondary sort, 156-159
    Version 3, 159-165
        determining location of rank statistics
            on each partition, 162
        filtering for rank statistics, 163
        map to (cell value, column index) pairs,
            160
        sorting and counting values on each par-
            tition, 161
        sorting on cell values, 164
        steps in the solution, 160

Version 4, 167-171
    aggregating to ((cell value, column
        index), count) on each partition, 167
    reducing to distinct on all partitions, 167
    sorting and finding rank statistics, 168
GPUEnabler package, 200
GPUs (graphics processing units), 200
GraphX, 10, 271
groupBy function
    changes in different Spark versions, 44
    on DataFrames, aggregates and, 43
    on Datasets, 66
groupByKey function, 18
    dangers of, 134
    in narrow versus wide dependencies
        between partitions, 90
    performance considerations, 139
    solution in Goldilocks example, 134
    why it fails, 136
groupByKeyAndSortValues function, 152
GroupedDataset object, 66
GroupedRDDFunctions class, 16
grouping operations on Datasets, 66
groupSorted function, 156

H

Hadoop
    input formats, using in Spark SQL, 61
    MapReduce, Spark versus, 7
    Yarn MiniClusters, 217
hash partitioning, 143
    groupByKeyAndSortValues function, 153
    HashPartitioner object, 144
hashcode function, 145
HashingTF, 224
    change in default hashing algorithm, 225
    using with Tokenizer in ML library, 237
HDFS (Hadoop Distributed File System), 216
    RDDs representing HDFS files, 16
    writing to HDFS store in Parquet format,
        263
high availability and stream processing, 270
Hive
    enableHiveSupport function, 29
    existing Hive Metastore, connecting to
        Spark, 32
    HiveServer2, 71
    loading and saving Hive tables in Spark
        SQL, 56

Spark SQL dependency, 30
    using plain old SQL queries on data, 49
HiveContext, 29, 32
    starting JDBC server from existing Hive-
        Context, 71
    using in Spark SQL, 30

I

if/else in Spark SQL, 42
Ignore (save mode), 61
immutability of RDDs, 14
implicit conversions
    causing problems with record types, 93
    functionality dependant on, in languages
        other than Scala, 177
    of iterators, 101
    with bad performance implications, 99
in-memory persistence, 13, 117
IndexToString, 238
inner joins, 82
integration testing, 216-217
    choosing testing environment, 216
        Docker-based environment, 216
        local mode, 216
        YARN MiniCluster, 217
intercepts, including in training a simple MLlib
    classification model, 229
intermediate object creation, 99
intersection function, 106
IPython, 181
isZero function, 110
Iterable objects, 142
iterative algorithms, large query plans and, 70
iterative computations, reusing RDDs in, 114
iterative solution (Goldilocks example), 130
iterator function, 15
iterator-to-iterator transformations with map-
    Partitions, 100-106, 108, 159
    space and time advantages of, 102
iterators
    groups created by groupByKey, 136
    in Scala, 101

J

Janino, 70
JARs (Java Archives)
    adding to class path, 186
    avoiding Hive JARs, 32
    building with sbt-jni, 197

for JDBC data sources, 53
Hive JARs for use in Spark SQL, 29
Java, 8
    accessing backing Java objects in PySpark, 184
    Iterable versus Iterator objects, 103
    iterator implementation, java.util.Iterator, 101
    object serialization, Tungsten versus, 50
    RDDs composed of Java objects, converting to DataFrames, 57
    Scala API versus Java API, 4
    simple Java JNI, 195
    System.loadLibrary function, 197
    writing Spark code in, 177
        converting RDDs between Scala and Java, 178
        Java APIs, 177
        Spark SQL and ML pipeline APIs, 179
        word count program example, 177
Java Native Access (JNA), 198
Java Native Interface (JNI), 176, 195-198
java.util.Properties object, 54
JavaBeans, RDDs composed of, converting to DataFrames, 57
JavaConverters object, 178
JavaDoubleRDD, 177
javah command, 196
JavaPairRDD, 177
JavaRDD class, 16
JavaScript, Eclair JS, 176, 192
JBLAS library, 195
JDBC
    data source for Spark SQL, 53
    JDBC/ODBC server in Spark SQL, 71
JdbcDialect, 53
JDWP (Java Debug Wire Protocol), 304
JNI (see Java Native Interface)
jobs
    anatomy of Spark jobs, 22-26
        DAG (directed acyclic graph), 22
        jobs, 23
        Spark application tree, 22
        stages, 23
        tasks, 24
    performance testing, 219
    scheduling in Spark, 19-22, 125
        default scheduler, 21
        in Spark application, 20

        resource allocation across applications, 20
        validation of, 219
join function, 18
joins, 75-86, 91
    co-located and co-partitioned RDDs, 146
    core Spark, 75-81
        choosing a join type, 77
        choosing an execution plan, 78
        speeding up by assigning a known partitioner, 79
        speeding up by using broadcast hash join, 80
    implementation by cogroup function, 141
    Spark SQL, 81-86
        broadcast hash joins, 85
        DataFrame joins, 82
        Dataset joins, 85
        self joins in DataFrames, 85
JPMML evaluator project, 232, 253
JSON, 193
    equivalent Spark SQL schema, 33
    loading and writing in Spark SQL, 52
    loading JSON data in Spark SQL, 32
    toJson function and streaming Datasets, 263
Julia (Spark.jl), 191
Jupyter notebook, 305
JVMs (Java Virtual Machines), 20
    including dependencies using Spark Packages, 188
    Tungsten and, 50
    user-defined functions written in non-JVM languages, 67
    using langauges other than Scala in, 176-180
Jython, PySpark and, 184

K

Kafka, 258
    DStream receiver, repartitioning, 259
    support by Structured Streaming, 263
key/value data, working with, 127-173
    actions on key/value pairs, 133
    choosing an aggregation operation, 138-141
        preventing out-of-memory errors, 140
    dangers of groupByKey function, 134
    Goldilocks example, 129-133
    Goldilocks example, Version 3, 159-165
    groupByKey solution to Goldilocks example, 134

why it fails, 136

multiple RDD operations (co-grouping), 141

OrderedRDDFunctions class, dictionary of operations, 149

partitioners, 142-149

    leveraging co-located and co-partitioned RDDs, 146

    PairRDDFunctions, mapping and partitioning functions, 148

performance issues, 127

repartitioning keyed data, 259

secondary sort and repartitionAndSortWithinPartitions, 151-159

    Goldilocks example with secondary sort, 156-159

straggler detection and unbalanced data, 165-173

keys function, 148

Kinesis, 258

KMeans model, 232

kontextfrei library, 208

Kryo serialization, 49, 290

    Tungsten versus, 50

L

LabeledPoint class, 223

    creating with with the label and vector of features, 227

labels

    encoding in ML library, 237

    requirements for LabeledPoint, 227

lambdas

    Java 8, Spark support for, 177

    Spark SQL expressions instead of, in DataFrame frunctions, 37

lazy evaluation, 11

    and debugging, 13

    performance and usability advantages, 11

    transformations and, 88

left anti joins, 84

left outer joins, 78, 82

    sample join in Spark SQL, 83

left semi joins, 84

libraries, 10

    adding to search path using JNA, 198

    language-specific and Spark-specific, using in PySpark, 188

limiting results, using sorting in Spark SQL, 48

linear algebra package, 234

linear models, persisting, 253

Local Checkpointing option, 122

local mode, 8

    developing and testing streaming applications in, 257

    using for integration testing, 216

    using for unit testing, 204

LocalRelation, 59

log4J, 303

logging, 301-304

    accessing logs, 303

    configuring, 303

    in Python, 323

logical plan (query optimizer), 69

LogisticRegressionModel, 232

lookUp function, 133

LRU caching, 14, 123

M

machine learning, 221-253

    choosing between Spark MLlib and Spark ML, 221

    ML and MLlib packages, 9

    modifying an existing algorithm, 252

    serving considerations in MLlib and ML library, 252

    with Structured Streaming, 265

    working with ML library, 233-252

        accessing individual pipeline stages, 241

        building a pipeline, 240

        data cleaning, 239

        data encoding, 236-239

        data persistence, 242-244

        extending ML pipelines with your own algorithms, 244-253

        getting started, organization and imports, 233

        models, 239

        pipeline stages, 234

        training a pipeline, 241

    working with MLlib, 222-233

        feature encoding and data preparation, 223-228

        feature scaling and selection, 228

        getting started, organization and imports, 222

        model evaluation, 232

        model training, 228

predictions, 229
  serving and persistence, 230-232
map function, 3, 18
  flatMap versus, 132
  in narrow versus wide dependencies
    between partitions, 90
  using on Datasets, 65
map-side combinations, aggregation opera-
    tions, 141
mapGroups function, 66
mapPartitions function, 107, 149, 153
  in Goldilocks example, Version 3, 160, 162
  iterator-to-iterator transformations with,
    100-106
  preserving partitionng information, 146
mappedRDD, 91
MapReduce
  Spark as alternative to, 7
  word count example, 12
mapValues function, 148
  preservation of partitioning information
    with, 146
Maven build manager, 10, 188
  adding Spark SQL and Hive components to
    builds, 31
memory errors, 137
  (see also out-of-memory errors)
  caused by cogroup, 142
  caused by key/value transformations, 134
memory management
  calculating executor and driver memory
    overhead, 279
  division of memory usage within executors,
    283
  Spark options for, 13
MemoryStreams, 258
MEMORY_AND_DISK_2 storage option, 125
MEMORY_ONLY storage level, 120
MEMORY_ONLY_SER storage option, 120
merge function, 110
meta-algorithms, ML library, 233
metadata
  checkpointing, 261
  checkpointing/streaming context recovery,
    270
  for Hive tables loaded into Spark SQL, 56
  for IndexToString transformer, 238
  machine learning models in internal Spark
    format, 231

MinMaxScaler (Spark ML), 239
missing data, working with on DataFrames, 42
ML library, 9, 221
  (see also machine learning)
MLeap project, support for PMML model
    export, 252
MLlib, 9, 221
  (see also machine learning)
  difficulty of implementing meta-algorithms,
    229
  PySpark interactions with, 182
MLUtils object, kfold function, 233
Mobius, 193
model training
  MLlib, 228
  training a pipeline in ML library, 241
  Word2Vec model, 225
models (machine learning)
  evaluation of, in MLlib, 232
  persistence and serving in MLlib, 230
    custom formats, 232
    exporting models to PMML formats, 231
    Saveable trait (internal Spark format),
      231
  persistence in ML library, 252
  Spark ML, 239
  tuning models in Spark ML, 242
multi-DataFrame transformations, 48
  set-like operations, 48
multiple actions on the same RDD, 115
MutableAggregationBuffer, 69
MySQL, including JDBC JAR in Spark Shell, 53

N
na function, 42
Naive Bayes algorithm
  constructing an estimator with minimal
    configuration in ML library, 239
  implementing a simple classifier, 249
  implementing using Structured Streaming,
    266
NaN values, isNaN function on DataFrames, 42
narrow dependencies, 15
  transformations with, 17
    coalesce function, 92
    dependency graph, 18
    implications for fault tolerance, 91
    in Spark job stages, 23
    narrow versus wide (example), 89

performance implications, 90
preservng partitioning information, 146
reusing RDDs, 117
Spark creators' definition, 88
native loader decorator, 197
NewHadoopRDD class, 16
noisy clusters, 124
Normalizer, using in Spark ML, 239, 241
notebooks, debugging in, 304
null values, isNull function on DataFrames, 42
numeric functions
Java-specific, and access to Scala equivalents, 179
RDD types and, 93
numPartitions function, 145

O

objects
deserialized Java objects, storing objects in RDDs as, 14, 119
intermediate object creation in functions, avoiding, 99
minimizing object creation, 94
reusing existing objects, 94
Python, and Java interoperability, 187
saving DStreams as, 261
off heap persistence, 116
off_heap storage option, 119
operators
in DataFrame API, 38
Spark SQL column operators, 38
Spark SQL Scala operators, 38
OrderedRDDFunctions class, 16, 127
defining implicit ordering for, 133
dictionary of operations, 149
how to use, 132
otherwise function, 42
out-of-memory errors
actions returning unbounded data to the driver, 133
caused by key/value operations, 127
on executors, from groupByKey, 137
preventing with aggregation operations, 140
output operations
DStream, 261
Structured Streaming, 263

P

packages, 255

(see also components and packages)
community packages for Spark, 256, 271-274
creating a package, 273
including Spark packages in applications, 60
Spark Packages system, 188
PairRDDFunctions class, 16, 127
cogroup function, 142
dictionary of mapping and partitioning functions, 148
how to use, 132
PairwiseRDD, 182
parallel-ssh, installing packages via, 188
parallelism value (SparkConf), 144
parameters (pipeline stages in ML), 235
explain params, 235
in custom transformers, 246
searching, 242
tuning parameters for models, 239
Parquet files, 54, 263
partitionBy function, 62, 143, 149
partitioner function, 16
partitioners
and key/value data, 142-149
custom partitioning, 145
HashPartitioner, 144
leveraging co-located and co-partitioned RDDs, 146
PairRDDFunctions, mapping and partitioning functions, 148
preserving partitioning information across transformations, 146
RangePartitioner, 144
Spark partitioner object, 144
custom partitioner, defining for Goldilocks example, 156
partitions, 10
changing number with coalesce operation, 92
discovery and writing functions in Spark SQL, 62
high cost for computing each partition, 116
in narrow transformations, 88
in RDD joins, 75
narrow versus wide dependencies between, 90
number and size of, 287
repartitioning data sources for stream processing, 259

speeding up joins by assigning a known partitioner, 79
partitions function, 15
PartitionwiseSampledRDD, 212
PCA (principal component analysis)
    feature selection in MLlib, 228
    in Spark ML, 239
performance
    considerations with aggregation operations, 138
    considerations with joins, 75
    Goldilocks example, review of solutions, 171
    issues with key/value operations, 127
    narrow versus wide transformations, 90
    PySpark DataFrames and Datasets versus RDDs, 183
    RDDs versus DataFrames, 27
    transformations, methods for improving, 159
    user-defined functions and, 67
    verifying, 217-219
        projects for, 219
        Spark counters for, 217
Perl Script, calling from pipe interface, 194
persist function, 14, 115
    StorageLevel argument, 118
persistence
    cost of, 114
    data persistence and Spark ML, 242-244
    model and pipelines persistence in Spark ML, 252
    persisting in memory, 117
    persisting RDDs, 115, 118
        when cost for computing each partition is very high, 116
    persisting to disk, 117, 120
persistencePriority function, 14
physical plan (query optimizer), 69
pip installations, 188
    installing PySpark, 189
pipe interface, calling other languages from Spark, 193
PipedRDD interface, 182
pipelines (Spark ML)
    accessing individual stages, 241
    building a pipeline, 240
    extending with your own algorithms, 244-253

creating custom estimators, 247
custom transformers, 245
pipeline and model persistence and serving, 252
parameters, setting for pipeline stages, 235
persistence in pipeline stages, 242
Pipeline object, 240
pipeline stages, 234
support for Structured Streaming, 266
training a pipeline, 241
transformers and estimators, 234
PipelineStage interface, 244
PMML (Predictive Model Markup Language) models, 230
    exporting a model to PMML formats in MLlib, 231
    persistence in ML library, 252
PMMLExportable trait, 231
predictions
    performing with MLlib, 229
    training a simple MLlib classification model for, 229
Predictor class, 249
preferredLocations function, 16
printSchema function, 33
programming languages, options with Spark, 175-201
    beyond Scala and the JVM, 180-193
        CLR (Common Language Runtime), C#, 193
        Eclair JS, 192
        PySpark, 180-189
        Spark.jl (Julia Spark), 191
        SparkR, 189-191
    beyond Scala, within the JVM, 176-180
    calling other languages from Spark, 193-201
        FORTRAN, 199
        getting to the GPU, 200
        using JNA, 198
        using JNI, 195-198
    future developements in, 201
    outside the JVM, 176
properties (RDDs), 15
property checking, using ScalaCheck, 213-216
    computing RDD difference, 213
psuedorandom number generators, creating, 107
Py4J, 181, 186
    and implementations of PySpark, 185

calling non-Spark JVM classes with, 186
Python, 8
    IPython, 181
    PySpark, 180-189
        accessing backing Java objects and mix-
            ing Scala code, 184
        DataFrames and Datasets, 183
        debugging, 305-324
        dependency management, 187
        how it works, 181
        installing, 189
        RDDs, 182
    round-tripping through RDDs to cut query
        plans, 70
    Scala performance versus, 4
    Spark ML parameter documentation, 235
    Spark packages, 273
    user-defined function performance penalty,
        avoiding, 67

Q

queries
    cutting large DataFrame query plans with
        Python, 185
    debugging Spark SQL queries, 71
    evil stream query manager example, 268
query optimizer, 69
    (see also Catalyst query optimizer)
QueueStreams, 258

R

R language, 8
    Spark support for, 175
    Sparklyr library, 191
    SparkR, 189-191
RandomDataGenerator, 211
RandomRDDs, 210
RandomSampler trait, 212
randomSplit function, 212
range partitioning, 144
    performance considerations, 152
    RangePartitioner object, creating, 145
rank statistics, 129
    (see also Goldilocks example)
RDD class, 16
rdd function, 178
RDDs (resilient distributed datasets), 3, 8,
    10-19
    changing partitioning of, 143

computing difference between, 213
converting between Scala and Java, 178
converting to data formats for use over pipe
    interface, 193
converting to/from Datasets, 63
data storage space, DataFrame versus, 50
DataFrames and Datasets versus, 28
DStreams, 257
functions on, transformations versus
    actions, 17
immutability and the RDD interface, 14
in-memory persistence and memory man-
    agement, 13
joins, 75-81
    choosing a join type, 77
    choosing an execution plan, 78
    speeding up by assigning a known parti-
        tioner, 79
    speeding up by using broadcast hash
        join, 80
lazy evaluation of, 11
    debugging and, 13
    performance and usability advantages,
        11
mock RDDs for use in testing, 208
operations with multiple RDDs and key/
    value data, 141
performance, DataFrames versus, 27
PySpark, 182
reading and writing in Spark SQL, 57
returned by transformations, types of, 92
reusing, 114-125
    cases for reuse, 114
    persisting and caching RDDs, 118
    types of reuse, 118
round-tripping through to cut query plans,
    70
sampling, 212
testing transformations, 204
transformations, 87
    (see also transformations)
types of, 16
wide versus narrow dependencies, 17
readStream function, 263
receivers, 258
recommendation algorithms, ML library, 233,
    239
recomputing RDDs, deciding if it is inexpen-
    sive enough, 117

record type informaton in RDDs, 93
reduce function, 3, 17
    object reuse with, 97
reduceByKey function, 18, 79, 81
    map-side combinations, 141
    performance considerations, 139
reduceByKeyAndWindow function, 261
registerJavaFunction, 184
regression algorithms
    ML library, 233, 239
    MLlib, 223
relational transformations (Datasets), 65
    multi-Dataset, 65
repartition function, 18, 92, 143
repartitionAndSortWithinPartitions function,
    150
    secondary sort and, 151-159
        how not to sort by two orderings, 155
        leveraging for groupByKeyAndSortVal-
        ues, 152
        using with Goldilocks example, 156
replication (storage level), 120
reset function, 110
resetAndCopy function, 110
resource allocation, 20, 278-290
    calculating executor and driver memory
    overhead, 279
right outer joins, 78, 82
    sample join in Spark SQL, 83
row equality, checking DataFrames for, 209
Row objects
    RDDs composed of, converting to Data-
    Frames, 57
    using with user-defined aggregate functions,
    69

S
sample function, 17, 212
sampleByKey function, 149, 212
sampleByKeyExact function, 212
sampling, 211
save modes (Spark SQL), 61
Saveable trait, 231
saveAsObjectFile function, 17
saveAsSequenceFile function, 17
saveAsTextFile function, 17
SBT
    adding Spark SQL and Hive components to
    builds, 31

sbt-jni package, 196
    nativeLoader decorator, 197
sbt-spark-package plug-in, 31, 273
    adding Spark SQL and Hive components to
    build, 32
Scala, 3, 8
    advantages for Spark development, 3
    flatMap operation on iterators and collec-
    tions, 132
    learning, resources for, 5
    Quasi Quotes, 70
    RDDs in, converting to/from Java, 178
    reasons not to use for Spark development, 4
    simple Scala JNI, 195
    Spark SQL Scala operators, 38
    type parameters, syntax of, 93
ScalaCheck, property checking with, 213-216
scaling features in MLlib, 228
schema function, 33
schemas
    adding schema information to data con-
    verted from RDDs to DataFrames, 57
    additional schema information in Datasets
    and DataFrames, 28
    DataFrames, working with as RDDs, 93
    inferring the schema from JSON data, 33, 52
    sampling schema inference, streaming and,
    263
    Spark SQL, basics of, 33-36
    specifying schema for local collection con-
    version to DataFrame, 59
secondary sort and repartitionAndSortWithin-
Partitions, 151-159
    using secondary sort in Goldilocks example,
    156
select operator, 41
    relational-style transformations with Data-
    sets, 65
selecting features in MLlib, 228
self joins, 85
    Datasets, 85
serialization, 119
serialization/deserialization
    Eclair JS and, 192
    in PySpark, 182
    Java serialization for models in MLlib, 232
    serialization options, 290
    SparK SQL benefits for sorting, 48

Tungsten serialization versus Kryo and Java
object, 50
using JNI with Spark, 195
set-like operations
DataFrame, 48
on Datasets, 65
on RDDs, 106
setParameterName function, 236
settings (see configuration settings)
setup overhead, reducing, 107-114
shared variables, 108
accumulators, 109
broadcast variables, 108
shuffle files, 91
reusing, 123
shuffle joins, 75
shuffled hash joins, 78
ShuffleDependency object, 15, 18
in Spark job stages, 23
ShuffledRDD class, 16
shuffles, 18, 88
avoiding performance problems with, 128
failures of, 128
shuffled read caused by groupByKey, 136
sinks, custom, for Structured Streaming, 264
basic custom sink for Naive Bayes training, 267
slideDuration, 261
sort function, 18
sortBy function, 130
sortByKey function, 150, 161
in Goldilocks example, Version 3, 160
RDD record types and, 93
sorting by two keys with, 151
wide dependencies, 91
sorting
in Spark SQL, 48
Tungsten data structures and, 50
sources (see data sources)
Spark
about, 1
components, 8
design principles, 7
in big data ecosystem, 8
job scheduling, 19-22
jobs, anatomy of, 22-26
libraries, 10
model of parallel computing, RDDs, 10-19
performance, importance of, 1

Scala and, 3
versions, 3
Spark Core, 8
Spark Jobserver, 219
Spark Packages, 188
Spark SQL, 9
components being built on top of, 256
data loading and saving functions, 51
data representation in DataFrames and
Datasets, 49
DataFrame API, 36-49
DataFrames and Datasets, 27
Datasets, 62-67
debugging queries, 71
dependencies, 30-33
extending with user-defined functions and
user-defined aggregate functions, 67
getting started with SparkSession, 28
JDBC/ODBC server, 71
joins, 81-86
broadcast hash joins, 85
DataFrame joins, 82
Dataset joins, 85
self joins in DataFrames, 85
performance in Python, 183
query optimizer, 69-71
Scala and Java interoperability, 179
schemas, 33-36
SQLContext and HiveContext entry points, 29
windowing, 46
Spark Streaming, 10
ML library and, 222
testing, 206
spark-perf package, 219
spark-sql-perf project, 211
spark-validator project, 219
Spark.jl (Julia Spark), 191
SparkConf object, 20
spark.default.parallelism value, 144
SparkContext, 15
broadcast function, 108
Py4J gateway, 186
resource allocation to executors, 20
setCheckpointDir function, 121
starting a Spark application on a distributed
system, 21
sparkling, 177
SparkListener, 217

Sparklyr library, 191
SparkR, 189-191
SparkSession, 15
   enabling Hive support in, 30
   getting started with, 28
SparkVector, 223, 230
   (see also vectors)
   returned by HashingTF tool, 225
sparse vectors, creating, 224
SQL
   plain SQL queries interacting with Hive
      data, 49
   Spark SQL, 9
   Spark SQL expressions, 37
SQLContext, 29
   creating, 32
   creating for testing, 210
   registering user-defined functions with, 67
stages, 23
   accessing in ML pipelines, 241
   performance implications of stage bound-
      aries, 91
   tasks in, 24
static allocation of resources, 20
status function, StreamingQuery, 270
storage levels, 118
   custom, 121
straggler tasks, 128
   caused by uneven partitioning, 144
stratified sampling, 212
stream processing with Spark, 257-271
   batch intervals, 259
   considerations for DStreams, 261
   considerations for Structured Streaming,
      262-270
   data sources, 263
   output operations, 263
   data checkpoint intervals, 260
   high availability mode, 270
   sources and sinks, 257
      receivers, 258
      repartitioning sources, 259
streaming (see stream processing with Spark;
   Spark Streaming)
StreamingActionBase class, 208
StreamingSuiteBase class, 208
StringIndexer, 237
StringIndexerModel, 238
strings

encoding string labels in MLlib, 227
handling string labels with StringIndexer in
   ML library, 237
IndexToString transformer, 238
simple HashingTF on RDD of strings, 225
StructField case class, 34
StructType case class, 35
Structured Streaming, 257
   batch intervals, 260
   considerations for, 262
      custom sinks, 264
      data sources, 263
      machine learning, 265
      output operations, 263
      stream status and debugging, 270
   data sources, 257
subtract function, 106
supervised learning
   in ML library, 236
      pipeline stage parameters, 239
   preparing MLlib features data for, 227
SWIG, writing wrappers with, 196

T
Tachyon, 119, 122
take function, 17
tasks, 20
   assignment of, 21
   number of, 24, 287
TaskScheduler, 22, 25
testing, 203-220
   getting test data, 210-213
      generating large datasets, 210
      sampling production data, 211
   integration testing, 216-217
      choosing testing environment, 216
   job validation, 219
   property checking with ScalaCheck,
      213-216
   streams for, 258
   unit testing
      factoring code for testability, 204
      general Spark unit testing, 204
      streaming, 206
      using mock RDDs, 208
   verifying performance, 217-219
Testing Spark: Best Practices (speech), 219
text files, saving DStreams as, 261
textual data, encoding for features

in ML library, 237
in MLlib, 224
this.type, 96
toDebugString function, 16
tokenizer, using with HashingTF, 237
toLocalIterator function, 206
Toree, 193
training
    machine learning algorithms not requiring, 246
    of Word2Vec model, 225
    required train functon for estimators, 247
transform function, 235, 236
    encoding string records in a custom map, 225
    implementation in custom transformers, 245
    repartitioning DStreams, 259
transformations, 87-126
    actions versus, on RDDs, 17
    DataFrame, 36-48
        beyond row-by-row transformations, 42
        for missing and noisy data, 42
        multi-DataFrame, 48
        simple transformations and SQL expressions, 37
    easier functional transformations with Datasets, 65
    in sinks, 265
    iterator-to-iterator, with mapPartitions, 100-106
        space and time advantages of, 102
    methods for improving performance of, 159
    minimizing object creation, 94
    multi-Dataset relational transformations, 65
    narrow versus wide dependencies, 17, 88-92
        implications for fault tolerance, 91
        performance implications, 90
        special case of coalesce, 92
    preserving partitioning information across, 146
    reducing setup overhead, 107-114
    relational transformations with Datasets, 65
    reusing RDDs, 114-125
        cases for reuse, 114
    stage boundaries, 24
    testing, 204
    types of RDD returned by, 92
Transformer interface, 244

transformers, 234
    creating custom transformers, 245
    data preparation stages, 237
    parameter values, 236
transformSchema function, 245
tree algorithms (MLlib), 223
treeAggregate function, 141
Tungsten, 50, 201, 290
tuning and cluster sizing (see configuration settings)
tuples
    RDDs not of type tuple, 16
    RDDs of, 127
    using arrays instead of, 97
types
    accumulator, 111
    collection and RDD members, 93
    compile-time strong typing with Datasets, 64
    Spark SQL types, 35
    typed implementation of select on Datasets, 65

U

union function, 106
unit testing, 203-210
    DataFrames, 208
    factoring code for testability, 204
    general, in Spark, 204
    mocking RDDs, 208
    regular Spark jobs, testing with RDDs, 204
    streaming, 206
Unix pipe, 193
unpersist function, 109
updateStateByKey function, 260
useDisk (storage level), 119
useMemory (storage level), 119
useOfHeap (storage level), 119
user-defined aggregate functions (UDAFs), 66
    extending Spark SQL with, 67
user-defined functions (UDFs)
    extending Spark SQL with, 67
    in HiveContext, 30
    Java UDFs, specifying return type, 180
    Python
        Jython and, 184

V

validation, job, 219

value function, 108, 113
values function, 148
Vector class, 223
    MLlib and ML library, 234
VectorAssembler, 237
vectors
    RDDs of SparkVectors, in MLlib predic-
        tions, 230
    working with Spark vectors, 224

W

when/otherwise functions, 42
wide dependencies, 15, 88
    transformations with, 17
        coalesce function, 92
        dependency graph, 19
        implications for fault tolerance, 91
        in Spark job stages, 23
        key/value operations, 127
        narrow versus wide (example), 89

performance implications, 91
windowDuration, 261
windowing functions, 46, 261
word count example, 12
    Java version, 177
    SparkR version, 189
Word2Vec, 224
    training a model, 225
    using a model, 226
Word2VecModel, 226

Y

YARN Resource Manager, 8
    using Python with, 324
    YarnMiniCluster, 217

Z

zipWithIndex function, 130

About the Authors

Holden Karau is transgender Canadian, and an active open source contributor. When not in San Francisco working as a software development engineer at IBM's Spark Technology Center, Holden talks internationally on Apache Spark and holds office hours at coffee shops at home and abroad. She is a Spark committer with frequent contributions, specializing in PySpark and Machine Learning. Prior to IBM she worked on a variety of distributed, search, and classification problems at Alpine, Databricks, Google, Foursquare, and Amazon. She graduated from the University of Waterloo with a Bachelor of Mathematics in Computer Science. Outside of software she enjoys playing with fire, welding, scooters, poutine, and dancing.

Rachel Warren is a data scientist and software engineer at Alpine Data Labs, where she uses Spark to address real-world data processing challenges. She has experience working as an analyst both in industry and academia. She graduated with a degree in Computer Science from Wesleyan University in Connecticut.

Colophon

The animal on the cover of *High Performance Spark* is a fire-tailed sunbird (*Aethopyga ignicauda*) native to Southeast Asia and the Indian subcontinent. Sunbirds are very distant relatives of the hummingbirds of the Americas and the honeyeaters of Australia.

As their name suggests, these birds (especially males) have very vivid coloring. Their tails and the back of their necks are red, their wings are green, their bellies are yellow and orange, and their heads are an iridescent blue. Male fire-tailed sunbirds are slightly larger than females, at an average of 15 centimeters long. Both members of a mating pair participate in feeding their chicks.

The fire-tailed sunbird's preferred habitat is conifer forest, where it consumes a diet of insects and nectar. The downward curve of its beak and a tubular tongue help it reach into flowers for food.

Many of the animals on O'Reilly covers are endangered; all of them are important to the world. To learn more about how you can help, go to *animals.oreilly.com*.

The cover image is from Wood's *Illustrated Natural History*. The cover fonts are URW Typewriter and Guardian Sans. The text font is Adobe Minion Pro; the heading font is Adobe Myriad Condensed; and the code font is Dalton Maag's Ubuntu Mono.

Learn from experts.
Find the answers you need.

Sign up for a **10-day free trial** to get **unlimited access** to all of the content on Safari, including Learning Paths, interactive tutorials, and curated playlists that draw from thousands of ebooks and training videos on a wide range of topics, including data, design, DevOps, management, business—and much more.

Start your free trial at:
oreilly.com/safari

(No credit card required.)